T0069996

Armchair Traveller
at the bookHaus

RICHARD TILLINGHAST is a native of Memphis, Tennessee. He first visited Istanbul as editor-in-chief of the travel guide, *Let's Go*, in the early 1960s. He holds a PhD in English literature from Harvard University and is the author of some fifteen books including *Finding Ireland*, an introduction to the culture of the country where he lived for a number of years. His 1995 book, *Damaged Grandeur*, is a critical memoir of the poet Robert Lowell, with whom he studied at Harvard. He has written on travel, books and food for the *New York Times*, the *Washington Post*, *Harper's Magazine*, *The Irish Times* and other periodicals. His poetry has been published in *The New Yorker*, the *Paris Review* and elsewhere; Dedalus Press in Dublin published his *Selected Poems* in 2009. He has received fellowships and grants from the John Simon Guggenheim Foundation, the Arts Council of Ireland, the British Council and the American Research Institute in Turkey. With his daughter, Julia Clare Tillinghast, he has translated into English selections from the Turkish poet Edip Cansever, collected in a volume called *Dirty August*. He currently divides his time between the Big Island of Hawaii and the Tennessee mountains.

An Armchair Traveller's History of Istanbul

City of Forgetting and Remembering

Richard Tillinghast

First published in Great Britain in 2012 by Haus Publishing Ltd
The Armchair Traveller at the bookHaus
70 Cadogan Place, London SW1X 9AH
www.thearmchairtraveller.com

A CIP catalogue record for this book is available from the British Library

print ISBN 978-1-907973-21-5
ebook ISBN 978-1-907973-28-4

Typeset in Garamond by MacGuru Ltd
Printed and bound in China by 1010 Printing International Ltd.

Jacket illustration: courtesy gettyimages

Contents

Part I

Arrival

I

First Impressions

ANYONE WHO KNOWS ISTANBUL will tell you that the best way to arrive in the Queen of Cities is by sea. On my first visit, I came here by boat from Greece. As we steamed up through the Dardanelles, W.B. Yeats's lines came to mind: 'And therefore I have sailed the seas and come / To the holy city of Byzantium'. We docked at Karaköy, home in Byzantine days to Genoese sailors. I remember the metallic surfaces that morning, the monotone grey, the harshness of the arrival hall where we disembarked and cleared customs. Istanbul does not present a welcoming face to newcomers – perhaps no great city does. It was clear that we were no longer in the Mediterranean, but had entered a climate more Balkan than Aegean, a city that seemed on the face of it to have more in common with Sofia or Belgrade, which were once part of the Ottoman Empire, than with those sun-drenched former seats of empire, Rome and Venice.

Few arrive in Istanbul nowadays the way I did back then. Times have changed; these days I fly like everyone else. And no matter how well I have planned my arrival, in a matter of minutes the city draws me into its own irrational and unpredictable way of doing things. So here I am in the passenger seat of a taxi, no seat belt, with a driver who hurtles through traffic in a way that would never be countenanced in Europe or North America. I have driven in Paris, in Rome, and even in Istanbul itself before the recent population explosion and the coming of the motorways, but I would not care to take the wheel on a road like this.

Lanes mean nothing to my cabbie, who says his name is Osman, nor to anyone else on the road. Because traffic is so congested this Saturday night, Osman drives most of the way on the right-hand shoulder, edging around lorries, weaving in and out among taxis and passenger cars at breakneck speed, sounding his horn almost continuously. We pass a truck with a cargo of onions just visible underneath an old *kilim* that has been tied down over them. At the edge of the motorway I catch a glimpse of a family of three, huddled in a primordial group on the edge of the road. The man wears black trousers and a white shirt and sports a moustache – the generic costume for an urban Turk of a certain class. His wife, wearing a head scarf, holds the baby. What is their story? Why are they standing there at the side of this dangerous highway?

The little family is a fleeting glimpse in the headlong rush of traffic. In Osman's cab the windows are rolled down: we are listening to Turkish *arabesk*, that haunting music that tells you that this is not Europe, and will never be Europe no matter whether they eventually admit Turkey into the EU or not. I am able to make out some of the words of the song. A man is singing about his father, dead now, a man like a lion, may Allah build him a fine tomb. My driver surprises me by asking my permission to smoke, and I say sure, go ahead, even though I loathe cigarette smoke. I dare not impinge upon the man's sense of who he is.

Osman thumps his chest and proclaims that he is a great driver. I tell him he drives like a lion. He reminds me of the *başıbozuk*, or *delibaş* irregulars who fought with the regular Ottoman armies when they captured Constantinople – 'broken-headed' or 'crazy-headed' free spirits, as out of control and fear-inducing as the wild cymbal crashes and wailing pipes the army bands played before they attacked. Finally we reach the city and drive along the Golden Horn, absorbed into the great fulcrum of energy that is Istanbul.

2

Istanbul and Constantinople

A CITY IS A LIVING BEING, with a memory of its own. The more we know of what Istanbul remembers, and even what it tries to forget, the more we enter into its essence. Istanbul has its characteristic sounds – ships' horns from the Bosphorus, the cries of seagulls, taxis hooting, workmen hammering away at copper and brass in ateliers around the Grand Bazaar, street vendors hawking their wares, and the call to prayer, that haunting recitation one hears five times a day, from before sunrise until after dark, knitting together the hours.

And Istanbul has its smells: lamb kebabs and corn on the cob roasting over charcoal braziers, diesel exhaust from boats and trucks, cigarette smoke, an indefinable aroma of drains from a city with a 2000-year-old sewer system; all of these odours dissolving in the bracing salt air of the sea. On a hot day one is refreshed by the acrid fragrance of fig trees, and the sweet perfume of acacias.

In early autumn, thousands of storks and large birds of prey fly over the city on their annual migration from Europe to Africa. In the spring, on their journey north, they return. The skies are full of them and the creak of their wings as they pass over. Storks are the anarchists of the bird world. They don't line up or form Vs as geese do – they straggle all over the sky. For the Persian-Jewish Istanbullu poet Murat Nemet-Nejat in his memoir *Istanbul Noir*, this migration is an emblem of larger patterns:

> ... Istanbul lies on the multiple migration paths of birds. More than the place where East meets West or Byzantium fuses with Islam, both of which are certainly true, Istanbul is a central location, a point of passage, in a natural movement that has

> been going on for millions of years, of which the Silk Road is the nearest human reflection. Istanbul has been destroyed and rebuilt, more precisely, re-imagined, innumerable times, creating its history of rich melancholy; but underlying these changes lies a deep, inescapable continuum, experienced just below consciousness. This dialectic between chaos and healing unity is at the heart of the city ...

The city's poets resolve this dialectic between chaos and healing unity. Many Istanbullus, as they are called in Turkish, can quote from memory 'I am listening to Istanbul', a poem by Orhan Veli. Here, in English, are a couple of stanzas:

> I am listening to Istanbul, my eyes closed.
> First a breeze lightly blows.
> The leaves on the trees
> Sway gently;
> From far, far away
> Come the bells of the water sellers, ceaselessly ringing.
> I am listening to Istanbul, my eyes closed.
> ... ...
> I am listening to Istanbul, my eyes closed.
> In my head, the drunkenness of times gone by,
> And a waterfront mansion with a deserted boathouse.
> Inside the vanished roar of winds out of the southwest,
> I am listening to Istanbul, my eyes closed.

In the words of the expatriate poet John Ash, a leading light among English-language poets working in the city, 'Istanbul is a city absorbed in constant contemplation of an enigma, so much so that sometimes it doesn't know itself. Is it Oriental or Occidental, secular or Muslim, ugly or beautiful, rich or poor?' Worldly sophisticates live a secular European kind of life here, side by side with transplanted Anatolian villagers guided by the dictates of the Qur'an.

And hidden everywhere, if you know where to look, remain traces of the minority populations that once made Constantinople – as most people of whatever religion or ethnicity called the city before the founding of the Turkish Republic in the 1920s – perhaps the most ethnically diverse city anywhere. Constantinople, *Kōnstantinoupolis* in Greek, had other names, too: Konstantiniyye in Arabic, Bolis in

Armenian, and Tsarigrad to White Russian émigrés who came here to escape the Bolshevik revolution. As the Turks tended to use Konstantiniyye as the official name for their city, you will encounter it in this book occasionally.

Every great city earns a variety of names and epithets. Like San Francisco, Constantinople came to be known simply as 'The City' (Greek: *hē Polis*, ἡ Πόλις; Modern Greek: *i Poli*, η Πόλη). This usage is still common in colloquial Greek and Armenian, I am told. The modern Turkish name Istanbul (pronounced Is-TAHN-bul) comes from a Greek phrase, *eis tin polis*, meaning 'in the city' or 'to the city'. Istanbul was the common name for the city in Turkish even before the conquest of 1453. The first Turks to arrive here, hearing the Greeks use the phrase, adopted it into their own lexicon without knowing precisely what it meant.

In 1930, with the introduction of a new postal system, the Turkish authorities officially requested that foreigners cease referring to the city by the traditional non-Turkish names and adopt Istanbul as the sole name in their own languages as well. If you sent a letter or package to Constantinople instead of Istanbul it was returned to sender by Turkey's PTT, which contributed to the eventual worldwide adoption of the new name. As the song has it, 'If you've a date in Constantinople, she'll be waiting in Istanbul'.

The New Rome

Designated as the capital of the Roman Empire in AD 330 by Constantine the Great, this New Rome became the eastern capital when the empire split in two. Constantinople, so called in honour of the man who transformed it from a provincial Greek port into a great metropolis, has one of the finest natural sites of any city in the world. Here is how Edward Gibbon describes the position of the city in *The Decline and Fall of the Roman Empire*:

> Situated in the forty-first degree of latitude, the Imperial city commanded, from her seven hills, the opposite shores of Europe and Asia; the climate was healthy and temperate, the soil fertile, the harbour secure and capacious, and the approach on the side of the continent was of small extent and easy defence. The Bosphorus and the Hellespont may be considered as the two gates of Constantinople, and the prince who possessed those

> important passages could always shut them against a naval enemy and open them to the fleets of commerce ... . Whatever rude commodities were collected in the forests of Germany and Scythia ... whatsoever was manufactured by the skill of Europe or Asia; the corn of Egypt, and the gems and spices of the farthest India, were brought by the varying winds into the port of Constantinople, which, for many ages, attracted the commerce of the ancient world.

In the history of Constantinople one encounters some memorable characters, ghostly players on the majestic and blood-soaked stage of this ancient city. First comes Constantine the Great, the city's founder: a ruthless soldier-emperor who fought his way to supreme power, becoming the visionary builder of a city that lasted more than a thousand years. The historian Cyril Mango attempts to put him in perspective: 'Constantine became a Christian saint ... and [was] made the subject of several hagiographic Lives that bear little relation to reality. Yet he killed both his wife and his eldest son, was baptised by a heretic, and, after his death, was accorded a pagan deification.'

The image of one of his notable successors, Theodosius I, a Spaniard who claimed descent from the Emperor Trajan, can be seen in the Hippodrome; carved into the marble pedestal of the Egyptian Obelisk. Surrounded by his retinue in the imperial reviewing stand, Theodosius is flanked by his two sons, Arcadius and Honorius, as well as by the Emperor of the West, Valentian, who would die before he made it past the age of twenty-one, probably murdered.

Others who wore the imperial purple also make appearances in this book – chief among them Justinian, builder of Haghia Sophia (Αγία Σοφία in Greek; the Turks call it Aya Sofya or Ayasofya), and Justinian's remarkable empress, Theodora, who was a prostitute in her younger days, and not a very classy one at that. Then there is the eleventh-century empress, Zoë, who was a niece of Basil II (of whom more later) and first promised in marriage to the Holy Roman Emperor Otto, though he died of a fever while she was en route to Italy for the wedding. She later married first Romanus III, then Constantine Monomachos. She had Romanus's face chiselled out of his mosaic depiction in Haghia Sophia and Constantine's face cemented in beside her. She can be seen in the south gallery of the great cathedral. Another emperor whose mosaic likeness is visible in Haghia Sophia is Alexander, who died playing polo while drunk.

The Ottomans

For their part, the Ottoman Turks, or *Osmanlıs*, were descended from Osman, 1288–1326, leader of a band said to consist of just four hundred warriors who fought and pillaged their way across Anatolia in the days of the Seljuk kingdom. These Turks' first religion was shamanistic; the shamans and dervishes who accompanied and inspired them played a key role in shaping the national character. The dervish, even today, remains an iconic figure for the Turks. Where we might say 'persistence pays', a Turk is as likely to come out with the proverb, *Sabreden derviş muradına ermiş* – 'The patient dervish reached his goal'.

First among the Ottoman rulers of Istanbul was Mehmed II, who reigned between 1451 and 1481 and came to be known as Fatih, the Conqueror, a ruthless man of great skill and vision and a ferocious warrior who was also a far-sighted planner. Mehmed conquered Constantinople for the Turks and began constructing the institutions that were to define it for the next five centuries. His son, Beyazit II, an ascetic man of mystical bent, reversed Mehmed's policy of modelling the empire on the civilisations of Greece and Rome, and looked instead to the Islamic regimes of the Arabs. Beyazit's quietistic reign gave way to that of *Yavuz Selim*, Selim the Grim, another great warrior who continued to expand the empire.

After Selim I came Süleyman the Magnificent, the greatest of all the sultans – though instead of 'sultan', the Ottomans preferred the Persian word *padişah* to describe their supreme ruler, 'the shadow of God on earth'. Süleyman's reign, 1520–66, was the territorial high-water mark of an empire that stretched from the Indian Ocean in the east, all the way across Asia Minor, north and west into the Balkans as far as the gates of Vienna, south again through the Middle East to Africa and the southern borders of Egypt, and west across North Africa to the Straits of Gibraltar.

What a pity that palace intrigue brought to the throne after him his son Selim II or 'Selim the Sot', a man as unfit to rule as his nickname implies. This was a man who, according to legend, lost his footing on the slippery marble floor of his imperial hamam in the Topkapı Palace after drinking in one draught a bottle of Cypriot wine, cracked his skull, and died in 1574. Unsurprisingly, he initiated the decline of this great empire – an eventful decline that lasted for almost four hundred and fifty years. When Mehmed VI, the last sultan, was bundled out the back door of the Dolmabahçe Palace onto a British warship in

1922 with his wives and concubines and sent into exile on the Italian Riviera, the 'sick man of Europe' had finally died.

FROM THE DAYS OF SÜLEYMAN, we skip ahead two centuries – certainly not because nothing noteworthy occurred during that period, but because the eighteenth century was a time of great change. The Ottomans seriously began to recognise that they were being eclipsed by the European powers and Tsarist Russia, and that they needed to adapt to a changing world rather than demanding that the world adapt to them. Furthermore, Ottoman architecture had now started to reflect the European baroque and rococo styles, with results over the next couple of centuries that range from the magnificent to the banal. Ahmed III, a sultan with a sense of beauty and luxury, and an open mind to what was happening in the world beyond his empire, ushered in the *Lale Devri* or 'Tulip Age' during the first thirty years of the eighteenth century.

In the early nineteenth century came Mahmud II, who attempted the daunting task of modernising the Ottoman Empire – an attempt doomed to failure as the empire had already begun its slow disintegration and the forces of history were working against it. Two rulers who came later in the nineteenth century – Abdülaziz and Abdülhamid II – are dark and tragic figures who are fascinating for their very failures. Perhaps sensing that modernisation and westernisation would ultimately be impossible in this tottering old top-heavy empire, they tried to turn back the hands of time and live on borrowed money in an autocratic past.

It took Turkey's great national hero, Mustafa Kemal – whose adopted name Atatürk means 'Father Turk' or 'Father of the Turks' – to salvage a Turkish nation from the wreckage of the Ottoman Empire. Atatürk, the first president of the Turkish Republic, was a visionary on the level of Ottoman predecessors like Fatih and Süleyman the Magnificent, and he defined modern Turkey just as surely as those men defined the Ottoman Empire. You see his face everywhere, on the currency, on the walls of barber shops and *köftecis*, which serve those delicious Turkish meatballs, police stations and *meyhanes*, taverns that serve food. Like his great predecessor, Mehmed the Conqueror, Atatürk was a complex man with some disturbing aspects to his personality, but he was everything George Washington and Winston Churchill were to their countries, and perhaps more.

The City's Greeks, Jews and Armenians

Part of Istanbul's uniqueness springs from its layering of historical periods, and the way the stories of its different ethnic groups and religions intersect, compete with and contradict one another. Byzantine history, Ottoman history and the stories of the city's Greek, Armenian and Jewish minorities are all part of a simmering stew. The Ottoman Empire was a multi-ethnic enterprise with at least as many Greeks, Jews and Armenians as Turks in the capital – not to mention Serbs and Croats from the Balkans, Albanians in their white skullcaps, Bulgarians and Magyars, Venetian merchants and Genoese sailors, Circassians, Persians, Arabs, turbanned Turcomans, Kurds and black Africans, and more recently, White Russians carrying suitcases stuffed with worthless rubles. A nineteenth century English traveller, Adolphus Slade, describes visiting a prison where a mosque, a synagogue and a church on the grounds were all necessary to answer the religious needs of the inmate population.

When Mehmed the Conqueror took possession of what had been the capital of the Byzantine Empire, it was severely depopulated, and he set about filling it with useful, productive citizens from the entire Mediterranean world. To that end he offered sanctuary to Sephardic Jews who were expelled from Spain under the Inquisition in 1492. Just as Americans whose ancestors came over on the Mayflower claim pride of place over more recent arrivals, the focus of Sephardic Istanbullu snobbery is the claim of having come from Spain on the 'first sixteen ships'.

Yet there had been Karaite Jews here in Byzantine days, living along the waterfront in Eminönü, until their neighbourhood was razed to make way for the Yeni Cami, the 'New' Mosque, at the end of the sixteenth century. ('New' is as relative a word in Istanbul as it is in Oxford, with its fourteenth-century New College.) Working-class Jews moved to Balat along the Golden Horn, next to the Greek neighbourhood of Fener, while the more prosperous gravitated to Galata, traditionally home to Genoese, Venetian, and other Italian sailors and traders. The Princes' Islands in the Sea of Marmara were home to many of these minorities as well. In the face of persistent Christian prejudice, the sultans stoutly defended the Jews. In 1840 Abdülmecid I issued a decree specifically stating that 'the Jewish nation will be protected and defended'.

A community of Jewish Istanbullus, many of them living in the Europeanised neighbourhood of Karaköy around *Bankalar Caddesi*,

'The Street of Banks', served the needs of the Ottoman bureaucracy, and many others worked in what would now be called the banking sector. The greatest of these families were the Camondos, Venetian Jewish financiers and property barons who came to the city in the eighteenth century. An 1881 property survey lists the Camondos as owners of ten *hans*, twenty-seven apartment buildings and houses, a theatre, fifty shops and two *yalıs* on the Bosphorus.

Tragically, the Camondos transferred their operations to Paris in the nineteenth century. When the Nazis went round in the middle of the night, pounding on doors and rounding up Parisian Jews, putting them on trains headed east on journeys from which few returned, these transplanted Istanbullus lacked the protection they would have had in Turkey under Atatürk. The last Camondos perished in Auschwitz. Their monument in Paris is the Musée Nissim de Camondo, dedicated to the decorative arts. This elegant mansion was given to the French people by Moise Camondo, born in Istanbul in 1860, in the name of his son Nissim, who died fighting for France in the First World War.

Elderly Jewish ladies may still occasionally be spotted playing bridge in the lobby of the Hotel Splendide on Büyükada, smoking cigarettes and keeping score in Ladino, the ancestral language of Sephardic Jews. The Jewish Museum in Karaköy is a good place to get a sense of this aspect of Istanbul's history.

Not that all was harmonious for Istanbul's minorites. In the early sixteenth century Selim I tried to close all the city's churches, until two aged Janissaries (from the Turkish *yeni*, 'new', and *çeri*, 'troops' – the elite corps of soldiers that served the sultan) were produced who were willing to testify that the city had capitulated rather than being conquered. According to the traditions of Islam, this meant that residents of the city must be allowed to keep their houses of worship. The wave of nationalism that would sweep the world in the nineteenth century ran counter to the Ottoman spirit, in which nationalities melded within a larger cultural and political entity.

As the Ottomans increasingly lost control of their subject peoples and were attacked from all sides as the century wore on, they reacted savagely. As Philip Mansel puts it in *Constantinople, City of the World's Desire*, 'On an average day in 1896 news arrived of riots in Crete, a rising in Lebanon, and an incursion of Armenians from Russia into eastern Anatolia.' These Armenians were massacred by Turkish peasants and soldiers, and roving bands of Kurds, and Istanbul's

Armenians were in danger too. A radical Armenian fringe allied to revolutionary movements in Tsarist Russia attacked not just representatives of the Ottoman establishment, but the Armenian Patriarch as well. In multi-ethnic Ortaköy they attacked Greeks. In 1895, two thousand insurgents armed with pistols and knives marched on the Sublime Porte, singing revolutionary songs and shouting 'Liberty or death!' Sultan Abdülhamid II was having none of it. The police opened fire on the crowd and many were killed.

In 1896, when Armenian revolutionaries wanted to bring the world's attention to the massacres of their countrymen, they forced their way into the Ottoman Bank in Karaköy armed with pistols, grenades and dynamite, killing several people, holding some 150 employees and customers hostage for fourteen hours, and triggering reprisals both from Sultan Abdülhamid II and from Turkish mobs outraged by the revolutionaries' actions. The police stood by while Armenians were beaten to death in the streets and on the docks. Carts carried the corpses away.

Wealthy Greeks, Turks and Jews were able to protect their employees and servants, so it was the Armenian poor who suffered the most. One would have expected the minorities to make common cause against their rulers, but this was not the case. Abdülhamid and the Greek Patriarch Joachim III had cordial relations with each other, exchanged gifts and conversed in Greek at Yıldız Palace. The Ottomans, as I have said, provided a safe haven for their Jewish population. In later years, however, 'wealth taxes' targeted Istanbul's Jews and Greeks, and many left rather than have their fortunes wiped out. In the 1950s, nationalist rioters smashed the shop windows of businesses run by minorities, Greeks in particular.

I have not succeeded in finding very much of a written record, in English at any rate, of the Greek and Armenian experience in Constantinople. We know that the Greek poet Cavafy, of whom more in chapter thirty-two, walked these streets as a child. The story of Greek Constantinople remains to be brought to the attention of English-language readers. When Istanbul looks at its past, it may see these 'minorities' out of the corners of its eyes, but they have rarely been the centre of the city's attention. That is why Elif Şafak's 2006 novel, *The Bastard of Istanbul*, was so important. It tells the story of a young American woman of Armenian heritage from San Francisco who visits Istanbul and discovers how interwoven her family history is with the city's history. Armenians played an important role in Constantinople's intellectual life, and the 2007 assassination of Hrant Dink, the outspoken Turkish-Armenian journalist, by a seventeen-year-old Turkish nationalist, brought 100,000 Istanbullus out into to the streets in a show of outrage. They carried banners reading *Hepimiz Ermeniyiz*, 'We are all Armenians'.

Greeks, Armenians and Jews are largely missing from present-day Istanbul, and the city is the poorer for their absence. While on the surface Istanbul endorses the Republican slogan, 'Turkey for the Turks', and has agreed to forget those who once enlivened the city, and made it a place where church bells filled the air alongside the Muslim call to prayer, where Hebrew script was inscribed above the doors of synagogues, where many languages were spoken and many religious festivals celebrated; old Istanbullus remember the Greeks, Armenians and Jews – and miss them. Many non-Christian Istanbullus celebrate a secular Christmas and even go to Midnight Mass at the Catholic churches of Santa Maria and San Antonio di Padua. These depleted communities remain part of the deeper memory of this city of forgetting and remembering.

A scene on the Galata Bridge between the old city and the new in 1878:

> *Behind a crowd of Turkish porters, who go by on a run, bending beneath the weight of enormous burdens, there comes a sedan chair inlaid with mother-of-pearl and ivory, out of which peeps the head of an Armenian lady; on either side of it may be seen a Bedouin wrapped in his white cape, and an old Turk wearing a white muslin turban and blue caftan; a young Greek trots by, followed by his dragoman dressed in embroidered zouaves; next comes a dervish in his conical hat and camel's hair mantle, who jumps aside to make room for the carriage of a European ambassador preceded by liveried outriders ... Before you have time to turn around you find yourself surrounded by a Persian regiment in their towering caps of black astrakhan; close behind comes a Jew, clad in a long yellow garment open up the sides; then a dishevelled gypsy, her baby slung in a sack on her back; next a Catholic priest, with his staff and breviary; while advancing among a mixed crowd of Greeks, Turks, and Armenians may be seen a gigantic eunuch on horseback, shouting* Vardah! (Make way!), *and closely following him, a Turkish carriage decorated with flowers and birds and filled with the ladies of a harem, dressed in green and violet and enveloped in great white veils; behind them comes a sister of charity from one of the Pera hospitals, and after her an African slave carrying a monkey, and a story-teller in the garb of a necromancer...*

– Edmondo de Amicis, *Constantinople*, translated by M.H. Lansdale

3

Istanbul As It Used To Be

ISTANBUL, WHEN I FIRST CAME HERE fifty years ago, was still the post-war backwater described by Orhan Pamuk in his *Istanbul: Memories and the City*; more like what can be seen in the old black and white photographs taken by Turkey's great photographer, Ara Güler, than the crowded metropolis it has since become. In those days its population numbered around one million, and it still conveyed the mood of *hüzün* or melancholy that Pamuk dwells on. I retain in my bones a memory of the old rattletrap buses pounding over cobblestones, and the bus tickets made of flimsy paper you would buy from a man who hovered around the bus queue. Once on board, you handed them to the conductor, and when he had accumulated a pile of these tickets he would strike a match and burn them in a tin tray by the driver's seat. This way of doing things wouldn't make sense anywhere else, but in Istanbul it seemed somehow normal.

In their nomadic early days, it is said, the Turks worshipped water, fire and air. Even today it is clear that these are Istanbul's three elements: water because the city is surrounded by water, divided between its European and Asian sides by the Bosphorus, that channel of unfathomable conflicting currents that runs between the Karadeniz, or Black Sea, into the Sea of Marmara and then into the Akdeniz, or White Sea, which is the name the Turks give to the Mediterranean. The old city, sometimes called Stamboul, is itself separated from the newer city of Beyoğlu by the Haliç, an estuary known in English as the Golden Horn. Air is predominant because the city is built on a series of hills, and to be in Istanbul is to be conscious of open spaces, distances and views.

Its other element, fire, has an essential connection to the life of the city. The Byzantines used their famous 'Greek fire', a kind of early napalm, as a weapon against their enemies in times of siege. The fires over which meat is grilled fill the air with a fragrance one catches everywhere. Fire shaped the life of the city for centuries. Churches, mosques and other public structures were built of stone and brick, but residences were made of wood, and great conflagrations periodically swept through whole neighbourhoods, reducing them to ashes.

Istanbul in the 1960s

When I first visited here, the black market currency exchange still thrived. The official rate ran to something like seven or eight Turkish lira for a dollar, but you could get twelve or thirteen if you knew where to change your money. I remember the *frisson* of slipping into a back room behind a shop in the Covered Bazaar and signing over a few travellers' cheques to a haggard-looking man in a shiny black double-breasted suit who would then hand over a sheaf of shopworn Turkish lira, which had clearly passed through many hands. The black market for money is a thing of the past now. You insert your bank card into a cash machine just like you do anywhere else in the world, and out come crisp *Türk Lirası*, Turkish Liras. One new lira equals one million of the old, eliminating the confusion of many zeros, and the absurdity of paying a man behind a little window 250,000 lira to use the public lavatory – a hole in the floor with a place on either side to plant your feet.

Without ever having heard the word back then, I had already become a *flâneur* in Istanbul, wandering around the city in a waking dream. For a few *kuruş* I would lunch on bread, a plate of *piyaz* – white beans served with raw onions and hot green peppers – and a bottle of cold water. No one drinks tap water in Istanbul, you don't even brush your teeth with it. I am told it will give you a headache. Wandering the streets at night I would enter a pastry shop called a *muhallebici* or *pastane* and order up a little plate of sticky sweet baklava and a tiny cup of bitter Turkish coffee, that strong, thick concoction that may be ordered either *sade*, sugarless; *şekerli*, sweet; or *orta şekerli*, medium-sweet.

On my own I would climb the steep cobbled streets of Galata, or stroll beside the Sea of Marmara, where rusting Soviet tankers steamed past over the glittering surface of the sea and a man with a day off from work would take his family to the shore, where they would go fishing, or spread out a blanket or *kilim* alongside the crumbling masonry of the Byzantine walls. There these descendants of Central Asian nomads would set up their charcoal braziers, slice up tomatoes, bread and cucumbers, and grill lamb on skewers just as their ancestors did on the Asian steppes.

I remember boarding the old Orient Express in Paris – though by my time it retained little glamour beyond its own name and the names of the places it passed through. Little flashes come back, impressions of sleeping on the floor of a train with wooden compartments and narrow corridors, catching a glimpse of the Stalinist state as we passed through Bulgaria. Soldiers came on board and stayed there from the border with Yugoslavia to the border of Turkey, waking the sleepers and intimidating the passengers with their brusqueness, heavy boots and loud voices. Early in the morning on one of these trips we looked out the window to see a brass band playing on the platform of the first station inside Turkey.

On that visit in 1967, did I drive overland or bring the Volkswagen by ship, its fenders dented from the thick ropes that were used to lift the car on board when we sailed from Piraeus to Crete, to Mykonos, to Rhodes? From this distance in time I can't remember. I do recall bathing in the Black Sea at Kilyos and then, later, smoking hashish on the roof of the Pudding Shop on the Divanyolu in Sultanahmet, Istanbul's way-station on the hippy trail to India in the '60s and early '70s. Late one night I went to the lavatory in a building in Çemberlitaş, when suddenly the light bulb hanging down on its cord began to swing rapidly back and forth. An earthquake was occurring.

In my student days I learnt to get around the city by bus. Then somehow I became middle-aged, and like the middle-class Turks whom I knew, I got into the habit of taking taxis everywhere. On recent trips I have started buying an *Akbil*, 'smart ticket', which Wikipedia defines aptly as an 'iButton on a plastic fob', and using it to take public transportation again, finding that the slow journeys are not only cheaper, but give me leisure time to relish sights glimpsed out the window of a bus, noticing street signs like *Peri Çıkmaz*, 'the cul-de-sac of the Fairy', which you pass on your left as you travel north on the coast road just beyond the Beşiktaş ferry landing. The *Akbil* is good on ferries, trams, light rail, etc., and you can top it up at machines located conveniently around the city.

If you take the bus up the steep slope from Beşiktaş toward Taksim you get a fleeting glimpse of how beautiful parts of the city must have been before the age of cement. You glimpse the lime-green of a mosque beside a ruined Ottoman mansion whose plaster walls still retain a lovely plum colour though all its windows are missing their panes – and beside these two, a gateway with a pointed arch leading who knows where. On a trip by bus or taxi up the Bosphorus on the European side, I like to look at the old Egyptian Embassy's summer quarters by the harbour at Bebek. It is an Art Nouveau mansion, now uncared-for, going seedy and weedy.

Going by bus down the slope that swings around from Taksim to the Atatürk Bridge, you see the downhill fringes of Beyoğlu streets that descend from Istiklal Caddesi, the main shopping street once called the Grande Rue de Pera, where Greek, Jewish, Armenian and Levantine merchants once lived in smart Art Nouveau apartment buildings. *Pera* means 'across' in Greek – the part of the city across the Golden Horn. Dilapidated and down-at-heel, paint blistering off old walls, an old wooden mansion in the Ottoman style survives here and there; you fear it will be torn down, hoping instead that it will be bought up and restored. Many of these now derelict apartment buildings are fantasias fronted with classical pilasters, round arches, projecting bays that imitate the old Turkish houses, which sent rooms out over the street with latticed oriel windows called *cumbas* in Turkish. Levantine architecture in the early twentieth century was eager to Europeanise, while at the same time keeping Orientalist fantasies alive. The city is a theatre of rot and renewal.

The black market money, the unfamiliar cuisine, the look of the people, the ancient cobbled streets climbing steeply above a harbour congested with ships and boats of all descriptions, the congress of stenches and fragrances that met one's nostrils, the wail of the call to prayer – all of this inspired a curiosity to understand a city I found both alluring and forbidding. Step by step over a period of almost half a century, I tried to piece together a solution to this puzzle by learning to read the language, attempting to understand the religion, studying both Byzantine and Ottoman history, educating myself about the art and architecture of the city, and finally trying to get a sense of why Istanbul is the city that it is.

4

Neighbourhoods

I VISIT ISTANBUL in all its seasons: in spring when the acacias and quinces are in bloom, or in summer when you look for shade under the plane trees and catch the astringent perfume of fig trees as you walk the dusty streets. Or else in autumn when you are disappointed to learn that the mosquitoes haven't died off yet, but delighted at the flocks of migrating storks that fill the skies. At first I used to book into a hotel in Sultanahmet, the historic quarter, because that was where most of the things I wanted to see were to be found, even though one was accosted by touts, rug salesmen and postcard sellers. I tried not to mind too much, because this is how some people make their living in a city where there is still great poverty. Later, when I came to town I would stay in Bebek or Arnavutköy, where I could stroll undisturbed beside the Bosphorus in the mornings and evenings, eat fish in restaurants along the coast road, and take a ferry across to the quiet waterside villages on the Asian side.

Like London or New York, once you get below the surface of its immensity, Istanbul is a city of neighbourhoods, villages whose outskirts have meshed with one another as the metropolis has grown. For glimpses of upper-middle-class Turkish life, go to Nişantaşı, where you can hobnob with Istanbullus who might be characters from Orhan Pamuk's memoirs or his novel *The Museum of Innocence*. Fatih, a short bus ride from Sultanahmet, has a conservative religious atmosphere. Walking these streets, shopping in the weekly market around the Fatih Mosque, you could almost be in a Turkish village. Traditionally the spiritual centre of Istanbul has been Eyüp, a suburb on the Golden Horn that has grown up around the tomb of Eyüp el-Ensari, a companion of the Prophet who was in the army that besieged Constantinople unsuccessfully in the seventh century.

The commercial centre of the old city was the bazaar quarter. The Kapalıçarşı or Covered Bazaar lies at the heart of the quarter, but it is surrounded by street after street given over to metal work and other light manufacturing, trade and commerce. In the Ottoman fashion, shops dealing in the same items clump together; so if it is inlaid backgammon sets or chessboards you are after, for instance, you will find any number of shops selling them side by side on Uzun Çarşı, Long Market Street, which plunges downhill from the Kapalıçarşı to the Spice Bazaar.

A survival from the early days when caravans brought goods over great distances to be sold in the capital are the *hans*, commercial warehouses where merchants could stable their pack animals, safely store their goods, and put up for the night. My favourite of these is the seventeenth-century Büyük Valide Han, the Great Han of the Queen Mother, on Çakmakçılar Yokuşu. To accommodate the religious needs of Persian merchants, there was a Shiite mosque on the grounds. I like to climb up to the roof for the view of the Golden Horn over domes out of which grass now grows.

Neighbourhoods along the Bosphorus still retain something of their original village flavour. Üsküdar on the Asian side of the city, a ferry ride across from Beşiktaş, has, like Fatih, a more conservative, Anatolian atmosphere than do those parts of the city on the European side of the water. A much-loved restaurant, Kanaat, is in Üsküdar. I'll get back to Kanaat later. During Ottoman times the annual Hajj, the pilgrimage to Mecca, set out from here, headed up by a white camel laden down with gifts from the Sultan. Üsküdar makes for a very pleasant ramble, as do Sultanahmet, Tünel and Asmalımescit, Fatih, Kanlıca and the upper Bosphorus.

Venturing out into the back streets

Apart from commercial areas, up-market parts of town and tourist centres like Sultanahmet, there is a kind of generic Turkish neighbourhood which I like very much. After I have settled into my hotel, unpacked and had a wash, I like to set out into the back streets. Once there, I feel I am really back in Istanbul. On one corner there'll be a *kebapçı* or *köfteci*, where shish kebabs, *döner* kebabs, *köftes* and the other versions of meatballs cooked on skewers are grilled over an open fire, served with bread and a *çoban salatası* or 'shepherd's salad' of chopped tomatoes, cucumbers, onions and hot peppers, and washed down with *ayran*, a delicious drink of yoghurt mixed with water. If you want beer, someone from the restaurant will usually go out and get a couple of cold bottles of Efes, the excellent Turkish lager. In fine weather you can eat outdoors. Your meal will cost you well under the equivalent of ten pounds. The pleasure of sitting outside in the temperate evening air, drinking a beer and eating a kebab! Scraps of music, whiffs of roasting lamb and ears of corn, and the aromatic tobacco of the *nargile* smokers blow past on the breeze.

Along the street are the *bakkal* or family corner shop, the *kasap* or butcher shop, and the *manav*, or greengrocer. There is always a barber shop with old-fashioned barber chairs and the generic calendar on the wall with an iconic photograph of Atatürk on it. Neighbourhoods like this are the *çarşı* or marketplace, the *meydan* or public centre or agora where the men of the quarter gather in small groups to smoke cigarettes, gossip and discuss the latest news. You will find the occasional *çamaşırhane*, or laundry, which is handy and much cheaper than having things laundered in your hotel. Then there are card rooms filled with men playing obscure games including one that seems to resemble hearts. Then comes the local mosque, and the religious men, sometimes wearing skullcaps, baggy trousers, long shirts and full beards, their moustaches clipped close, as the Prophet's is said to have been.

The road will be cobbled or paved with bricks, lined in many places with ancient *çınars*, plane trees, some of which have been provided with little protective walls of whitewashed brick and wire fencing, and there is the occasional crepe myrtle or oleander as well. In many places grape vines have been trained to grow across the narrow streets to provide a natural arbour. As you stroll along, people will naturally be curious about you; if you greet someone with *Iyi akşamlar*, 'Good evening', they will greet you in return and be pleased that you know a little Turkish. If you say *Selamün Aleyküm*, 'the peace of God be with you', they will be even more pleased, because you will be showing that you respect their religion. These streets are full of men. When they go home they enter a world where women rule, but the *meydan* is a masculine space.

Stray cats loiter, and people come out to feed them. They feed them more or less anything, or so it seems. Is there anywhere else where cats will eat cucumbers and tomatoes and bread? I suppose they must be very hungry. The Prophet Muhammad was said to have been fond of cats. In one of the hadiths, the legendary stories of the Prophet, it is said that once when it came time for him to get up and leave some of his friends, a cat was asleep on his robe. So he asked for a pair of scissors and cut out the portion of the robe where the cat was sleeping, so as not to disturb the creature.

In this ancient city, history is never far away. I like to stay in Fener, the old Greek neighbourhood along the Golden Horn. It's only two ferry stops from the Galata Bridge and if you are in a rush, a taxi to Eminönü, the centre of the old city, costs five liras, or about £1.20. If you walk along the coast road you will see remains of the Byzantine sea walls, where both the Crusaders, and later the Turks, made their assault on the city. One night, in a neighbourhood called Cibali, I came across a low gate cut into the wall just above Kadir Has University, where there is a marker which I will translate as follows: 'Here on the 29th of May 1453, an officer from Bursa, Cebe Ali Bey, broke an opening through the city wall. Because he entered here, people call this quarter Cibali.' Not far from this gate is the Gül Camii, or Rose Mosque, which the Constantinopolitans crowded into on that fateful day in 1453, in a vain attempt to escape their fate. When Ottoman troops burst into the original Orthodox church, they were charmed and bemused to find that the Greeks, mostly women and children, and men too old to fight, had filled the sanctuary with roses; and because the Turks love roses, perhaps they showed some mercy.

Mecidiyeköy

There are parts of Istanbul that it would never occur to most of us to visit – places that are not conveniently located, scenic, or of historical interest. One winter I spent some time in such a neighbourhood: Mecidiyeköy, which is a subway ride past Taksim on the new side of the city. On cold mornings I would wrap myself in a duvet on the seventh floor overlooking the maze of streets that wander through this neighbourhood, which is home to some of the more than twelve or fifteen million people who have crowded into Istanbul in the last half century. None of the buildings here even existed in the years when I first came to the city. Grass once grew on these steep hills that are now lined with undistinguished six- and seven-storey poured-concrete apartment blocks. Sheep grazed here, and vegetable plots flourished, producing food for the city's markets. The precipitous slopes, called *yokuş* in Turkish, though paved, look as though someone simply dumped a few truckloads of hot asphalt at the top and let it run downhill.

On a snowy morning there I would be awake early. While a baby tried out its first syllables in the adjacent flat, from down in the canyon-like streets below you could hear an occasional automobile horn, tires spinning in the snow, and men shouting instructions to a driver trying to get his car unstuck: *Gel! Gel! Gel!* ['C'mon back! C'mon back! C'mon back!']. A black and white cat would pick its way one paw at a time through the snow across the red-tiled roof of the building next door for a better view of what was going on in the street below. Later, after people had gone off to work, quiet would return, the mid-morning silence broken only by the repetitive cries of street vendors making their rounds: the man who calls out *simit!*, the hard, chewy, delicious sesame roll available everywhere in Istanbul; or the junk man with his pushcart, calling *Eskici, Eskicii!*, or the scrap-metal man, the *hurdacı*.

Tourists stay in Sultanahmet because that's where the ancient church of Haghia Sophia stands, with the Blue Mosque directly across the park from it, and the Covered Bazaar just a few blocks up Divan Yolu, which has been a main street in the city for two thousand years. Visitors and residents alike turn up in Tünel and Asmalımescit at night for the restaurants and night life. A trip to Üsküdar is a great excuse to get out on the water, with the added attraction of being the only place in the world where you can go from one continent to another by ferry. While Mecidiyeköy has little to interest visitors, at the same time it's nobody's slum. It is a working- and middle-class enclave crowded with people doing whatever they need to do to put food on the table. People work really hard in Istanbul to make ends meet. Staying in an apartment where the hot water supply is not always reliable and the radiators are often not very warm contributes to one's sense of what life must be like for most Istanbullus.

The gas-burning heating unit in our apartment that winter, called a *Kombi*, never seemed to come on when it was most needed, though I translated the manual into English and my son and I fiddled with it endlessly. On the balconies of the building I could see outside my bedroom window, the occupants stacked firewood and bags of coal. Every now and then a woman wearing a colourful headscarf would come out to rummage in a burlap bag for a few bricks of coal. Once or twice during a snowstorm I fantasised about breaking up the furniture and burning it for warmth, as in a Russian novel.

To venture out into the storm, trudging through the snow in the streets, past plastic bags full of rubbish, is to see the city not as a tourist destination, a place of charm and exotica, or even as the post-imperial metropolis Istanbul has been since the last sultans threw in their lot with the losing side in the First World War. An entire sociology may be read in the sight of a woman wearing high, spike-heeled boots inching her way sideways up an icy *yokuş* in Mecidiyeköy.

5

Türkçe

THE LANGUAGE WE KNOW AS TURKISH is called *Türkçe* in the native language of *Türkiye*, or Turkey. While it is unlikely that a short-term visitor to Istanbul will have the time or inclination to learn much of the language, some familiarity can be both helpful and interesting, and a few words and catchphrases can take you surprisingly far. My own Turkish is rather slow and halting since I am never in town long enough to get much practice, but still I am often told that I 'speak beautiful Turkish' – a great confidence builder no matter how untrue it is! People's faces light up when they hear a foreigner speaking or even just trying to speak the language.

While Turkish is the first language of some 83 million people worldwide, it has little currency outside Turkey itself or among the Turkish residents of Northern Cyprus, some parts of Iraq, Greece, Bulgaria, the Republic of Macedonia, Kosovo, Albania and parts of Eastern Europe. *Türkçe* can also be heard among immigrant groups in Western Europe, Germany in particular. Related Turkic languages are also spread across the southern tier of what used to be the Soviet Union, stretching from the Black Sea across Azerbaijan, Turkmenistan, Uzbekistan, Tajikistan, Kyrgyzstan and Kazakhstan on the western borders of Tibet.

To give you an idea of how close these languages are to Turkish, I found that an Azeri I once met at a cocktail party and I could converse if he spoke Azerbaijani and I spoke Turkish. No doubt the cocktails helped. For readers with a scholarly bent, these languages are part of the Turkic-Altaic language family. Turkish is not part of the Indo-European language family which comprises most European languages, nor is it a Semitic language like Arabic. This is because, before they began to migrate westward, the Turks were a group of nomadic tribes who herded sheep on the western marches of China.

Grammar and pronunciation

So much for the history and classification of the language. While the English sentence naturally structures itself around a subject-verb-object pattern, Turkish traditionally likes subject-object-verb. The information the sentence wants to convey accumulates, once the subject has been stated, in anticipation of the verb, as in the sentence *Ahmet bugün şehirde bir masal bana anlattı* – Ahmet told me a story today in town – literally 'Ahmet today in town a story to me told'. Before revealing what the action of the sentence is, Turkish fills us in on when and where and to whom it happened. But these rules do not always apply; words can be placed in differing orders for emphasis.

Turkish pronouns do not reveal gender; the pronoun *o*, for example, can mean he, she, or it, depending on the context. In Turkish there is no verb 'to have', one of the most common verbs in English. So how does one express possession or ownership? This is done by inflecting – adding the right ending – to the word that identifies what is owned, and then using that very common Turkish expression, *var*, 'there is'. 'I have a car' becomes *Arabam var*, 'My car exists'. The opposite of *var* is *yok*, 'there is not'. *Arabam yok*, 'I don't have a car', literally 'My car does not exist'. Again unlike English, Turkish lacks prepositions; every word is inflected: *arabada*, 'in or on the car'; *arabadan*, 'from or out of the car'; *Arabamı sürüyorum*, 'I am driving my car'.

Turkish is an agglutinative language, meaning that one word gets tacked onto the end of another to express meaning. Thus the word *çamaşırhane*, used in a previous chapter, tacks *hane*, 'house' or 'place', onto *çamaşır*, meaning 'laundry', to signify a place where laundry gets done. The relation between two nouns may also be articulated in a slightly more specific way by the use of the 'possessive couplet'. The meeting place of the Mevlevi dervishes in Tünel is called the Mevlevihanesi, literally 'the Mevlevi, their house'. The *i* on the end of the word, preceded by the buffer consonant *s* to avoid having two vowels in a row, indicates that the second word pertains to the first.

This may well be more than you want to know. But it does explain why you will sometimes see an *i* on the end of a word, and sometimes not. *Cadde* means avenue; *sokak* means street. The *i* on the end of a word completes what is called the possessive couplet, showing that the word is connected to what comes before, in this case the name of the street or avenue. When an *i* gets tacked onto *sokak*, it becomes *sokağı*, as in the television program *Susam Sokağı*, the Turkish version of the American TV show for children, 'Sesame Street'. Turkish doesn't like harsh sounds, so the *k* gets softened to a *ğ*, called a 'soft g'. And *Bankalar Caddesi* is The Street of the Banks.

Place names like *Aya Sofya*, 'Holy Wisdom', or *Divan yolu*, 'the Street of the Divan', are sometimes written as two words, sometimes as one, *Ayasofya*, or *Divanyolu*. *Büyük* means big, *küçük* means little. One of the city's most notable churches, Saints Sergius and Bacchus, converted into a mosque, has become known as the *Küçük Ayasofya*, The Little Haghia Sophia, because of its supposed resemblance to the great church. You will see the name of the mosque and the street it has given its name to, written as either *Küçük Ayasofya* or *Küçükayasofya*.

Something that makes Turkish a pleasant language to listen to is vowel harmony, whereby the vowels in successive syllables get changed to follow the pattern of what comes before. The plural is formed by adding *–lar* or *–ler*, for example, as in *arabalar*, 'cars or carriages', and *kalemler*, 'pens'. Consonants also change in the interest of euphony. The last letter of *kebab*, for example, changes to produce the word *kebapçı*, maker or seller of kebabs. When *Mehmed* becomes 'Little Mehmed', the *d* changes to *t*, and the word is spelled *Mehmetçik*. D and t, which linguists called dentals, sometimes find themselves used interchangeably. Mahmud and Mehmed are sometimes written Mahmut and Mehmet, for instance. The *yumuşak g*, or 'soft g', can be confusing. It is unpronounced, and only serves to lengthen the previous vowel. The neighbourhood of *Beyoğlu* is pronounced something like Bay-oh-loo.

Then there are the vowels that do not occur in English. The umlauted *ü* in Atatürk's name, for instance, is pronounced by rounding the lips and saying the English vowel u. The umlauted *ö* in the first syllable of *köprü*, 'bridge', sounds a bit like the u in 'cup' if you try to push the sound right to the front of the mouth. Then there is the undotted i, written as *ı*. This sounds a bit like the English sound *uh* when pushed to the front of the mouth. To distinguish the capital undotted I from the capital dotted I, Turkish uses this character: İ. The dotted capital I can appear rather peculiar to our eyes, and I have not used it in this book in names like Ibrahim and Istanbul.

Grammatically, Turkish does not express gender. The context has to tell us, for example, whether *onun evi* means 'her house' or 'his house'. *Kardeş* means 'sibling', but can be made more specific by saying *erkek kardeş*, 'boy sibling' or *kız kardeş*, 'girl sibling' – in other words, brother or sister.

Sometimes Turkish uses the plural where English uses the singular. When someone wants to wish you a good journey they say *Iyi yolculuklar*, literally 'Good journeys'. Or *iyi akşamlar*, literally 'good evenings', where we say 'have a good trip' or 'good evening'. Incidentally, when I give the plurals of Turkish words, I don't use the Turkish endings – that would be too confusing to readers unfamiliar with the language. So in this book the plural of *yalı*, a wooden mansion on the Bosphorus, is given as *yalıs*, not *yalılar*. The plural of *dolmuş*, a shared-ride taxi, in this book, is *dolmuşes*, not *dolmuşlar*.

Useful pleasantries

These observations only scratch the surface. *Türkçe* is a fascinating language for many reasons, perhaps chiefly because of how different it is from English. One thing about it that comes in handy is that the spoken language is filled with common pleasantries that can be used as formulas in certain situations. In restaurants you will often hear your waiter and your fellow diners say *afiyet olsun!*, the Turkish equivalent of *bon appetit!* If someone is sick or going through a bad patch, you say *Geçmiş olsun!*, 'may it pass', or something like 'get well soon'. If you pass someone who is working you can say *kolay gelsin*, literally 'let it come easily', just as the French say *bon courage* in a similar situation. *Kolay gelsin* is also a common informal farewell, like 'Take it easy' in English.

If *günaydın*, 'good morning', or *iyi akşamlar*, 'Good evening', prove to be too difficult to say, then *merhaba*, 'hi', works too, even if it is more informal. *Teşekkür ederim*, 'thank you', is a mouthful, and *çok teşekkür ederim*, 'thank you very much', even more so. *Sağ olun* (formal) or *sağ ol* (informal), 'may you be healthy, or strong', work fine. Learn a few of these pleasantries and you too will find you speak 'beautiful Turkish'.

Part II

Roman and Byzantine Constantinople

6

Constantine the Great

IN THE FOURTH CENTURY, what Shakespeare called 'the most high and palmy state of Rome' was entering a perilous period of her history. The Roman Republic had long since given way to the Roman Empire, which was surrounded on all sides by enemies envious of her wealth and power. Territories in Asia Minor and what we call the Middle East, which the Romans had in the second century seized from the Persians, were now threatened by a resurgence of Persian power under a new dynasty, while to the north, in Europe, barbarian tribes were on the move.

The days of anything resembling representative government, when the emperor was chosen by the Roman senate, an elite body of Italian aristocrats, were gone with the wind. Now the empire had become in effect a military dictatorship whose leader was chosen by acclamation from within the ranks of the army. In the words of the historian Peter Sarris, 'one ineffectual emperor after another was deposed and murdered by his own soldiers'. Sarris goes on to say that Constantine's rise to power 'can only be understood in the context of the brutal and opportunistic manœuvring of ambitious men which characterised the politics of the later Roman Empire'. Even to call the empire Roman anymore is misleading, if we picture a centralised realm governed from Rome. The soldier-emperors, who were increasingly unlikely to be Roman in origin, were constantly mobile as the army fought campaigns in Asia Minor, North Africa, the Balkans, or Northern Europe.

To address the decentralisation of the empire, which could no longer be governed by one man, the Emperor Diocletian, voluntarily relinquishing the reins of power in 305 and retiring to his farm on the

Dalmatian coast to grow cabbages, introduced a system of governance called the Tetrarchy, whereby the empire was administratively divided into east and west, with a senior and junior emperor (Augustus and Caesar respectively) in charge of each. While this arrangement in theory made the top-heavy empire easier to govern, in reality, considering the power-hungry generals who were appointed to these offices, it simply created a system whereby four ambitious men were placed in a position to fight against each other until the strongest man won.

A curious statue representing the Tetrarchy, carved from Egyptian porphyry, stands near the southwestern corner of St Mark's Cathedral in Venice. This statue, with its brutish figures of four warriors, bearing none of the grace of the Græco-Roman sculptural tradition, the stone itself coloured an anti-luminous maroon, offers a sobering image of the reality of power in what the Roman Empire had become by the time of Constantine's early days. Dressed and posed identically, each grim-faced man grasps the hilt of his sword in one hand while with the other he grips the shoulder of his co-ruler, as if each is determined to prevent the other men from making the first aggressive move. None of the majesty or mystique which mention of the Roman Empire may conjure up in our minds attaches to these blunt, graceless warriors. It's as though they are posed for some sort of ritual time-out, and at a pre-arranged signal, they will come out fighting. Which is exactly what they did.

The Roman Empire and the new religion

Constantine's circumstances and the trajectory of his rise to power give some indication of the geographical spread of the Roman Empire. He was born in what is today the Serbian town of Niš, located in the Roman province of Dacia. His father Constantius won the attention of Diocletian through his inspired generalship and was appointed as a Caesar with the assigned task of putting down a rebellion in a faraway province on the northwestern fringes of the empire, called Britain. Constantine followed in his father's footsteps and, fighting by his father's side, distinguished himself in campaigns both in the eastern provinces and in northern Europe. When his father died, the troops raised him on their shields and proclaimed him Augustus.

Inevitably the time came when Constantine would march south across the Alps to confront his rival Maxentius. The inevitable showdown took place just north of Rome where the Milvian Bridge crossed the Tiber. The legend of Constantine claims that on the eve of the battle, the young commander had a vision that was to inspire the rest of his career as a soldier and eventually as emperor. This vision, or rather the legend of it, would change the course of history. His official biographer, the historian Eusebius, reports: 'He said that at about midday, when the sun was beginning to decline, he saw with his own eyes the trophy of a cross of light in the heavens, above the sun, and bearing the inscription Conquer by This (*Hoc Vince*). At this sight he himself was struck with amazement, and his whole army also'. That night Christ appeared to him in a dream and commanded that the symbol of the new religion should appear on the shields of Constantine's troops. Inspired, so the story goes, by this vision and dream, he threw his men into battle against Maxentius, and even though outnumbered, they won a famous victory.

Constantine's vision of the Cross has become one of the set pieces of Christian legend and has often been illustrated in European art. One of the most attractive early representations is a ninth-century miniature in three panels: the topmost shows Constantine asleep on a sumptuous bejewelled couch, dreaming of the cross, the middle panel shows him routing his enemies at the Milvian Bridge, while the third shows his mother Helena's discovery of the True Cross in the Holy Land years later. Perhaps the most sublime depiction is Piero della Francesca's *Dream of Constantine*, a series of frescoes in Arezzo showing the emperor asleep in his tent, watched over by bodyguards, surrounded by the tents of his bivouacked army. The painting conveys an air of dignified mystery – the emperor dreaming, his companions looking as though they had fallen into a trance.

An air of mystery is appropriate to the occasion of Constantine's vision. There are reasons to doubt whether it actually happened at all. The appearance of the cross in the sky, supposedly witnessed by the entire army, was not corroborated by any other observer. Eusebius makes no mention of the vision when he tells the story of the famous battle in his *Ecclesiastical History*, written during Constantine's lifetime, and only records it in his *Life of Constantine*, written many years after the emperor's death. If in fact the entire army saw what Constantine saw, then, as John Julius Norwich archly comments, '98,000 men kept the secret remarkably well'.

In *Pagans and Christians*, a study of the transitional period in the Mediterranean world when paganism was giving way to the new monotheistic religion of Christianity, Robin Lane Fox focuses instead on the second part of Constantine's experience, the appearance of Christ in a dream, commanding that the symbol of the cross appear on the shields of his soldiers when they went into battle the next day. In the world of paganism, occasional appearances by gods did occur, a phenomenon the Greeks called *epiphanos*, from which we get our word 'epiphany'. What was different about Constantine's experience was that the symbol of the cross came first, rather than the appearance of a walking, talking human form, which would have been a more familiar vision in pagan religious life.

These epiphanic appearances of the immortals, larger than life, aglow with strength or beauty and carrying supernatural authority, will be familiar to readers of the *Iliad* and the *Odyssey*. Lane Fox suggests that only with the coaxing of committed Christians would Constantine have come to associate the man in the dream with Christ: 'Perhaps ... he had dreamed of a conventional type of divinity, a young man of outstanding beauty, dressed in shining robes. He could hardly have been more specific, as no artistic image focussed his dream and nobody knew what Christ had looked like.'

Choosing Christianity as the official religion of the empire made good political sense. Because of its early identification with Rome, it strengthened a sense of the empire as Roman, as a way of distancing it from the barbarian influences that had crept in. Christianity also gave the empire a moral and spiritual focus that was in danger of being lost under the rule of the 'barrack emperors' – amongst whom one could be forgiven for including Constantine himself. Thirdly, it put political power into perspective by eliminating an older cult that saw the emperor himself as a god. Though no one doubted that Constantine was the most powerful man in the known world, he went even further in his assertion of authority when he announced that he was 'God's man' – not a god in his own right as some previous emperors had declared. Constantine comes down in history as eminently capable, decisive and masterful, and absolutely sure of his mission. We may get some sense of how he saw himself from Eusebius's *Life of Constantine*:

> With such impiety pervading the human race, and the State threatened with destruction, what relief did God devise? ... I myself was the instrument he chose ... Thus, beginning at the remote Ocean of Britain, where the sun sinks beneath the

> horizon in obedience to the law of Nature, with God's help I banished and eliminated every form of evil then prevailing, in the hope that the human race, enlightened through me, might be recalled to a proper observance of God's holy laws.

Once he had defeated his western challengers, this energetic young campaigner turned to the east and dispatched his last remaining rival, Licinius, whose power base was Asia Minor. Amazingly, as one of history's quirky little footnotes, six fourth-century silver dishes have survived, bearing the inscription *Licini Avgvste Semper Vincas*, 'Licinius Augustus, may you always be victorious' from the period when Licinius was eastern emperor and Constantine western, and they were at peace. In the centre of the dish, surrounded by a laurel wreath, is the crudely carved SIC X SIC XX, 'As ten, so twenty', evidently celebrating Licinius's ten years as Augustus in the eastern empire and making a hopeful prediction for the future. The plates were discovered in 1901 in Niš, Constantine's birthplace. Silver, and weighing exactly one Roman pound each, they were called *largitio* dishes. One of these may be seen in the British Museum. The museum catalogue describes the dish nicely:

> Dishes like this were presented by the emperor to high-ranking soldiers, civil officials and faithful allies on special occasions. Thus when Licinius celebrated the beginning of his tenth year in office, he marked the occasion by taking vows for a second ten years and also by issuing commemorative tokens like this dish. These were known as *largitio*, a Latin word meaning largesse (the liberal bestowal of gifts) but also bribery!

By the time Licinius was defeated and put to the sword, Rome's day as the seat of imperial power had clearly passed. Its location had become too insecure to defend against barbarian incursions. Not only that, but the eastern empire was now more populous and prosperous. The focus of world trade had shifted to the place where Europe met Asia. Perhaps that was why Constantine set his sights on the eastern empire. By fusing Roman imperial power and its traditions of administration and organization with the new world religion of Christianity, Constantine created a new amalgam which would endure during the entire ascendancy of the Byzantine Empire. The division between secular and sacred, what is owed to Caesar as opposed to what is owed to God, has little to do with how these people thought. The emperor was styled 'the faithful in Christ Emperor of the Romans', the 'equal of the apostles'.

A new city and a new civilisation

With his position secure, and with a new religion to give him moral backing and inspire his subjects, Constantine set about consolidating his base of power in a new capital city, to be called Nova Roma Constantinopolitana; the New Rome, the City of Constantine. The good sense of choosing the Greek town of Byzantion as his headquarters was confirmed by the city's impregnability to attack for more than a thousand years. Surrounded almost entirely by water, it could be defended on its short landward side by the construction of a defensive wall. Legend has it that Constantine himself paced out the position of the walls. His entourage became increasingly alarmed by the amount of territory he was encompassing as he walked across the seven hills of the city. When asked how long he intended to keep going, he is said to have replied, 'Until he who walks before me stops walking'.

He set about building his capital city with a large public gathering space, or forum, the equivalent of what existed in Rome. Next came the Hippodrome, a huge open-air arena designed to hold the entire population of the city when they assembled to watch horse racing, gymnastics, games, displays of wild animals, theatre, acrobatics and so on. This was the New Rome's answer to the old Rome's Coliseum. Constantine also built temples, palaces and mansions for the high government officials who followed him here. Roads and squares were laid out, aqueducts and cisterns to provide the city's water supply and public baths for its citizens. All of it was richly adorned with fine marbles, precious metals and statuary. Here is how Gibbon in *The Decline and Fall of the Roman Empire* describes the new capital:

> Some estimate may be formed of the expense bestowed with Imperial liberality on the foundation of Constantinople by the allowance of about two million five hundred thousand pounds for the construction of the walls, the porticoes, and the aqueducts. The forests that overshadowed the shores of the Euxine, and the celebrated quarries of white marble in the little island of Proconnesus, supplied an inexhaustible stock of material, ready to be conveyed ... to the harbour of Byzantium. A

> multitude of labourers and artificers urged the conclusion of the work with incessant toil .... By [Constantine's] command the cities of Greece and Asia were despoiled of their most valuable ornaments. The trophies of memorable wars, the objects of religious veneration, the most finished statues of the gods and heroes, of the sages and poets of ancient times, contributed to the splendid triumph of Constantinople.

What the ancients called the Euxine, we call the Black Sea – Karadeniz in Turkish. The modern name for the island of Proconnesus is Marmara, and it is surrounded by the sea of the same name, which the ancients called the Propontis.

Constantine may have founded one of the greatest cities in the world, but he gets low marks from Gibbon:

> The dress and manners which, towards the decline of life, he chose to affect, served only to degrade him in the eyes of mankind. The Asiatic pomp which had been adopted by the pride of Diocletian assumed an air of softness and effeminacy in the person of Constantine. He is represented with false hair of various colours, laboriously arranged by the skilful artists of the times; a diadem of a new and more expensive fashion; a profusion of gems and pearls, of collars and bracelets; and a variegated flowing robe of silk, most curiously embroidered with flowers of gold.

Interestingly for the man who made his mark in history by establishing Christianity as the state religion of the Roman Empire, Constantine throughout most of his years on the throne entertained a certain ambivalence toward his adopted religion. Many of his subjects, particularly among soldiers in the army, remained convinced pagans, and Constantine could not afford to alienate them. While no doubt the western world was moving toward belief in a single deity, there was still some doubt as to the identity of this being.

When Constantine began minting coins in his own name as emperor, some of them honoured Apollo, the sun god, called 'Sol Invictus', the Unconquered Sun, while others showed Constantine side by side with the sun god. When he assigned a name to the first day of the week, which was to be a holiday, he called it Sunday, the Sun's Day, not as the Latins had it, Domenica, the Lord's Day. He saw

Christ not as the suffering advocate of humanity who was sacrificed to ensure the salvation of mankind, but rather as Christ the victor, the one who triumphed over death, just as Constantine himself had attained victory over his enemies and now single-handedly ruled a newly united Roman Empire.

Constantine placed his main church cheek by jowl with the royal palace, dramatizing the hand-in-glove relationship between church and state. *Basileia* (imperial power) and *sacerdotium* (priesthood) were linked by position – just as they would continue to be in cities influenced by Byzantium such as Venice and Moscow. But just as Constantinople declared itself through architecture a Christian city, in its culture it retained something of the classical heritage of Greece and Rome. Roman schoolboys learnt about grammar and history through the poetry of Homer; boys in the schools of Constantinople were also educated through tales of the epic war under the walls of Troy and of Odysseus's wanderings.

Thus did the pagan world give way, by degrees, to the Christian world. In building his imperial city, Constantine provided temples for pagan worship alongside churches, and pagan rites continued to be celebrated during his reign. The city has a long history of accommodating diverse beliefs. In the Muslim era the all-pervading influence of the dervishes and their Sufistic tolerance softened an authoritarian Islam. Partly too, both Greeks and Turks entertained a substratum of folk beliefs which preceded and coexisted with the orthodox teachings of whatever religion was ascendant at the time. Pilgrims in present day Istanbul good-naturedly ignore the Şeyhülislam's rules about how Muslims should behave at *türbes*, those mausoleums the Turks regard as holy places. Muslim peasant women flock to the old Greek holy wells to pray for healing. And I have yet to find in the Holy Qur'an any reference to the ubiquitous *nazar boncuğu*, that blue bead that the Turks put on every building, on bracelets, necklaces, keychains and fridge magnets to ward off the Evil Eye.

Paganism certainly did not come to an end in the time of Constantine. In the Metropolitan Museum of Art in New York City, I found a curious epigram written as a petition to Christ in the early eleventh century by one John Mauropous: 'If perchance you wish to exempt certain pagans from punishment, my Christ, may you spare for my sake Plato and Plutarch. For both were very close to your laws in both teaching and way of life even if they were unaware that you as

God reign over all. In this matter only your charity is needed, through which you are willing to save all men while asking nothing in return.'

Constantine was a ruler, not a theologian, and he quickly saw how divisive theological hair-splitting could be to his newly reunited empire. He moved to establish an orthodox definition of what Christians should believe. With the development of orthodoxy, rival theories became known as heresies. The most distracting of these arose from a churchman from Alexandria called Arius. Like many of the heresies, Arius's theory had to do with the nature of Christ: was he human, or divine, or a bit of both? According to Arius, Christ did not partake of God's nature, in that his being was not eternal, as God's was; he had been created by God for a specific purpose, the salvation of the world. Thus he was perfect man, though he was not divine, and as such he was subordinate to the Father. It was partly to deal with issues like this that Constantine called a universal council of the Church to meet at Nicæa, a council he presided over in person. Eusebius makes much of the Emperor's entrance into the council chamber:

> And now, all rising at the signal that indicated the Emperor's entrance, at last he himself proceeded through the midst of the assembly like some heavenly Angel of God, clothed in a garment which glittered as though radiant with light, reflecting the glow of a purple robe and adorned with the brilliant splendour of gold and precious stones. When he had advanced to the upper end of the seats, he at first remained standing; and when a chair of wrought gold had been set for him, he waited to sit down until the bishops had signaled to him to do so. After him the whole assembly did the same.

Constantine was a military man and a ruler. At his urging, the bishops refuted the Arian doctrine and declared that Christ is *homoousios*, con-substantial with the Father. This is why, to this day, Christians reciting the Nicæan Creed from the Book of Common Prayer assert that they believe in 'one Lord Jesus Christ, the only-begotten Son of God; Begotten of his Father before all worlds, God of God, Light of Light, Very God of very God; Begotten, not made; Being of one substance with the Father'. For reasons that have been the cause of debate among historians, Constantine delayed being baptised into the faith until he was on his death bed. When the sacrament had been administered to him, he is said to have exclaimed,

'Now I know in very truth that I am blessed; now I have confidence that I am a partaker of divine light'.

The world's marketplace

We tend to view the Byzantine Empire in terms of its art and architecture, to admire the political and military mastery that allowed it to dominate the world for almost a thousand years. It was equally important as a centre for trade. The twelfth-century description of the city by one Benjamin of Tudela, a Jewish merchant from Córdoba, invokes a vanished world of trade and commerce:

> All kinds of merchants come from Babylon and Shin'ar [in Mesopotamia], from Persia and Medea, from all the kingdoms of Egypt, from the land of Canaan, from the kingdom of Russia, from Hungary, from the land of the Petchenegs [Romania], from Kazaria [the Caucasus], from Lombardy and from Spain. It is a tumultuous city; men come to trade there from all countries by land and by sea. There is none like it in all the world except for Baghdad... . They say that the city's daily income, what with the rent from shops and markets and what with the customs levied on merchants coming by sea and by land, reaches twenty thousand gold pieces.

To understand the sources of Constantinople's magnificence, its power and its glory, one must understand how well it exploited, from earliest times, its secure position between Europe and Asia. It was said that two-thirds of the world's wealth was concentrated within the impregnable walls of this great city – *the* city, as the Greeks called it. Caravans reached Constantinople over land routes across the entire Middle East, from places with names to conjure with – Samarkand, Bokhara, Transoxiana, Khorasan and Persia. In some cases their laden camels reached the capital through trading centres such as Antioch and Aleppo. Those great Russian rivers, the Dnieper and the Don, swollen with snowmelt from the northern steppes, brought timber and furs from the kingdoms of Muscovy and Kiev down to ports like Trebizond on the Black Sea, and the docks along the waterfront in Constantinople were kept busy unloading ships that sailed here from as far east as the Bay of Bengal and as far north as the lands of the Vikings, each cargo paying taxes.

Raw materials from all over the known world – rare woods, luxury goods, precious stones and metals – debouched into the city's ateliers and warehouses. Silk and leather came from Peshawar in what is now Pakistan, incense from Arabia. Pepper, nutmeg, cloves, cinnamon and jewels were brought here by ship from India and Cathay. Africa supplied, through trade routes up the Red Sea and via the Mediterranean port of Alexandria, slaves, cotton and corn, gold, ivory, amber and ebony. Fish were shipped from as far away as the North Sea, woolen goods from Bruges, honey, furs, skins and slaves from Eastern Europe, flax from Egypt, cotton from Syria and Armenia.

Constantinopolitan craftsmanship set a standard unequalled in Europe and the Near East. To create the illuminated manuscripts Byzantium was famous for, saffron, alum, indigo and gum were imported to make pigments. An army of expert artificers, craftsmen in precious metals, painters, stonecarvers, workers in mosaic, scribes, weavers, seamstresses, dyers, tailors and button makers all plied their trades profitably between the Marmara and the Golden Horn. And of course manpower was unlimited. The eastern provinces of the empire were densely populated; new people flocked to the capital in search of work. And like ancient Greece and Rome, the Byzantine Empire was built on slavery.

In the Middle Ages, Byzantium, or the Roman Empire as it was called at the time, had immense prestige throughout the world. Early on, the Venetian doges were vested in robes given to them by the Byzantine emperor, who also gave his daughters in marriage to solidify alliances. Orthodox monasteries as well as merchants and traders spread the religion and culture of the empire from Asia Minor throughout the Balkans, into Italy and even as far afield as Sicily.

What remains

Few physical traces of Constantine the Great remain in the city that bore his name for sixteen hundred years, though the basic outlines of the streets as he laid them out have been retained. The course of the Mese, so called because it ran through the middle of the city, has not changed. *Mese* means 'middle' in Greek. The Ottomans retained the Mese as the main street of their city, changing its name to Divanyolu, because the street led in the days of the sultans to the *divan* or council chamber within the Topkapı Saray. (*Yol* or *Yolu* means street.) Despite how busy it is, the Divan Yolu is a street of great charm because of the Ottoman mausolea and old cemeteries that line it from Sultanahmet to the bazaar quarter. I like to drink tea in the Balkan Turk *çay bahçesi* in the garden behind an old cemetery on the right-hand side.

Nearby is the *türbe* of Mahmud II, the reforming sultan from the early years of the nineteenth century. The cemetery surrounding his *türbe* is home to a wonderful collection of monuments to members of the Ottoman royal family and other notables from the declining decades of the empire's last century. The tombs of famous writers are adorned with marble ink wells and quill pens. An admiral's tomb sports the model of a ship. Further down the street, the Column of Constantine, fashioned from six drums of porphyry sitting atop a block of marble, called by the Turks *Çemberlitaş*, the 'Burnt Column', has recently been cleaned and repaired. Even spruced up, however, it is a sad-looking stump of a thing. The statue of Constantine in the guise of Apollo which originally sat on top of it was destroyed during a storm in 1106, and it has been subjected to other indignities in the centuries since then. Today it lends its name to a tram stop.

Constantine, 'Equal of the Apostles', built a mausoleum for himself as part of his Church of the Holy Apostles, a cruciform building that served as the model for St Mark's Cathedral in Venice and many other Byzantine churches. Here Constantine was buried after lying in state at the Great Palace for three months in a gold coffin covered by a purple pall. The last remains of several of his successors were entombed here as well. Mehmed the Conqueror chose the site of the Holy Apostles, standing as it does atop one of Istanbul's seven hills, for his imperial mosque, and the Church of the Holy Apostles was pulled down and its materials used to build the mosque. Fatih's mosque itself was destroyed by an earthquake in the eighteenth century, and the mosque that occupies the site dates only from that time. Porphyry sarcophagi, some of which held the bones of Byzantine royalty, can be seen around the grounds of the Archæological Museum. I once saw one of these being used to house an air-conditioner.

7

Justinian and Theodora: A walk through imperial Constantinople

THE CHURCH OF HAGHIA SOPHIA was the spiritual centre of Constantinople, as we shall see, but the Hippodrome, or as it is called in Turkish, the *At Meydanı* or 'Horse Grounds', was the city's public centre. In its heyday it was nearly 427 feet wide and 1476 feet long, with 40 rows of seats and a capacity of 100,000. As the name implies, horse races were run here, and the early Constantinopolitans were mad about sports, horse racing in particular. The Hippodrome was also where public demonstrations took place. Constantinople had a very contentious citizenry. The Nika Revolt in AD 532 saw a clash of political rivalries between merchant guilds called the Greens, the Blues, the Reds and the Whites. During the revolt the imperial palace and Haghia Sophia sustained massive damage, and Justinian the Great was at the point of being forced off the throne. Justinian vacillated, but his wife Theodora, who was made of sterner stuff, pleaded with him to be resolute. As you shall see a few pages further on, Procopius sometimes described Theodora in distinctly unflattering terms, but in this instance he presents her in a heroic light:

> Every man who is born into the light of day [she said] must sooner or later die; and how could an Emperor ever allow himself to be a fugitive? May I myself never willingly shed my imperial robes, nor see the day when I am no longer addressed by my title. If you, my Lord, wish to save your skin, you will have no difficulty in doing so. We are rich, there is the sea, there too are our ships. But consider first whether, when you reach safety,

> you will not regret that you did not choose death in preference. As for me, I stand by the ancient saying: the purple is the noblest winding sheet.

Justinian marshalled his forces and managed to seize power again. When he did so, he was determined to deal the rebels a decisive blow. He instructed his troops to seal off the gates to the Hippodrome when it was full of people. What followed was a bloodbath. More than 30,000 people were massacred on Justinian's orders.

The royal couple

The Emperor Justinian himself was born in the Balkans, in the Roman province of Thrace. His mother tongue was probably Thracian, a language which would become extinct well before the end of the first millennium. His uncle and patron, Justin, who was emperor before he was succeeded by his nephew, also sprang from the Thracian peasantry, and was probably illiterate. Justin possessed a wooden stencil into which was cut the word LEGI, 'I have read it'. He would trace the word out in purple ink, and since only the emperor was allowed to use purple, this would make it clear, when it appeared on any document, whose imprimatur it was. Made possible by expertise passed on from the dying culture of classical Greece, backed by the shrewdness, high ambition and treasure of an emperor who was not very far from the mud and thatch of a life among the Balkan peasantry in a remote province of the old Roman Empire, itself being destroyed; the great Church of Haghia Sophia was built in just five years and consecrated on 26 December 537.

If Justinian's peasant background strikes us as an unlikely preparation for one who would become the head of this powerful empire, the pedigree of his Empress Theodora is even more surprising. Theodora was not the kind of girl you would want to take home to mother. Few empresses could boast having a bear-keeper as a father, or a circus performer and acrobat as a mother. Yet such was Theodora's parentage. The sixth-century Byzantine historian Procopius's account of her in his *Secret History*, which contains all the juicy bits he had to leave out of his official chronicles, is certainly among the most scandalous descriptions of a ruler ever to see the light of day. Here is a paragraph from the *Secret History* concerning Theodora's early years:

> Now for a time Theodora was still too immature to sleep with a man or to have intercourse like a woman, but she acted as might a male prostitute to satisfy those dregs of humanity, slaves though they were, who followed their master to the theatre and took the opportunity to indulge in such bestial practices; and she remained some considerable time in a brothel, given over to such unnatural traffic of the body ... But as soon as she reached maturity she joined the women of the stage and became a harlot, of the kind that our ancestors used to call 'the infantry' ... The wench had not an ounce of modesty, nor did any man ever see her embarrassed: on the contrary, she unhesitatingly complied with the most shameless demands ...

The historian John Julius Norwich calls him a 'sanctimonious old hypocrite', but it's hard to believe Procopius was making all this up. While in some ways Constantinople was indeed the Holy City, it clearly had its seamy side as well. Those lords and ladies of Byzantium that Yeats wrote about didn't spend all their time in rapt contemplation of the divine mysteries.

Justinian was perhaps the greatest of the Byzantine emperors after Constantine. In addition to rebuilding Haghia Sophia, he worked tirelessly as an administrator. Palace officials referred to him behind his back as 'the sleepless one': his relentless energy kept him on the job at all hours. He reorganised the bureaucracy of the state, tried to eliminate kickbacks and corruption, and unified the civil and military authorities in the provinces. Perhaps his most important work was to establish a set of laws known as the Code of Justinian, in which Roman law was laid out systematically and encyclopædically in many volumes. His ambitious goal of regaining for the empire territories that had been lost to Germanic invaders such as the Visigoths and the Vandals was achieved thanks to the leadership of a remarkable general named Belisarius, who embodied the traditional Roman martial virtues. In 534 he retook North Africa and then, after a twenty-year war, he brought Italy back under Byzantine control.

The Hippodrome

On the right-hand or west side of the Hippodrome as one walks along it away from Ayasofya, is the Museum of Turkish and Islamic Antiquities, housed in what was the private palace of Ibrahim Paşa,

Grand Vizier (Turkish *vezir*) under Süleyman the Magnificent. Just as Süleyman's favourite and beloved wife, Roxelana, was of Russian – or more precisely, Ruthenian or Ukrainian – origin, Ibrahim, his intimate friend, was a Greek convert to Islam who rose to become the most powerful man in the empire and was married to Süleyman's sister Hadice. He eventually overreached himself, however, and Süleyman had him assassinated after thirteen years as Vizier, then confiscated his wealth and property. The palace is large even as it stands today, and yet at one time it was about twice its present size. Inside is a splendid collection of carpets, calligraphy, miniatures and so forth. It also houses a good café, as well as a museum shop with fixed prices, for those who are nervous about *pazarlık yapma*, or bargaining.

Today the Hippodrome is less a centre in its own right than a place one passes through on the way to other places. The curious Fountain of Kaiser Wilhelm II, built at the end of the nineteenth century, is a worthy structure that imitates the forms of Ottoman architecture with a curiously North-European ungainliness. It is as if an Ottoman architect went to sleep one night and woke up speaking German. The long, thin strip that runs down the centre of what can be imagined as a long oval race track, with the Palace of Ibrahim Paşa on one side and the cafés and souvenir shops on the other in front of the west gate into the Sultanahmet Mosque, is called the *spina*, or spine, of the Hippodrome.

In the centre of the *spina* is the Serpentine Column, which Constantine the Great brought here from Delphi in the Peloponnese. Before you reach the Serpentine Column, you come to the Egyptian Obelisk. This huge monument, weighing 800 tons, didn't survive the journey by sea to Constantinople intact; only the upper third made it here. It was erected in the Hippodrome by Theodosius the Great, a remarkable man and the last of the Roman emperors to rule over both east and west before the eventual demise of the Western empire and the ascension of the Eastern or Byzantine.

What is especially worth looking at here is the marble base on which the obelisk rests. This block of stone has been carved with ceremonial scenes of the Emperor and his family in the Kathisma, the royal viewing stand that would have stood on the eastern side of the Hippodrome. The carvings are much eroded, but on the north side the Emperor can be seen supervising the transportation and erection of the obelisk, a huge engineering feat in its time. Men with ropes slung over their shoulders are dragging the column along, while others are turning a capstan to wind ropes. On the west side Theodosius receives homage from a group of kneeling captives, who in their Persian head-dresses stand out from the imperial party in Roman dress, togas and so forth – a reminder that those people we call Byzantine thought of themselves, at least during their first few centuries here, as *Rhomainoi*, or Romans. At Theodosius's side are his western co-emperor Valentinian II and the Emperor's two sons, Honorius and Arcadius, who would later become emperors of West and East respectively. On the South side they are watching a chariot race. We see the faces in the crowd, and along the bottom, dancing maidens and musicians.

My favourite parts of the monument are the faces of Theodosius's bodyguards, with their spears and wild moustaches, all of which gives us something of the flavour of this empire in which nothing was assured, not even the lives and security of its rulers. Whatever impressions we may have of the grandeur and majesty of empire, whether Roman, Byzantine, Ottoman or any other, the fact remains that, as Mao Tse-Tung wrote, 'Political power grows out of the barrel of a gun' – or the point of a knife. Valentinian, immortalised here in stone, lost out in a power struggle with the Gauls and was found dead in his private apartments on 15 May 392, aged twenty-one. As John Julius Norwich writes in *Byzantium: The Early Years*, 'Much trouble was taken to prove that his death was the result of suicide ...'

Though the Hippodrome remains as a vestigial reminder of the imperial capital, almost nothing else has survived of the lavishly decorated, sprawling but interconnected series of structures that made up the conglomerate that Constantinopolitans called the Sacred Imperial Palace. The Great Palace covered the wooded slopes that descended down to the Sea of Marmara and the Golden Horn. Gardens and churches lent an air of beauty and sanctity, while summer houses, fountains, a riding school and polo grounds, swimming pools and ornamental ponds brought refreshment. Stables, kitchens and storerooms existed to support the secure and luxurious existence of the Byzantine upper classes. Here the emperors and their courts maintained a way of life determined by ritual and ceremony – described in detail in his *Book of Ceremonies* by that most learned of the emperors, Constantine Porphyrogenitus, who also may have borne the most elegant name of all the emperors. This vanished world is here for travellers with the imagination to picture what is no longer visible.

8

The Holy City

W.B. YEATS NEVER VISITED ISTANBUL, but the poems he wrote, inspired by his reading and his exposure to Byzantine art, have made 'Byzantium' an enduring emblem of the Holy City. Yeats's introduction to Byzantine art came through the mosaics he saw in Palermo and Ravenna. Although it might seem ironic that he never saw with his own eyes the city he made sacred for us through his poems, in a way he didn't need to. The Byzantium that still lives in the world through its art and architecture occupies a kind of eternal present, inspiring wonder and a sense of majesty similar to the effect of the great poems by the Irish master. Yeats was moved by the hieratic mosaic art of Byzantium, and his invocations of the figures depicted in this art marry the shimmering, rippled surface made of thousands of tiny squares of colour, with the spiritual import of what is depicted. His lines about 'sages standing in God's holy fire, / As in the gold mosaic of a wall' beautifully render the relationship between what is pictured and its meaning.

Byzantine art, and the early Italian religious art of the thirteenth and fourteenth centuries that imitated it, appeal to us for their very static and artificial qualities, rather than for the imitation of life that would later come to typify European art before modernism. The last stanza of 'Sailing to Byzantium' captures that sublime artificiality:

Once out of nature I shall never take
My bodily form from any natural thing,
But such a form as Grecian goldsmiths make
Of hammered gold and gold enamelling
To keep a drowsy Emperor awake;

Or set upon a golden bough to sing
To lords and ladies of Byzantium
Of what is past, or passing, or to come.

Yeats's images were inspired by accounts of the artificial trees that visitors to the court described in the throne room; gold and silver leaves and branches covered with fruit fashioned of rubies, emeralds, turquoise and sapphires, where little mechanised golden birds perched and sang.

Imperial Constantinople

Architectural drawings and digital models give us a clear picture of what imperial Constantinople probably looked like. To the north of Haghia Sophia and downhill a bit, stood the church of Haghia Eirene, 'Holy Peace', second in importance only to the great church of Holy Wisdom itself. This much hasn't changed, though Haghia Eirene is now enclosed within the walls of Topkapı Palace. There seems to have been an arcaded forum or agora in the position now occupied by the *meydan* in front of Haghia Sophia. Constantine the Great laid out this plan in the fourth century. At the western end of the agora stood a marble marker called the Milion, which marked the spot from which all distances in the empire were measured. The marker is still there today, but it looks battered and pathetic, and the tram lines divide it from the *meydan*. Because the surface of the ground has risen over the centuries, what with earthquakes, accumulation of rubble and the construction of new roads, you have to look down into a little well to see the base of the once-famous marker.

From this point began the Mese, which led to the Golden Gate in the city walls, and there began the road to Rome, a thousand miles away. Nearby is the Sunken Palace Cistern, the *Yerebatan Saray Sarnıcı*. Even when constructing a cistern, the Byzantines built on a grand scale, with 336 columns forming a kind of underground temple. The remains of ancient statuary are sometimes put to odd uses in Istanbul. Here two enormous gorgon's heads have been employed as the bases of columns, one of them lying on its side, the other upside down. The very existence of the place was forgotten, only to be rediscovered by a French antiquarian, Peter Gyllius, in 1545, when he observed that residents of the neighbourhood lowered buckets through holes in their floors to draw up water and sometimes even fished through the same holes. Soft lighting and new-age music give the place a kind of mystique that everyone seems to enjoy, making it the perfect place to retreat down into on a hot Istanbul day.

Archæologists are still making new discoveries in Sultanahmet. Downhill from Haghia Sophia stood the Great Palace of Byzantium, and excavations are going on there now, behind the Four Seasons Hotel. Mosaics and fragments of statuary from the Great Palace of Byzantium that were discovered in excavations carried out in 1935 are displayed in the small Mosaic Museum off Torun Sokak, the 'Street of the Grandchild'. It can be accessed from the Arasta Bazaar. The palace has been but a memory for centuries, its marble perhaps used for the pavement of the Sultanahmet mosque. The stone was quarried on the island of Marmara, which is visible from rooftop terraces in this neighbourhood. Marble has been extracted from the seemingly inexhaustible quarries on the island from classical times right up to the present. Once when I examined the pavement of the mosque courtyard, I was struck by how big and irregularly shaped the slabs of marble were, as though the builders had salvaged huge blocks, sawed them to size and fitted them into place.

Byzantium as spiritual imperium

For the traveller who reads history, Byzantium remains a palpable presence. While crossing the big open space in front of Haghia Sophia at night, I often think of lines from 'Byzantium', the second of Yeats's sublime poems on the city:

> The unpurged images of day recede;
> The Emperor's drunken soldiery are abed;
> Night resonance recedes, night-walkers' song
> After great cathedral gong;
> A starlit or a moonlit dome disdains
> All that man is,
> All mere complexities,
> The fury and the mire of human veins.

Two empires have come and gone from this stage. Yet there remains a sense of grandeur about the setting – a grandeur not wholly effaced by tourism or the passage of time.

At midnight on the Emperor's pavement flit
Flames that no faggot feeds, nor steel has lit,
Nor storm disturbs, flames begotten of flames,
Where blood-begotten spirits come
And all complexities of fury leave,
Dying into a dance,
An agony of trance,
An agony of flame that cannot singe a sleeve.

Astraddle on the dolphin's mire and blood,
Spirit after spirit! The smithies break the flood,
The golden smithies of the Emperor!
Marbles of the dancing floor
Break bitter furies of complexities,
Those images that yet
Fresh images beget,
That dolphin-torn, that gong-tormented sea.

Yeats was a great reader of Neo-Platonist philosophers like Plotinus and Proclus. In Byzantium he found an image of what he called Unity of Being:

> I think if I could be given a month of Antiquity and leave to spend it where I chose, I would spend it in Byzantium a little before Justinian opened St Sophia and closed the Academy of Plato. I think I could find in some little wine-shop some philosophical worker in mosaic who could answer all my questions, the supernatural descending nearer to him than to Plotinus even, for the pride of his delicate skill would make what was an instrument of power to princes and clerics, a murderous madness in the mob, show as a lovely flexible presence like that of a perfect human body... .

If he had been able to find someone in Constantinople who could answer all his questions, Yeats would have been lucky indeed. For several centuries Byzantium was plagued with theological controversy that threatened the stability of the state. The particular point of dispute revolved, as I have said, around the exact nature of Christ. As a member of the Trinity, was he God, man, or something in between? To the Arians, Christ was more human than divine. To the Monophysites, Christ had only one nature, and that was divine. Constantine the Great, as befitted a practical-minded ruler busy with the affairs of state, struggled to reach a compromise.

That a question like this should occupy the minds of not only the learned, but even the man in the street, may at first glance seem incredible to us today; but one has only to stop and consider the blood that has been shed, and continues to be shed, in the name of religion even in our own day to get some sense of it. Philosophical and theological disputation has occupied the minds of scholars and clergy in several religious traditions – think of Talmudic wrangling, think of the lengthy debates engaged in by Tibetan monks, think of the Catholic theologians of medieval Europe, think of Islamic philosophers like Avicenna in the late Middle Ages. St Gregory of Nyssa's account of discussions in late fourth-century Constantinople regarding the divinity of Christ and his relation to God the Father is vivid and memorable:

> The whole city is full of it, the squares, the market places, the cross-roads, the alleyways; old-clothes men, money changers, food sellers: they are all busy arguing. If you ask someone to give you change, he philosophises about the Begotten and the Unbegotten; if you inquire about the price of a loaf, you are told by way of reply that the Father is greater and the Son inferior; if you ask 'Is my bath ready?' the attendant answers that the Son was made out of nothing.

Yeats's poems and his prose remarks from *A Vision* provide a good preparation for a visit to the Church of Holy Wisdom. It is a building of great power, presence and dignity. For the task of rebuilding the earlier church that the Byzantine mob destroyed in the Nika riots of 532, the Emperor Justinian chose as his architects two mathematical physicists, Artemius of Tralles and Isidorus of Miletus. Isidorus had been head of the Platonic Academy which Justinian closed. This brief recitation of names gives us a glimpse into the mélange of cultures and nationalities that made up the Byzantine Empire. Artemius and Isidorus, those learned men, provided a link to classical Greece and all its knowledge and expertise. The Emperor's choice of his architects significantly tied the Eastern Roman Empire, whose capital city Constantinople was, to the Hellenistic world. This composite, cobbled together out of high ideals, expediency, and the demands of power and prestige, survived and flourished all the way through the Middle Ages.

9

Looking at Byzantine Art

TWO IMPERISHABLE MONUMENTS of Byzantine art are found in Istanbul. Both are churches – Haghia Sophia and the Church of St Saviour in Chora, called the Kariye Camii. Pictures of Haghia Sophia cannot prepare the visitor for its sheer size inside and the impression of space and light it encloses. It is, in the words of Robert Byron, a 'leviathan of architecture'. Most of the mosaic decoration has been lost. Still, the beauty of its form and the richness of its marble columns, revetments and flooring are powerfully evocative. While the Kariye is a very pretty church on the outside, its interior is what draws visitors, who come to see its mosaics and wall paintings, which Robert Byron calls a 'microcosm of craftsmanship'. In addition to these two masterpieces of macrocosm and microcosm, a bonus is the Mosaic Museum with its collection of early pavement mosaics excavated from the ruins of the Great Palace of Byzantium.

The geographical reach of Byzantine art

W.B. Yeats, as we know, never came to the place his writings have defined for so many readers. I too first encountered Byzantine art in Italy, in the churches of Ravenna on the mainland and in Palermo and Cefalù in Sicily, and then later I drove over the bad roads and rocky tracks of Greece, Macedonia and Serbia, straining the suspension of my little Volkswagen, to see gem-like monastic churches whose interior walls are decorated with Byzantine frescoes. It was an experience like no other – to be greeted with smiles of welcome by the bearded, black-clothed monks, given a glass of cold water, a little piece of Turkish Delight, and a shot of *slivovitz* on a brass tray, and then to go into the church and look at the candle-lit frescoes and icons.

When the Ottoman Turks occupied Asia Minor and Thrace and eventually conquered Constantinople, the metropolitan centre of Byzantium changed forever, and many of its monuments were destroyed or put to other uses. Of the Boucelon, the Byzantine palace built with access to the Emperor's private harbour and yacht basin on the Sea of Marmara, all that remains is a forlorn shell with four big marble-framed, empty windows inserted into brick and stone-work walls that look out to sea. To get a sense of the immense splendour of the imperial palaces of Byzantium, one needs to travel to Sicily and have a look at the chamber of King Ruggiero in the twelfth-century Palazzo Normano in Palermo, decorated in the imperial style by Byzantine craftsmen. The floors are marble, with intagliated patterns fashioned from polychromatic stone. Round medallions of porphyry like those that adorn the exterior walls of Venetian palazzi are set into the pavement. Little gilded, marble-topped tables have been placed sparingly here and there.

As one's eye ascends, the walls are revetted, as in Haghia Sophia, with slabs of cool, veined marble. Above these panels rises an arched ceiling supported on marble columns. The glory of the room is its mosaics high up on the walls and on the ceiling where, glowing against a shimmer of gold, the stylised shapes and greenery of orange trees and palms refresh the eye on sweltering Sicilian afternoons. Centaurs confront one other with bows drawn, leopards and peacocks strut, lions are worked into cartouches on the arches that divide the squinches, griffins pose in heraldic stylization. The room carries an air of majesty, sumptuous yet uncluttered, the cool colours of marble and the restrained paintwork of the doors rising to the magnificence of the gold mosaics. If one can picture chambers decorated with this sort of opulence, then it may be possible to imagine what the Great Palace of Byzantium looked like.

Because the Ottomans maintained a policy of letting the *millets*, or ethnic communities, within the empire manage their own affairs and practice their religious life autonomously, churches had a better chance of survival than the imperial palaces and the mansions of the wealthy. Even when, as was frequently the case, churches were converted to mosques, the fabric of the buildings has remained intact; with stout roofs overhead to keep out the ruinous weather. Almost all the Turks have done in converting a church to a mosque is to build a minaret for the call to prayer, and to place inside the mosque a *minbar* pulpit for preaching during the Friday services and a *mihrab* niche orientated toward Mecca, the direction of Islamic prayer.

I remember my first glimpse of another converted mosque, the Myrelaion ('the place of myrrh'), or Bodrum Camii, in Istanbul. I had sought it out on a smoky autumn afternoon in the streets of the garment district on the Marmara side of Divan Yolu not far from the Laleli Mosque, and it was not easy to find. But as soon I saw it, I exclaimed inwardly: 'This is not a mosque, it's a church!' It has the plain brickwork exterior of many Orthodox churches, and like the Gül Camii in the Küçük Mustafa Paşa neighbourhood, it rises tall and imposing. The survival of these buildings, even if their interiors have been altered, their mosaics removed, destroyed or plastered over, stands in stark contrast to what happened in the British Isles, when after the dissolution of Roman Catholic monasteries under Henry VIII, cloisters and roofless sanctuaries were left to deteriorate into picturesque ruins.

Classical to Byzantine

Byzantine art is by origin a fusion of several strands of influence at play in the eastern Mediterranean in the early years of the first millennium AD. It continued on one level to be the art of the Roman Empire: an art of power, designed to inspire awe. Its ability to dazzle and impress was greatly enhanced by the adoption of elements from the traditions of the Middle East – Persian and Syrian – which portray their subjects not with an approach that calls for visual realism, but with an eye to conveying the psychological and spiritual significance of what is portrayed. This work is always eager to highlight, to exaggerate, to abstract. The art and culture of Byzantium enjoyed enormous prestige throughout the Mediterranean and the Middle East. The Persians pulled down a newly built palace when the Byzantine envoy remarked of it: 'The upper part will do for birds and the lower for rats.'

From the fourth century on, the Roman Empire became a Christian enterprise where Church and state were equal powers. The Church attained wealth and power from the state because it sanctioned the right of the state to govern; the state gained a kind of sanctity because it ruled by divine right. Cyril Mango summarises Byzantine art in these terms:

> Whereas Early Christian art tended to be ostentatious and, if judged by classical standards, incompetent, Byzantine art infused into the old forms its distinctive spirituality and elegance. It forsook naturalism without falling into total abstraction and always retained a certain understanding of the draped human figure. It took over a tradition of bright polychromy and turned it into a palette of superb richness and harmony that was later inherited by the Venetians.

This art pleases by its geometric purity: the perfectly round halo that surrounds the head of Christ, Our Lady, or some warrior saint, the patterned border ringing the shield that a saint holds, the opulence of the fabrics in which emperors, empresses and courtiers are vested, as well as their jewellery and other accoutrements. Perhaps what is most striking about the figures portrayed in this art is their gaze. The eyes in Byzantine mosaics are wide open, slightly larger than they realistically could be, and they communicate directly to us. We not only see the work of art, it sees us.

Predominantly attracted to pattern and design, Byzantine art is by nature conservative. It instinctively resists change. Maintaining the status quo was an inherent if usually unspoken ideal. Originality, all-important in Western art, was not prized. Up until the late twelfth century we know the names of only one or two artists. When we look at Western art, we focus on style, that quality that distinguishes one painter or sculptor from another. Hearing the names Botticelli, Michelangelo, Titian, Ingres, Turner, Constable, Picasso, Matisse, Modigliani, Pollock, Rothko, our mind's eye instantly conjures up an image of their individual stylistic distinctiveness. The Byzantine artist, by contrast, was not trying to express his individuality, he was fashioning an object for the glory of God, or the emperor, God's representative on earth.

While Greek and Roman art from the classical period observed, understood and celebrated the beauty of the body, draped or nude, Byzantine art turned its back on realism. As Robert Byron writes in *The Byzantine Achievement*, 'Of the numerous European cultures whose monuments our taste considers great, Byzantine representational art was the first to discover that principle of interpreting, instead of reproducing, perceived phenomena, which in our time has come to underlie all artistic expression.' No doubt the taste for abstraction in modern art has made us more ready to appreciate the abstract qualities of Byzantine art.

Though the millennium-old Byzantine Empire finally came crashing down over five hundred years ago, fragments of its art can be found throughout the world – not primarily in Istanbul, as I have said, but in museums and in churches built in the Byzantine style in many other countries. Outstanding works adorn the churches of Cyprus, Chios, Mistra and Daphni in Greece, as well as in former Yugoslavia, Mount Sinai, and Russia. The late ninth-century mosaics in the church of Haghia Sophia in Thessaloniki have extraordinary grace and beauty.

So the lover of this art will want to travel – to Greece and Macedonia, to Sicily and Russia, to the monastery of St Catherine in the Sinai desert, as well as to the church of Haghia Sophia in Trabzon on the Black Sea, which can be reached by boat from Istanbul. Remaining fragments are to be found, as well, in the collections of the world's museums – in Paris, Berlin, London, New York and in Washington at Dumbarton Oaks. Illustrated manuscripts, reliquaries, gilded enamel book covers, miniature mosaics, jewellery, cups and goblets, coins and medallions, textiles, and private devotional items: though on some level these items represent the lesser products of Byzantium's artistic efforts, they carry the same distinctive *élan* as the major works.

Icons and iconoclasm

In terms of detached paintings, the world of Byzantium is best known for its production of the icon, a form perfected by Constantinopolitan artists and then continued in places like Crete, Venice and Russia. The icon museum in Venice and the Byzantine art museums in Athens and Thessaloniki have choice collections. The Byzantine icon is the basis of Italian religious painting of the early Renaissance. Few are left in Istanbul other than the remarkable mosaic icons in the Orthodox Patriarchate, one of which is a copy of the original image of the Mother of God, *Hodegetria*, 'The guide who shows the way', at one time the most beloved and valued icon in the city, said to have been painted by St Luke himself. Constantinopolitans were convinced that it brought their armies victory in battle and protected the city from attackers.

When the Emperor Manuel I returned from a victorious campaign against the Hungarians in 1167, the parade route from the Golden Gate to Haghia Sophia was draped with gold and purple cloth for the procession. Prisoners of war marched before the soldiers and notables. The chronicler Niketas Choniates commented: 'When the time came for the emperor to join the triumphal procession, he was preceded by a gilded silver chariot drawn by four horses as white as snowflakes, and ensconced on it was the icon of the Mother of God and unconquerable fellow general of the emperor. The most glorious and most great emperor was mounted on a stately horse arrayed in the imperial regalia.' The *Hodegetria* was carried with great ceremony along the walls of the city during the final battle in May 1453 and stored in the church of St Saviour in Chora near the imperial palace at Blachernae. Ottoman soldiers rushed into the church and ripped the icon from its setting, hacking it into four pieces.

There is even an instance of an icon switching sides in battle. During the Crusader assault on the city in 1204 Emperor Alexios V processed around the city with the icon called *Nikopoios*, 'Maker of Victory'. Both emperor and icon were taken captive by one of the Crusaders, Henry of Flanders. After they came out of the battle victorious, the Crusaders claimed that the icon had brought them success, so they took it home along with many other boatloads of booty, and it may now be seen in the museum of the Cathedral of Saint Mark's in Venice.

This might be a good moment to comment on the centrality of Mary in the religion of Byzantium. While in the West she is thought of as the Virgin Mary, Our Lady, the Blessed Virgin, and so on, in the Eastern church she is invoked as *Theotokos*, 'the God-bearer'. No doubt her place in the human imagination represents a survival of the ancient Mother Goddess from an earlier religion. In the *Akathistos*, a popular hymn from Byzantine times, she is called 'mother of the unsetting star, dawn of the mystical day, rock that quenches thirst, column of fire, tent of the world, flower of immortality, land flowing with milk and honey, impregnable wall'. The word *akathistos* means 'not sitting', meaning that worshippers stood to sing it.

HISTORICALLY SPEAKING, icons probably derive from Roman funereal portraits that used the encaustic technique of mixing pigments with wax to give a lifelike glow and translucency similar to the effect that artists of the Italian Renaissance achieved in their oil paintings. Icon painters also used little tricks to make their subjects seem more lifelike, turning the figure at a bias from the frontal view, making one eye look in a slightly different direction from the other, having the eyebrows or moustache slightly crooked. In a sermon given when the mosaic of the Mother of God on the apse in Haghia Sophia was dedicated, the Patriarch Photius commented, 'You might think her not incapable of speaking ... to such an extent have the lips been made flesh by the colours.'

Though the Greeks and Romans kept small-scale statues of their gods and goddesses in their homes, there is really no precedent in classical art for the central role that icons came to play in the artistic and religious life of Byzantium. Icons were felt to have healing or curative values. Some were even thought to have been 'not made by hands', to use the Biblical phrase. It is not uncommon to find an icon, like the *Hodegetria*, that tradition says was miraculously produced by St Luke. When one is looking at an icon one is receiving a benediction. Blessings are felt to flow through the eyes of the sacred personage into the eyes and heart of the beholder.

Given the hold that icons had, it is no wonder that they eventually met fierce opposition. Theologians inevitably invoked Old Testament strictures against 'graven images', and finally the seventh-century emperor Leo III responded by prohibiting icons altogether. Though his removal of an icon of Christ from the Chalke gate of the Great Palace caused riots, his military success against the Arabs was taken as a sign that God was on his side. His immediate successors continued his policies during the Iconoclastic period. Thousands of icons were destroyed, and the damage done to the Byzantine artistic legacy was immense.

We have no hope of understanding Byzantium unless we understand that what are to us minute theological distinctions were to many people more important than life itself. Among the *iconodules*, literally 'those who served icons' – in other words lovers of icons, – images of Christ, his Mother, and the saints and prophets, were important because they affirmed Our Lord's full humanity. This is what the Trinity is all about, and the sense of God as man is one of the things that distinguished Christianity from Islam, its monotheistic rival in the Middle East, whose art focussed on calligraphy and geometrical pattern.

Architecture

Let us distinguish between three types of buildings: the Greek temple, the Gothic cathedral and the Byzantine church. The Greek temple – think of the Parthenon – is a superbly realised embodiment of rational perfection. The eye of the viewer does not remain static, yet its movement is absorbed by what it sees, by the way the proportions of the temple, its colonnades, its pediment and architrave, fit together and complement each other. The Parthenon is a supremely human building; its proportions even imitate those of the human body. The great gift of classical Greece to humanity is a sense of human perfectibility.

The achieved goal of the Gothic is, on the other hand, to raise us out of what Yeats called 'the fury and the mire of human veins'. In the soaring spires of the cathedral at Rheims, at Notre-Dame in Paris, even among the traffic and tourists at Westminster Abbey, rationality is not an issue. Our eye and our spirit rise toward heaven, and if the supporting columns get thinner and the arches more pointed, the loss of sturdiness and stability is not a problem. Even the flying buttresses developed in the Île-de-France and employed in England at Bath Abbey look so airy that we forget their engineering purpose is to keep the walls, thinned out by the inclusion of so much stained glass, from collapsing under the weight of the church's height.

I got my first glimpse of a Byzantine church when I went to Venice and saw Saint Mark's Cathedral, probably the best-preserved example in the world of what the churches of Constantinople would have looked like in their prime. While the naïve eye may be our most trustworthy resource, it can also let us down. On first exposure to Saint Mark's, I was disappointed. My idea of a cathedral was Gothic – a spired building reaching to the clouds. I had just come from seeing the cathedral of Notre-Dame in Paris with its soaring Gothic arches. My eye had not yet been trained to look at domes or rounded arches. And where, realistically, would one's eye have received such preparation? No one had taught me how to look at a cathedral that was not Gothic. Saint Mark's, like any other example of Byzantine architecture, does not 'soar'.

When I first saw Saint Mark's I had not yet read John Ruskin's *Stones of Venice*. Ruskin characterises the basilica as 'a Book of Common Prayer, a vast illuminated missal, bound with alabaster instead of parchment, studded with porphyry pillars instead of jewels, and written within and without in letters of enamel and gold'.

The metaphor is a subtle one, because while it invokes prayer, it is really about the church as a work of devotional art, adorned not only with the handiwork of Venice's finest artists and craftsmen, but also with marbles, icons and reliquaries. Many of these were plundered from the sack of Constantinople that took place during the Fourth Crusade. If the church is like a prayer book, then, like the physical form of any book, it is self-enclosed and delimited. Saint Mark's gives an impression of hugging the ground from which its domes rise harmoniously from below to above.

Part of enjoying Byzantine churches means learning to appreciate the beauty of marble – an appreciation that runs through all Mediterranean cultures. When preparing slabs of marble for revetting, or covering, the walls of churches, the stonecutters of Byzantium liked to slice blocks of marble on the bias, so as to reveal currents of colour that lay hidden beneath the surface. They would chisel a shallow groove along the top, fill the groove with sand, and then two men would saw back and forth with a long piece of string, progressing at the rate of about two inches per day.

When it comes to the interior columns in the churches of Constantinople, many of these amazing marbles were salvaged or plundered from pagan temples. Both Constantine and Justinian commandeered building materials from all over the empire. Part of the genius of Venetian craftsmen, in their turn, has to do with how skilled and adaptive they were in imitating the art and design of the cultures they absorbed. They reproduced both the decorative patterns of Islamic art and the brilliance of Byzantine motifs, which build on a classical talent for graceful decoration and a Middle Eastern sense of art as a statement of royal and supernatural presences.

Ceremony and splendour

While the Greeks and Romans liked to decorate the outsides of their temples, and while the churches of the Italian Renaissance dazzle the eye with their courses of polychromatic marble, with the Byzantines the opposite is true. Compare the splendour of the Basilica of Santa Croce in Florence with the plain brick churches of Ravenna, or the Fethiye Camii (Church of the Pammakaristos) in Istanbul, whose brick exterior, though pleasingly patterned, gives little hint of the gold mosaic surfaces within. As with all early church art, the purpose of these richly adorned interiors was twofold: to instruct and to dazzle.

Few people were able to read the Bible, so the pictures in churches taught them about the Creation, Adam and Eve, Noah's flood, the Crucifixion and so on. The depictions of the saints, prophets and church fathers made these presences come alive before the eyes of worshippers. Now these interiors are stripped and plain, 'bare ruined choirs where late the sweet birds sang'. Imagine, though, what high mass was like inside a building that shimmered with gold, where the air was filled with incense, with the sound of bells chiming at the elevation of the host, and the deep-throated chanting of priests and monks.

Anyone who wants some sense of what this was like can attend a service at the Greek Patriarchate in Fener on the Golden Horn, where there is much incense, much chanting, and much genuflection and kissing of icons. The effect of Byzantine artistic splendour and ecclesiastical ceremony on visitors to Constantinople during the Middle Ages can be gauged from a contemporary account left in 987 by the ambassadors sent by Prince Vladimir of Kiev, who was trying to decide whether the official religion of his new kingdom should be Muslim, Roman Catholic or Orthodox. This is what the ambassadors reported to their prince:

> We knew not whether we were in heaven or on earth. For on earth there is no such splendour or such beauty, and we are at a loss how to describe it. We know only that God dwells there among men, and their service is fairer than the ceremonies of other nations. For we cannot forget that beauty. Every man, after tasting something sweet, is afterward unwilling to accept that which is bitter, and therefore we cannot dwell longer here.

Prince Vladimir chose to make Orthodoxy his state religion, and while Byzantium perished in its place of origin, Russia became a new Byzantium, even adopting the Byzantine double eagle as its symbol.

That most splendidly named emperor, Constantine VII Porphyrogenitus, has left us an exquisite account of court protocol in his book, *De Ceremoniis*, written for the edification and instruction of his son and successor. A Byzantine emperor's life was conducted with a kind of ceremony that, while it inspired awe, also carried religious symbolism. When the emperor dined, twelve guests were seated with him, while the rest of the company were seated at other tables, twelve to a table. They ate off plates of gold, enamelled and bejewelled. The floors of the banqueting hall were strewn with sweet-smelling roses, rosemary and myrtle, whose fragrance filled the air while they dined. The emperor's vestments reflected the changes in the church's liturgical calendar: in the Advent season he was robed in blue, on All Souls' Day his garments were black, and at Easter he was decked in the colours of the Resurrection.

Three periods of Byzantine art

Yeats wrote in a prose piece about 'Great Byzantium ... where nothing changes'. On first exposure to Byzantine art, the viewer is attracted by what seems to be the static quality that Yeats invokes, but looking closer, one sees that it did in fact change and evolve. Let me risk being pedantic here and suggest that it might be useful to recognise three separate periods of Byzantine artistic production. The first period, from the mid-fourth to the mid-sixth century, consolidates the art of the classical period and evolves it to a place where, in the words of one art historian, 'One is no longer in the classical world' – that historical moment where the figures depicted are no longer realistic in the classical mode of Greek and Roman art, but become something distinctive, arresting, easily recognised and unforgettable once seen. This phase saw the creation of the stunning mosaics in Ravenna, which established a standard of hieratic art that is quintessentially Byzantine.

Constantinople was home to workshops and factories that produced finely woven textiles, as well as jewellery and enamel work whose refined and exacting technique came to be imitated in Europe during the Middle Ages, especially in France, where *cloisonné* enamelling is one example of how the civilisation of Byzantium influenced and informed the European Middle Ages. No other culture has employed wall mosaics as extensively as did the artists and craftsmen we call Byzantine. Representations of royal personages, stories from scripture and pictures of saints and bishops were executed using tiny squares of oven-baked glass to form compositions in vivid colours against a shimmering background of gold that took advantage of curved ceilings and arches to give the whole a more dynamic look. To make the golden tiles that formed haloes and glittering backgrounds give an impression of being in constant motion, tiles were glued in at differing angles so the light of candles or sunshine could play over them. So important is technique and craftsmanship to this art that some in the Middle Ages even denied that mosaic art was art at all. The ninth-century Arab scholar al-Djahiz commented, 'The ancient Greeks were men of learning, while the Byzantines are artisans.'

Mosaic artists from Constantinople from time to time executed projects in other parts of the Mediterranean, such as the Great Mosque of Damascus, and the Dome of the Rock in Jerusalem, built during the Iconoclastic period when the services of mosaic craftsmen were less in demand in the capital. Later examples include churches and palaces built in Palermo and Cefalù by the Norman kings of Sicily. The iconoclastic prohibition against portraying human subjects resonated with a similar reluctance among the Muslims – though Islamic doctrine was not nearly so absolute as is sometimes claimed; in their palaces and manuscript albums, Muslim rulers commissioned and enjoyed depictions of the human body, erotic and poetic.

It is hard to get close enough to mosaics to appreciate the intricacy of the technique, but magnified pictures are available, and one can see how different sizes and slightly varying colours of mosaic tiles, or tesserae, fit together to produce effects such as facial colouration and shading. Mosaic was the medium of choice where affordable, but elsewhere, churches, particularly in the Balkans, were decorated with wall paintings and murals. These can be seen in the little monasteries and Orthodox churches of Greece, Serbia and Macedonia which I have mentioned.

In the Roman world, mosaics were mainly applied to floors and pavements. The preservation of the earliest mosaics in Istanbul we owe to archæologists who discovered in Sultanahmet mosaics from the floors of the Great Palace of Byzantium probably dating from the sixth century. These mosaics mostly depict animals, or hunting and sporting scenes. A boy tries to get his donkey to drink; a bear gorges on a stag; a lion and an elephant fight; young men engage in a mock chariot race. In our urban and technological age we have sadly lost touch with the natural world and the central role it has traditionally played in the human imagination. The poet Richard Wilbur evokes this connection when he asks, 'What should we be without / The dolphin's arc, the dove's return, / These things in which we have seen ourselves and spoken / ... In which we have said the rose of our love and the clean / Horse of our courage?'

The Church of San Vitale in Ravenna

Perhaps the most commonly recognised and appreciated images from the first period of Byzantine art are the mosaics from the church of San Vitale in Ravenna, particularly the monumental processional portraits of Justinian and Theodora, surrounded by courtiers and churchmen, accompanied by imperial bodyguards, one of whom bears a shield emblazoned with the Chi-Ro Christian symbol which Constantine had established two centuries previously as the emblem of the Roman Empire's new state religion. The figures represented in these mosaics supposedly form part of a procession, but really what they do is to stand statically in a row, looking face-on at the viewer. As much as we are looking at them, they are looking at us. We have their full attention.

Eye contact between subject and viewer is at the heart of Byzantine art. One might use the Sanskrit word *darshan*, usually applied to an interview with a holy man or woman, to give a sense of what is going on here. Everything is sumptuous, beginning with the gorgeous *chlamys*, the robe which only highly-placed personages were allowed to wear. Justinian's is purple, the colour of Byzantine royalty, and it is pinned at the shoulder with a jewelled clasp and pendants. His crowned head is surrounded by a nimbus of gold, and he holds a golden liturgical bowl which he is presenting to the church. He is accompanied by Maximanus, the presiding bishop. Even the footwear here is elegant and graceful. The picture is framed with jewelled borders.

The Empress Theodora and her entourage look even more stunning. While we are confronted here again by a row of standing figures facing us frontally, the Empress and her train occupy a little less of the total space of the mosaic panel than Justinian and his entourage. What this arrangement does is to allow more space for decoration and ornamentation around the figures in the procession. A lovely, fluted golden dome with a green mosaic ceiling arches over Theodora's head. A swag of fabric striped white, blue and red hangs over the heads of her ladies, who are outfitted in gorgeous robes of varying colour and design – a reminder of the sumptuousness of Byzantine weaving and fabric decoration. Though her attendants are accoutred, as is fitting, a degree more modestly than the Empress is, they too wear eye-catching jewellery. They look out at us, aloof and soulful. A marble fountain on a pedestal topped with an acanthus capital flows beside them. If Justinian's panel speaks of the majesty of power, Theodora's is all about the majesty of beauty.

The second phase of Byzantine art runs from the ninth century, after the Iconoclastic period with its prohibition against figural representation was finally repudiated in 843, right up to the Fourth Crusade in 1204, when the Venetians and their allies from Northern Europe plundered everything that could be ripped off and melted down or taken home – including the lead roofs of churches – destroying much of the city in the process. In the late ninth century the exquisite mosaic rendering of the Madonna and Child in the apse of Haghia Sophia was created, followed by several other important though fragmentary mosaics that grace the great church. We shall look at these works in the next chapter.

St Saviour in Chora

The final phase in the art of the Byzantine Empire runs from the restoration of Greek rule under the Palæologue Dynasty in 1261 until the Turkish Conquest in 1453. During these two centuries, when the death knell had sounded for all who had ears to hear it, Byzantine art nevertheless enjoyed a late flowering which produced the great mosaics in the Church of St Saviour in Chora, now known as the Kariye Camii. *Chora* in Greek signifies something like 'in the fields', as the church was built outside the city walls. The name St Saviour in Chora is the Constantinopolitan equivalent of London's St Martin-in-the-Fields. Originally the church of the monastery that once flourished here, it was constructed in the eleventh century, and would be considered a beautiful building on its own merits even if it weren't filled with great art. The Byzantines loved puns, and the church's name had a double meaning, because it can also mean 'container of the uncontainable', a reference to Mary's role in carrying the Son of God in her womb.

The Chora fell into disrepair during the Latin Occupation, and in the early thirteenth century a man called Theodore Metochites undertook its restoration and redecoration. A mark of how low the empire's fortunes had fallen by then is that this work was overseen and paid for not by the emperor, but by a private citizen. Still, Metochites was not just any private citizen. He was a scholar and author in his own right, an erudite man who rose to be Grand Logothete, or head of the imperial Treasury, and later Prime Minister. He knew that the empire was barely able to keep the wolf from the door, and he makes this clear in his poetry:

> Anatolia has departed from the Roman state! O this destruction! O this loss! We live in a few remnants of a body that formerly was so great and beautiful, as though the majority of the most vital members had been severed. And we continue to live in shame and derision, wholly incapable of the means of existence and life.

Metochites is said to have been the richest man in Byzantium, second only to the emperor. He restored and rebuilt the fabric of the church and commissioned the mosaics and wall paintings, even providing ecclesiastical furnishings, silver eucharistic vessels and wall hangings, and books for the monastic library.

This munificence does not necessarily mean that Metochites was a nice man. Byzantium's riches were based in part on its highly efficient system of taxation, and Metochites rose as high as he did because of the zeal with which he pursued revenues for the state. In 1328 he was removed from office during a palace coup and banished to Thrace, where he languished for two years, complaining miserably about the bad food and undrinkable wine. Eventually he was allowed to return to Constantinople to become a simple monk in the monastery whose patron he had been, and here he died in 1332. The image of Metochites one carries away is of this great patron of the arts kneeling before the enthroned Christ, presenting a model of the church. His robe is of the finest fabrics that the looms of Constantinople could supply, and he wears on his head an enormous turban of great *chic*.

The monumental style of Byzantine art in the early middle ages, preserved in the churches of Ravenna, gives way here to a vibrant, dynamic burst of kinetic energy. To look up into the dome of the inner narthex of the Chora, where the Presentation of the Virgin at the Temple in Jerusalem is depicted in a series of images about the life of the Mother of God, is to be overwhelmed by a swirl of figures, patterns and rich colours – haloed figures, an angel in mid-air bending down to feed Our Lady with manna during her vigil at the Temple, the roofs and canopies of the architectural backdrop curved and moulded to fit their circular placement under the dome of the building, all of it fused into a unity by the dazzling background of gold mosaic.

In the Miracle at Cana, huge wine jars fill the lower reaches of the elongated pendentive. Elsewhere, in a scene from the Massacre of the Innocents, a Roman centurion, balancing on one foot, reaches out across an arch, his right arm stretching out threateningly with his sword, his right leg extending behind him. Art historians inevitably invoke the term Mannerism to describe the way the human figure is elongated and bent into the overall composition. To my mind there are strong parallels to the Romanesque sculpture of Burgundian France which can be seen in the churches at Vezelay, Autun and Auxerre.

Though parts of the decoration are damaged or missing, there is enough remaining for one to appreciate the beautiful marble revetments that once covered the walls of the *naos*, the Greek word for the central worship space inside the church. Built alongside the church itself is the *Parekklesion*, a side chapel built to contain the tombs of Theodore Metochites and other notables. Here the medium is not mosaic but wall painting, and the arches, soffits and domes are covered with brilliantly rendered scenes in a sumptuous colour scheme of deep blues and blacks highlighted with orange, red and gold.

The twelve segments of the ribbed dome where the Virgin and Child look down from a central medallion are occupied by haloed attendant angels, the ribs of the dome decorated with varied ornamentation, patterned with a richness and variety that exemplify the Byzantine eye for design. This eye for design extends to the robes of the church fathers, bishops and scholars who stand around the arch, their vestments decorated with boldly rendered crosses.

The Last Judgement, where the enthroned Christ is surrounded by saints, evangelists and prophets, while below him on one side the saved are ascending and, on the other, the damned are being prodded by devils down into a lake of fire, is a work of broad scope, brilliantly composed to fill the challenging architectural space. Overhead hovers an angel who holds the 'scroll of heaven', which looks like a conch shell, rolled up to signify the end of time. In the dome of the apse is the Harrowing of Hell, one of the great works of Byzantine art, or indeed of any art. A muscular Christ, enveloped in a dazzling aura of white light, strides forward to pull Adam and Eve from their tombs, wrenching our first parents up into the realm of Christian salvation. Byzantium, like every expression of power and wealth on earth, eventually fell – less than a century and a half after these great works were executed – but its vision and imagination live on in St Saviour in Chora, whose art is one of the supreme expressions of the human spirit.

10

Haghia Sophia and Ayasofya

As one walks toward Haghia Sophia from the Sultanahmet tram stop through snow at the end of February, or on a fresh June day with a breeze off the Sea of Marmara, the church resembles a broad-shouldered mountain with foothills clustered round. The huge, unsightly buttresses erected to keep the dome from collapsing obscure one's view of how it must have originally been designed to look. Yet all the dependent structures – the Ottoman *türbes* or mausoleums, the domed library, the house where the mosque's official astronomer worked, the airy *şadırvan* built by Mahmud I in 1740 when Ayasofya was a mosque, support the pre-eminence of the central dome and pay homage to it.

A word about directions: The 'new' part of the city centred around Beyoğlu lies across the Golden Horn to the north of the old city around Sultanahmet. Haghia Sophia, like most Christian churches, lines up on an east-west axis, and the Blue Mosque lies to the south of the great church. The big doors through which one enters are on the western end.

The *türbe* that Sinan built for Selim II is the masterpiece among Haghia Sophia's dependent structures. The minarets that the sultan's architects added are outriders guarding the assertiveness of the building's bulk. This majestic church, despite sections of its dome having collapsed at least twice, has withstood the onslaughts of time. Perhaps part of its endurance is owed to the builders' having mixed the spittle of holy monks into the mortar they built with – or perhaps it was Mehmed II's having added a hair from the beard of the Prophet Muhammad when he was having the structure repaired.

Mahmud I's baroque *şadırvan* or ablutions fountain, where

Muslims washed themselves ritually before going into the mosque to pray, would be worth a visit even if there were no mosque or church here. It is an octagonal building. Eight widely spread arches supported by willowy columns of grey marble hold up a wide, low-pitched canopy roof, its wide-spreading eaves giving protection against both the heat of a summer's day and Istanbul's rainy winters. The undersides of the eaves are fretted with slender strips of wood, and along the tops of the little walls above the eight arches, you can make out a narrow band of red, white and green design.

Paralleling this band of decoration, just beneath it, runs another strip of horizontal lozenges – emerald green – on which verses from the Qur'an are inscribed in low relief, picked out in gold. The lightness of this bagatelle of a building is further enhanced by our being able to see right into the fountain itself, which is enclosed by a grille of gilded metal rising up into the dome by way of light, curving branches fashioned from wrought iron. The whole is topped by a little dome with a gilded finial, echoing the more powerful domes of the church itself.

I felt I was finally beginning to get somewhere in my understanding of Ottoman architecture when it dawned on me that the Turks' origins as a nomadic people account for many things about them, including their style of building. The chief model for much Turkish domestic architecture is the tent. Look at the pavilions of the Topkapı Palace and you will appreciate that even in their settled days the Turks felt most comfortable in places that could open themselves to the breezes of summer and, when the weather cooled off, could be simply heated with a charcoal brazier. The low divans around the walls of their pavilions served as couches during the day and beds at night. Bedding was rolled up and stored in built-in cupboards.

The Turkish word *konak*, or mansion, originally meant, as the Redhouse Dictionary has it, 'a stopping place, a place to spend the night while travelling; a bivouac or temporary encampment.' We might even pause to consider the etymology of the word *pavilion*, which is related through Old French to the Latin word *papilion*, meaning both 'butterfly' and 'tent'. Many of the Turks' most delightful domestic buildings are light as butterflies. The *şadırvan* of Mahmud I itself is modelled on a tent, its broad roof held up by thin columns as utilitarian as tent poles.

Entering the great church

One is used to entering Haghia Sophia's precincts, running the gauntlet of the touts, postcard sellers and guides offering their services, through a gate opening off the big open space or *meydan* that lies along the south of the complex, a vantage point that pairs it up with the Blue Mosque across the park with its fountain and garden. So it is hard to grasp that the church was designed to be approached through a portico on its west side, a portico that no longer exists. An act of historical imagination is needed to eradicate the little street with its hotel, tea garden and shops that now parallels the church on the west, and to mentally dig up the tram tracks that run uphill from the ferry landings at Eminönü, past the train station and Gülhane Park, in order to imagine the Emperor approaching the arcade that once preceded the entrance.

Christian churches are customarily built on a west-east axis, with the altar at the east end facing the rising sun. In our democratic age one enters Haghia Sophia with little self-consciousness from the exonarthex and then through the narthex – outer and inner porches – into the nave through the Imperial Door, which once was reserved for the Emperor and the Patriarch. Looking up, one sees the first of the surviving mosaics in Haghia Sophia, showing either Leo the Wise or his son, Constantine Porphyrogenitus. Scholars differ as to which emperor this is who prostrates himself before Christ, as no identifying inscription exists to inform us.

I like the theory that it is Leo, who reigned for twenty-five years in the late tenth century. While the emperor was God's representative on earth, in spiritual matters he sometimes had to defer to the Patriarch as head of the church. The church could (and can) get a bit stiff when a question of divorce arises. Leo was married four times, and the Patriarch used his power to deny him entry into Haghia Sophia. The mosaic, executed six years after his death, shows Leo's repentance and subsequent reinstatement into the ranks of the saved thanks to the good graces of the Virgin, who is shown here in a medallion on one side of Christ, whilst a Recording Angel appears in a matching medallion on the other side of Him, making sure the transaction gets written down.

Once inside, I take off my hat. I am standing in a building that is a millennium and a half old. I want nothing to obstruct my vision as I look up into the dome, which the ancients saw as being suspended from heaven on a golden chain. The circle of the dome, the half-circles of the round arches and tympanum – pierced with dozens of little windows that fill the place with sunlight, thronged with dust-motes that by filling the space, define it visually – are like a series of wheels turning as the eye follows them, in perpetual motion. In the words of David Talbot Rice in his little book, *Byzantine Art*, Haghia Sophia 'seeks for the infinite rather than the finite'.

Space needs to be qualified or articulated in some way before we can apprehend it. This is true even of the Grand Canyon. What is most immediately obvious about Haghia Sophia is the huge volume of space it encloses. I have read that the dome is as tall as a fifteen storey building. As the church was being finished, that space was made dazzling by the application of mosaics which covered its entire inner surface. Its appearance would have been similar to the shimmer of gold in Saint Mark's Cathedral in Venice. At one time a surface of four acres was covered with gold mosaics. The apex of the dome is 56 metres from the ground. It is recorded that Justinian exclaimed, upon entering the church when it had been completed: 'Glory be to God, who has found me worthy to finish so great a work, and to excel thee, O Solomon'.

One can picture what this interior space must have looked like when illuminated by hundreds of beeswax candles and perfumed by clouds of frankincense from the altars. The massive circular chandeliers, each of which holds two dozen or more clear glass oil lamps the size of your hand, have been electrified; but still the low-wattage light they project through ancient, hand-blown glass lamps, glistening on a marble pavement worn smooth by fifteen centuries of Christian and Muslim feet, is one of the loveliest sights in existence. Robert Byron writes enchantingly of the church's interior:

> ... it is the light, the formless, unbegotten radiance of no visible source, which brings harmony to these elements [the mosaics, the marbles, the architectural forms] – almost, it might be said, transfigures them. In a Gothic cathedral, there are only cavernous shadows and dramatic rays; in a Classical, the windows are of blatant, hygienic convenience. But in St Sophia, an exquisite luminous mist seems to envelop the whole church, diffused from innumerable small windows set along the cornice of the dome, and in the walls elsewhere. Shadows are not; only depths.

Once one has had time to absorb its overarching magnificence, hundreds of smaller details inside the church strike the visitor. Above the huge central door, one's eye falls on a black and white marble plaque the size of two chess boards set one above the other against the wall. On the plaque is pictured a book propped on a throne, its pages lying open, framed by tiny classical pillars and an arch. Poised above the book, a dove representing the Holy Spirit hovers in mid-air as it descends onto the opened pages of the book.

Moving in and out from the nave into aisles which are divided off by arcades, you walk, as among the trunks of mature trees in a grove, among verd antique and porphyry columns that support the lower arches, each column bound for support with a collar of lead at top and bottom. I always go back into the apse, into what would have been a little space behind the altar when the building functioned as a church, to look at the panel of fifteenth- and sixteenth-century Iznik tiles picturing the Kaaba in Mecca, facing in the direction in which Muslims pray. There is just this one little panel, only a few feet tall and a couple of feet wide, inserted discreetly into the marble revetment under an arch, with sea-green tiles, and flowery plumes of decoration like elongated paisleys. Someone has repaired a broken bit by inserting a tile of completely different design – a single tile that would fetch several hundred pounds in an auction house in London.

I don't know what lens would open wide enough to take in Haghia Sophia's sense of space and light. Perhaps the large-format camera that Ansel Adams used to photograph the Sierra Nevada would be up to the job. I like to climb up to the gallery in an attempt to get a better feeling for the size of the place, and look up into the dome from there. Then you walk to the east end of the gallery and try to get a good view of the mosaic of the Virgin with her child on her lap in the half-dome of the apse. This powerful image dates from 867 and was the first mosaic executed after the defeat of the Iconoclasts. From up here one can also get a good look at the huge figure of the Archangel Gabriel in the south arch of the apse, and the few fragmentary feathers of the Archangel Michael's wings that remain. I gaze in wonder at the six-winged angels depicted in the east pendentives, trying to remember whether they are seraphim or cherubim, and which of the two dwell closer to the throne of God.

While most guidebooks will tell you that the Turks plastered or painted over Haghia Sophia's mosaics, the facts are a little different. Mehmed the Conqueror, that man of religious tolerance, ordered that the angels' faces should remain uncovered, and recent research has shown that even the massive representation of Christ Pantocrator that filled the main dome of the apse remained uncovered until the time of Ahmed I in the early seventeenth century, when a reaction against figural representation set in. Even then, figural mosaics not visible from the main floor of the mosque were not covered up.

While one is up in the gallery, it is interesting to look for the initials visitors to the church carved into the marble railings at some early date. That they are Greek letters for some reason lends these acts of vandalism a little class. If you look carefully you may find the strange carvings in the south gallery supposedly put there by Vikings at a time when those fearsome Northmen served the Byzantine Emperor as bodyguards, as well as the carved ship on a pillar in the north gallery near the mosaic portrait of the Emperor Alexander. This man was so notorious that when he visited his predecessor and brother, Leo VI ('the Wise', he of the four wives, who is seen grovelling in the mosaic in the Imperial Gate), on the latter's death bed in 912, the old emperor's dying words were, 'Here comes the man of thirteen months'. Leo's words were prophetic: Alexander reigned for thirteen months and died of apoplexy while playing polo drunk. It *can't* be intentional, but Alexander is depicted in the mosaic with so livid a countenance, you'd swear his portrait was executed when he had a hangover.

Situated at the head of the west gallery, looking down the whole length of the church toward the high altar at the east end, is the *loge* reserved for the Empress of Byzantium. She had the best seat in the house. From the intricate lace-work of the white marble capitals to the verd antique columns arranged in groups of threes on either side of the *loge* – deliberately fashioned smaller than the tree-trunk pillars one sees elsewhere in the building – to the delicate lamps that flank the spot where she sat with her entourage, it is clear from the design, scale and materials that this *loge* was specifically designed with the Empress in mind. A circle of green Thessalian marble set into the pavement marks the spot where her throne stood.

The perfidy of the Franks

Walking round the south gallery, one stops for a moment at the tomb of Henricus Dandolo, the Doge of Venice who personally led the Frankish troops of the Fourth Crusade in their sack of

Constantinople in 1204. Dandolo is one of the great heroes of the Venetian Republic; he was ninety years old and practically blind when he led the siege. In fixing a date for the demise of Byzantium, people tend to focus on 1453, when the city fell to the Ottoman Turks, but the real catastrophe for Constantinople came two and a half centuries earlier, and the destroyers were Christians like the Byzantines themselves. The Byzantines despised and mistrusted the Franks just as thoroughly as the Franks hated the Byzantines. The Doge resented Byzantine incursions along the Dalmatian Coast, which Venice regarded as her own. In 1171 the Emperor Manuel I Comnenus arrested all the Venetians in the city and confiscated their wealth, which was considerable.

The mutual enmity between the Orthodox and Roman Catholic churches goes some way toward explaining the barbarity of the Crusader sack of Constantinople. But the fires that reduced half the city to smouldering ashes, and the rape of women, including nuns, are enough to extinguish any idealistic notions one might have had about the Crusades. The French share alone of what was plundered amounted, in Gibbon's words, to 'seven times the annual revenue of the kingdom of England'. The plunderers led mules to the altar of Haghia Sophia, the easier to load them down with liturgical vessels. They dressed their horses in ecclesiastical garments from the vestry of the church. Drunken soldiers sang bawdy songs in the sanctuary of the church and sat a prostitute on the patriarchal throne. It will be recalled that both Constantine and Justinian had brought the choicest statuary of the classical world to the capital. These the Crusaders destroyed; where the statues were of gold or bronze, they were melted down to be recast into portable bars and coins. Much of Byzantium's classical heritage was destroyed forever.

Constantinople had been famous for its holdings of Christian relics – objects of veneration to medieval worshippers, as anyone who has read the *Canterbury Tales* knows. These were distributed throughout the lands from which the Crusaders came. The body of St Andrew went to the city-state of Amalfi in Italy, and the heads of St Clement, St James the brother of Christ, and St John the Baptist were brought back to cities in France and Germany. The Latin Emperor Baldwin II used the Crown of Thorns to pay part of the money he owed to Venice, and then the Venetians sold the relic to St Louis of France, who built the Sainte Chapelle in Paris to house it.

Once they had seized the city, the Franks more than made back what they had lost. During the interregnum, it is estimated that the annual income of the Genoese, who traded from their base in Galata, was seven times greater than what the Byzantines themselves earned. The city's treasures, including several sacred relics such as a stone supposedly from the tomb of Jesus, were looted, and carried away to Venice and other parts of Europe. There are several stunning Byzantine art works in the Treasury at Saint Mark's, including an unforgettable gold and enamel depiction of the Archangel Michael. The warrior saint stands with both elegantly shod feet firmly planted, a look of serene assurance on his face, and he holds in his right hand a sword, the pommel of which is a perfect pearl. Though the Byzantines regained power in Constantinople later in the thirteenth century, the Empire was never so powerful again. When they retook their city, Dandolo's bones were dug up and thrown to the dogs in the street. Conducting tours for his classes at the University of the Bosphorus, the late Godfrey Goodwin, author of the classic book *Ottoman Architecture*, would invite any student who felt so moved to spit on Dandolo's grave.

The Empress Zoë

This part of the church, the southeast gallery, was given over to the imperial family. They could enter from the Great Palace by way of a staircase through a doorway, remains of which are still visible. Two mosaics on the east wall of the gallery tell yet more history. One shows the Emperor Constantine IX Monomachos and the Empress Zoë, the other shows John II Comnenus and his consort. I have already told something of the story of the Empress Zoë in chapter two, but this was a complicated tale. One doesn't have to look too closely to see that the tesserae around the heads have been interfered with.

Disappointed in love when her husband-to-be, the son of the Holy Roman Emperor Otto, died while she was sailing to Italy for their wedding, Zoë continued to play a role in Byzantine dynastic struggles. Of royal blood in the Macedonian line as niece to Basil II the Bulgar-Slayer, she could provide legitimacy to claimants to the throne where there was no clear succession. This was the case when Romanus III, a candidate for the purple, was proposed for the throne. There was a problem: he was already married. So he was given a choice: in the words of John Julius Norwich, 'Either there was an immediate divorce and Romanus married Zoë, in which case he would receive the rank of Caesar and, in due course, *basileus* [emperor]; or his eyes would be put out.'

You can guess what choice he made. But things didn't work out. After they were married, Romanus not only denied her the pleasures of the marriage bed, but took a mistress. Zoë in the meantime fell in love with a young man named Michael, at the time still in his teens, while Zoë was now in her fifties. Shortly afterward, Romanus had the misfortune to drown in his bath, a drowning that was quite possibly aided by a dose of poison. Zoë's reaction is recorded by the contemporary historian Psellus as follows: 'By this time the shouts of those who had first discovered him brought many people running to the spot, among them the Empress herself, unattended and making an immense show of grief. She gazed long at her husband; then, satisfied that he was past help, went away.'

After various other dynastic complications during which Zoë was exiled to a nunnery on Büyükada in the Princes' Islands, and her mosaic portrait in Haghia Sophia effaced, she found herself once again Empress, this time as the consort of Constantine IX Monomachos. Upon returning to the throne she had her face restored to the mosaic and the face of Romanus II replaced by that of the new emperor. He is seen holding a bag of money; she bears a scroll, both apparently bearing witness to their contributions to the church. Between them Our Lord has a stern expression on his face. It is no wonder.

The mosaic to the right of this one shows the eleventh-century emperor John II Comnenos, 'John the Beautiful', and his empress Eirene of the Comnenian dynasty, posed like the royal pair in the other panel as donors to the church, decked out in jewel-studded garments, with crowns to match. This time the Emperor and Empress appear on either side of the Virgin Mary with the Christ Child. Byzantium had no fixed protocol for royal succession, so dynasties tried to find ways of keeping the throne in the family. One method was to appoint one's son as co-emperor.

That is what this mosaic is about. To the left of the Empress appears their son Alexios. His inscription emphasises that he, like his father, is *porphyrogenitus*, 'born in the purple' – a reference to the purple birthing chamber where the mothers of Byzantine royalty were installed when they were about to give birth. John was called beautiful not, apparently, for his looks but rather for his character and virtue. He was also a highly successful general who won victories both in Anatolia and in the Balkans. But Alexios unfortunately died before he was able to ascend the throne.

Also in this part of the church is a partially-damaged mosaic showing Christ with his right hand raised in a gesture of blessing, while on either side of him stand his Mother and John the Baptist. This type of holy picture is called a *Deësis*, or Intercession, because John and the Blessed Virgin are pleading with Christ to intercede with his Father for the salvation of mankind. Despite the damage to the lower part of the mosaic, this thirteenth century work is one of the greatest and most affecting examples of Byzantine art in all the world. It is part of the renaissance that occurred in the latter years of the empire, and is related in style to the mosaics at the Kariye Camii.

Unlike most of the other mosaics in Haghia Sophia, this picture exudes gravitas and compassion. While the royal portraits inspire awe and impress us with the majesty of those portrayed, the faces of Jesus, Mary and John the Baptist project a sorrowful compassion for the human condition. One can speculate about whether this is evidence that some of the more 'human' interpretations of Christianity prevalent in medieval Europe at this time, emphasising Christ's suffering and compassion rather than his majesty as part of the godhead, had found their way to Constantinople. Perhaps this newfound softening of the divine image owes something to the developments in Italian art of the early Renaissance.

Haghia Sophia and the fall of Constantinople

Though admittedly the Turkish conquest of Constantinople in 1453 and the Fourth Crusade, two centuries earlier, rank as the city's greatest catastrophes, it must be said that the early history of Haghia Sophia is also filled with destruction, both natural and man-made. Here is how John Freely and Hilary Sumner-Boyd sum up this history in *Strolling Through Istanbul*:

> The first church was completed c 360, in the reign of Constantius, son and successor of Constantine the Great, and was dedicated to Haghia Sophia, the Divine Wisdom, an attribute of Christ. The church was burnt down on 9 June 404 during a riot by the supporters of St John Chrysostom, the Patriarch, who had been removed from his see by the Empress

> Eudoxia, wife of the Emperor Arcadius. A new church was later built on the same site by Theodosius II, son and successor of Arcadius, and dedicated on 10 October 415. This structure ... was destroyed by fire on 15 January 532, the first day of the Nika Revolt. Justinian began work on the present church just a month after the end of the rebellion, on 23 February.

Nine centuries later, by the time of the Turkish conquest, Constantinople was no longer the glittering capital city it had been in its prime. The marauding Turks had drastically reduced its tributary territories in Asia Minor and southeastern Europe, and the city itself had become seedy and weedy, its population much depleted, and many of its buildings deserted and in disrepair. Some quarters resembled ghost towns. Still, the loss of Constantinople and of Haghia Sophia, the centre of Orthodox Christianity, can hardly be overestimated, as 'The Last Mass in Haghia Sophia', by C.A. Trypanis and translated by Richard Stoneham, makes dramatically clear:

> God rings the bells, earth rings the bells, the sky itself is ringing,
> The Holy Wisdom, the Great Church, is ringing out the
> message,
> Four hundred sounding boards sound out, and two and sixty
> bells.
> For every bell there is a priest and for every priest a deacon.
>
> To the left the emperor is singing, to the right the patriarch,
> And all the columns tremble with the thunder of the chant.
> And as the emperor began the hymn to the Cherubim,
> A voice came down to them from the sky, from the archangel's
> mouth:
>
> Cease the Cherubic hymn and let the sacred objects bow,
> Priests take the holy things away, extinguish all the candles;
> God's will has made our city now a Turkish city.
> But send a message to the West, and let them send three ships:
>
> The first to take the cross, the second to remove the Gospel,
> The third, the finest, shall rescue for us our holy altar...
> The Holy Virgin was distressed, the very icons wept.

> Be calm, beloved Lady, be calm and do not weep for them;
> Though years, though centuries shall pass they shall be yours
> again...

Legend has it that the priests who had been chanting at the altar gathered up the sacred eucharistic vessels and moved toward the southern wall of the sanctuary, which opened miraculously and swallowed them up. In many Greek hearts the name of this city is still Constantinople – a Greek, Christian city existing in a kind of neverland. On the day that Constantinople is restored to the Greeks, according to this legend, the south wall of the church will open again and produce the vessels that are sequestered there.

SULTAN MEHMED II, who would become known as Fatih, the Conqueror, was just twenty-one years old and had been sultan for little more than two years when he conquered what was then, though in great decline, still the most illustrious city in the world. He made his triumphal entry late in the afternoon of Tuesday 29 May 1453, a scene described by the seventeenth-century Turkish chronicler Evliya Çelebi in his *Seyahatname*, or Narrative of Travels:

> The sultan then having the pontifical turban on his head and sky-blue boots on his feet, mounted on a mule and bearing the sword of Muhammad in his hand, marched in at the head of seventy or eighty thousand Muslim heroes, crying out, "Halt not conquerors! God be praised! Ye are the conquerors of Constantinople!"

John Freely takes up the narrative:

> The Conqueror rode directly to Haghia Sophia, the Great Church that was as renowned in Islam as it was in Christianity, and when he arrived there he dismounted and fell to his knees, sprinkling a handful of earth over his turban as a sign of humility. Fatih then surveyed the church and ordered that it be immediately converted to Islamic worship .... Tears fell from his eyes [wrote his biographer, Kritovoulos of Imbros] as he groaned deeply and passionately, 'What a city have we given over to plunder and destruction!'

The refreshment of baroque and rococo

This massive pile of stone can absorb a frightful amount of cold. It is possible, when one of the guards is not looking, to open a window from the gallery to get a view to the sunny outdoors. From the south gallery may be seen a skyscape of dome after dome after dome. In the foreground are two *türbes* in the congeries of buildings that surround the cathedral – big domed octagons topped with gilded finials, answered across the park at a distance of two hundred metres by the domes of the Sultanahmet Mosque.

From the north gallery there is a view across to the dome of Haghia Eirene, which was the most important imperial church in the city before Haghia Sophia was built in 576. And sometimes it is possible to open one of the little windows at the eastern end of the north gallery, beyond the mosaic of the drunken emperor Alexander, and gaze out over the fountain of Ahmed III, to my mind the most pleasing creation of the Turkish baroque style in Istanbul. Built in 1728 at the very end of Ahmed III's reign, its hipped roof slopes down at a forty-five degree angle, its four little dome-shaped lanterns, one on each declivity of the sloping roof, with a slightly larger lantern crowning the roof, each of these sporting with a flourish a gilded finial. Along the upper walls, underneath the eaves, runs a calligraphic frieze of inlaid scarlet marble, with emerald green tiles. Underneath this frieze are other, parallel bands of decoration in tile and inlaid stone.

The pavilions of paradise must resemble the fountain Ahmed III built. Islam came into being in the desert, and water plays a sacred role in its rituals, architecture and symbolism. What might logically have been square angles at the corners of this lovely rectilinear building swell out on each of its four corners to form semi-circles with little grilled windows where cold spring-water was handed out to thirsty mosque-goers or petitioners approaching the Topkapı Palace, whose grounds stretch out to the north behind Haghia Sophia. Green being the sacred colour of Islam, how fortunate that shades of this colour, whether matching the opacity of jade, the brilliance of an emerald, or the freshness of a newly opened leaf, is set off so perfectly by calligraphy picked out in gold. Thus it was that the artists in the employ of the sultans and pashas of Istanbul found a way to marry the simplicity of Islam's desert origins to the sumptuousness achieved by the Ottoman Empire, successor to Rome and Byzantium.

Ahmed III, who caused this fountain to be built, was one of the first sultans to turn his gaze toward Europe, both for political support and for æsthetic inspiration. During their first few centuries the Ottomans were invincible, and they carried themselves with the assurance and the arrogance of power. But imperial power ebbs and flows, and by the end of the seventeenth century the Ottomans began to be seriously threatened from without and within. A close look at the tensions that troubled the sultanates of Ahmed III, Mahmud II and their successors helps one understand their reactions to these threats.

The Vestibule of the Warriors

In through the Imperial Gate, out through the Vestibule of the Warriors. This is the passageway where part of the emperor's bodyguard waited for him while he attended services. The rest would leave their weapons here and go into the church with him. In the lunette above the doorway leading to the narthex is a dedicatory mural that shows the Virgin Mary enthroned, with the Christ Child on her lap, one of Byzantium's two most illustrious emperors on either side of her. To her left Constantine, whom the inscription in Greek identifies as 'great emperor among the saints', presents a model of the walled city that he founded. To her right, robed and accoutred in an equally sumptuous manner, stands Justinian, 'the illustrious emperor' as his inscription calls him, presenting a model of the great church.

The mosaic, dating from near the end of the tenth century, is thought to have been commissioned by Basil II, known as *Bulgaroctonos*, 'the Bulgar-Slayer', for his ruthlessly effective campaigns against these enemies who had attacked the empire from the west. He was pure soldier; no aura of imperial majesty or sanctity surrounded him. According to John Julius Norwich, 'Basil was ugly, dirty, coarse, boorish, totally philistine and almost pathologically mean. He was in short, profoundly un-Byzantine'. In an age when warfare was known for being brutal, Basil plumbed new depths of savagery. This is how Gibbon describes his treatment of Bulgarian prisoners of war:

> His cruelty inflicted a cool and exquisite vengeance on the fifteen thousand captives who had been guilty of the defence of their country. They were deprived of sight, but to one of each hundred a single eye was left, that he might conduct his blind century to the presence of their king. Their king is said to have expired of grief and horror; the nation was awed by this terrible

example, the Bulgarians were swept away from their settlements, and circumscribed within a narrow province; the surviving chiefs bequeathed to their children the advice of patience and the duty of revenge.

Presences

After an hour or so of being caught up in the power that Haghia Sophia exerts, along with reminders of the complex, devious and often brutal history of the Byzantine Empire, it feels good to go outside and sit out where the courtyard of the cathedral once was, among bits of classical statuary and architectural fragments, and drink little cups of strong, sugary tea. Turks love roses as much as they love tea, and the rose bushes here are well tended and pruned, winter leaves and debris cleared away. Rather than rushing out again into busy Istanbul, it is good to rest here and be sensible of what one has absorbed from a visit to the massive old cathedral, which embodies so much of great architecture's ability to make us feel happy.

Inside, within an immense volume of captured air, are the spirits of the Greek mathematician and geometrician who designed this marvel, the Emperor who caused it to be built, his remarkable Empress, ghostly archangels, the feathers of whose wings have not quite been eradicated from the walls, the Emperor's Viking bodyguards who sailed all the way here from the icy fjords of Norway, and the bored churchgoers who, perhaps to relieve the tedium of the protracted Orthodox liturgy, carved their initials into the white marble railings. Here are Leo the Wise with his four wives, here is the pale visage of the Emperor Alexander, who enjoyed his last moments of existence drunk, galloping on a polo pony, and the mosaic portrait of the Empress Zoë, who when her first two husbands died, had their faces chiseled off the wall and replaced by the visages of their successors in her affections. We might even remember the brutal but effective Basil the Bulgar-Slayer.

Finally come those who destroyed Byzantium in the name of more recent empires: the empty tomb of the brave, avaricious Doge of Venice, who ordered his men to lift him off his ship and stand him blind among the Crusaders attacking the city walls, and Sultan Mehmed II, in his enormous turban and his sky-blue boots, weeping over the city his troops had destroyed, quoting Persian poetry about the transitory nature of our lives.

Part III

Ottoman Istanbul

11

Mehmed the Conqueror

WHO WAS THIS MEHMED, this ruthless conqueror who sported sky-blue boots and quoted Persian poetry? On the one hand visionary and cultivated, but at the same time violent and ruthless, he was a dangerous and headstrong man. To read the life of his father, Murad II, is to be astonished by the scope of the man's energy and ambition. Murad laid the foundations of everything the empire was to become, and in the meantime fathered three sons, of whom Mehmed was the third, and not his father's favourite, but eventually destined to become sultan after his older brothers died young. Mehmed's mother was probably a Christian slave girl. Mehmed's impulsiveness worried his father, who wanted to retire from practical affairs and enjoy the pleasures of the harem, evenings of poetry and music, and philosophical discussions with scholars and wise men. Murad was forced to come out of retirement twice in order to straighten out various difficulties that his son had got himself into.

Ultimately the Ottomans would become the defenders of Islamic orthodoxy, and the sultan would be not only *Padişah* but also *Halife* or Caliph, spiritual head of Sunni Muslims. But in their earliest years they were nomads and border fighters with a religion of primitive nature worship. Not only do their architecture, their cuisine and their music owe something to their nomadic origins, but their spirituality seems to have this source as well. Persia and Anatolia, when the Turks migrated across these lands, contained a heady and vibrant mixture of tribes and religions, with shamanistic holy men and dervishes who lived half in the world of the *djinns*, or spirits, and half in the world of men. The dervishes were also great warriors, bearing some resemblance in this regard to heroes of the American Plains

Indians like Crazy Horse, who was both a mystic and a warrior. I myself, as recently as forty years ago, attended *semas* where Turcoman dervishes, in the mountains between Turkey and Iran, would go into a trance brought on by hours of chanting and then run skewers through the flesh of their arms and cheeks, without bleeding, and would hold live coals against their flesh without appearing to be burnt.

Zoroastrianism and Christianity bubbled in a rich stew with what was at the time the new religion of Islam, along with remnants of the old Greek and Roman paganism and who knows what other folk religions. By the fifteenth century, orthodoxy was starting to win out among the Ottomans, however, and Prince Mehmed's elders became alarmed when he associated himself with the views of a Persian dervish who preached an affinity between Islam and Christianity. The Grand Mufti, head of the orthodox clerics, denounced the dervish from the pulpit and then turned him over to the incensed mob, who burnt the poor dervish at the stake. It was said that the Mufti, in his excitement, came too close to the flames and singed his beard.

But if these unorthodox tendencies led observers to a low opinion of the young man, all doubts were dispelled when he came to the throne. His *idée fixe* was to lay siege to Constantinople. Having been dealt a mortal blow by the Fourth Crusade in 1204, Byzantium was now an empire only in name, its once-centralised power dispersed. A branch of the old ruling family reigned in the kingdom of Trebizond on the Black Sea, and Greek despots affiliated with Constantinople ruled on the Peloponnesian peninsula and elsewhere. Western observers at the coronation of John VI Cantacuzenos and his Empress in 1347 noticed that the imperial jewels in their crowns were made of glass.

The queen of cities

Many Constantinopolitans had left the city during the Latin occupation, and nine outbreaks of bubonic plague in the fourteenth and early fifteenth centuries laid waste to many more. Essentially Constantinople had become a city-state with a depleted population of not more than 80,000 inhabitants. The Crusaders had stripped the lead off the roofs of the city's churches and sold it for ready cash, so that many churches were no longer maintained. Only Haghia Sophia retained its former magnificence. So great was the destruction left by the Crusaders that within its still formidable walls the once-great city was now reduced to a scattering of hamlets interspersed with gardens and orchards where nightingales sang and wild roses bloomed in the hedgerows. With the Ottomans occupying the lands from which Byzantium once drew its substance, the empire was starved. The most prosperous of the settlements in the capital were those inhabited by foreign merchants and traders, including the Genoese and the Venetians.

Still, the city occupied a strategically unrivalled position and was the key to the Ottomans' ambitions of building an empire with territory in both Europe and Asia. No one could be acknowledged by the world as heir to the Caesars, Alexander the Great, and the emperors of Byzantium, as well as, in Persian terms, *Padişah*, Vice-Regent of God on Earth, until he controlled Constantinople, the New Rome – and this was the goal Mehmed set for himself. Behind its hitherto impregnable walls, the Greeks, who could muster only about 8,000 soldiers, even including the Italian volunteers who joined them, put up a stalwart fight, but the Ottomans' superiority in numbers and military technology were sufficient to defeat them. Ottoman troop strength is estimated at about 150,000, with another 50,000 camp followers.

One of the most bizarre episodes of the battle was the Turks' ingenious transportation of ships overland from the Bosphorus to the Golden Horn. The Greeks had sealed off the mouth of the Horn with a brass chain supporting a boom of pontoon floats that prevented the Turks from entering the waterway. The chain, amazingly, survives and may be seen in the military museum in Istanbul. Mehmed had his engineers construct a road that crossed the hill of Pera from what is now Tophane down to the Golden Horn, effectively bypassing the barrier. The Turkish ships were tied onto cradles, lowered into the water, dragged ashore by pulleys, and then pulled over the newly constructed road by teams of oxen. Oarsmen rowed the air in a kind of pantomime, and sails were hoisted, while fifes and drums played, turning the transport into a strange and gay martial parade. Once afloat in the Golden Horn these ships could protect the Ottoman troops with their cannons and muskets while they assaulted the Byzantine sea walls.

The final assault on Constantinople took place on the fateful day of 29 May 1453, once the huge cannons of Mehmed's artillery had weakened the walls sufficiently for the Turks to make their final assault. It must have been a terrifying scene for those inside the walls. The Ottoman infantrymen, javelin-throwers and archers were chanting *La-ilaha ill'allah, Muhammad-an-Rasul-ul-lah* ['There is no God but Allah, and Muhammad is His Messenger'], pipes and trumpets blared, and cymbals crashed. The Turks' torches and campfires rendered the scene as bright as day. While some of the troops were setting fire to the wooden stockades the Byzantines had erected along the barricades, others were mounting ladders with which to scale the walls. Inside the walls church bells were pealing, gongs sounded, and the sacred icons and relics were paraded through the streets by terrified Constantinopolitans in the hope that their magical powers would once again deliver the city from destruction. The Turks made their final assault, breaking through the walls, and the city was theirs, with the carnage and shock and awe described in the previous chapter.

The new empire

Once he had conquered the city, Mehmed immediately set out to rule, and he proved himself as adept a planner and administrator as he was a warrior. The first thing he did was to lay the groundwork for a multicultural empire by organizing his subjects into *millets*, or nations, self-governing communities under his own ultimate authority as absolute ruler. Continuing to be as interested in what we would call comparative religion as he had been as a callow youth, he had the Greek philosopher George Amiroutzes prepare a treatise for him outlining what Christianity and Islam have in common. There was freedom of worship for his Christian subjects under a Greek Orthodox Patriarch.

As Patriarch of the Greeks he chose the monk Gennadius, who at the time of the Conquest had become the slave of a rich Turk. Mehmed was impressed with the man's learning, and soon had him enthroned in the Church of the Holy Apostles, with his own civil court, his own prison, and with complete authority over the Orthodox community. An assiduous student of the history of the empires he had supplanted, Mehmed was particularly interested in the exploits of Alexander the Great (*Büyük İskender* in Turkish) and had Arrian's life of Alexander read aloud to him every day, as well as Herodotus, Livy, Quintus Curtius and other Greek and Roman authors. The Greek original of Arrian's biography still resides in the library of the Topkapı Palace.

Mehmed later had the Church of the Holy Apostles demolished when he decided to build his own mosque on the site – a great pity, because it was by reputation one of the great churches of Constantinople, and the burial place of the emperors. When the Church of the Holy Apostles was torn down, Gennadius and his Patriarchate were moved to the Convent of the Pammakaristos, which the Turks call Fethiye Camii, in the old Greek neighbourhood of Fener. The church has since been made into a museum, and has, in fragmentary form, some stunning mosaics.

Tolerance, however, was only one side of Mehmed's personality. At the battle of Başkent in 1472 he engaged in hand-to-hand combat with his arch-enemy Uzun Hassan [Hassan the Tall], striking Hassan so hard with his sword that a piece of the man's heart fell to the ground. Mehmed then spent three days after the battle ended personally supervising the execution of prisoners. He was kindly disposed toward the Greeks – in fact he spoke Greek and had, so legend would have it, been tutored by Greek scholars under the very walls of Constantinople during the siege. He was considering making one of the Byzantine emperor's chief ministers, Lucas Notaras, governor of the city. What follows is not a pretty story. It seems that Mehmed, very much in his cups at a banquet, sent a messenger to Notaras's house demanding that the minister send his fourteen-year-old son for Mehmed's pleasure. Notaras refused, and the Sultan immediately had Notaras, his son, and his son-in-law put to the sword. Then the three decapitated heads were put on display on the banqueting table.

Mehmed set out on annual campaigns to capture territory both in Asia and in Europe. He rode at the head of his armies, and no one but he knew their destination. As the Ottoman historian Lord Kinross puts it, 'Questioned once by a general as to the objective of his next campaign, he replied that if a single hair of his beard knew his intentions, he would pluck it out and cast it into the fire'. On these campaigns he secured his Anatolian lands and conquered practically the whole of the Balkans, which would remain under Ottoman control until the Balkan wars of the nineteenth and early twentieth centuries.

Mehmed transformed a loose federation of Anatolian border-fighters who rode into battle for plunder and pillage, into a centralised theocracy with himself at the top as absolute monarch. As you enter the Seraglio grounds through the *Bab-i-Humayun* or Imperial

Gate, you see an inscription in Ottoman Turkish which translates as follows: 'Sultan Mehmed ... Shadow and Spirit of God amongst men, Monarch of the terrestrial orb, Lord of two continents and of two seas. And of the east and the west, and conqueror of the City of Constantinople.'

Chillingly, this grand monarch institutionalised, among other things, the practice of fratricide in the royal family: 'For the welfare of the state', his edict read, 'the one of my sons to whom God grants the Sultanate may lawfully put his brothers to death. This has the approval of a majority of jurists.' Ruthless and pitiless as this practice was, it addressed (if observed dispassionately) the vexed question of dynastic succession which troubles the exercise of power in many political systems. The later and in some ways more humane solution, which amounted to putting the heirs to the throne under house arrest in the Harem at Topkapı, served the state less well since it tended to turn these heirs into weaklings at the mercy of palace intrigue, with no experience of real life, and little notion of how to govern an empire.

Mehmed oversaw a system of government whereby the Grand Vizier, appointed at the pleasure of the Sultan, was chief executive. It turned out to be a very sound arrangement. While many Grand Viziers displeased their sultans and lost their heads, others ruled wisely and well for years. Some of the viziers who figure in this book are Ibrahim, Süleyman the Magnificent's over-reaching brother-in-law; Sokollu Mehmet Paşa, who later served under Süleyman; and the whole family of Köprülüs, who rose in the ranks after being recruited from their native Macedonia – or abducted, depending on how you look at it – for the *devşirme*, the annual levy of youths from territories the Ottomans had conquered.

Technically at least, everyone in the Ottoman state was a slave of the Sultan, the shadow of God on earth. The Turkish word that translates as 'slave' is *kul*, and carries fewer negative connotations. Old-fashioned people will still sometimes sign themselves as *Kulunuz*, 'Your slave', in the same affectedly polite way that people used to style themselves at the end of a letter, 'Your obedient servant'. Through the *devşirme* system, which Mehmed's father Murad II instituted, teams of scouts fanned out once every seven years through the lands the Ottoman armies had conquered, picking out the brightest and worthiest children between roughly the ages of ten and twenty, and bringing them to Constantinople, where they were converted to Islam.

The most talented and quick to learn were enlisted in the palace school at Topkapı, where they received training that would allow them to enter the bureaucracy and run the government. Others became Janissaries. Kara Khalil Çendereli, founder of this elite corps, bluntly stated the Ottoman position: 'The conquered are slaves of the conquerors, to whom their goods, their women, and their children belong as lawful possession.'

The rural populations from which these children were taken had mixed feelings about the practice, as is reflected in the terms for it that were used in their respective languages. Some saw the system as Ottoman revenge on populations who had resisted being conquered. The Greeks, rather neutrally, called it *pædomazoma*, 'collection of children'; to the Armenians, it was *mankahavak*, ' child-gathering'. In Romanian it was *tribut de sânge*, 'tribute of blood', and in Bulgarian it was *kraven danak*, 'blood tax'. For some families it must have been a horrible experience. And yet others bribed officials to choose their sons, seeing it as an opportunity for advancement, a way to escape from the mud and thatch, famine and deprivation of feudal Eastern Europe. It offered such immense opportunities to the boys who were chosen that Muslim families sometimes tried to smuggle their own children into the *devşirme*. Godfrey Goodwin, the architectural historian, puts the practice into a larger geopolitical perspective:

> This levy has caused more indignation than it warrants.... The real objection was that the system deprived the provinces of their best men, for the recruiting officer sought out those who were the healthiest, the most intelligent, and the best looking. From the point of view of the Ottoman government, this wisely reduced the possibility of unrest and rebellion since it deprived the Christian areas of their natural leaders.

The Ottoman enterprise was a curious one in many ways. Technically it was a slave society, and everything depended on the sultan's pleasure. The civil and military organisation made possible by the *devşirme* allowed the Ottomans to disarm any system of rank or privilege among the Turks themselves that might have developed from an aristocracy with hereditary rights. The conflict between centralised government and a landed aristocracy with hereditary privileges was one the Byzantines had struggled with before, not always satisfactorily, and perhaps as the Ottomans came to govern former Byzantine lands, they learnt from the experiences of their predecessors.

The positive side of what may strike us as a monstrous system is that it produced a thorough-going meritocracy, where the son of a Serbian peasant could rise to become the most powerful man in the realm. Certainly it is hard for us to understand a system in which one could technically be a slave and yet be rich, powerful and influential. 'For', Goodwin remarks, 'great officer of State or not, Viceroy of Damascus, Governor of Belgrade, Lord Treasurer or Grand Vezir, these men were slaves, and proud to be slaves, with responsibility only to their sultan and to God.'

Ottoman society was an inflexible hierarchy, where everyone had his place and knew exactly what that place was. It is an approach to life that in the European understanding of things would appear to be quintessentially medieval. Perhaps these resemblances between the European and Middle Eastern Middle Ages hint at some basic unity that exists among all traditional societies. Perhaps Mehmed's approach to hierarchy shows how much he modelled his new society on the Byzantine Empire which he had inherited.

One striking manifestation of this hierarchical organisation can be seen in the dress code that the Ottomans dictated. Different ranks, different *millets*, could be distinguished by the colours and styles of their turbans, robes, sashes and shoes. Traces of this system could still be seen in the late nineteenth century when the Italian traveller Edmondo de Amicis catalogued on the Galata Bridge that spanned the Golden Horn what he called, in M.H. Lansdale's translation, 'all the footwear of the world':

> from that which obtained in Eden to the latest Parisian fashion: the Turk's yellow slippers, the red slipper of the Armenian, turquoise-blue of the Greek, and black of the Israelite – sandals, high boots from Turkestan, Albanian leggings, low-cut shoes, *gambas* of Asia Minor horsemen, a gold-embroidered slipper, Spanish *alpargatas*, feet shod in leather, satin, rags, wood, crowded so close together that in looking at one you are aware of a hundred... .

By tradition, each ruler learned a trade or craft – perhaps as a way of relaxing and of working with his hands, acquiring a kind of expertise not open to the warrior and monarch that he otherwise was. The notorious late-nineteenth-century Sultan, Abdülhamid II, became an expert cabinet maker and learned the art of inlaying mother-of-pearl, tortoiseshell, ebony and ivory into veneered surfaces. Some of his pieces can be seen in the Yıldız Palace, others in the Beylerbeyi Palace, and the workmanship is very fine. Selim the Grim, interestingly, learned to be a goldsmith, as did Süleyman the Magnificent. What skill did the fearsome Mehmed choose? Gardening! He looked after the gardens at Topkapı. He was extremely proud of the cucumbers he grew, and one day became enraged when he found that someone had picked one of his prize vegetables. Suspecting one of his gardeners, he cut the man's stomach open, and found there the remains of the prize cucumber.

What are we to make, finally, of Mehmed the Conqueror? As we have seen, he was an unspeakably violent, impulsive man, as well as a powerful and effective general and a gifted, far-sighted ruler. The same man who flew into a rage and cut open his gardener's belly to confirm his suspicions about the fate of his cucumber was said to be fluent in Turkish, Greek, Arabic, Latin, Persian and Hebrew, a student of philosophy and theology and a lover of poetry, as we have seen, who could quote it for pleasure.

The drunken sodomite who commanded the summary decapitation of Lucas Notaras, Notaras's fourteen-year-old son and his son-in-law, and ordered that their severed heads be placed on his banqueting table, was also the able administrator and tolerant man who granted freedom of religion to all faiths at the same time as the Spanish Inquisition was torturing Jews and forcing them to convert to Christianity. As L.P. Hartley famously wrote, 'The past is a foreign country. They do things differently there'.

12

Mehmed the Conqueror and Gentile Bellini

THE TWENTY-SEVEN-YEAR PERIOD from 1453 to 1480, beginning with the Turkish conquest of Constantinople and culminating in a remarkable portrait of Mehmed II painted by Gentile Bellini, proved to be pivotal for two empires: the Ottoman and the Venetian. It also occasioned a turning point in the relations between Venetian and Islamic art, and particularly in the life of Gentile, son of Jacopo and brother to Giovanni Bellini.

To see this early period when Constantinople was the Ottoman capital in terms of a clash of civilisations, or even of religions, is to misread what was going on. True, the declared goal of Muhammad's religion was either to conquer or to convert the infidel. But the reality was more a process of assimilation and accommodation than conflict. The Ottomans were not fanatics. In terms of religion, the policy was one of toleration. Many of the empire's rulers, administrators, architects, admirals and other important figures were Greeks, Armenians, Serbs, Macedonians, Albanians and Bosnians. Mehmed was well aware that the conquest of Constantinople made his people heirs to a great tradition reaching back from Byzantium to Rome and from there back to classical Greece.

What the Ottomans wanted was to enhance their new enterprise's power and prestige. This was the impulse behind inviting Spain's Jews, when they were expelled in 1492, to make a new home within the Ottoman Empire, where some of their descendants still live. Italian metal-workers, cartographers and artists were brought to Istanbul. Leonardo da Vinci was invited to the sultan's court, though there is no record that he ever went, and one of Michelangelo's unfulfilled projects involved building a bridge to span the Bosphorus.

As for Venice, which began as a client state of Byzantium during the period when the western Roman Empire was being destroyed by barbarian invasions, her foreign policy throughout a long and profitable history might be summarised as 'make money, not war'. By masterminding, financing and providing a navy for the sack of Constantinople in 1204 during the Fourth Crusade, Venice had already siphoned off much of Byzantium's fabled wealth.

Neither the Venetians nor the Crusaders seemed to mind killing fellow Christians and looting their city, despite the Crusaders' having set off from Europe with the stated aim of freeing Jerusalem from the infidel. 'Doge', the Venetians' name for their leader, was borrowed from Byzantium and derives from the Latin *dux*. In a sense the Ottomans and the Venetians were joint heirs to the old empire. The Venetians, with the help of knights from Western Europe, had already cut the legs out from under the empire in the thirteenth century; in 1453 the Turks simply finished the job.

A scant ten years after their successful siege of the ancient capital of Byzantium under the twenty-one-year-old Sultan Mehmed II, 'the Conqueror', the Ottomans found themselves at war with the Venetians – a surprising turn of events, since the Venetian merchants doing business in Constantinople had not only survived the fall of Byzantium, but wasted no time in renegotiating and enhancing their trading position with the Ottomans and squeezing out the Genoese, their only serious rivals. But when Mehmed seized Greece and Bosnia, the Venetians were more or less forced to go to war.

By the terms of the peace treaty they signed with the Ottomans in 1479, they gave up a significant amount of territory and agreed to pay a heavy tribute. In the resulting atmosphere of *détente*, the Turks sent a delegation to Venice and Mehmed asked for the services of 'a good painter'. Gentile Bellini was the most prominent official artist in Venice at the time, having recently been commissioned to paint the large canvases that would decorate the Council Chamber in the Doge's Palace. It was a measure of how seriously the Doge took the Sultan's request, that in 1479 he sent Gentile, who was to stay in Istanbul for two years, after which he returned to the Serenissima. Tradition has it that he became an intimate of the Sultan's. According to one story, the Sultan, critical of Bellini's depiction of a severed head in one of his paintings, provided a freshly rendered example as a model for a depiction of the beheading of John the Baptist. It is known that Bellini was housed close to the Topkapı Palace, a quarter that will be familiar to readers of Orhan Pamuk's *My Name Is Red* as the headquarters of the official court painters of the time.

It is well to remember that Mehmed, despite his violent and sometimes barbarous nature, was a very well-educated man by any standards. He was not unfamiliar with the history of Italy. The Italian antiquarian Cyriaco of Ancona, with whom Mehmed studied in his tent beneath the walls of Constantinople, by one account 'gave him tuition in the historians of classical antiquity and the chronicles of the popes and the Lombard kings'. In addition Mehmed studied with George Amiroutzes, Grand Chamberlain to David Comnenos, Emperor of the Byzantine kingdom of Trebizord. There was more continuity in the regime change of 1453 than one might have imagined.

Bellini's portrait of the sultan

The best-known result of Bellini's stay in Istanbul is his portrait of Mehmed II now owned by the National Gallery in London. The Turks were the terror of Europe until late in the seventeenth century, when their advances were finally repelled at the gates of Vienna in 1683 – a campaign to which we owe the croissant, concocted by Viennese bakers in imitation of the crescent moon on the Turkish standard, Mozart's opera, *The Abduction from the Seraglio*, and the few bars of Turkish martial music that Joseph Haydn wrote into his 'Military' Symphony, No 100 in G Major. When the Turks first stormed into the consciousness of the Mediterranean world, few Europeans even knew what they looked like. Portrait painting was not widely practiced in the Islamic world, and that is one reason why Bellini's portrait has such historical significance.

The picture presents the Sultan as a Renaissance prince, with an introspective air typical of Venetian portraiture. Mehmed's white turban, the red conical hat around which it has been wound, his fair skin and brown beard, and sumptuous red gown with its fur collar – all of this stands out against a background of black. Bellini has chosen to frame him inside an elaborate Venetian arch decorated with motifs taken from Roman art. The Sultan is said to have been pleased by Bellini's mastery of perspective in his depiction of the arch, showing that the Ottoman prince was aware of the revolution in Renaissance art brought about by the use of perspective, which was traditionally missing from Persian miniatures.

On either side of the arch three crowns are placed, standing for Mehmed's three kingdoms: Asia, Trebizond and Greece – a reminder of how differently the fifteenth century saw the world and the relative importance of its geographical divisions. Mehmed had a keen interest in all things classical, Christian and European and assembled a notable collection of Christian icons, classical and Christian manuscripts, and works of art, including this and other paintings by Bellini. Included in his collection was an album of drawings by Jacopo Bellini that Gentile had given him. A large part of Bellini's assignment was to provide paintings to decorate the newly constructed Topkapı Palace. What a pity it was that Beyazit II sold his father's treasures in the Grand Bazaar, and that they were then scattered throughout the world. The bad luck represented by this sell-off is matched by the catastrophic fire in the Doge's Palace that destroyed the large canvases Bellini painted for the Grand Council Chamber.

The seated scribe

In addition to his portrait of Mehmed, another work Bellini painted whilst in Constantinople is an exquisite picture of a seated scribe rendered in brown ink, now owned by the Isabella Stewart Gardner Museum in Boston. Having done the drawing in ink, Bellini proceeded to decorate it with watercolours and gold paint in a manner imitative of Islamic techniques. We can safely assume that the scribe was a page in the Topkapı Palace school.

Gentile's *Seated Scribe* was evidently not painted in response to a commission, nor would most people call it a major work of art. But the eye never tires of looking at it. Sumptuous fabrics, along with jewels, spices, gold, rare woods, apes, Turkish and Persian carpets, and other luxury exotica – all of them emblems of wealth and elegance – were Venice's stock in trade; they often appear in paintings. This scribe's robe, his purple velvet collar, his crimson sleeves, elaborately pleated, are a study in sumptuousness. But it's the look of perfect concentration the scribe brings to his task that enchants the viewer, his eyes so focussed they look almost blank. He is probably a member of the Kalemiyye, the prestigious school whose graduates typically rose to occupy prominent positions in the Ottoman hierarchy.

Once executed, the drawing acquired a history of its own. It was sent as a gift to a Persian court in Tabriz, where it was mounted in one of the albums of drawings that were popular at princely courts in the Middle East. Princes perused them for pleasure, and artists studied them in order to learn. In the sixteenth century someone added a fanciful spray of stylised flowers to the upper left-hand side of the drawing and a cartouche in the upper right-hand corner which identifies the drawing as 'The work of Ibn-i-Mu'azzin [son of the Muezzin], who is one of the well-known masters of Europe'. The attribution is ambiguous and probably misleading, but visually the beauty of its calligraphy and its pleasing scarlet border decorated with flowers enhances the work. Painted by Gentile Bellini as an homage to Islamic art, the picture became absorbed into the tradition of that art, thus gaining a new life in that exquisite *mélange* of diverse cultures that characterised the eastern Mediterranean in the early modern era.

13

Looking at Islamic Art

TRYING TO FIND a common ground for the artistic accomplishments of the varied groups of people who profess Islam may be an absurd endeavour. Still, the Prophet Muhammad said that 'God is beautiful and He loves beauty', so perhaps one should try. Then we can go on to see how these descriptions specifically fit what one sees in Istanbul, Queen of Cities. These diverse but linked cultures flowered gloriously for over twelve hundred years. After the death of Muhammad in AD 632, empires that conquered under the banner of the new faith, which was the third 'revealed' religion to come out of the Middle East, spread rapidly.

By the year 750, Islamic empires stretched from the borders of what is now India to the Atlantic Ocean. Of these the largest was the domain of the Umayyads, centred in Damascus, who were succeeded by the Abbasids, whose capital was Baghdad. The green tide of Islam reached its high-water mark under the Ottomans, during the sultanate of Süleyman the Magnificent in the sixteenth century. This civilisation, in turn, went into serious decline with the breakup of the Ottoman Empire in the years leading up to and following the First World War, when large areas of the Middle East and North Africa were divided up between Britain and France and their allies.

Architecture

The first Islamic art that a traveller notices is architecture, and architecture is the quintessential art of Islam. Beginning with the Dome of the Rock, built between 684 and 692 in Al-Quds (Jerusalem) under the Umayyad dynasty, Arab architects absorbed the achievements of Roman engineering and adapted Roman and Byzantine forms. Expertise in constructing round Romanesque arches travelled from Italy both to the eastern Mediterranean and northwest into pre-Gothic Europe. The great imperial mosques built in Istanbul by the Ottoman architect Sinan and others were largely modelled on the cathedral of Haghia Sophia, itself a bridge between classical antiquity and medieval Byzantium. In turn Islamic architecture provided models for the Gothic style, which began by imitating the Islamic buildings traders and crusaders would have seen in Moorish Spain and the Holy Land.

Many pages of this book are devoted to a discussion of the individual mosques that dominate Istanbul's skyline. The call to prayer punctuates the day, even for non-religious Istanbullus. Here I'll make just a few general observations about mosques. In designing a mosque, the architect's first task is to determine the *qibla*, *kible* in Turkish, the direction of Mecca, toward which one faces when performing *namaz*, the ritual prayers. At an earlier period in history it was a job for astronomers and geographers. Nowadays all one need do is go to www.qiblalocator.com, type in one's postal code, and the *qibla* is provided in seconds.

Looking at mosques, one might not at first appreciate the huge engineering feats that are required of the builders. A good architect is at once an artist and an engineer. The problem boils down to how one supports a circular dome atop a square room. Since the purpose of a mosque is to assemble a large group of worshippers in one large space, it is important that the space is not filled up with walls and columns to support the weight of the dome which, being hemispherical, wants to push out against the vertical supports holding it up.

The answer, from Haghia Sophia onward, has been to construct massive piers which in their turn hold up wide arches that carry the dome's weight. The downward thrust of the piers is then strengthened by round weight-towers, and the arches are buttressed by semidomes that help keep the weight of the dome from collapsing the building outward. Istanbul is extremely vulnerable to earthquakes, so the builders dug down until they found a solid subsurface, and then built a strong foundation up from there, using rubble and cement. Once one has grasped the enormity of the engineering problems, it is interesting to look at a mosque like the Süleymaniye and notice how the great architect Sinan did things like building beautiful galleries on the north and south sides of the mosque to mask the huge buttresses that were needed there to prop up the piers.

I am not suggesting that one needs to think like an architect to comprehend the accomplishment of these mosques, but some notion of the engineering involved does give a slightly different perspective, as well as a greater appreciation. Add to this that everything had to be accomplished by hand, without today's jackhammers, power saws and drills, cement mixers and so on. Think what was involved in the quarrying, cutting and shaping of all the stone that was required. Imagine the work needed to construct wooden frames to support domes and arches as they were being shaped. Consider the task of pouring molten lead, rolling it out, cutting and shaping it into the triangular segments that make up one of those beautiful lead roofs atop the domes, which is then capped with a gilded brass finial called an *alem*, and decorated with the Islamic crescent. The labour, the expertise, and the skill and knowledge that went into building these awe-inspiring creations was all for the glory of Allah.

'Graven images'

A common but understandable misconception is that the Qur'an prohibits portrayal of human forms. In fact, this prohibition appears nowhere in the Qur'an, but is a product of custom and tradition. Because Islam saw itself as the successor to Judaism and Christianity, it absorbed into its traditions one of Judaism's Ten Commandments: 'Thou shalt not make unto thee any graven image, or any likeness of any thing that is in heaven above, or that is in the earth beneath, or that is in the waters beneath the earth' (Deuteronomy 5:8). Both Muhammad and the Old Testament prophets were trying to convert idol worshippers to monotheism. Yet though this prohibition lacked the force of Qur'anic authority among Muslims, it came to have a powerful and destructive life of its own.

Distrust of images is a trend running though all three of the great revealed religions. Though the notion that the divinity is ineffable and that the true name of God is unutterable may have originated in Judaism, it has continued to resonate. The Iconoclasts in Byzantine times who destroyed irreplaceable icons, believing that no one should attempt to depict the holy personages of Christianity; Cromwell's soldiers who smashed the faces of religious statues and shattered hundreds of stained glass windows throughout the British Isles;

the teenage Taliban recruits who dynamited statues of the Buddha in Bamiyan in Afghanistan – all these enthusiasts, or fanatics if you will, have been prompted by similar impulses.

Islamic artists have tended to see evidence of God's infinitude in the multiplicity of natural forms. A pattern of vines or flowers leads quite naturally to a geometric exploration of pattern, seen as a visual manifestation of divinity. The origins of a geometrical, pattern-obsessed Islamic style emerged, as mosque architecture did, from the art of classical antiquity. In tenth-century marble capitals from Cordoba in Moorish Spain, Roman acanthus motifs had already started to morph into less naturalistic, more geometrical forms which served the purpose of decorating surfaces. Around the top of these capitals commonly run friezes of Arabic script from the Qur'an – never mere decoration, but occupying a space somewhere between art and revelation. Anyone who looks at Iznik tiles will see this merging of the natural world with an idea of pure geometry. And despite the caveat I have just given, it is true that the glories of Ottoman art have mostly to do with design and pattern.

Calligraphy

Muslims, like Jews and Christians, are as the Qur'an says, 'People of the Book'. Even when God dictates the book, someone has to write His words down, and Muhammad himself was the first to do so. Since the Prophet wrote in Arabic, it is no wonder that that language is held in such reverence, and that calligraphy is the most honoured of the arts. Of course at first there was no such thing as a printed book. Even when the printing press was introduced into the Ottoman Empire, it was introduced by Christians and Jews. The *ulema* fulminated against it, and even issued *fatwas* against its very existence, managing to make it illegal in the empire between 1483 and 1729.

The Qur'an says, 'The first thing that Allah created was the pen, and He said to it: "Write! So it wrote what is to be forever."' This is how, in Islamic belief, the holy book came into being. Keep this reverence for the art of writing and its instruments in mind when viewing the pen-and-ink sets in the Museum of Turkish and Islamic Art and the Sadberk Hanım Museum. The space between art and revelation which calligraphy occupies has evolved over the centuries after God's revelation to his prophet. The first commonly used script, instantly recognizable once one has seen it, is called Kufic, characterised by rigidity and a severely horizontal orientation, with the shafts of the Arabic letters rising perpendicularly. Kufic appeared at least as early as the eighth century, and takes its name from the city of Kufa in Iraq.

As Islam grew and its arts developed, other varieties of script evolved. Artists were clearly looking for something softer, more flowing and curved, and they developed something called Nashi, in which the individual letters flow into one another more freely than in Kufic. It is at this point that pages of Qur'anic text start to evolve from simple transliteration of scripture to designs that can be considered works of art in their own right. The *thuluth* script used in Iznik ceramic plaques to adorn mosques and *türbes* is a variation of Nashi.

One doesn't have to know the names of the various scripts in order to appreciate them. A good place to see beautiful examples as well as to learn something about the techniques and instruments used in the art is the Museum of Calligraphy in Beyazit Square, housed in the former *medrese* of the Beyazit Mosque complex. At this writing it was closed for renovation, but perhaps by the time you read this it will have opened again.

The Bektaşi order of dervishes, with their heterodox views, often leaning toward Shiism, developed a style of calligraphy wherein Arabic texts form pictures. A lion often appears, as an image of Hazrat Ali, the fourth Caliph, whom Shiites venerate. The aleph, the first letter of Ali's name, is sometimes elongated with a sweeping brush-stroke to form the hull of a boat for which other letters form oars – a symbol of the boat of salvation provided by the brotherhood. The conical dervish hat sometimes also appears, or the stork, considered sacred. Another popular form of calligraphy is called *aynalı*, 'mirrored', where two bits of text appear, each mirroring the other. One does not have to be an expert on the symbolism, however, or the numerological mysticism of Islam, to appreciate the ingenuity of these works. Calligraphy is a living tradition in the city. You may see calligraphers practising their art in the Sahaflar Çarşısı, the Booksellers' Bazaar, where many of the booksellers are dervishes.

Art and the nature of God

Though the Qur'an and the Hadiths are full of stories, Islam is a less narrative religion than Hinduism, where we find vivid characters like

Radha and the blue-skinned Krishna, depicted in scenes from their ecstatic courtship. Or Judaism, peopled by patriarchs like Moses, who stood tongue-tied before the manifestation of God in a burning bush, and later held his staff aloft to part the waters of the Red Sea so that the Israelites could cross dry-shod to safety. Or Christianity, with characters like Peter, who denied his Lord three times before the cock could crow, as prophesied; or Judas, who betrayed Him with a kiss. There is less emphasis on an anthropomorphic 'jealous God', or a 'God the Father' in Islam; Allah is a more abstract entity with ninety-nine names, each capturing one facet of the whole. No divinity is claimed for Muhammad, a mere human, God's messenger.

True, a narrative does surround the revelation of the Qur'an to Muhammad, and there are stories about the lives of the Prophet, his family, and the early history of the faith; but the religion emphasises the substance rather than the circumstances of the revelation. After all, the speaker in the Qur'an is God himself! Islam is founded, like Buddhism, not primarily on a narrative, but on a set of assertions about the nature of reality. This orientation is particularly striking when one compares Islamic art with Byzantine painting or with the medieval and early Renaissance Italian art that derived from Byzantium. Christian art celebrates stories like Christ's passion and the story of Mary, who though a woman, in some mysterious way became the Mother of God.

A fabulous body of work was created during the Ottoman centuries based on the wealth derived from this vast empire, the traditions of design and craftsmanship of its peoples, and the skills of the painters, architects, tile workers, stonecarvers, weavers and calligraphers who were drawn to the patronage of the sultans. Ottoman craftsmen of the seventeenth century executed embroidery of exquisite taste and delicacy. Kaftans sewn for Ottoman princes have great poignancy for anyone who knows that the nineteen younger sons of Sultan Murad III were strangled late one night in 1595 to prevent dynastic disputes when their half-brother Mehmed III came to the throne. As in Renaissance Florence, Rome, Milan and Venice, the utmost artistic delicacy often lives side by side with cruelty and brutality.

Turkish rugs

As Turkish tribes migrated west into Anatolia, they brought their sheep and goats along with them. They were a pastoral people who depended on the milk and meat of their flocks and herds. Along with their animals they brought their looms, because their women wove clothing, saddle bags for camels and donkeys, bags to carry grain in, curtains, covers for cushions and beds, and the fabric for their tents and floor coverings, from the wool of these same animals. These weavers made durable knotted rugs, and since the artistic impulse is universal, their rugs not only provided shelter and warmth, but were one way they expressed their sense of beauty. Over the centuries they evolved the technique of making dyes from natural substances. Scarlet came from the ground root of the madder plant; a different shade of red came from cochineal insects. Blue came from the indigo plant. A certain shade of brown is derived from walnut husks. Of course some colours in these rugs are achieved simply from the colours of the wools themselves. Stylised animals such as camels and birds were part of their designs, as were flowers, stars, and mythological creatures such as dragons and phoenixes. One rug might represent a garden, another might show the towers of a city. The paisley-shaped motif, representing – according to whom you talk to – either a pear or a bush, or a pine-cone – is particularly attractive.

To make a rug, called a *halı*, the Turks and their cousins who settled in the Caucasus used a knot called the Ghiordes knot, which is accomplished by looping the yarn round two warp-threads (the threads going lengthways) and then bringing the yarn out between them and snipping it off to produce the pile, which is what gives rugs thickness and makes them pleasant to walk on barefoot and to sit on. The Turkish knot, because it is doubled, is stronger than the *senneh* knot used in more refined Persian rugs and Ottoman court carpets, which is more compact and thus allows for a denser weave. The average weaver can tie eight hundred or a thousand of these knots per hour. Flat-weave or tapestry-weave rugs called *kilims* are woven without a pile. Lighter than *halıs*, they were light enough to be rolled up and used as prayer mats, or to decorate a wall or drape over a divan.

It did not take long for Westerners to recognise the attraction of Anatolian rugs, and soon Italian merchants were bringing them into Europe, where their beauty and the esteem in which they were held are attested by their appearance in European paintings. Simone Martini, working at the beginning of the fourteenth century, includes Turkish rugs in his religious paintings, so we know that the trade had begun at least that early. Several patterns are known by the names of painters who included them in their paintings. Collectors refer to certain carpets as Holbeins, Bellinis, Crivellis, Lottos, Ghirlandaios and Memlings. It is not unusual for the throne on which the Virgin Mary is seated with the Christ Child on her lap, to be resting on a fine Anatolian carpet. Henry VIII and Cardinal Wolsey were among the first collectors in England to come to love these rugs, which they had shipped over in quantity from Venice. In Holbein's striking and enigmatic *The Ambassadors* at the National Gallery in London, two men lean against a high cupboard over which is draped a 'Holbein' rug. For centuries in Britain these rugs were called simply 'Turkey carpets'.

I bargained for and bought my first Turkish rug in the Covered Bazaar in 1964, an Uşak prayer rug which was later stolen from me when my house was burgled. I can still picture it vividly. Over the years I have continued to buy rugs in Istanbul, but I am not at all sure there are many bargains to be had anymore. Part of the problem is that buying a rug has become part of the tourist experience in Istanbul. Included in the price of the carpet is the experience of sitting in a carpet shop as the shop boys – often cousins from the country – bring out and unroll rug after rug and you drink cup after cup of tea and chat with the rug merchant.

Another issue is that prices in Turkey are determined not only by the value of an item but by who the buyer is in relation to the seller. Family and friends have one price, people from the same town or neighbourhood another good one, other Turks pay a bit more, Turkish-speaking foreigners do a bit better, and finally you as a tourist pay the highest price of all, even when you have finished bargaining. The best deal I ever got for rugs was at a shop in Şişli where I went with a Turkish friend, one of my former students. The merchant had been a student of my student's father, a professor of mathematics at Istanbul University, and the discount I was accorded was a very good one. Nowadays I do most of my rug shopping on eBay. Much less atmospheric, but probably a much more sensible way of doing business.

Whether one is in the market for a rug or simply enjoys seeing them in museums, the Turkish rug is a surpassingly beautiful thing. The richness of colour; the command of geometrical pattern; the mastery of field; the way the different elements of the composition are brought together to create an entire visual environment – it is amazing that all this should be part of what is essentially a folk art.

We think of refined technique as being typical of 'high' art, but the designers and weavers of these rugs need concede nothing to the makers of poems, paintings and string quartets.

Ceramics

The tile-makers at Iznik (formerly Nicæa, where the Nicæan Creed was formulated in the fourth century), fashioned ceramics both for the flat tiles used to cover the walls of mosques and palaces, and for the rounded surfaces of bowls, bottles, mosque lamps, plates and so on. They favoured stylised floral designs such as the tree of life, carnations and tulips, which lent their name to the *Lale Devri* or Tulip Period, a flowering of culture and luxury in Ottoman court circles in the eighteenth century.

Yet one of the strangest and most attractive of these designs is what the Turks call *çintemani*, derived from a Sanskrit word meaning 'precious jewel'. *Mani* is the same word that occurs in the Tibetan Buddhist mantra, *Om Mani Padme Hum*. The individual dots of the pattern bear a remarkable resemblance to the *nazar boncuğu*, the blue bead seen everywhere in Turkey, which wards off the Evil Eye. The wavy lines and three dots deployed on these tiles carry all the elegance of Chinese design, and I think they must derive from the Chinese porcelains that were such an influence on Turkish ceramic design. The most exquisite examples of these tiles in Istanbul are to be found at the tomb of Eyüp el-Ensari and in the Harem at the Topkapı Palace.

The Ottoman sultans' collection of Chinese ceramics at Topkapı is one of the most comprehensive in the world, and the designs, colours and glazes of that work provided an inspiration, both technically and æsthetically, for Iznik pottery in all its glory. Earthenware pottery was already being produced in Iznik before the Ottomans made the decision to encourage this industry with lavish subsidies in the second half of the fifteenth century. At first the royal patrons of the workshops and kilns at Iznik wanted blue and white pottery resembling what they had imported from China and used in the sultans' banquets at Topkapı.

Iznik craftsmen were already skilled at making what is called fritware (from Italian *fritta*, 'fried') where, at high temperatures, a hard ceramic core is achieved by combining silica, fine white clay and other ingredients. The most commonly used early technique is called *cuerda seca*, a Spanish phrase meaning 'dry string', because a cord was laid down to keep pigments in one area from bleeding into other parts of the composition. Though tiles employing the *cuerda seca* method are more common in Bursa, an earlier Ottoman capital, than in Istanbul, they can be seen here too – in the *türbes* on the grounds of the Şehzade Mosque and on the walls of the Çinili Köşk in the Archæological Museum complex. The Çinili Köşk, once an outlying part of the Topkapı Palace complex, now one of three units that make up the Archæological Museum, is perhaps the best place to lose oneself in enjoyment of Iznik ceramics of all periods.

After the *cuerda seca* period, one of those seemingly miraculous breakthroughs resulting from the discovery of new techniques occurred – in this case involving the use of pigments and glazes. Artists and craftsmen have always gravitated toward centres of wealth and power. As Persian power declined and the Ottoman imperium came to dominate the Near East, craftsmen from cities like Tabriz and Isfahan migrated to Edirne, Iznik and Istanbul, bringing with them a technique of underglazing through which they were able to paint vivid designs on hard ceramic surfaces, cover them with a transparent glaze, and fire them at high kiln temperatures. A golden age began, lasting little more than a century, during which brilliantly coloured and designed tiles, mosque lamps, drinking vessels and plates were produced in Iznik with a more fluid and dashing style than is seen in the older *cuerda seca* work.

From the beginning, cobalt blue was the pigment that saw the most use. One of my favourite pieces at the Çinili Köşk is a blue and white china bowl with a ribbed knob in the centre for extracting the juice from a lemon. An ordinary version of this implement is found in most kitchens. The one in the Çinili Köşk, though a simple, utilitarian piece, is delicately painted with floral designs. I envy the cook who squeezed lemons with it to make lemonade during the hot Turkish summers, or to flavour *zeytinyağlı* meze.

An austere blue and white palette did not, however, satisfy Ottoman taste for very long. The Turks lived actively and passionately, and were most at ease on horseback or drawing a bow. They were not Confucian mandarins sipping tea in a garden pavilion. Craftsmen in Iznik began grinding turquoise and blending it with cobalt blue. Turquoise, after all, the blue-green hue of the waters of the Aegean, is the quintessential Turkish colour. What other colour, what other stone, takes its name from a country? Anyone who has swum off Turkey's Aegean beaches has bathed in waters the colour of turquoise. In the mid-sixteenth century Ottoman ceramicists developed a lovely sage green that they applied as an underglaze, eventually finding a way to develop a bright emerald green that superceded sage.

At around this same time some genius in the Iznik potteries discovered Armenian bole, *bolus armenus*, a red clay found in Armenia. Perhaps the tile makers discovered it in the ateliers of their fellow craftsmen, because bookbinders employed it for colouring, and it could also be found in the kits of gilders, where it was used to form a base for gold leaf and to enrich the depth and lustre of binding. Some writers refer to Armenian bole as having the colour of flame or coral, but to my eye there is a bit of rust in it, perhaps owing to the iron oxide in its composition.

However the craftsmen at Iznik created their pigments and glazes, their handiwork produced some of the glories of Ottoman art. By contrast with the austerity of Chinese porcelain, with its celadon and blue and white colouration, the craftsmen based in Iznik created a world of lavish richness – the purity of their high-cloud whites contrasting with deepwater blues, a green that seems to come from the heart of a big emerald, and that understated Armenian bole, an earthy red that speaks of some substantive kinship with the clay from which the tiles are made.

All of these objects demonstrate the great variety of ornament used in Iznik wares, for example the immensely popular tulip, lush, plump peonies and carnations, spiky and scrolling leaves and bold epigraphic ornament. The apogee of the tilemaker's art coincided with the high-water mark of the Ottoman Empire militarily, politically, economically and in terms of its international prestige. The art declined, just as much else in the life of the empire did, in the late sixteenth century.

Islamic art and European decorative art

Most major museums in the world have some Iznik ceramics in their collections. In Istanbul the best place to see Iznik wall tiles is in mosques. The Blue Mosque takes its name from the colour of its tile revetments, though the best of these are in the galleries, and the galleries are hard to gain access to. The interior of the mosque of Rustem Paşa, one of Süleyman the Magnificent's grand viziers, at the foot of Uzun Çarşı Street in the market district of the old city, is famous for being entirely covered in tiles, and they are of a very high quality. Rustem Paşa collected tiles and stored them in preparation for the construction of his mosque. To my eye the best use of tiles in a mosque is in the Sokollu Mehmet Paşa Camii, where they are used more sparingly, and one's eye can focus on them with greater discrimination. I also like the Çinili Cami, or Tiled Mosque, at the top of the hill in Üsküdar, a short walk from Sinan's exquisite Atik Valide Camii.

Ceramics of the Safavid dynasty in Persia, some of whose artisans migrated to Turkey to work at Iznik, can be seen in the tile panels on display in the Jameel Gallery of Islamic Art at the Victoria and Albert Museum (V&A) in London, in the Islamic wing of the Staatliche Museum in Berlin, and in the sumptuous Islamic galleries of the Metropolitan Museum in New York. Elegant sybarites depicted on Persian ceramics eat their sweetmeats off blue and white Yuan and early Ming Dynasty plates and pour their wine from pitchers of similar design, rendered in unmistakable detail. Persian poetry by Hafez and Firdausi in praise of wine, love, drinking parties beside melodiously flowing streams, or the pleasures of the chase, often served as subject matter for scenes like these. This sybaritic strain within Persian and Ottoman culture aroused the suspicions of orthodox Muslims, and there was a proverb, 'He who reads Persian loses half his faith'. But Ottoman high culture was based on Persian culture in the same way that Roman culture was inspired by the Greeks, and the imperial collections at Topkapı are full of figurative art.

Anyone coming into contact with the art of the Islamic world will immediately see the influence that its glorification of pattern has had on European decorative arts, particularly on the Arts and Crafts tradition in Britain and its Commonwealth as well as in the United States. In architecture there are Orientalist fantasies like the Royal Pavilion in Brighton and the Anglo-Indian masterpieces Sir Edward Lutyens created along Raj Path in New Delhi. Looking at exquisite seventeenth-century Persian *cuerda-seca* tile panels from the Safavid dynasty depicting aristocrats picnicking, with silk-gowned figures of young pages and serving girls, their figures sensuously curving, their facial expressions mysterious, one cannot help but speculate about Islamic influence on Art Nouveau and even the Pre-Raphælites. No wonder the Greek, Jewish, Armenian and Levantine merchants who grew rich on trade within the Ottoman Empire took so readily to

Art Nouveau style when they came to build their sumptuous private mansions and apartment buildings along the Grande Rue de Pera in Constantinople.

It is perhaps harder to draw a line between sacred and secular in the Islamic world than in the Judæo-Christian tradition. But especially when delighting in art from the Ottoman and Safavid courts, including the poetry mentioned above and the ceramics inspired by it, I sometimes wish there were some word other than 'Islamic' to cover this art. I can't think of a single word that would serve better, but all the same it can be misleading if it suggests that all this art is of a religious nature. The only 'Islamic' element in Safavid ceramic depictions of idealised aristocratic picnics, Mughal and Persian miniature paintings, or sumptuous Ottoman silks and eye-delighting Iznik tiles, may be the notion that God manifests Himself fully in His creation, which is, for that reason, worthy of the artist's full attention and effort.

14

Sinan, Imperial Architect

ANY MENTION OF THE GLORIES of Ottoman architecture during the reign of Süleyman the Magnificent and his immediate successors must include Mimar Sinan, who held the office of Architect of the Abode of Felicity for fifty years during the empire's most vibrant and expansive period. *Mimar* is the Turkish word for architect. The Abode of Felicity is what the Ottomans called Istanbul. Like his royal patron and employer, Sinan was a man who, it seems, was born not only to exercise power, but to enlarge upon the powers invested in him. At almost a hundred, his death was said to be the result of an accident!

Like many notable figures in the history of the Ottoman Empire, Sinan was not a Turk, but rather an Anatolian Greek or Armenian – perhaps the latter since the account books for the Süleymaniye Mosque, still extant, are written in Armenian, and since the architect was known for his preference for Armenian stonemasons. Among the few things known about his origin is that his father was a stonemason. In any case, Sinan was a product of the *devşirme*, the youth-levy which brought so many talented young men into the Janissaries and the imperial civil service. Sinan did not, as might be expected of someone whose talents must have been evident to the recruiting officers for the *devşirme*, enter the palace schools with which we will acquaint ourselves in the next chapter, but rather became a soldier in the Janissary corps.

So great was his scope that he took control of every aspect of civil engineering not only in Istanbul but throughout the empire. This architect of the Ottoman Empire's most sublime buildings also developed an efficient sewer system in the capital and organised a system of fire prevention. His office grew to encompass so many facets of imperial management during this period of expansion and consolidation that he became a law unto himself, exercising greater power and authority than the minister under whom he nominally served, and sitting on meetings of the *divan* at the Topkapı Palace. He claimed over three hundred buildings as his own work, not including many other projects that he oversaw but deemed not important enough to mention. In a Turkish miniature that survives from 1579, a dignified-looking bearded gentleman whom tradition identifies as Sinan stands among workers on a building site, holding a measuring stick and keeping a watchful eye on three workers building Süleyman the Magnificent's *türbe*.

The young man would have learned carpentry and basic building skills on one of the projects the Janissaries were assigned at home when not at war. He fought in some of Süleyman's major campaigns in Rhodes, Belgrade, and at the Battle of Mohacs in Hungary, rising in the army to become an officer of both infantry and cavalry. As to the relation between his eventual profession and his service in a rifle corps, the architectural historian Godfrey Goodwin comments: 'It is good training for an architect to start his career by learning how to find the weak points of structures in order to knock them down.' Sinan impressed the Sultan with his engineering skills when he built pontoon bridges for the army on campaign in eastern Anatolia. From there he was ordered to complete tasks such as inserting new windows into an old mosque in Edirne and adding a room in a palace. He went on to build a castle on the Danube and fashion formidable stone bridges and roads to link widely scattered provinces of the empire.

Architect for the Ottoman inner circle

Once he had done his journeyman work and was established as master of works in the capital, Sinan took it upon himself to bring order to the growing metropolis. He mandated enclosed stoves in the city's tinderbox wooden dwellings and saw to it that the water supply was made plentiful and safe. The empire was still young then, and the building trades were not yet organised, so it was up to Sinan to recruit and train workers. Records show him putting together a guild of four hundred skilled carpenters in Istanbul – no small task in the early sixteenth century when the Ottomans had made the city their own only fifty years before. Nomads and gypsies were pressed into service to do the heavy lifting, and more than once he persuaded the admiral of the fleet to lend him a force of Christian galley-slaves to perform unskilled labour at the palace.

Among his early works in Istanbul are the *külliye*, or complex of charitable and educational buildings, that he was commissioned to erect for Haseki Hürrem, Süleyman's favoured wife, known in the West as Roxelana. The word *külliye* describes the complex of charitable institutions through which the mosque distributed alms to the poor – a hospital for the sick and ailing, a soup kitchen, a school, cells for scholars and dervishes, rest houses for travellers. These institutions mirrored the social services networks provided by monasteries in Byzantine times. Sinan's magnificent hamam, across the *meydan* from Haghia Sophia, has been restored and is now offering five-star bath packages complete with massage and aromatherapy. Reservations may be made online.

Other buildings of the *külliye* are spread about the quarter. The *medrese*, or religious school, can be found next to the Yeşil Ev hotel on Kabasakal Caddesi, the Street of the Bushy-Bearded One. It houses an attractive centre for Turkish handicrafts, run by the municipality. Near the ferry landing in Beşiktaş, where today some of its dignity is sacrificed by its proximity to the taxi stands and bus ranks, he built the severe and compact *türbe* of the great Ottoman admiral, Hayreddin Barbarossa. Born on the island of Lesbos, the admiral was in today's more nationalistic or ethnic way of looking at things, a Greek – though he and men like Sinan were first and foremost Ottomans, and proud of it.

Now that it had become clear what a gifted builder Sinan was, and how capable he was of undertaking such a variety of tasks, other projects were quickly assigned to him. Among these the place of honour lay in mosque building, which was how the members of Süleyman's inner circle expressed their pious and charitable impulses as well as their desire to memorialise themselves for posterity. This inner circle encompassed the Sultan and his immediate family as well as the larger, institutional family he gathered around himself, drawn from his palace school in Topkapı. These two 'families' melded together through the Ottoman practice of marrying the sultan's daughters and sisters off to rising members of the ruling bureaucracy, thus helping to create a loyal inner cadre that combined meritocracy with the claims of kinship. All of Sinan's most notable mosques were commissioned by this inner circle.

The Şehzade Mosque

Mehmed, Süleyman's eldest son by Roxelana, died from smallpox at the age of twenty-two while the *Padişah* was campaigning in the Balkans. Süleyman was prostrate with grief. When the prince's body arrived in Üsküdar, it was greeted by a crowd of black-clad mourners from among the high officials of the realm. Dervishes chanted hymns while the prince's coffin was ferried across the Bosphorus and carried to the Beyazit Mosque, at that time the most important mosque in the city, where the funeral was held. Alms and free food were distributed to the population. At the graveside, Süleyman wept for two and half hours, clinging to the coffin and not allowing it to be buried. For the mourning period of forty days he attended prayers beside the grave and with his own hands distributed alms to the poor.

To commemorate his favourite son, the *Padişah* commanded Sinan to build the Şehzade Mosque. Şehzade means 'child of the shah (sultan)' or prince. In this, his first really important commission, Sinan built his royal master a mosque which expressed the oneness and greatness of God, and the grandeur of Süleyman's kingdom, and which became, with the prince's adjoining *türbe*, a kind of temple of death. Sinan records in his autobiography: 'as soon as His Majesty's noble order reached me, I gathered together masons and stone cutters and the foundations of the building were laid at an auspicious hour.' The mosque complex was to include a Friday mosque, a religious school, hospice, guest house, and Qur'an school. At the laying of the foundation, alms and meat from the animals that were sacrificed during the ceremony were distributed throughout the city.

Sinan built not only a powerful building, but a powerful symbolic synthesis. In the mosque itself, the Şehzade celebrates the unity of God, while his *türbe* represents a vision of the Muslim heaven. Anyone entering the mosque will be awed by an overwhelming sense of interior space – perhaps even more so than in Haghia Sophia, where the space is divided by rows of columns that create side aisles. Sinan rests his massive dome on four mighty pillars, without the intervening columns that create exedras or side chapels in a Catholic church. Where Haghia Sophia is designed to move visually and ceremonially from the western entrance to the eastern altar, with its central worship space channelled by side aisles, here the orientation is lateral, so that the parallel ranks of men lined up for prayer can face in the direction of Mecca. Where an Orthodox church bows to a hierarchical sanctuary reserved for the clergy, the mosque makes a statement about the equality of men in the eyes of God.

A great architect is equal parts engineer and artist. In this building, Sinan's first major work, it must be said that the engineer predominates. Architecture in Istanbul was haunted by the presence of Haghia Sophia, a constant reminder of Byzantine greatness and the genius of her architects. The engineering problem facing Anthemius of Tralles and Isidore of Miletus, whom we met in chapter ten, was how to sustain the enormous weight of a broad dome without collapsing the building. Their solution was to erect four massive piers, set a drum holding up the dome on these piers, and then to position four semi-domes on the four sides to distribute the weight pressing down from above. This was the solution Sinan adopted in the Şehzade Mosque.

A plan of the mosque with annotations written in at crucial points, apparently in the architect's own hand, in which a compass has been used to draw circles showing how its different parts harmonise geometrically, has been discovered buried in the foundations of the mosque. To get a glimpse into the mind of this great architectural visionary, you might try to find it online. Because these sites change so frequently, I dare not give you the URL where I found it. But the search is worth the effort.

One can see changes in the nature of the Ottoman enterprise in Sinan's plan for this mosque. Earlier, the descendants of Osman spent most of their time on the move, and a mosque had to accommodate not only worshippers, but also travellers. As a result it was customary to build *tabhanes*, hostelries where these wayfarers could be housed and fed without charge for three days. *Tabhanes* were often built flanking the central space of a mosque. This arrangement appears in the mosque of Beyazit II. Perhaps it is not a coincidence that Beyazit was a mystic and a follower of the dervishes. Visually the unity of the older mosques suffers from the spread-out effect of the *tabhane* side-wings. As Mehmed the Conqueror and his descendants increasingly consolidated their control, developed a self-renewing bureaucracy, army corps, and civil service, and defined themselves as champions of Sunni orthodoxy as Caliphs of the Islamic faith, this consolidation was reflected in their mosque architecture.

If engineering trumps artistry in this mosque, so be it. The overall effect is awe-inspiring. And due to the magnanimity of Süleyman's benefaction, the *külliye* is extensive, spread out over the neighbourhood, even though some of its functions no longer operate. If you go out through the *avlu* or courtyard, you enter a kind of park, though it looks a little unloved. There was room here in Sinan's day for caravans to camp under the trees. The mosque must have fallen into disrepair in the middle years of last century, because Aziz Nesin describes riding his bicycle inside the mosque back in the 1940s. Don't try this!

The türbe of Şehzade Mehmed

In the heart of this vast complex, tucked behind the massive mosque with its domes and semi-domes, minarets and arcades, stands the *türbe* of Şehzade Mehmed, one of Sinan's choicest early creations and proof that he was just as adept at minute decorative detail as he was at the grand sweep of an imperial mosque. While the mosque stands, manly and four-square, making a statement about power and authority, the mausoleum makes a more subtle statement about youth and grace. If Sinan the engineer was in charge of the mosque, it was Sinan the poet who set his hand to the *türbe*. Set among funerary cypresses, grape vines and the roses that Turks love so much, the octagonal building is lavish in its decoration and in the materials employed.

Octagonal in shape and revetted in marble, the *türbe* is decorated with detailed flourishes in terracotta and breccia. As distinguished from the smooth lead dome of the mosque itself, the dome of the mausoleum is fluted, and so is the drum that surrounds and supports it. The teardrop-shaped mullions of the windows and the reddish voussoirs of the arches surrounding them lead us into a realm of detailed articulation that Sinan deliberately eschewed on the exterior of the mosque.

After a long period during which Şehzade Mehmed's *türbe* suffered from neglect, the decision was made to surround its porch with glass, and while this may have been necessary, it nevertheless gets in the way of the easy flow between inside and outside which makes the building so much a part of its garden setting. The poetry of the *ensemble* prompted Godfrey Goodwin to some of his own most poetic descriptive writing:

> The noble door is flanked by panels of Iznik *cuerda seca* tiles in which full blue, primrose, white and a fresh green predominate. The inscription over the door grants a foretaste

of the overwhelming beauty of the interior, which is paneled to the level of the dome with a heavenly meadow of magnificent faience tiles in which are set the upper stained-glass windows delineated in fragile plasterwork under the painted dome of eternity. The sarcophagus has lost its brocade covers and the candles no longer burn, but a richly inlaid wooden cage still encases the symbol of man's death. Doors and casements are equally handsomely inlaid. The tomb is not large and the tiles are overwhelming but without vulgarity or any weakening of their force. Sinan was able to use the finest work of the early Iznik period to create his mirror of paradise, and the unprecedented beauty of this sepulchre must have been a consolation to Süleyman when he came, in a kaftan of black watered silk, into this room of the apple-green colour of youth.

Royal patronage

Süleyman the Magnificent was the Ottoman architectural patron *par excellence*, but Sinan was also commissioned to create major works by members of the sultan's family and inner circle. Who were the human beings behind the names in Ottoman history? Starting at the time of the conquest, we know about Mehmed the Conqueror, a soldier, visionary, Renaissance prince, and practical thinker with a brilliant sense of organisation, whose complex nature included a chillingly savage side. We know about Mehmed's son Beyazit II, a man of spiritual strivings who rejected his father's broad-minded spirit of inclusivity and directed the Ottoman project in the direction of Muslim orthodoxy. Then came his son Selim, with that forbidding sobriquet, 'the Grim', a great conqueror who brought the holy cities of Mecca and Medina into the empire, along with much treasure. Selim the Grim was Süleyman's father.

Three or four names stand out among the cast of characters by which Süleyman the Magnificent was surrounded, and they each had a role to play as patrons of Ottoman architecture. First comes Roxelana, whom legend has made a romantic heroine. A girl of the harem, she was abducted from her native Ruthenia for the slave trade by Crimean Tatars and brought to Istanbul. What medieval geographers called Ruthenia covered parts of Ukraine, eastern Russia, western Poland, Belarus and Slovakia. The name she is known by, Roxelana, means The Ruthenian One. Süleyman was smitten by her, wrote poetry to her, and elevated her to a position not granted to royal consorts since the days of Orhan, the first of the Ottoman *padişahs*.

Roxelana may indeed have been the romantic heroine of Orientalist legend, but there is also a darker side. It would seem that she used her influence over the Sultan to have his favourite, his Grand Vizier Ibrahim, strangled, and his vast wealth and properties confiscated. Ibrahim's position came to be occupied by Rustem Paşa, a Bosnian Croat from a village near Sarajevo. Later she turned her husband against his more capable son in favour of the disastrous Selim the Sot, her own son.

Süleyman and Roxelana's only daughter, Mihrimah Sultan, was introduced to Rustem, a graduate of the palace school at Topkapı and a rising young man in the Sultan's service, at the circumcision celebrations for her young brothers, Beyazit and Cihangir, when she was seventeen. At first Roxelana didn't like Rustem, because of his homeliness – not surprising in the son of a swineherd – and she spread the rumour that the young man had leprosy. But at a crucial moment a louse appeared on the young man, a sure sign of his health, apparently, because according to the medical wisdom of the day, lice were not attracted to lepers. Rustem made an impression on the *Padişah* by leaping from a window to retrieve something that had fallen from the ruler's hand.

Assiduous, non-leprous, and of high intelligence, this young son of a Croatian swineherd rose quickly in the imperial ranks and soon married Mihrimah. Mihrimah and Roxelana used their influence with Süleyman to have the Sultan's son-in-law made Grand Vizier. Rustem was a financial wizard, but his tight-fistedness won him many enemies, and one of several unflattering nicknames for him, derived from the incident recounted above, was The Louse of Fortune. Sinan built a famous mosque for Rustem at the bottom of Uzun Çarşı Street near the Spice Bazaar and decorated it with the many fine Iznik tiles the Vizier had collected. As the Sultan's only daughter and the wife of the Grand Vizier, Mihrimah became fabulously wealthy, and was able to commission two mosques from Sinan – the Iskele Mosque in Üsküdar and the Mihrimah Sultan Mosque in Edirnekapı near the land walls. Sinan finished the Iskele Mosque a couple of years before he began work on his greatest mosque in Istanbul.

The Süleymaniye Mosque

Soon after Sinan had completed the Şehzade Mosque, Süleyman the Magnificent commanded him to begin preparations for a new mosque on Istanbul's third hill, one that would be, according to a contemporary observer from Persia, 'peerless and unique on the face of the earth'. Marble panels were removed from the Hippodrome, marble and granite columns requisitioned from classical sites all over the empire, and 150,000 gold pieces were minted from the treasury to pay the workers, two thousand of whom were kept busy in good weather. Sinan took up residence on site, and Süleyman himself was close at hand to keep an eye on things. The Sultan was fifty-four years old and had been on the throne for thirty years. His view of the world had become more solemn, with thoughts of last things crowding into his mind. Successful military campaigns under his father, Selim I, and during his own reign, culminating in the sack of Baghdad, Rhodes and Belgrade, had filled the imperial coffers. He wanted to build a supreme monument to be remembered by, and to be buried there alongside his beloved Roxelana.

Natural topography made the third hill a commanding location, rising on a ridge overlooking the Golden Horn and lining up along the Istanbul skyline both with the complex of buildings on the first hill at Topkapı and on the fourth hill where the Fatih Mosque stood. Working with the lie of the land and artfully enhancing it, Sinan set about terracing the hillside so that the surrounding structures of the *külliye* would build up pyramidally to the central dome of the great mosque. *Medreses* and a hamam were built below the mosque facing toward the Horn, and Sinan inserted shops into their lower floors. Standing or sitting along the outer wall of the mosque complex facing across toward Beyoğlu, one looks down onto a street lined with the successors of these same shops, and across the domes of the hamam in the direction of the Galata Bridge.

With the decline of the Ottoman Empire, the institutions of the *külliye* long ago became derelict. One can but imagine what a bustling, purposeful place the Süleymaniye was in its prime. The gatehouses along the precinct walls were once tenanted with a community of gifted and learned men who saw to various duties and enlivened the life of the institution. There were, according to Seyyid Lokman, a court historian who worked under Murad III later in the sixteenth century, 'exhilarating rooms for distinguished brethren among the literati and calligraphers, provided with endowed books entrusted to a librarian'. The mosque astronomer occupied rooms in the monumental portico leading into the mosque courtyard. The mosque's penetralia, its arcades and back rooms tucked away here and there, would have been used by mosque officials for purposes lost over time. Sometimes when the mosque is more or less empty of visitors, a custodian will appear at your elbow and offer to take you up a hidden stairway to a belvedere that offers a wonderful view of the Golden Horn. Go on along, and give the man a tip. He will be grateful, and the view is worth it.

There can be no doubt that in building the Süleymaniye, Sinan set out to rival Haghia Sophia. The great mosque had a more centralised focus, in contrast to the attention given to subsidiary spaces in the Church of Holy Wisdom and its focus on the altar and sanctuary where priests performed the eucharistic rites. In contrast to the arcades that allow for side aisles and *exedrae* in Haghia Sophia and, as we shall see later on, in the Church of Saints Sergius and Bacchus, Sinan has created a configuration on either side of the central worship space composed of three arches, the centre one very tall, rising to the base of the big tympanum which, pierced with windows, brings light into the building from the sides. Each of these two triumphal arches is supported by a pair of granite columns, sourced from Baalbec, Alexandria and Constantinople itself, each weighing eleven tons.

In addition to its focus on austerity and centrality, the mosque eschews the gold mosaics, icons and other decorative features that give Haghia Sophia its air of sanctity and mystery and hide the architectural structure that supports its massive arches and vast dome. With its white stone interior and lack of subsidiary spaces, the Süleymaniye is more sober, rational and open than the great church; a more light-filled place of worship. The transparency of its architectural logic and the severity of its decoration reflect the austere and reflective mood of the great monarch's last years.

At the same time the mosque is famous for the brilliance of the decorative features it does contain. Both here and in the *türbes* of Süleyman and Roxelana, the calligraphy is stunning. Hasan Karahisari, the greatest calligrapher of his age, and Karahisari's pupil, Hasan Çelebi, designed the Iznik tile roundels on the *qibla* wall, and were responsible for the magnificent panels of *thuluth* work in the mausolea. It is a pity not to be able to read what is written here. Foreigners like myself are excluded from an understanding of these texts by our ignorance of Arabic and Persian. And because of Atatürk's language reforms, very few Turks, even, can read the old script. The inscriptions largely promulgate the orthodox Sunni view of religion that the Ottomans espoused. Literate worshippers would be able to read Qur'anic injunctions such as 'worship at fixed hours hath been enjoined on the believers', and 'recite that which hath been revealed to thee of the Scripture, and perform worship'.

As visitors to great buildings such as the Süleymaniye, we are likely to miss out on some of the more subtle and arcane meanings their architects have built into them. I am thinking of the occult symbolism expressed in the design of Durham Cathedral, and the mystical narrative of the maze at Chartres. Süleyman's mosque embodies its own esoteric meanings, related particularly to the continuity between interior and exterior features. The four minarets are said to symbolise the fact that Süleyman was the fourth Ottoman sultan to reign in Constantinople, while the presence on the minarets of ten *şerefe*, or balconies, where the call to prayer was recited are meant to call attention to the fact that Süleyman was the tenth sultan in the lineage. The study of numerology was very popular with the mathematically-minded Ottomans.

An inscription above the gate leading into the mosque courtyard invites us into the realm of paradise. Entering the mosque from the courtyard, one's eye is drawn to the *qibla* wall, facing toward Mecca. According to Gülru Necipoğlu in her masterly book on Sinan, this interior wall's 'floral Iznik tiles and stained-glass windows create an illusion of transparency, as if the funerary garden visible from the ground-level windows is continuous with the mosque interior'. The stained-glass windows were designed by the most highly regarded glass maker of the period, a man with the colourful sobriquet of *Sarhoş* Ibrahim, Abraham the Drunkard. The chronicler Evliya Çelebi wrote that the mosque was filled with the fragrance of flowers from windows on the lower level facing the gardens, 'perfuming the minds of the congregation as if they had entered heaven'.

The mosque has a clear narrative: from the aforementioned calligraphic inscription above the courtyard gate that invites one into the precincts of heaven promised to believers by the Qur'an, through the worship space where prayers are performed in accordance with the mandates of the holy book, to the southeast wall of the building. This wall, with its illusion of transparency, invites our attention out into the garden, with the beautiful *türbes* that Sinan designed for

Süleyman and Roxelana, bringing us to this botanical representation of paradise.

And once we enter that funerary garden, we are not likely to be disappointed. Roxelana's *türbe* is perhaps the more successful of the two, since what it sets out to achieve is somewhat less ambitious than Sinan's attempt to build a mausoleum for the great Süleyman. The recurring motifs here are beauty and grace, the final resting place of one who was addressed by her royal husband in verse as 'my spring, my joy, my glittering day, my exquisite one who smiles on and on'. A floral theme is established by the panels of Iznik tiles flanking the entrance, which represent gardens in spring. The artistic medium is perfectly suited to what it is called upon to express.

The Iznik floral patterns that cover the walls were mirrored beautifully by the fresh flowers cut daily from the garden surrounding the *türbes* and placed in vases provided for that purpose. Revenues from the shops and ateliers built on the ground floors of the adjoining *medreses* helped pay for the upkeep of those religious schools. Whatever flowers and fruits were left over from decorating the mausolea were sold to the public and the proceeds put into the coffers of the foundation that ran the Süleymaniye.

Sinan's most successful attempt at building a royal *türbe* is not Süleyman's but rather the tomb of the great man's altogether less impressive son, Selim, on the grounds of Haghia Sophia. Perhaps even the great Sinan found himself intimidated when faced with building a memorial to the magnificent one, who died in 1566 before the walls of Szigetvar, a fortress in Hungary which blocked the Ottoman army's advance toward Vienna. Roxelana's mausoleum has a pleasing modesty, and feels simple despite its sumptuousness. The interior of her husband's *türbe* is crowded with the catafalques of the sultan and members of his family, with their covers of green baize and, in Süleyman's case, the enormous turban he wore in life. It is a sombre, even oppressive room despite the sheer beauty of its materials, with calligraphic panels executed in Iznik tiles, and a beautiful painted ceiling. The light filters dimly in through stained-glass windows that fill the arches supporting the dome.

The porch surrounding the *türbe* is a nice touch, and it is pleasant to walk around it, particularly when the roses are in bloom in the garden. The Ottomans had a particular genius for cemeteries, and there are many of these cities of the dead in Istanbul. This little cemetery is one of the most pleasing. The roses blooming here in the spring around the tombs of Süleyman, Roxelana and other notables either mock the brevity of human life or symbolise its renewal in paradise, depending upon one's beliefs.

To view the crowning glory of Sinan's architecture, it is well worth making a day trip to Edirne, where he built his masterpiece, the Selimiye Mosque. For a sample of his more utilitarian work as an engineer and builder, one can visit Büyükçekmece, a suburb of Istanbul, where Sinan built a bridge to span the estuary there. Commissioned by Selim II, the bridge is over 2,000 feet long, a majestic seven-arched structure that is still in use today.

As for the man whose buildings epitomise the Ottoman Empire in its prime, he is buried near the Süleymaniye Mosque in Istanbul, in the garden of the house just on the other side of the mosque complex, where he lived until his death some twenty years after that of his patron. His *türbe* is a modest one.

15

Topkapı Palace

TOPKAPI PALACE can be difficult to take in, and sometimes I despair of getting a good look at the place because of the crowds that pass through here during the tourist season, particularly when the cruise ships are in town. The Seraglio, as it is called in Italian, a version of Turkish *saray*, is familiar to music lovers from Mozart's opera, *The Abduction from the Seraglio*. Topkapı has entered the European imagination as a place of legend. Its storied Harem is the stuff of fantasies, both male and female. On a visit the palace can strike one as a barren assemblage of architectural oddities thronged by peculiarly-dressed people with cameras until one gets a sense of how it functioned as a centre of empire. The three or four thousand residents of the *saray* in its prime governed the empire, led it in wars, prayed, caroused, attended to the necessities of life, made love, schemed, murdered, consumed thousands of meals cooked in the palace kitchens, amassed countless bags of gold, silver florins, aspers and dinars, and guarded the fabulous spoils of war its warrior-sultans brought back from their military campaigns.

During the Ottoman Empire's glory days the centre of power in the world had not yet shifted to northern Europe, Britain, and the New World. England, Wales, and Scotland were separate, warring kingdoms when Mehmed II built his palace here. Ireland had not yet been brought to heel by Elizabethan soldiers and adventurers. America remained a wilderness, an uncharted region of forests, jungles, bottomless rivers, deserts and impassable mountain ranges still awaiting the fateful arrival, almost exactly forty years after the fall of Constantinople, of its first European voyagers and explorers. The Indian subcontinent, innocent of European designs, was still a loosely knit assemblage of princely kingdoms. Only China, not yet eclipsed by the British and American empires, was a world power, then as again today, a high civilisation majestically remote, many weeks by sea to the east.

The plan of the palace

When approaching the palace through the Imperial Gate after a visit to Haghia Sophia, at first one may not notice that this complex of buildings sits on a promontory. Topography is not always obvious in an urban area. Given the reality of the city as it has grown, it is still amazing to consider that as originally conceived, the palace and its grounds occupied the entire northeastern tip of the peninsula where Constantinople is situated. No ferry boats docked and disembarked at Eminönü, no trains chugged in and out of Sirkeci Station, no Galata Bridge connected Stamboul and Pera. A wall two and half kilometres long surrounded this vast area, connecting up with the Byzantine sea walls. Around the palace proper were extensive hunting grounds where the sultans and their courtiers and favourites rode their Arabian horses, honed their skills with bow and arrow, and loosed their falcons to bring down the birds of the air. Orchards and gardens filled with roses as well as produce for the imperial table grew on the slopes below the promontory where Mehmed built his *saray*.

Fatih Mehmed's choice of this prominent location atop the first of the city's seven hills was important more for symbolic and æsthetic than for practical reasons. Five years after taking Constantinople he visited Athens, where he was particularly eager to see the Acropolis. Steeped as he was in classical ideas from his reading and from conversations with his Greek tutors and advisers, he intended the first hill of Constantinople, which was styled *zeytenluk* ('the olive groves') in old Turkish, to be Constantinople's new acropolis. Konstantiniyye, the Turkish name for their new capital, stood at the point where Europe and Asia, the Black Sea and the Mediterranean came together. This carried symbolic value for a ruler who styled himself 'Sultan of the Two Continents and Emperor of the Two Seas' in the inscription he commanded to be rendered in gold calligraphy against an emerald green field above the Imperial Gate. It was Mehmed's plan to reconquer the lands of the old Roman and Byzantine empires and to rule as the Byzantine emperors had ruled.

According to his official biographer, a Greek chronicler called

Kritovoulos, Mehmed personally sketched out plans for his new palace. Then he invited European architects and engineers to his new capital to get their ideas. Interior decorators, builders and painters from Florence and Venice came to assist. At Fatih's request the Venetians, as we have seen, dispatched the painter Gentile Bellini to work for the Sultan. Intellectually and æsthetically, Mehmed's city lived and breathed and had its being as part of a world of power, ideas and commerce reaching from the city states of Italy to Asia Minor and beyond, to Persia and even north to the distant steppes of Russia. In that fifteenth-century world, our more recent ideas about an impermeable border between a Christian Europe and an Islamic Middle East can be inaccurate and misleading.

When it came to how Ottoman rulers would comport themselves and how their subjects would regard them, they worked out an elaborate ceremony that took its cues from those ancient rival Middle Eastern empires, Byzantium and Persia, along with the courts of the Umayyads of Damascus, the Abassids of Baghdad, the Mamluks of Cairo and the Timurids of Central Asia. The western civilised world still centred around the Mediterranean. Distinctive as it was, the Ottoman Empire can best be seen not as a new power that destroyed Byzantium – which in its own day straddled east and west and partook of both – but as the continuation, in altered guise, of that once-great empire. In many surprising ways it was, as the Irish say, 'the same, only different'. Both Byzantine and Ottoman notions of how a sovereign should conduct himself and be thought of by his subjects centred on a sense of the majesty of the ruler, who remained an object of awe and veneration assured by his inaccessibility.

Topkapı is a series of courts through which one moves from a public parade ground to the most private inner sanctum. Foreign visitors reported viewing the Sultan sitting cross-legged on a throne like an idol, speaking to no one, surrounded by an aura of worshipful veneration, thinking his own private thoughts. Except for occasions of state, he seldom appeared in public. In his presence a reverent silence was considered *de rigueur*. As in the medieval Abassid court in Baghdad which served as one of the Ottomans' models, during court proceedings an attendant stood by with a bow and arrow to 'shoot down any crow or bird lest they disturb the proceedings with their ominous crowing and noise'.

In the early years of their migrations, the Ottoman ruler was a ghazi, غازي or *ġāzī*, a nomadic tribal chief who won fame and treasure by his raids on neighbouring lands, preferably but not invariably belonging to the infidels. Mehmed II was a ghazi who made the successful transition to head of state of a vast multi-ethnic, multi-religious empire run by a well-organised bureaucracy. A century later, Henry VIII would make himself dictator-king by subduing the landed English barons and supplanting them with his 'new men' in an aristocracy of merit answerable only to the sovereign. Mehmed went even further. For one thing, he was answerable to no parliament.

As we have seen, his government was an extension of his household, a centralised organisation of household slaves exercising absolute power autocratically. Graduates of his palace school, taken from their families in the provinces and brought to the capital to be trained as pages, were raised with total loyalty and obedience to the Sultan. They were dependent upon him for all the necessities of life, and even for life itself, and were groomed to govern and administer his empire. The members of this cadre who rose to the very top of the Ottoman governing elite were married off to royal daughters and sisters. Mehmed eliminated any chance that the religious hierarchy might be a power on its own, putting the religious scholars and graduates of the *medreses* on salary, thus making them employees and dependents of the state. It was a policy of Atatürk's, too, to keep the imams subordinate to secular authority.

The interior of the palace

But let's not get ahead of ourselves. It is best to approach Topkapı court by court, for that is how it is laid out, and that is how it functioned from the days when Mehmed II was the first *padişah* to live and reign here, followed by his successors Beyazit II; Selim I, the Grim; Süleyman the Magnificent; Selim II, the Sot; and Murad III, to name the succession up to the end of the sixteenth century. By the eighteenth century the sultans began to abandon Topkapı, except on occasions of state, in favour of the pleasure palaces they built along the Bosphorus. They later decamped altogether and moved across the water to the Dolmabahçe Palace.

As we have noticed in looking at the *şadırvan* of Mahmud I outside Haghia Sophia, the Turks tended to model their architecture on the encampments of their nomadic days. For this reason the word 'palace', with its European associations of a single massive building, does not accurately describe Topkapı Sarayı, which resembles in some ways the arrangement of tents, some very elaborate and glittering with bejewelled gold cloth that the imperial army pitched when the sultan was on campaign. Some of these tents were devoted to military and service functions, others given over to the private household of the ruler.

Though much has been erased, lost, or destroyed in the history of Istanbul, much has also been preserved. The Military Museum in Harbiye, a short taxi ride from Taksim Square, is worth a visit if only to see the sultans' tents which are preserved there and to hear the military band that plays daily in front of the museum. Kritovoulos states that the buildings of the palace were designed 'with a view to variety, beauty, size and magnificence'. The styles of its different structures reflect not only the nomadic traditions of the Ottomans themselves, but the architectures of the cultures they conquered and saw themselves as supplanting.

The First Court

One enters the first court through the *Bab-ı Hümayun*, the Imperial Gate mentioned above. The niches around the entrance sometimes displayed the heads of traitors and rebels as a warning to any who might challenge the authority of the sultan. Weapons were on exhibit both as a show of power and to indicate that one was entering a realm where peace and tranquility reigned. Bows and arrows, swords, guns and pikes hung here. Fifty or so *kapıcıs*, or gate-keepers, slept in rooms above the portal to guard the entrance to the palace. The first court is a vast open space, and it had many uses during Ottoman years. It is sometimes called the Courtyard of the Janissaries, as it was here that these elite troops would assemble when the army was not on campaign. At Fatih Mehmed's funeral in 1481, the court accommodated some twenty-five thousand slave soldiers from Mehmed's service, along with two hundred handsome pages from the palace school – perfumed, their hair curled, elegant amidst the rough-hewn soldiery. It must have been quite a show.

If we could see the first court as it looked in those times, it would look quite different from the appearance it presents today as an open, park-like space. We would see exotic animals here – elephants and giraffes, the elephants caparisoned in rich fabrics studded with jewels. Likewise, visitors in bygone days remarked on the smartly outfitted cavalry officers who rode here on parade, their tack ornamented and bejewelled. Along with the cavalry and the menagerie of exotic animals, the first court was home to a congeries of temporary buildings whose construction made no pretension to the elegance of the inner parts of the *saray*. Firewood was piled here and there, and stables were provided for the oxen who hauled the wood. Imagine how much would have been required. Almost all the rooms had their own fireplaces or stoves. The kitchens alone must have burned many trees to cook food for the palace's inhabitants.

Workshops for all kinds of skilled labour of use to the palace's ongoing construction plied their trades: engineers and architects; blacksmiths, carpenters, locksmiths and stonecutters; silversmiths and polishers of precious stones; painters, glaziers and joiners; luthiers; weavers and tailors; bootmakers; makers of fine velvet, engravers on ivory. A well yielded fresh water, and a waterwheel built by Sinan turned, providing water for the baths and latrines. A small mosque or *masjid* answered the spiritual needs of those who worked hereabouts. The first court also held an infirmary for the imperial pages, some of whom would feign illness or bribe the attendants into letting them stay there, for the infirmary offered a more relaxed, less supervised atmosphere than did the palace school, watched over by its grim eunuchs.

Here the pages could relax with their friends, drink wine and listen to music. The air of the first court was redolent with the smell of freshly baked bread, for the bakeries were originally situated here. The Church of Haghia Eirene, second only to Haghia Sophia in Byzantine days, was stripped inside of its glorious mosaics and fine marbles, its vestments, icons and eucharistic vessels, and converted into an armory and makeshift military museum filled with captured weapons, Byzantine relics, antique banners and shields. The deconsecrated church stood as a mute witness to the turning of fortune's wheel. Today St Eirene looks dusty, unloved and desolate. The building is open at odd times nowadays, and provides a fine venue for concerts of jazz and classical music.

Through the Gate of Salutation into the Second Court

One enters the second court, and thus the palace proper, through the *Bâb-üs Selâm*, which means The Gate of Salutation in Arabic and which the Turks called, more plainly, the *Orta Kapı* or Middle Gate. The Italianate appearance of the towers is a reminder that as

Mehmed built his empire, his enterprise was ruled by ideas from at least three distinct traditions. The first was Byzantine, that ornate and storied but empty shell he was coming to occupy; the second, border-fighter nomadic Turkish, with its absorption of the Persian and other Middle Eastern kingdoms through which the Turks had passed on their journey westward. The third of these three traditions embodied the new ideas of the Italian Renaissance. Behind the Byzantine and Italian traditions lay the Roman Empire and the classical past which influenced both the Ottomans and the civilisation of fifteenth-century Italy.

Only persons on official business could get past the guards stationed at this towered gate, who lined up ceremoniously as official visitors entered the second court. Only the sultan himself could ride a horse within the palace grounds. The battered paving stones under the arch of the gate, the big, open fireplaces where the soldiers warmed themselves on cold Istanbul nights, when chill and rain blew in from the Bosphorus and the Sea of Marmara, tell a story of the life of those who kept watch here. The porter in *Macbeth* comes to mind.

Dormitories for the *kapıcıs* flanked the gate on either side, and on the floor above was their *masjid*, *mescit* in Turkish – the word used for a prayer space less grand than a mosque – so that the gatekeepers could perform their obligatory five daily prayers without straying too far from their posts. Like the Imperial Gate, the Gate of Salutation was a place where weapons were displayed. Bows and arrows, battle axes, swords and shields, gilded for show, hung beside and above the gate. At one time a small gaol held government officials who had broken the law, and it was here as well that the aforementioned executioner had his living quarters.

Just outside the gate, the *Cellat Çeşmesi*, or Fountain of the Executioner, provided water where the grim man who dispatched traitors and miscreants to the next world could wash the blood off his axe and his hands – another Macbethian touch. Black Ali, Chief Executioner at the time of Murad IV, was said to have at his disposal 'seventy-seven instruments of torture – nails, gimlets, razors, matches for scorching ... different powders for blinding, clubs for breaking the hands and feet'. The whole *ensemble* – the undoubtedly intimidating *kapıcıs*, the bristle of weapons, the gaol, the dark-visaged executioner with his axe – must have put the fear of God into all who passed under the arch.

If the first court was a parade ground, menagerie and

higgledy-piggledy collection of service buildings, workshops and storerooms, the second court was the administrative centre of the palace as well as providing the first veiled intimations of the private areas that lay beyond. From the small open space just inside the gate, a variety of paths radiate in different directions. I seem to recall being told at some point that the little gate to the far left, hardly noticeable, was where the bodies of those who died inside the Topkapı Sarayı were carried out. One path on the left leads to the Harem's carriage gate on that side of the court, for the women of the palace were allowed to pass through the *Orta Kapı* in the royal carriages.

Another leads to the Harem entrance proper, two others to the *divan* chamber, while two on the right lead to what were once the palace kitchens. What a lot of cooking went on there! Someone has uncovered the yearly inventory of ingredients from the year 1640 and has ascertained that the cooks went through 1,130 tons of meat, 92 tons of spinach, 14 tons of yoghurt, 265 tons of rice, and so on. Topkapı's amazing collections of Chinese porcelain and imperial costumes are displayed in the kitchens now. The broad, central path leads straight to the third gate. It is called the Sultan's Way, and one can easily picture *Il Gran Turco* traversing it on horseback.

In such an imposing place as this, perhaps one does well to focus on out-of-the-way things like the sultans' carriages. Though these vehicles are hard to see in their poorly-lit glass display cases, they do give a sense of the style in which, even as late as the reign of Abdülaziz in the mid-nineteenth century, the sultan and his family were still sallying forth. Particularly interesting are the carriages built especially for ladies. Even when on the move, their privacy was preserved by the same lattice-work that can be seen in the *haremlik* windows of Ottoman houses. Were they protected and precious members of what used to be called the weaker sex? Or simply prisoners of male dominance? Perhaps a bit of both.

In the eyes of the West, the idea of the seclusion of women can seem puzzling or even odious. The word 'harem' is derived from two related Arabic words, حرم or *ḥaram*, denoting a 'forbidden place, something that is sacrosanct'; and حريم or ḥarīm, 'a sacred inviolable place'. The conception goes against our ideas about personal freedom and equality of the sexes. It also goes against the great Atatürk's ideas about the kind of country modern Turkey should be. And it goes against the ideas of the millions of non-headscarf-wearing Turkish women among the better-educated and more prosperous levels of society. Other Turkish women seem to like it, however, for the way it grants them privacy and respect. Few would deny that Turkey is largely a male-dominated society; but many Turks would also be quick to assert that in the home it is a different story.

As a visitor to Topkapı, one enters the palace's forbidden or sacred inviolable place, the Imperial Harem, through the Carriage Gate next to the *divan* along the upper left side of the second court. Approaching the palace from outer to inner, however, I like to see the third court first and then come back to the Harem. In any case there is usually a delay in admission, so it is best to secure a Harem ticket and return at the time specified on your ticket.

The centre of power

To get on with our look at the second court: other oddments here include the massive acanthus capital parked on the ground in the courtyard, just in front of the carriages – a colossal chunk of Marmara stone, deeply undercut, that once held up some enormous early Byzantine entablature, perhaps from the φόρος Θεοδοσίου, the Forum of Theodosius in Beyazit Square. This part of the palace grounds has been the repository for archæological findings for a very long time. This same capital is described as having been in the same place from the earliest days of the *saray*. The outline of a mosque lamp has been delicately carved into an old tombstone beside two plane trees, for the open ground here also served as an open-air prayer space. Off to the left side of the main path a fountain built during the reign of Mehmed II and repaired under Ahmed III in the Tulip Age has been placed outside the gift shop. Charmingly, to my eye anyway, the old tiles have been cemented in randomly. There is an old well just inside the *divan* chamber. This place is full of ghosts.

Dominating the administrative centre of the palace from above, and situated at the outer edge of the Harem, the Tower of Justice rises above the *divan*, or Council Chamber, where the Grand Vizier looked after the quotidian cut-and-thrust of government. Originally the tower was lower, but in the early nineteenth century Mahmud II had it rebuilt in its present form, which has a vaguely Palladian look. From this tower the *padişah* could watch executions being carried out in front of the Executioner's Fountain. As condemned men begged for forgiveness, the sultan would open one of the shutters in the tower to signify that he was listening to their pleas.

The sovereign governed by proxy through his Grand Vizier, and could observe the Vizier's deliberations unobserved by looking through a curtained window between his private quarters and the Council Chamber. In her fascinating scholarly study, *Architecture, Ceremonial, and Power: The Topkapı Palace in the Fifteenth and Sixteenth Centuries*, Gülru Necipoğlu puts it succinctly: 'although invisible, his presence was always palpable'. This autocratic ruler kept his own counsel and pursued his pleasures in his private gardens, pools and pavilions, attended by his pages and courtesans, among whom he bathed and feasted, read and wrote poetry, listened to the music of stringed instruments, enjoyed the pleasures of the harem, and practiced archery and the sports of the chase. In the decadent days of the sultanate the Valide Sultan, or Queen Mother, the power behind the throne, was the watcher through this gilded grille.

Right at the foot of the tower, in the Council Chamber, the Grand Vizier, flanked on the *divan* by his lesser viziers and the representatives of the non-Muslim *millets* or ethnic communities, heard petitions, made his decisions, and saw to the business of governing this vast empire. The Council Chamber, with its loggia and overhanging roof, was a version in stone, wood, lead and tile, of the consultation tent the sultan pitched when out on campaign. Under Mehmed the chamber was a much more modest affair than the building we see today, which his grandson Süleyman the Magnificent ordered to be rebuilt in a grander style while he was away on campaign in Hungary in 1526.

Murad III had the Council Chamber redecorated in the closing years of the sixteenth century, and though the chamber was repaired and reworked over the centuries, it retains the imprint of those years when the Ottoman Empire still ruled much of the civilised world. Leaded domes and marble columns replaced the simple pyramidal roof and wooden posts of the old structure. The walls were revetted in beautiful Iznik tiles, the *divans* covered sumptuously, a golden globe was hung from the ceiling to signify the world the House of Osman ruled, and the best rugs from Turkish, Persian and Caucasian looms lay underfoot. When the European-influenced fashion for a rococo æsthetic made itself felt in Istanbul, it turned out to be a style not unharmonious with classical Turkish architecture. The rich cream and gold fretwork of the ceilings in the Council Chamber and under the roof of the Gate of Felicity, the curlicues and flowing lines of the painted details, the rosettes and pastel colours, add grace, even if a yawn of decadence and self-satisfaction can be faintly heard.

Further inward was the outer treasury, crowned with eight leaded domes, where the empire's vast revenues from its far-flung provinces were recorded and stored. This was before the era of banks. The treasury was secured with many locks and sealed with wax bearing the *tuğra*, or official monogram and signature, of the *padişah*. A rare foreign visitor to see the treasury opened, wrote in 1573, during the reign of Selim the Sot: 'from it they took out a large quantity of their coin in leather sacks to pay the Janissaries. In it is reportedly a large quantity of gold and silver coins, precious stones, jewelled objects of gold and silver such as swords, decorated knives, and other objects. I have heard ... that there is a grand quantity of gold bars left from the past emperors.'

The focus of the second court, the thing one sees at the end of the Royal Way running up its centre, is the *Bâbüssaâde*, to give it its Arabic name, or Gate of Felicity in English. This is a broad canopy crowned with a prominent dome, with the spreading eaves of its roof supported by marble columns, flanked by a colonnade of alternating green and white columns that form an elegant arcade joining the Council Chamber with this ceremonial gate. The domed canopy reproduces the large, open umbrella-like tent under which the sultan would sit to hold court while on campaign. Though already grand in the time of Mehmed, Ahmed III remodelled it in the early eighteenth century. Charming depictions of idealised bucolic scenes have been painted on panels on either side of the gate, adding to the air of elegance.

A liminal space between outer and inner, the Gate of Felicity was where the accession of a new sultan was announced, and where the Sacred Banner of Islam was unfurled when the imperial armies went to war. This was where important holidays were celebrated, and where the sultans' funerals were held when their reigns – glorious, uneventful, ignominious or catastrophic as the case might be – came to an end. Mehmed made frequent appearances here in the early years of his reign, but as gout and corpulence overtook him, he came out from his private quarters less frequently. And as Ottoman court protocol increasingly ossified in later centuries, the appearance of the *padişah* here, or in any other public space, became more and more rare.

Whatever faults may be attributed to the sultans of the House of

Osman – and there were many – they cannot be accused of lacking a sense of style. When one of these rulers made an appearance at the Gate of Felicity, a throne covered with gold cloth and sparkling with diamonds, sapphires and emeralds the size of horse-chestnuts, was brought out from the recesses of the third court and set up here, along with sumptuous carpets and hangings. Horsemen whose mounts sported jewel-bedecked saddles and tack lined up in front of the colonnade, while a military band played music similar to what one can hear these days at the Military Museum in Harbiye.

Through the Gate of Felicity into the Third Court

From the Gate of Felicity and beyond, one enters precincts where at one time visitors rarely set foot. As the heroic age of the Ottoman Empire ended with the death in 1566 of Süleyman the Magnificent, his son and his grandson retreated more and more into the privacy of these inner courts, enjoying the pleasures of life in the harem, the baths and private gardens of the inner courts. A Venetian observer in the time of Murad III, Süleyman's grandson, wrote that 'Sultan Selim, father of the present Grand Signor, initiated the following opinion: that the true felicity of a king or emperor did not consist in military toils and in operations of bravery or glory, but in idleness and tranquility, in the satisfaction of the senses, in the enjoyment of all comforts and pleasures in palaces filled with women and buffoons, and in the fulfillment of all desires for jewels, palaces, loggias, and stately constructions'. In the seventeenth century, during the 'Reign of the Women', the Valide Sultan, or Queen Mother, was frequently able to manipulate her son and exercise power in the back-rooms of the Harem, abetted by the palace eunuchs in an unseemly stew of palace intrigue.

And who were these eunuchs, one might ask? Their very existence, the custom of castration, the word *eunuch* itself even, with its un-Englishlike sound, remains one of the most disturbingly outlandish features of the Ottoman system. Yet the custom is an ancient one, going back as far as records were kept. Every ancient culture from China to Rome seems to have had eunuchs. The Bible refers to them more than once. Their presence is mentioned at the Byzantine court, and at least one prominent Byzantine general was a eunuch. The etymology is Greek and means 'bed keeper'. Eunuchs, having no offspring and no access to power through the army or the aristocracy, were thought to be well suited to look after the person of the ruler and, in particular, his womenfolk, around whom their sexual incapacity made them a safe presence.

The ubiquity of the custom does not make it any less barbaric. Topkapı had its black eunuchs and its white eunuchs, and they served different functions, the former to guard the women of the harem, the latter to look after the pages in the palace schools. The Qur'an forbade castration of male Muslims, so these unfortunates came either from Christian communities in the Balkans or from Africa. Caravans reached Istanbul from its far-flung provinces, and those sent annually to the capital by the governors of Egypt brought African slaves as part of their tribute.

Young boys about eight years of age from Abyssinia and Sudan were taken to a Coptic monastery along the caravan route in Egypt where the monks chained the boys to tables to perform the operation. After the deed was done, the monks stuck a piece of bamboo into the genital area, then submerged their victims in hot sand up to the neck to cauterise their mutilated parts. Ten per cent of them survived! The no-doubt traumatised, miserable and disoriented ten per cent then continued their journey to the slave markets of the great city, where they fetched a high price, many of them brought into service at the *saray*. Clearly neither the moral constraints of the religion of Muhammad nor those of the religion of Christ were enough to curb the inborn human impulse to ruthlessness and savagery.

Venetian diplomats were shrewd observers, and they saw that the days when the sultans became increasingly cut off from the realities of government coincided with the beginnings of decline. Morosini, a visiting diplomat from the Serenissima, wrote in a report to his superiors during the reign of Murad III, 'this sultan does not, in my opinion, live so desireable a life, for he stays almost continually enclosed in his seraglio in the company of eunuchs, boys, dwarves, mutes, and slaves… . In the morning he arises quite late from bed and … comes out of the women's quarters, where he sleeps each night …' Morosini goes on to relate how the Sultan spends little time with his viziers, preferring to practise archery, listen to music and have comedies performed before him, and be entertained by his mutes and buffoons. 'Then he always reenters the harem for dinner with the approach of night, both in the summer and winter.'

The Royal Court

Visually, the transition from the second court to the third says something about both æsthetics and ceremony, because unlike the entrances to the two other courts, the massive doors of the Gate of Felicity do not open into an open space. Instead one immediately faces another building, colonnaded on all four sides, with broad overhanging eaves sweeping outwards, forming what to the Western eye is an enchanting Orientalist fantasy. This is the *Arz Odası*, which translates as the Chamber of Petitions or Audience Hall, in my view the most elegant and pleasing small secular Ottoman building in Istanbul. Süleyman the Magnificent restored and renovated the structure his father Selim I and his great-grandfather Mehmed II had built on this site. Later, Ahmed III and Mahmud II, respectively, redecorated and restored this gemlike building.

This little *köşk* – the Turkish word from which we get *kiosk* – modest in size, but decorated with breathtaking sumptuousness, was just the kind of place the Ottomans liked. Broad eaves covering the arcaded porches that surrounded it on all four sides kept off the rain and shaded it from the rays of the sun. Breezes could blow in through the many doors and windows. The Chamber of Petitions reflects the broad sweep of Ottoman taste in architecture and interior decoration from the great days of its beginnings in the fifteenth century to the grand C Major of Süleyman the Magnificent in the sixteenth, when the empire reached its apotheosis of power and greatness, to the rococo elegance and dying fall of the eighteenth and nineteenth centuries, when what was pleasing to Europeans also pleased the Turks.

Whereas in the Council Chamber the sultan was unseen and all-seeing, here his exalted personage sat on a raised dais covered with black velvet sewn with patterns of gold, over which lay leopard and lion skins – symbols of power and kingliness. Much of the old opulence has vanished from the throne chamber, but at one time, or so early observers report, its fireplace was of solid silver covered with gold, and its ceiling was painted an ultramarine blue studded with golden stars. Even the walls were plated with gold and decorated with emeralds, rubies and pearls. Set into one wall was a little fountain, with a solid gold drinking cup chained to it. Emblems of kingship decorated the throne, which bristled with bows and arrows, a sword and a penbox like those on display in the Museum of Turkish and Islamic Arts, showing that the sultan was, like the Prophet Muhammad, a man both of the sword and the pen.

Life at the Ottoman court was ritualised to the highest degree. While he awed foreign ambassadors and visiting statesmen in his throne room, on other occasions the *padişah* might sit out in the colonnaded forecourt in front of his *köşk* on a special canopied throne inlaid with ebony, ivory and mother-of-pearl. On the eve of a *bayram*, or religious holiday, he ceremonially received the greetings of palace officials, who would come here to kiss his hand, after which he distributed presents and gold coins. Before he walked down the marble-paved path that led from the Privy Chamber in the northwest corner of the third court over to the Chamber of Petitions, pages from the palace school would wash the path down with rosewater, vinegar and lemon juice so that the sovereign's feet did not have to tread on an impure surface. Gülru Necipoğlu beautifully sums up the difference between the Chamber of Petitions in its glory days and the building we see in the twenty-first century:

> Gone are the marble revetments, star-studded ceilings, elegant tiles, precious furnishings, rare fabrics, and gilded objects inlaid with jewels that made it legendary. One can no longer hear its playing fountains nor see the rich curtains and stained-glass windows that made it a dark, flickering, mysterious space, glittering with gold and gems. It was the culmination of every embassy's passage across the increasingly secluded thresholds and forecourts of the palace, the site of the final encounter with the sultan in majesty. The impact of its opulent interior, glistening, shining, and sparkling with ornaments, was dazzling. Despite its small scale, unusual in imperial architecture, this miniature building was not meant to express modesty but, on the contrary, unshakable confidence in the sultan's imperial grandeur.

One gets the sense that the Chamber of Petitions, situated right on the edge of his private quarters, was perched as close to where he had to perform his public duties as the sultan was prepared to go. From here, where he sat in state and received either his own viziers or the emissaries of foreign governments, he could retreat into his private quarters, which were originally located in the Privy Chamber in the northwest corner of the court. Ahmed III, a modern-looking sultan from the early eighteenth century, chafed under the dead hand of the elaborate court ceremonies that had built up over the centuries. In a rare glimpse of a *padişah* as a human being, we find him complaining to his Grand Vizier: 'if I go up to one of the chambers, forty Privy Chamber pages are lined up; if I have to put on my trousers, I do not feel the least comfort, so the swordbearer has to dismiss them, keeping only three or four men so that I may be at ease in the small chamber.'

Ahmed III's Library

Ahmed, one of the most notable architectural patrons among the sultans, built his *Enderûn Kütüphanesi*, The Library of the Inner Palace, a few steps behind the Chamber of Petitions. One can easily imagine this learned, pleasure-loving gentleman spending contented hours in the comfort of his gemlike little eighteenth-century building among his books and collections of Persian miniatures. At one time, before they were moved to the Palace Library, more than 3,500 manuscripts lived here. Significantly, the library, revetted in grey marble, faces not toward the public part of the *saray*, but back toward the inner recesses of the sprawling palace complex. Standing at the base of the entrance staircase is a fountain, elegantly arabesque, which would have cooled this garden courtyard with its flowing waters and been a pleasure to hear as background music for the sultan while he was inside in the company of his books.

In terms of the building's structure, it is clear that the sultan's architect, Mimar Beşir Ağa, must have been responding to what was being built in Europe at the time when he drew up his plans. When viewing the sombre-looking library from the outside, the balanced geometry of neoclassical European architecture comes to mind. The way the rectangular windows on the lower level rise to taller, arched windows on the floor above will be familiar to anyone who has seen the Georgian buildings of London or Dublin. The porch, with three bays whose arches are supported by slender columns, leaded domes topping each arch, is reached up short flights of stairs on either side, like the *piano nobile* of a Georgian building. Yet in case we needed a reminder that we are in Istanbul and not London, the arched windows rise to points, and leaded domes crown each of the four rooms of this cruciform building, with elegant gilded finials atop each of them.

Inside, the library is a little paradise for the exercise of quiet contemplation. Niches for books and manuscripts alternate with cabinets whose wooden doors gleam with elaborate patterns inlayed in mother-of-pearl, tortoiseshell and ivory. The upper walls captivate the eye with Iznik tiles from the sixteenth and seventeenth centuries that form interlocking arabesque patterns of tulips and peonies, carnations and roses in Armenian bole, turquoise and cobalt blue against a field of glistening white. The total effect is probably not available to us from this distance in time – the quiet elegance of the patterned woodwork, the Iznik tile revetments at the same time sensuous and cool, the sound of water flowing in the fountain outside. Around the walls, low *divans* are arranged, and it is easy to imagine sitting here and reading the choice collection of Arabic and Persian texts with their depictions of scenes from the literature that formed the core of traditional learning, both religious and secular, that was the common heritage of Islamic peoples inhabiting the Middle East in its days of glory.

On these pages filled with flowing calligraphy and finely-coloured illuminations enhanced by the dazzle of gold leaf, Majnun viewed Leyla from the tower of his palace and fell fatefully in love. Dervishes sat contemplating the ninety-nine beautiful names of God in mountain fastnesses whose stylised rocks glowed puce and violet, rose and lavender. Warriors mounted on Arabian steeds jousted above fields of flowing Persian verses. On his Night Journey from Mecca to the Al Aqsa Mosque in Jerusalem, from there to the Seventh Heaven and thence back to Mecca, the Prophet himself, his face veiled – because what artist would dare try to depict him? – rose up through the heavens on the mythological steed Buraq, البراق or *al-Burāq*, meaning 'lightning', a winged white horse with a human face who, one poet tells us in a lovely phrase, 'could place his hooves at the farthest boundary of his gaze'. He bucked when Muhammad came to mount him. But the Angel Gabriel put his hand on Buraq's mane and said: 'are you not ashamed, O Buraq? By Allah, no one has ridden you in all creation more dear to Allah than he is.'

On the threshold of the Inner Palace

Beyond Ahmed III's library, the third court housed the pages who were studying and being trained in the palace school which provided the Ottoman government with bureaucrats and officials, men of letters and scholars. Their numbers also included musicians, archers and falconers, trainers of hunting dogs and squires of the royal stable – the Ottomans were keen hunters – and even stokers responsible for heating the water for the sultan's bath. Here some among them learned how to care for the *padişah*, how to wrap his turban, shave him, cut his nails and wait on his table. Their dormitories occupied the north range of the court, diagonally across from the sultan's private quarters, where now the relics of the Prophet astonish the faithful and the faithless alike.

The Privy Chamber, a spacious four-roomed suite in the Ottoman style, each of its rooms covered by a dome, was built in the late sixteenth century to replace a somewhat less grand structure that housed the sultan's living quarters from the time of Mehmed. As the sultans moved their households into the harem and began spending more time in its labyrinthine fastnesses, the Privy Chamber became a repository for holy relics of the Prophet Muhammad. The empire became more centred on Islam with the accession to the throne of Beyazit II, a pious man. Beyazit was followed by his son Selim I, a great campaigner who in 1516–1517 conquered the Mamluk Kingdom with its capital in Cairo, and brought all of Egypt and the western part of the Arabian Peninsula along the Red Sea, as well as what is now Syria, under Ottoman control. In Turkish, Syria is still called by the old name of *Şam*.

Having already conquered Asia Minor and the Balkans, the Ottomans now became the dominant power in what we call the Middle East, which included the Hejaz, site of the holy places of Islam. Possession being nine-tenths of the law, Selim now made bold to assume the role of Caliph, spiritual head of Islam. The Sharif of Mecca granted him the title *Khâdim ül Haramain ish Sharifain*, or Servant of the Holy Cities of Mecca and Medina. This meant that along with their military might, the Ottomans could add a spiritual justification to their hegemony in the region. Among the calligraphic decorations, executed in Iznik tiles, that grace this room where the holy relics are displayed are verses from the Sura of Victory from the Qur'an, promising victory in battle to the faithful and a triumphal entry into paradise. Most iconic of the relics of the Prophet was the green Banner of Islam, which the sultan first carried into battle in the late sixteenth century against the Hapsburgs, whose fortunes in this contest between empires began to rise at the same moment those of the Ottomans fell into decline.

Among other booty that Selim brought back, the cloak of the Prophet Muhammad (the Holy Mantle), two swords, some battle sabres and a bow that the warrior-prophet had wielded, plus a fascinating autographed letter offering a choice to the residents of a city he was besieging: either convert to Islam or expect to die in combat. A cast of his footprint indicates what a big man he must have been. The swords of the Four Caliphs are also on display here, as is the prayer rug belonging to the daughter of Muhammad and the staff that Moses used to part the Red Sea, as well as one of the Prophet's teeth and a hair from his beard! The curators of the museum have been able to maintain an atmosphere of reverence in this dimly lit space by banning photography and having an imam on-site to intone scripture.

The Inner Palace

The buildings that surround the third court are bound together in an architectural unity by the columned portico that surrounds the entire inner area. The styles of the individual buildings, however, express the cultural diversity of the Ottoman enterprise. The Privy Chamber is fronted with the pointed arches and *muqarnas* capitals, with their stalactite decorations, of the Moorish Islamic tradition. Across the way, fronted with an Italianate loggia, its walls formerly decorated with Byzantine mosaics, stands a complex of buildings that contained both a sumptuous bathhouse and the sultan's treasury. The Mamluk style of its ornate doorway is a reminder of Selim I's conquest of the Mamluk capital of Cairo.

Mehmed II built an aviary in the third court, and beside that a bath of the kind we call Turkish. According to a fifteenth-century poem by Cafer Çelebi, the Sultan liked to relax beside the pool 'while the naked, well-proportioned bodies of the handsome bath attendants who served him made the "mouths of the fountains water", and the hot floors, burning with desire, kissed their bare feet'. Given the proximity of the women of the harem, accessible on the other side of his Privy Chamber, one is tempted to compare this part of the *saray* with those paradisal gardens described by Robert Lowell in his sonnet about Attila the Hun, 'stocked with adolescent beauties, both sexes for simple nomad tastes'.

The inner palace was a labyrinth, and its customs and doings were multifarious. Also in this part of the *saray* could be found a mosque and a music room, the chief eunuchs' recreation room – one can only wonder what that was like – and a place where the palace mutes (their services were prized since they could not go about telling tales) were taught sign language. Selim the Sot had the baths rebuilt after they were damaged in an earthquake, one of many with which Istanbul has been afflicted. A weak and superstitious man, he was rattled by a concatenation of events he saw as portents: the appearance of a comet, an earthquake in Constantinople, floods on the Arabian peninsula that endangered the holy places in Mecca, and above all, and most alarming for a man with Selim's bibulous habits, a fire in the *saray* in Edirne that destroyed his wine cellar. His reign lasted a mere eight years.

Architecturally of a piece with the baths was what was called the Inner Treasury, to distinguish it from the more operational Outer Treasury in the second court, which functioned as a sort of bank for the receipt of imperial revenues and a paymaster's clearing house where the Janissaries were paid. Selim the Grim, grandson of Mehmed II and father of Süleyman the Magnificent, was a great warrior, notable for his campaigns against the Safavid Persian capital in Tabriz and the Mamluks in Cairo. From these campaigns he returned enriched not only by the holy relics mentioned above, but by other more worldly spoils of war. In those days, when you defeated an enemy on his home ground, you brought back his treasures, and Tabriz and Cairo had been very rich indeed.

And not only rich but cultivated – because these princely states were home to workshops where calligraphers, painters and gilders, workers in precious metals, ceramics and weaving, and all other skilled craftsmen in the traditional decorative arts plied their trades. The sultan's wealth was reflected not by his bank account but, in a very literal sense, by his treasures. Wealth in those days before the euro, credit swaps, the Dow and the FTSE, was a less abstract proposition.

The Treasury today puts on display a selection of items still in the palace collection, and in this case a little stands for a lot, because as in any museum there is more in the permanent collection than can be displayed at any given time. The Ottomans loved jewels, the more ostentatious the better. The famous Topkapı dagger with its huge emeralds, around which the plot of the movie *Topkapi* revolves, is here. Open the emerald on top and a watch is revealed. This was made for Mahmud I. The *Kaşıkçı Elması*, or Spoonmaker's Apple, an 86 carat diamond, was worn by Mehmed IV in the aigrette of his turban. It is the fifth largest diamond in the world, and it is surrounded by other sparklers that set off its heart-shaped chunky brilliance. Then there is the ebony throne of Murad IV, inlaid with ivory and mother-of-pearl.

All of these items are talking history, but I especially like looking at the gold aigrette that Süleyman the Magnificent made for himself. As we know, he chose goldsmithing as his part-time *metier*.

The Ottoman treasury contained such stuff as dreams are made on: urns heavy with gold and silver coins, trunks overflowing with jewels. An inventory from the archives at Topkapı that was carried out by order of Beyazit II contains page after page enumerating prayer rugs, chessboards and backgammon sets inlaid with mother-of-pearl, ebony and tortoiseshell, swords, shields and helmets, gilded and jewelled tack, precious stones of all hues, carats and cuts, and illuminated manuscripts from the ateliers of Cairo, Baghdad, Tabriz, Isfahan and points east; elephant tusks and rhinoceros horns, sharks' teeth, incense burners, shoes and swords. Beyond the bibelots, *objets d'art* and weapons, precious raw materials were warehoused in the treasury: turquoise and lapis lazuli, ivory and ebony, sheets of gold leaf, paper, silks and velvets, marble from far-flung quarries, sandalwood, mahogany and other fine woods. The royal craftsmen in the outer court would have come here for these things, all carefully enumerated by the palace staff.

The poets and novelists are our truest guides to the mysteries of past times, and no one has given us a more vivid sense of the Inner Treasury than Orhan Pamuk in his masterpiece, *My Name Is Red*. Here the man we as readers know simply as 'Black' is led through the treasury by one of the palace dwarves in the early seventeenth century. What are for me the greatest of treasure troves have gone missing from the palace, scattered to the four winds almost a century ago. Mehmed the Conqueror, that man of vaulting ambition, gargantuan appetites and omnivorous curiosity, was not only a great warrior and practical visionary, he was also a great collector of manuscripts, early printed books, rare maps, and albums of paintings not only by artists in the Persian and Timurid traditions but by European, or as the Byzantines and Ottomans called them, Frankish painters. These included the Venetian master, Gentile Bellini, as well as Costanza da Ferrara, who executed a famous bronze medallion of Mehmed II.

Of Mehmed's five wives, three were certainly Christians, at least by upbringing, as they were members of the Byzantine royal family. Through them the *ghazi*, this warrior of Islam, became conversant with the Christian faith. Gentile Bellini reported that the sultan lit candles before the religious paintings in his collection. One can only wonder what he made of the superstitious Christian belief in relics, which had been so much a part of the religious life of Byzantium. In any event, he owned a large number of relics, most of which must have been preserved from Haghia Sophia and other Byzantine churches. It is known that relics from the Great Palace of Byzantium and the Monastery of St John the Baptist fell into the Conqueror's Hands. Two of these relics remain in the Topkapı treasury – the skull and the humerus of St John the Baptist. It is said that on one occasion Mehmed II became very angry when his royal librarian stepped on a marble stone in the library to reach a book on a high shelf. The stone, the outraged Mehmed told his trembling librarian, was the cradle in which Isa (Jesus) slept!

When the Venetians, always out for a bargain, offered him thirty thousand ducats for the stone, Mehmed II replied that he would not part with it even for a hundred thousand ducats. His relics were, he said, 'more precious than money'. So it would appear that Mehmed II genuinely did revere these relics, as he revered his collection of classical manuscripts. Regrettably his son, Beyazit II sold them in the Grand Bazaar. How one would have liked to have been there to haggle over them! Beyazit offered the books to European rulers in return for favours and sometimes gave them as gifts to the Franks. There must be some bibliophile, somewhere in the world, who would have a sense of what has become of these books. A few remain, a paltry remnant but treasures in themselves, in the Topkapı library.

Life and art in the Harem

Having had a look round the third court, I like to go back to the second and enter the Harem. Unfortunately nowadays one finds oneself part of a herd here even though the numbers of visitors are supposedly controlled. Despite the exoticism with which legend has exalted these now cold and empty halls and rooms, the Harem does not feel like a happy place. The lives of most of its inmates – I use the term deliberately – must have been miserable. Very few of these women were ever chosen to be consorts of the sultan. Most of them simply worked as servants, sleeping three or four to a room in dormitory-like quarters which, like college dormitories, were presided over by a head matron. They were essentially slaves, incarcerated within a place and a system organised for the pleasure of one man, the sultan, and watched over by eunuchs whose outlook, given what they had been subjected to, could not have been sunny.

Like the imperial pages, the women of the harem were subjected to a detailed training programme through which they were taught to read, write, sew, play music, dance and tell stories – a highly prized quality in the Islamic world, as we know from the story of Scheherazade and the *Thousand and One Nights*. They would line up along what is called the Golden Path, because here the sultan would throw gold coins to them as he passed by. The protocol was for him to toss a handkerchief to whichever girl he most fancied, and that meant she got to sleep with him that night. She would then be carefully prepared for her big night. Servants would bathe and perfume her, and the eunuchs would then lead the lucky girl to the royal bedchamber, where female musicians provided background music for the occasion.

A girl could better her station here. Once she had slept with the sultan, her fortunes in this claustrophobic world began to rise. She suddenly had status, and was given her own room. Though she was still a slave, other, lesser slaves were assigned to wait on her, cook for her and serve her meals. She even had her own eunuch to guard and protect her. If she became pregnant and presented the *padişah* with a child, better yet, for then she had a crown to wear and moved into a larger apartment with a larger staff to attend her. What a bustle, what shock waves of admiration and envy must have attended each change in status! If she were the first to give the sultan a male heir, then she had really arrived. And if her son acceded to the throne, she was suddenly queen bee in this airless hive. If she played her cards right and was skilled at manipulation she might rise to become the most powerful person in the Ottoman Empire. As unlikely a scenario as this may seem, it is exactly what happened to more than one woman from the Harem.

TO THINK OF THE HAREM as simply an elegant supply-house of gorgeous slave girls for the pleasure of their master, however, is to see only part of the picture. The word *harem* in Turkish usually means simply the women's apartments, and this can as easily apply to a humble dwelling as to a palace. It has to do with a distinction between what is public and what is private. The *selamlık* in a traditional Turkish house was the public area where guests could be received; the *haremlik* was the interior, more domestic zone where only members of the family were allowed. This applied just as much to the sultan's household as to anyone else's.

That said, a memoir left by his Italian court physician records that Murad had forty wives, called *haseki* in Turkish, with digs in the harem. One hardly need guess what Murad got up to, as records show that he left twenty sons, two daughters who were married off to viziers in the imperial government, and twenty-seven unmarried daughters – not to mention all those children who must have died in infancy. Murad's mother, Nurbanu, was the first of the powerful women of this period. Sources differ as to whether she was a Venetian or a Spanish Jew.

Whatever her precise origin, she effectively ruled the empire from her elegant chambers in the harem as the power behind the throne of a drunken husband and a son some people would call a sex addict. Nurbanu carried on an extensive correspondence with Marie de Medici and the Doge of Venice in pursuit of a foreign policy favourable to the Serenissima. As long as Sokollu Mehmed Paşa, whose mosque we shall look at in Chapter 20, held the office of Grand Vizier, it really didn't matter how the sultan spent his time, but as soon as Nurbanu began exercising her influence over her son to curb Sokollu's powers, and especially after the death of this remarkable Grand Vizier, the empire became rudderless.

Nurbanu was succeeded in her position as the power behind the throne by a woman nicknamed Safiye, meaning The Pure One, but whose real name was Sofia Baffo. Daughter of the Venetian governor of Corfu, Safiye had been captured by pirates and presented as a gift to the sultan in Constantinople, where she entered the harem. She was possibly a cousin of the Venetian lady who would become her mother-in-law. Succeeding Nurbanu, Safiye was known as the *Yeni Valide* or New Queen Mother when her son ascended to the throne, and when she built her mosque in Eminönü, the mosque was called the Yeni Valide Camii, or New Queen Mother's Mosque.

Over the years this was shortened to Yeni Cami, or The New Mosque, and its position at the Stamboul end of the Galata Bridge makes it one of Istanbul's most easily recognised landmarks. Safiye corresponded with Queen Elizabeth of England, and Gloriana even presented the Valide Sultan with a carriage in which, once she had had the customary *haremlik* shutters and latticework added to protect her privacy, she liked to drive from the palace into the city, a practice that shocked the more old-fashioned and led to unseemly gossip.

The predilections of what would become an entire lineage of

incompetence and fecklessness were hardly a secret to those in the know. Some sultans liked women, some liked boys, some liked both. Some wrote poetry, some were serious collectors of manuscripts and *objets d'art*, some devoted their days to the pleasures of the hunt, or the harem. A scurrilous couplet that did the rounds about the sultan popularly called *Deli İbrahim*, or Ibrahim the Mad, and his son Mehmed IV, runs like this: *babası am delisi, oğlu av delisi* – 'his father was c**t-mad, / The son is hunt-mad'.

Ibrahim liked his lovers large, whether male or female. One of his favourites – commentators differ as to the gender of this individual – was an Armenian called *Şekerparçe*, Lump of Sugar, who was said to weigh over three hundred pounds. Ibrahim liked *Şekerparçe* so much that he gave him or her a government pension and the title of Governor General of Damascus. Hearing a rumour that another fox may have got into the henhouse, Ibrahim had 280 members of his harem drowned in the Bosphorus. He amused himself by feeding gold coins to fish living in the palace's pool.

Sinan's work at Topkapı

If the empire suffered from being led, or more precisely not led, by sultans who were loath to leave this paradise of the senses, and who turned the affairs of state over to the queen mother and her retinue of sycophants and eunuchs, architecturally Topkapı gained. Sinan still held the post of head architect even after the death of Süleyman the Magnificent, and the rooms he designed for Murad III are breath-takingly sumptuous, as is the *türbe* he built for Murad's father Selim II on the grounds of Haghia Sophia. As the locus of power moved inward within the *saray*, it focused on three centres within the Harem: the sultan's private living quarters, his throne room and audience chamber, and the quarters of the Valide Sultan. All three of these areas became architecturally resplendent.

It doesn't seem to have mattered to Sinan whether he was building for the majestic Süleyman, for his bibulous son Selim, or for his randy grandson Murad. Until his death at the age of ninety-seven, Sinan just kept on creating buildings whose grandeur of design and architectural daring were matched by the sumptuousness of their interior furnishings – their revetments of the finest tiles the ateliers of Iznik could produce, the richness of the gilded bed canopies and other wooden constructions, the characteristic long strips of *thuluth* calligraphy proclaiming verses from the Qur'an or lines of Persian poetry. Though parts of these rooms have been redecorated in the rococo style, the tiles, the stained-glass windows and the decoration of the dome in Murad III's audience chamber are largely unchanged from when Sinan built them in the sixteenth century. Murad III's bedroom pavilion gives us the truest sense of the style and elegance that were favoured by Ottoman taste in its most magnificent period, when Sinan worked his magic as a builder and oversaw the interior decoration of those extraordinary rooms.

The great architect brought to this domestic setting the same gift for making an impression simultaneously monumental and refined that makes a mosque such as the one he built for Sokollu Mehmed Paşa such a perfect marriage of the great and the small. The ceramic tiles, that give the pavilion's inner walls a sheen and present the eye with an arabesque of infinite design, are the finest work from Iznik's best period. The posts of the gilded canopies over the low platforms for sleeping and sitting are carved with the same kinds of botanical designs as the Iznik tiles that cover the walls. Their carving and gilding, though probably of a later date than the age of Sinan, give the room an air of Orientalist fantasy which was the genius of the Ottoman decorative arts. A *soba*, or enclosed stove, the pointed design of whose hood is reminiscent of the peak of a minaret, stands between the two canopies.

Set into the walls are delicately arched marble niches, gleaming inside with tilework. These small arches, along with those of the canopies, mirror the larger arches of the stained-glass windows and the grand arches that rise to support the dome. The windows filter the light that enters the chamber, adding to the air of mystery created by the gleaming surfaces, gilded woodwork and intricately patterned tile panels. The bands of calligraphy executed in Iznik's choicest white against a background of deep, deep blue, would have given double pleasure to those literate enough to read them, for calligraphy of this type is both decoration and evocation of the poetry it quotes. But the glory of the room is its dome, still decorated in arabesques that strike a balance between intricacy and grace, picked out in gold leaf against a dark background.

Sinan's royal patrons wanted things done with the choicest materials, and wanted the job done fast. The Sultan's agents were authorised to go out into the city and requisition antique marble columns and revetments from private mansions, for which the owners were paid on the spot, and to bring them to Topkapı for the construction of a royal bath. Proconnesian marble for these jobs was quarried on the island of Marmara from the same quarries that supplied the stone for the buildings of classical antiquity as well as for the palaces and churches of Byzantium. A decree went out for porphyry to be brought, and another for six-hundred masons and carpenters to report posthaste to the palace. To ensure that there would be no shortage of manpower, Kılıç Ali Paşa, admiral of the Ottoman navy, was ordered to supply galley slaves to work on Sinan's projects.

Murad also provided sumptuous apartments for the Valide Sultan and for his consort Safiye, who would live here permanently when her son Mehmed III ascended to the throne. His nineteen brothers were strangled on the night of his accession, following the charming Ottoman custom, the purpose of which was to ensure an orderly transition of power. As a dutiful son, the Sultan visited his mother to pay his respects every morning. She in turn took an active hand in choosing his concubines. The reasoning was that if an inexhaustible supply of beautiful virgins could be found, and if the *Padişah* spread his affections around amongst them, no head wife would emerge to challenge the power of the Valide Sultan. Furthermore, if these consorts were the Valide Sultan's protégées, they could also report to her whatever secrets it was to her advantage to know. And if the Sultan was exhausting himself with sensuous pleasures, power and influence would remain in the hands of his mother and her network of courtiers and eunuchs who controlled the flow of patronage within the empire. The Valide Sultan's quarters, redecorated in the baroque and rococo styles in the seventeenth century, give an impression of opulence part Middle Eastern, part Parisian and part Viennese – a gorgeous European imitation of classical Ottoman style that lies somewhere between pastiche and parody. I love it.

Perhaps the most successful blending of classical Ottoman tradition with rococo fancifulness is the dining room of Ahmed III, built in the early eighteenth century. This dining room brings to mind other densely-decorated smallish chambers such as the William Morris room at the V&A museum in London. Ahmed chose to have the walls of this charming little room decorated with paintings of fruits and flowers that form patterns endlessly pleasing to the eye. There are no calligraphic panels here, no quotations from the Qur'an or Persian poetry. And yet the room is unmistakably Ottoman in its saturation of intricate design.

The fireplace is hooded with a dome that suggests an ogee arch – a shape reminiscent of the domes of Tudor and Jacobean buildings – but the surface of the hood is undercut to give an effect of arabesque lacework. And the wall niches echo the shapes seen in rooms previously built for Murad III and other sultans of the palace. Drawers are fitted between niches and panels depicting vases of peonies, roses, poppies and other flowers. The parts are drawn together by a simple diamond pattern in red and black. A cheerful frieze of red and pink fully blown blossoms, interspersed with stylised dark green cypresses, runs around the lower reaches of the ceiling above the cornices – a look that strikingly foreshadows some of William Morris's fruit, flower and wreath designs.

The Fourth Court: stately pleasure domes

Leaving the Harem and passing again into the innermost sanctums of the palace grounds, one finally reaches what in Ottoman days were the sultan's private gardens, enhanced by some of the broadest and most exquisite panoramas in Istanbul. Gardens were, for these formerly nomadic people whose ancestors had crossed the steppes, mountain ranges and deserts of the ancient Middle East on horseback, earthly paradises that both symbolised the life that, the Qur'an promised, awaited believers after death, and the perfect setting on earth for a life of contemplation and ease. Delimited as Topkapı is by its position within the modern city that has grown up around it, one needs to remind oneself that at one time the buildings of the *saray* were surrounded by acres of gardens, including hanging gardens descending in terraces from the back walls of the Harem down to where the Archæological Museum stands today.

At the heart of all this, the jewel in the crown is a small triad of structures that brought together some of the most meaningful elements of life for the Ottoman dynasty – religious, political, military and recreational. The Revan and Baghdad kiosks and the Sünnet Odası, or Circumcision Pavilion, with the tiny but exquisite İftariye Köşkü in their midst, all stand within the range of the sound of water from the nearby fountain. *Sünnet*, or circumcision, the ritual by which a Muslim boy becomes a man, is central to the life of Islam. The tiles with which the front wall of this structure is revetted are among the finest in Turkey and, in their variety of styles, form a museum-in-miniature of the ceramic art.

The appeal of one's favourite buildings tends to cast reflected glory onto the architectural patrons who caused these buildings to be built. Sinan's masterpieces are eternally associated with his great royal patron, Süleyman the Magnificent, and with his daughter Mihrimah Sultan, as well as with his Grand Viziers, Sokollu Mehmed Paşa and Rustem Paşa – though, as we know, Sinan could work equally well under royal nonentities such as Selim the Sot and Murad III. Murad IV, who had the Baghdad and Revan pavilions built, was described even by an ardent admirer, the traveller and chronicler Elviya Çelebi, as 'the most bloody of the Ottoman Sultans'. Never was there a prince, according to Elviya Çelebi, 'so athletic, so well-made, so despotic, so much feared by his enemies, or so dignified'.

Coming to the throne during the Reign of the Women, when the sultanate was overwhelmed by chaos caused by weak leadership, corruption, palace coups and factionalism, Murad set things right by force. It was said that he could shoot an arrow so forcefully that it penetrated a sheet of metal four inches thick; could leap at full gallop from one horse to another; and hit with his javelin a raven perched atop a distant minaret. When a giant in the Persian army challenged any man among the Ottoman forces to single combat, Murad went out to meet him and with one stroke of his sword clove the giant's head in two from crown to chin.

But his thirst for blood became an addiction, and it is said that over twenty-five thousand of his own people were slaughtered at his command, many by his own hand. One of his favourite sayings was, 'vengeance never grows decrepit, though she may grow grey'. The portrait of Murad in the gallery of *padişahs* next door to the Pavilion of the Holy Mantle in the third court depicts him as a great warrior of the faith – handsome, muscular, dashing, black-bearded and wearing a magnificent plumed headdress, his ready hand on the hilt of his sword.

This is the man on whose orders the Baghdad and Revan pavilions, which epitomise peace, leisure and a life of refined contemplation, were built. Murad's passion for drink was as powerful as his passion for blood, and he died after an especially ferocious binge, at the age of twenty-eight. Ironically, in view of his military exploits, his companions on this drinking bout were Persian, just as Atatürk's companions on his last night on the town were Greek.

The two pavilions built between 1635 and 1638 by Murad IV celebrate his two great victories over Persia, the Ottomans' traditional rival on their eastern front. In the first great campaign Murad captured the city of Erevan in the Caucasus, and in the second he recaptured Baghdad, a city proverbial in Middle Eastern culture as the cynosure of refinement and wealth under the Abassid Caliphate. The two pavilions visually exemplify the Ottoman ideal of luxury and leisure, and their furnishings are breathtaking *ensembles* of the best decorative arts of the mid-seventeenth century. The Revan Köşkü, tucked away as it is off to one side of the grand colonnade that runs alongside the Pavilion of the Holy Mantle, was originally designated as a site for the forty-day retreat that is at the heart of dervish practice, where the novice sequesters himself and recites the *zikr*, repeating a mantric phrase like *Allahu Akbar*, 'there is no power or might except in God', or *La ilaha ill'Allah*, 'there is no god but God'.

That the sultans had a *köşk* built for this express purpose tells us something about how inseparable religion was from the Ottomans' understanding of the world, and, more particularly, the impact that dervish mysticism had on military traditions. How exquisite it must have been for the Sufi to sit cushioned here on the low *divans* that line the interior walls, his eye running across the lines of sacred *thuluth* (*sülus* in Turkish) calligraphy that traverse the upper ranges of the walls, fingering his prayer beads and repeating the names of God until he reached the place where he understood what the mystic al-Hallaj meant when he wrote, 'I saw my Lord with the eye of the heart. I asked: *who art Thou?* He answered: *thou*.'

It almost doesn't matter that by the time the Revan Pavilion was built, the quality of the Iznik tiles was not what it had been, because the overall effect, especially of the turquoise tiles which cover the exterior of the pavilion, complemented by its marble revetments, is of coolness, grace and sumptuousness – qualities that lie at the heart of this great architecture. The best view is from the garden below with its fountain and roses, looking up to the delightful little balcony with its marble balustrade. From here one can see how the four sections of the cruciform structure project from the core of the building.

Both the Iftar Pavilion and the exquisite Circumcision Pavilion were built by order of Murad's brother Ibrahim the Mad, who succeeded to the throne despite Murad's deathbed order that Ibrahim be strangled. His aides assured the dying Sultan, too weak to rise from his bed, that the deed had been done, and the great warrior died with a satisfied smile on his handsome face. While Murad was violent and bloodthirsty, Ibrahim, as his sobriquet implies, was insane and incompetent, ruled by irrational whims, most of them of an erotic nature, as we have seen. He would die a bloody death at the hands of palace insiders after a reign of only eight years, to be succeeded by his 'hunt-mad' son Mehmed IV. Fortunately for the fortunes of the empire, while Mehmed spent most of his forty-year reign on horseback, day-to-day government passed into the hands of the supremely capable Köprülü dynasty of Grand Viziers.

At the edge of the terrace graced by these two airy pavilions, the wide, overhanging eaves of their domed roofs supported by arches mounted on slender posts of marble topped by the chevron capitals that Ottoman architects favoured, stands the gorgeous little İftariye Köşkü, the Iftar Pavilion. The *iftar* is the meal one eats to break one's fast during the holy month of Ramadan. This bijou looks to be made of gold, but is in fact fashioned of gilded copper and tin alloy. The Turkish word for this type of small building is *kameriye* and it is associated with the moon, which may be why the little structure is sometimes called 'the moonlight seat'. The kiosk is built in the shape of a garden arbour, in this case fitted out with marble seats and a marble balustrade, where the sultan and his favourites could enjoy the sunset on Ramadan evenings while waiting for the sky to darken and the evening gun to sound – the point at which the day's fasting ended and the night's feasting could begin.

The Iftar Kiosk and the terrace of the Baghdad Pavilion facing out over the Golden Horn command wonderful views over Istanbul, which is one reason Mehmed originally decided to build his palace here. The view is in many ways much the same as when the Conqueror first gazed upon it in 1453, with the ruins of the Great Palace of Byzantium all around him. I like to think of him here, standing amongst the smoking ruins of the city he had captured and intended to make his capital.

He wanted to look out, as visitors can still do today, and see the waters of the Golden Horn gleaming to the west, with Pera and its Galata Tower that the Genoese built in the Middle Ages standing above it to the north, orchards and vineyards stretching up toward what is now Taksim Square – and then the broad channel of the Bosphorus that divides Europe from Asia curving up toward the Black Sea. Out to his east stretched the Marmara Sea, with the Mediterranean and its as-yet-unconquered lands falling off to the east. The hills were wooded then, with a few Byzantine churches and monasteries dotted here and there, the twin fortresses of Anadoluhisarı and Rumelihisarı commanding the straits below Bebek. Mehmed was then just twenty-one years old, lord and master of all he surveyed.

16

The Archæological Museum and the Çinili Köşk

SOME MUSEUMS OVERWHELM US with the size of their holdings. Entering them, we feel as though we are being given an assignment we can never complete. This describes how I feel about the British Museum, the Louvre, the Metropolitan Museum – institutions that command our respect but somehow fail to win our affection. Smaller museums like the Cloisters in New York City, Sir John Soane's Museum in Lincoln's Inn Fields in London, and the Sadberk Hanım in Istanbul are more knowable, and one thinks of them fondly. Istanbul's Archæological Museum, like the V&A in London, falls somewhere in between.

Over the years during which I have been going both here and to the V&A, I have carved out my own little museum-within-a-museum from their vast holdings. When I think of the Archæological Museum – made up of three separate buildings – what I look forward to seeing are the small but choice holdings of Greek sculpture from the archaic period, and both Greek and Roman sculpture of the Hellenistic period. This is all contained within a few rooms on the right-hand side of the main museum building on the ground floor.

The rest of the museum, as well as the Museum of the Ancient Orient, which contains treasures from the ancient Middle East, I am guilty of visiting more out of duty than enthusiasm. And by not paying homage in the main museum building to the Alexander Sarcophagus from the fourth century BC, no doubt I am missing something as well. But there you are. The building I absolutely adore is the *Çinili Köşk*, or Tiled Pavilion – I love the way its Turkish name looks and sounds. But when I anticipate a trip here, what I most look forward to is having tea in the museum's *çay bahçesi*, an outdoor café, one of the loveliest in the city.

The art of Attic Greece

First to those rooms one sees upon turning right at the entrance to the main building. Displayed here are artworks surviving from the most pristine and innocent period of Greek art – called 'archaic' – in the sixth century BC, when Attic Greece first illuminated the barbarous rocky coastlines of the Mediterranean world with a vision of beauty that has stamped itself on the human imagination from that day forth. Here a maiden, or *kore*, and a young man, or *kouros*, radiate what the Turkish poet Edip Cansever called 'the gladness of living'. The whiteness of the marble, their facial expressions at once serious and as fresh as those of children, still astonish with their purity. All are fragmentary, yet even with a statue whose face is missing, we feel, in the words of Rainer Maria Rilke's poem, 'An Archaic Torso of Apollo':

> We will never know his magnificent head,
> the ebb and flow of his youth –
> an orchard of ripening fruit,
> yet his fire has not diminished,
>
> incandescent light radiates
> from his torso...

In the next room are some naïve and charming works from the early period when Persia ruled Asia Minor. I love the charioteer, his horses' necks ornamented with what may be called necklaces, their manes braided into patterns; a funeral procession dominated visually by a large cartwheel in the centre of the composition; the primitive rendition of a king and queen eating and drinking, attended by serving men. Further on are Attic grave stelae representing scenes from life – a young athlete, a Thessalian myrmidon, a father giving a farewell blessing to his sons. In the next room Roman statesmen and philosophers present a series of distinguished visages from a civilisation that disappeared centuries ago.

What draws me back over and over again to this part of the

museum is a larger-than-life head of Sappho – a Roman copy, we are told, of a work from the Hellenistic period, found in Smyrna far before its name was changed to Izmir, several centuries back before Constantinople became the capital of the Roman Empire. Her nose is chipped and she is generally a bit the worse for wear, but still the great Greek lyric poet from Lesbos – in honour of whose island we name a variety of love – looks out frankly at visitors from the twenty-first century. Her lips are full and sensuous. The eyes in her marble face have been chiseled to look wide open. It is clear from the expression in them that she has learned a lot over the centuries but that she is keeping her own counsel. Sappho's face has a kind of beauty that Yeats called 'as cold and passionate as the dawn.'

The tea garden

After I have visited my favourite sculptures here, I go back outside and sit in the little *çay bahçesi*. What makes this tea garden so fetching is that it is an open-air sculpture garden *avant la lettre*. I spend almost as much time in the tea garden as I do in the museum proper. Admittedly it may seem odd to fly all the way to the other side of Europe just to sit and drink tea, but one does a lot of walking in Istanbul, and it's good to sit in a quiet place, relax, and absorb what is there to be absorbed.

The bits of sculpture displayed in the tea garden must have been deemed not worthy of inclusion in the museum's indoor collections. Their random placement among the café tables and chairs makes them even more poignant – easier to appreciate and not as distanced as items in the museum may be with their identifying labels, and the saturnine guards keeping an eye on you. They represent the residue of the vanished classical, Byzantine and even Ottoman civilisations.

Over there is the head of some unknown figure from the pantheon of Greek paganism, his nose bashed in. Here, in broken stone, one may hear old Triton blow his wreathèd horn and see Laocoön and his sons wrestle with the serpents Poseidon has sent to strangle them. Blocks of stone carry inscriptions in Greek or Latin, a few of which I can read the easy parts of. Fanciful Byzantine capitals from churches and palaces that disappeared centuries ago stand here and there. Ottoman fountains, now dry, have been set outside, presumably because there is no other place to put them. Two gorgons' heads are ready to turn the viewer to stone.

The Çinili Köşk

The Çinili Köşk, or Tiled Pavilion, is architecturally unique in Istanbul for representing the Timurid style, whose name derives from their great leader Tamurlane, a descendant of Genghis Khan. The Timurids were a warlike Turkic-Mongol tribe, similar to the Ottomans in that they swept out of the far reaches of the Middle East beyond the Northwest Frontier, conquered territory and carved out empires for themselves. Their capital cities were Samarkand in modern day Uzbekistan and Herat in what is now Afghanistan, home at one time to the most renowned school of miniaturists in the world. Little is left of their distinctive architecture, but what there is is unforgettable, like the mosques in Isfahan and the shrine of Hazrat Ali in Mazar-i-Sharif. Unlike the Ottomans, the Timurids built *eyvans*: large, open, pointed arches that sheltered prayer spaces, and they covered the exterior of their buildings with turquoise tiles similar to those that have been used here.

The Timurids were great rivals of the Ottomans during Osman's sons' early days, and Tamurlane's army defeated them in the battle of Ankara at the beginning of the fifteenth century, a humiliating defeat for both the Turks and their sultan, Beyazit I – called *Yıldırım*, the Thunderbolt, for the speed with which he mobilised his troops and attacked the enemy. Beyazit was taken prisoner and, according to contemporary accounts, used as a footstool by the victorious Tamurlane, chained in a cage which was wheeled around when the army moved. The defeat dealt Ottoman ambitions a severe blow. Yıldırım Beyazit was left humiliated and broken, his nerves shot. But after the great Tamurlane himself died, the Timurid empire went into swift decline, while Beyazit's sons engaged in open civil war against each other. However, Ottoman fortunes rose from the ashes of defeat, culminating in their eventual conquest of Constantinople under Beyazit's great-grandson Mehmed II, Fatih.

A theory about the buildings in the Topkapı complex is that their differing architectural forms and details represented to some degree a triumphal allusion to the civilisations the Ottomans had conquered on their way to becoming masters of the world. Some of these details were mentioned in the previous chapter. The presence of the Archæological Museum's main building, built in 1891 by the same architect who designed the Pera Palas Hotel, gets in the way of our being able to visualise that the Çinili Köşk was once a grand garden pavilion down the hill from the palace proper, a pleasure palace where the sultans could retire at some distance from their official residence and enjoy themselves. As there is nothing at all Byzantine about it, the supposition is that it must have been designed by a Persian architect.

The exterior walls are ornamented with turquoise and royal blue geometric tiles in the *cuerda seca* style that speak more of Transoxiana than of Constantinople. The spindly columns of the two-storey arcaded portico give the building an archaic delicacy that seems slightly foreign here. The plan is a Greek cross, with a high-ceilinged central space flanked by two *eyvans*. Displayed within are some glorious Iznik plates, mosque lamps, and bowls with exquisite renderings of flowers, using the Armenian bole previously mentioned, leaves and more abstract patterns against a background of sumptuous white. The same motifs occur on some tile panels on the walls, as well as fine examples of the *thuluth* calligraphy, executed in tiles, that the Ottomans were famous for.

All architecture proceeds from the outside in – a secret space is hidden within every great building. A Gothic cathedral, with its arches and stained glass windows, its aisles and vaulted ceilings, eventually leads us up to the altar where the eucharistic mysteries are enacted. In the *Çinili Köşk*, when we pass into the back galleries we enter a modest shrine to the museum's first Turkish director and *eminence grise* in its formative years, the artist and archæologist Osman Hamdi Bey. Recessed into the wall is the peacock fountain that appears in one of his paintings. Osman Hamdi Bey was one of the most distinguished figures of the Ottoman Empire's last years. The son of a Grand Vizier, a Greek from the island of Chios, he was brought up at the heart of the Ottoman establishment. Whilst studying law in Paris, where he married his first wife, a Frenchwoman, he came up with the idea that Turkey must have a great museum like the Louvre, and on his return to his homeland he worked to accomplish this goal. As an archæologist, he is responsible for unearthing some of the most important objects in the museum.

As a painter he is best known for the charming Orientalist picture called *The Tortoise Trainer*, which is on view at the Pera Museum. The painting shows a dervish surrounded by tortoises he is training by means of a stick and bits of lettuce he has placed on the floor. Tortoises with candles on their backs walked about in the Sultan's and Grand Vizier's gardens during famous *soirées* in the Tulip Age. The situation depicted in the painting is very droll: the task is obviously beneath the dignity of the dervish, with his grey beard, scarlet robe, and elaborate turban. The picture is said to be Osman Hamdi Bey's ironic comment on his work as a teacher of painting in Istanbul.

17

In the Shadow of the Blue Mosque

To the east of the At Meydani is the massive and awe-inspiring Blue Mosque, as Western visitors to Istanbul call the Sultanahmet Camii. Sinan died in 1588, with all his great mosque-building behind him: he had practised as an architect, as we have seen, throughout the forty-year reign of Süleyman the Magnificent, on through that of his son Selim II, and halfway through that of the next ruler, Murad III. Sinan's office passed to Mehmed Ağa, who built the Blue Mosque. Everyone who comes to Istanbul visits the Blue Mosque, and this means that during the tourist season it can become so crowded and frenetic that any chance of catching a quiet moment inside simply disappears. One is surrounded by the unlovely sight of tourists with their bare legs and arms covered by ungainly shawls to satisfy the demands of the mosque's keepers that people be dressed modestly. To be fair, no one envies these men their jobs, but at times they can be a bit brusque.

Even Godfrey Goodwin, who wrote the definitive book, *Ottoman Architecture*, admits that the exterior of the great mosque is more successful than its interior. Mehmed Ağa was not as resourceful as Sinan in integrating the huge piers that support the dome into the rest of *ensemble*, so one is overly aware of their size within the otherwise pleasing interplay of arches, walls covered with tiles, and columned arcades. In addition the original stained glass was allowed to deteriorate and has been replaced by reproductions that introduce a light that is too garish. Furthermore, the stencilling on the ceilings is not original, and lacks the subtlety and mastery of colour of the seventeenth-century work. What *is* extraordinary here are the blue Iznik tiles with which the lower parts of the walls have been revetted.

Those in the galleries are particularly fine, but just try getting up there on a crowded day in summer!

Part of the genius of the imperial mosques is their artful massing of domes, and it is a delight to stand at the foot of the steps leading up to the courtyard's western entrance, where the half-domes can be seen rising by degrees to support the central dome of the mosque. The courtyard occupies as large an area as the mosque itself, and it is a pleasure just to sit here or wander about – except when plagued by postcard vendors – and drink it all in. This is a lovely spot on a moonlit night. I also like to catch a view of the mosque from different vantage points around the neighbourhood. Sitting in the park between the Blue Mosque and Haghia Sophia and watching the *Son et Lumière* show on a summer night can be fun – I find something suitable on my iPod and ignore the loudspeakers.

Some of the dependent structures from the old Sultanahmet *külliye* survive. The wooden buildings along the north wall of the mosque enclosure give an indication of what Istanbul must have looked like before the age of concrete, and the *kilim* museum housed in what were the royal apartments to the northwest of the mosque is worth visiting as much for building itself as for its collection of rugs. I also love to sit in a café somewhere and take my *keyif*. *Keyif* is an old Turkish word for pleasure, and I think it must be derived from Arabic. To 'take one's *keyif*' is a Turkish way of describing complete, sybaritic relaxation – the Turkish equivalent of the Italian *dolce far niente*. *Keyifim yerinde*, literally 'my pleasure is in place', is a lovely way of saying that life is good.

Life in modern Turkey is of course more fast-paced and competitive than it was during the Ottoman period, but when I see a group of Turks taking their *keyif*, my sense is that they know how to abandon themselves to the pursuit of happiness better than most of the world does. I have two pictures that capture this pursuit in a pleasing way. One is a reproduction of a Persian painting – ink and watercolour – that I bought years ago at the Museum of Turkish and Islamic Antiquities. If there were a Turkish title, it would probably be *Sarhoş*, 'drunk' – but pleasantly, not sordidly so. A barefoot, elegantly dressed young man reclines against a pillow with a jug of wine in his hand, the cup on the ground before him. He has unbuttoned his shirt and relaxed the sash or cummerbund that would have bound his kaftan at the waist. His turban lies on the ground, and on his head an elegant little skullcap sits atop his flowing locks. He leans on his elbow and his eyes are closed in pleasure, a little smile on his plump, handsome face.

The other picture, a reproduction of an old *carte postale* from the late Ottoman period, does have a title: *Le professeur chez lui*, 'the professor at home'. Interestingly, he too is barefoot, lying stretched out on an old prayer rug. The professor is propped on his elbow like the young man in the other picture, and he is reading a book, no doubt a book of poetry. His other hand idly clutches his *tespih*, or prayer beads. On a little table inlaid with mother-of-pearl sits a tray with a cup of Turkish coffee, a glass of water and a *nargile*. He would seem to have all the elements necessary for contentment.

A café I like is just a few steps past the north entrance to the Blue Mosque, on Mimar Mehmed Ağa Caddesi (the avenue of the architect Mehmed Ağa). The *Derviş Aile Çay Bahçesi* or Dervish Family Tea Garden, is a lovely spot, shaded by *çınars*. You can drink a glass of tea, smoke a *nargile* (water pipe), read the newspaper, or play a game of *tavla*, or backgammon. Even though this is a tourist neighbourhood that doesn't mean it's not a pleasant place to spend some time. If you leave the *Derviş Aile Çay Bahçesi* through the entrance diagonally opposite the one you would have entered it by, from Mimar Mehmed Ağa Caddesi, you find yourself on Kabasaba Sokak, The Street of the Bushy-Bearded One.

I like the Istanbul Handicrafts Market that is located here in an old theological seminary that has been rescued from dereliction and beautifully restored. This is the *medrese* built by Sinan for Roxelana that I mentioned in an earlier chapter. As in the Caferağa Medresesi, the craftsmen have their workshops in what were the cells of the old seminary, and you can see them at work doing calligraphy, working on musical instruments, and so on. This place has decent prices, and is a pleasant alternative to the hustle and bustle of the Covered Bazaar. The Hotel Yeşil Ev, or Green House, is next door. Though you may pay more for it here than in other neighbourhoods, they serve a lovely quiet lunch in their back garden and do a really nice plate of *zeytinyağlı* vegetables stuffed with savoury rice.

18

Ahmed III

KEEPING UP with the forty-odd Ottoman sultans, not to mention the eighty-eight or ninety Byzantine emperors, would be a tall order. Constantine the Great, Justinian, Mehmed the Conqueror and Süleyman the Magnificent are familiar names. Another of the sultans, Ahmed III, keeps cropping up in relation to the architectural gems that were built during his reign. His dates as sultan are 1703 to 1730, at which time, under pressure from the Janissaries and a restless population, he abdicated in favour of his nephew, Mahmud I, who built the *şadırvan* on the grounds of Haghia Sophia which we have previously discussed.

Ahmed III was perhaps the first sultan to make a concerted effort to strengthen the empire's ties with Europe, and not only that, to understand and emulate the Europeans. Ottoman power had been on the increase since about 1302, when a Turkish army under Osman I defeated the Byzantine army at the Battle of Bapheus on the southern shores of the Marmara Sea – though the fortunes of Byzantines and Ottomans swung back and forth continually during those early years. The Ottomans were already a mighty power even before they conquered Constantinople in 1453, and their victories, the territories they ruled, and the wealth they amassed continued to increase. But in 1683 when their deepest foray into Europe failed at the gates of Vienna, the tide began to ebb.

Now it was no longer the age of warfare, but the age of diplomacy: in 1699 the Treaty of Karlowitz brought the conflict between the Ottoman Empire and the Austro-Hungarian Empire to a peaceful conclusion, at least for the time being. At this point greater threats were coming from the burgeoning power of Sassanid Persia to the east, and from Tsarist Russian to the northeast. Ironically, Ottoman weakness *vis-à-vis* the power of Russia under Catherine the Great was to bring them a kind of security they were incapable of winning themselves on the battlefield. As Ottoman armies suffered more and more disastrous losses against Russian forces, the Western powers decided that, to secure the balance of power, they had to step in and prop up the tottering 'sick man of Europe', as the Ottoman Empire would come to be called. The decline of the Empire would last for a further two hundred years. One loss followed another with almost sickening regularity, and what Gibbon wrote about Rome might be said of the Ottoman Empire:

> The decline of Rome was the natural and inevitable effect of immoderate greatness. Prosperity ripened the principle of decay; the causes of destruction multiplied with the extent of conquest; and as soon as time, or accident, had removed the artificial supports, the stupendous fabric yielded to the pressure of its own weight.

By then the Ottomans had relaxed some of their more draconian practices. Imperial fratricide was no longer carried out. Instead, potential heirs to the throne were kept in the *kafes*, or 'cage', in Topkapı Palace – a term that requires some explanation, as these young men were not kept in an actual cage but rather under luxurious house arrest, with all the pleasures of the harem at their disposal. This was undeniably preferable to being garroted with a silk handkerchief, or smothered with a pillow, or drowned in one's bath. However, life in a gilded cage was clearly not proper preparation for a potential head of state, and in fact few of the later sultans turned out to be great rulers along the lines of Mehmed the Conqueror, Selim the Grim or Süleyman the Magnificent.

Ahmed III and the Tulip Age

Before he ascended to the throne, Ahmed III had spent sixteen years in the *kafes*, though his earliest years had been at his father's court in Edirne, where he could ride and hunt and enjoy life away from the rigid rituals of Topkapı. Furthermore, his uncle Selim III had taken him under his wing, as the two men shared a modernising impulse. However, Ahmed seems to have drunk deeply of the pleasures of the harem. The names of fourteen of his wives are on record, and he fathered about forty children, including three sets of twins.

Ahmed's Grand Vizier, who bore the impressive name of Yirmisekiz Çelebi Mehmed Efendi, brought back engravings of Louis XIV's palace at Versailles on his return from a diplomatic mission to France. Ottoman architects began to take notice of European architectural developments, and how they were softening the powerful lines of their classical architecture, making it more fanciful and flowing. This explains the gloriously extravagant fountain situated behind Haghia Sophia, as well as another fountain built along the quay in Üsküdar by Ahmed III that now looks a little forlorn and unloved, stranded in the midst of traffic.

Perhaps emulating the royal displays of European monarchs like Louis XIV, Ahmed and the members of his entourage went in for lavish entertainments and building projects. In 1721 Ahmed III built his *Sa'dabad*, 'Abode of Felicity', on the banks of The Sweet Waters of Europe, a stream that flows into the Golden Horn north of the holy suburb of Eyüp. With its pavilions, pools and fountains, this must have been a glorious place in its day, but it was built of less permanent materials than stone and sadly has not survived.

The Sa'dabad was the site of some of the most lavish displays of the *Lale Devri*, the Tulip Age, which began under Ahmed III. The Tulip Age saw the rise of the famous craze for this flower, which was native to the steppes. Ahmed's second Grand Vizier and son-in-law, Nevşehirli Damad Ibrahim Paşa, was said to have planted 500,000 tulip bulbs in his own garden in what is now Yıldız Park. When they were in bloom he would light the garden pathways and entertain the Sultan and his entourage at soirées there. The French ambassador wrote of these nights: 'the colours and reflections of the lights in mirrors make a marvellous effect. The illuminations are accompanied by noisy music and Turkish music lasts through all the nights that the tulips are in flower. All this is at the expense of the Grand Vizier, who during the whole tulip time, lodges and feeds the Grand Seigneur and his suite.'

From these accounts of his reign and from the marvellous portrait of him at the Topkapı Palace, Ahmed III would appear to have been a pleasure-loving man. His suite in the Harem contains some of the most beautiful decorations to be seen there, with their lovely murals of fruits and flowers. He was also responsible for two beautiful libraries, one at Topkapı and another adjacent to his *türbe* in the streets around the Yeni Cami. When a storm of unrest began to brew as a result of inflation and food shortages, Nevşehirli Damad Ibrahim Paşa suggested that the *Padişah* ride at the head of his army in a campaign against Persia. But there is something comical about the notion of this portly, mild-looking sybarite in the saddle, rallying the troops, and instead he quietly handed over power to the son of his brother Mustafa, who became Sultan Mahmud I, under whom work began on the Nurosmaniye Mosque, the huge baroque edifice that dominates the skyline on the eastern side of the Grand Bazaar.

19

A Walk through Sultanahmet beyond Haghia Sophia

FROM THE FOUNTAIN OF AHMED III behind Haghia Sophia, there are four ways to walk. The first is down the hill on İshak Paşa Caddesi, the Street of İshak Paşa, which leads down toward the Sea of Marmara and the Byzantine sea walls. İshak Paşa was a wealthy and powerful Turk, Murad II's best friend and closest adviser, and served briefly as Mehmed II's Grand Vizier. His mosque stands nearby, and the former hamam from its *külliye* forms part of the Empress Zoë Hotel in the oddly-named Ak Bıyık Street, White Moustache Street.

Sultanahmet is an ancient neighbourhood, and one has only to walk a block or two away from the main tourist attractions to find oneself in amongst local people whose lives have nothing to do with the tourist trade. İshak Paşa is lined with old houses and makes a nice walk down to the Marmara. One goes outside the Byzantine sea walls through the *Ahırkapı*, the stable gate, so-called because in Ottoman times horses were brought through this gate to the imperial stables at Topkapı. A stroll outside the walls gives one a good look at what is left of the Byzantine fortifications here.

Also starting from the fountain of Ahmed III, one can walk south along the east side of Haghia Sophia to the *meydan*, i.e. the open space in front of it, where you will find a tea garden, cash machines, postcard sellers and taxi rank. Or, continuing north past the fountain, one can proceed straight through the big archway into the Topkapı Palace. Finally, one can turn left and follow Soğukçeşme Sokağı, The Street of the Cold Fountain, along its row of old houses built with their backs right up against the walls of the palace grounds.

I like to take this route, following this street as far as the first turning to the left, Caferiye Sokağı.

On the left-hand corner, opposite the fountain of Ahmed III, stands a wonderfully extravagant Turkish rococo gateway leading into the garden behind Haghia Sophia. Some people feel that Turkish architecture became decadent once it passed its classical period and came under the influence of baroque and rococo styles from Europe – and perhaps it did. The mosques and palaces of the classical period are characterised by dignity and balance. But to me the decadence and rococo extravagance of later Ottoman architecture is part of the charm.

Another amazing if over-the-top example of the Turkish rococo style in all its glory is visible from the tram line that runs up from the waterfront at Eminönü to Sultanahmet, on the right-hand side of the tracks. This is what used to be called The Sublime Porte, the gateway to the offices of the Grand Vizier, where the business of the Ottoman government was conducted after its offices were moved outside the *saray*. Ambassadors from foreign countries presented their credentials to these offices, and thus 'The Sublime Porte' was how the Ottoman government was referred to, just as Whitehall stands for the British government, the White House for the US government, and the Kremlin for that of Russia.

The current gateway dates from early Victorian days, and has just the kind of panache that was so dear to European painters of the Orientalist school – though in terms of how the gate looks today, the word sublime does not spring to mind. The broad canopy over the gate, like the wide brim of a stylish but eccentric woman's hat, is a delight. The Sublime Porte is of a piece with the gateway to the rear of Haghia Sophia on Soğukçeşme Sokağı and the *şadırvan* of Mahmud I.

Back on Soğukçeşme Sokağı are rows of old wooden Ottoman houses that have been restored. Recent visitors would hardly recognise the decrepitude into which the city had fallen before a historic preservation movement after the Second World War began to restore it. While Istanbul's monumental structures were built of brick and stone, most of its ordinary houses were built of wood. The first time you see them it is hard to place their style. They have a cottagy, Victorian Gothic look, with carpenter-gothic 'gingerbread' detailing. Their little turrets are occasionally topped with onion domes that look Russian – perhaps because so much Russian architecture derives from Byzantine roots. Because there were so many wooden buildings in the city, and old wood dries out, particularly when left unpainted, fire was a great danger.

One of the prettiest features of old Turkish houses is the way their upper stories project out over the street. Commonly the upper part of the house was given over to the *haremlik*, the women's quarters to which no men other than members of the family were admitted. The windows were finely latticed, so that those inside could look out and strangers could not look in. These buildings, facing out over the back of Haghia Sophia, are painted in shades of lime green, cerulean and cobalt blue. Soğukçeşme Sokağı, with its overhanging trees and cobblestone pavement, is a quiet little corner within the bustle of Sultanahmet. So is Caferiye Sokağı, with its small hotel and garden café, the street one turns left onto and follows back to the *meydan*.

This fragment of a neighbourhood, like many others in old Stamboul, gives a hint of how the city must have been at some period in the distant past – before the Crimean War, let's say, or even earlier, in the Tulip Age. Just past the turning into Caferiye Sokağı a cobbled lane plunges downhill. A little sign points to the Caferağa Medresesi. Here a modest café is housed in a *medrese* built by Sinan. In a medrese, cells for the students were arranged around a courtyard, and today these cells contain little workshops for traditional handicrafts and music that one can explore after resting and having a glass of tea.

20

A Gem by Sinan, and the 'Little Ayasofya'

A SHORT WALK is all it takes to be free from the touristy atmosphere around Haghia Sophia, Topkapı and the Blue Mosque. I like to walk along the western side of the Hippodrome in front of the Palace of Ibrahim Paşa, whose architecture, with its broad Ottoman eaves, is mirrored in the more recent buildings of Marmara University that face the *meydan* from the south.

Once one has entered the little street that leads south toward the Marmara Sea off the square at its southwest corner, one has left tourist Istanbul and re-entered the town itself. At the end of this street there is a school. The caretaker in the sentry box will generally just wave visitors in to see the view (*manzara*) over the Sea of Marmara from here. It's a great place to be at sunset.

Downhill to the right stands the dome of the Sokollu Mehmed Paşa Mosque, while just below, toward the water, one sees the minaret and distinctive pumpkin-shaped dome of the mosque people call the *Küçük Ayasofya*, or Little Haghia Sophia, because of its supposed resemblance to the great church. Built just before Haghia Sophia, this is the sixth-century Church of Saints Sergius and Bacchus, honouring two Roman centurions whose adherence to the new faith of Christianity was the cause of their martyrdom. I like to sit on a bench at the edge of the school courtyard and look at the freighters ranged in the harbour below before walking downhill to look at the mosque, one of Sinan's finest.

Sinan built the mosque for Grand Vizier Sokollu Mehmed Paşa, who married one of the granddaughters of Sultan Süleyman the Magnificent, Princess Esmahan. The story is that the vizier had the mosque built in honour of his wife, but it is by his own name that it has come to be known. As we know, Grand Viziers were in most instances products of the Ottoman meritocracy and not usually Turkish. Ibrahim Paşa, whose palace stands on the west side of the Hippodrome, was Greek in origin. Before his fall from power he served Süleyman as a military commander and was known for his skill as a diplomat.

As for the founder of this mosque, Sokollu Mehmed Paşa, né Sokolović, he was a Bosnian Slav whose father had been a priest; he was said by some to have been of Bosnian royal blood and by others to have come from a family of the minor aristocracy. Mehmed had served as an acolyte in the church as a boy and was brought to Constantinople as a young man in the *devşirme*. Sokollu Mehmed Paşa served under Süleyman and continued in office under his disaster of a son, Selim II, as well as under Selim's successor, Murad III. His wife Esmahan, having grown up in the palace, is said to have mocked Sokollu Mehmed for being a country bumpkin from the Balkans.

Murad, under the influence of those who resented Sokollu Mehmed's prominence, unwisely curbed the vizier's power, so he was not able to govern as effectively during his last years in office. This period marked the beginning of the long Ottoman decline. During Selim's reign, the *devşirme* system deteriorated, with Muslims finding ways of introducing their sons into the schools in which the civil service was trained. The numbers of the Janissaries swelled with inductees whose relatives had bribed their sons' ways in, thus destroying the *esprit de corps* of this elite unit. While Selim and Murad enjoyed the pleasures of the bottle and the harem, talented men like Sokollu Mehmed tried, not always successfully, to keep the empire on course. The stories of these men's careers show us, in case we needed reminding, how inaccurate it is to think of the Ottoman Empire as 'Turkish'; it was an international and multi-ethnic enterprise. After Sokollu Mehmed Paşa was assassinated in 1579 by a mad dervish, the Venetian ambassador commented that 'with Mehmed Sokollu, Turkish virtue sank into the grave.'

Sokollu Mehmed Paşa's Mosque

The mosque, which was built during 1571–72, is a short walk downhill from the school with the beautiful view of the Sea of Marmara. Because the hill where the Hippodrome, the Blue Mosque and Haghia Sophia are situated, descends so sharply to the old harbour at

Kadırga, Sinan's mosque is approached by way of stairs on two sides. The mosque and its courtyard, dependent structures and cemetery occupy their own little plateau. To approach the mosque from the best of all possible angles, the thing to do is to descend along its high walls to the bottom, then turn left and enter through the lower gate. From here you climb up the stairs, their marble worn from the feet of many worshippers over the centuries, and as you climb you see rising above you the exquisite little domed *şadırvan*, and rising above that, the multiple domes of the mosque proper.

Ottoman mosque architecture at its best combines large and small arches and domes with little decorative touches that lend grace to the overall monumentality of the building. Underneath the roof of the *şadırvan* the *voussoirs*, those wedge-shaped stones that combine to form an arch, alternate warm, buff-coloured stones with a cinnamon-red marble, adding a touch of ornamental gaiety to the domed fountain. Lead is a poor cousin to silver and gold, but on a dome it has a beauty of its own, and the imperial mosques seen from the outside present a clustering array of little supporting domes that lead up to one main dome. These leaded domes are at their most beautiful in the rain. The roof of the *şadırvan* at the Sokollu Mehmed Paşa Mosque fans out its broad eaves to offer shelter to those performing their ablutions at the taps issuing from the fountain.

Around the courtyard range what used to be the cloistered cells of scholars who lived next to the mosque, each cell framed with an ogee arch, which gracefully varies the mosque's pattern of round arches and domes. Each cell had its own stove and wall niches where the scholars' books and personal belongings could be stored. Nowadays these rooms house a *medrese*, or religious school for boys in the neighbourhood. A large part of their education is given over to memorising the Qur'an, and when school is in session you may hear them chanting away in Arabic, a language few if any of them can understand.

The mosque is sometimes locked, but the caretaker (*bekçi*) is usually not hard to find. One can just wait for him to show up, or one can ask someone for him (sign language is effective). I like visiting the mosque with friends, so someone else can listen to the *bekçi* telling them things I have already heard. Once inside, Sinan's mastery of space makes itself evident. In the Atik Valide Mosque in Üsküdar, another of Sinan's small masterpieces, one's vision widens to include the broad spread of the place. Here, as in Haghia Sophia, our eyes are drawn up into the space created by the high dome, and the two half-domes on either side that support it. The pleasure of being inside the mosque is immense, and perhaps this pleasure derives from the way geometric shapes interact with and play off one another. Five-bayed arcades on the west wall of the mosque, as well as to the left and right as one faces in the direction of prayer, support galleries that run along three sides of the mosque interior.

Overhead, in the side aisles, wooden fretting forms geometrical designs, and in places, remnants of the original painted decoration can be seen, much finer than in the restored areas. The interior decoration is both unified and various. The eye moves delightedly from the patterns of fretted wood overhead to the painted designs, to the stalactite ornamentation under the supporting rims of the semi-domes, to the rich blues, reds the colour of fresh blood, and snowy whites of the tiles, all produced during the finest period of Iznik craftsmanship. The midmost of the arches forming each of the lateral arcades is truncated to allow space for a rectangular calligraphic plaque above it.

Unlike the Rustem Paşa Mosque at the foot of Uzun Çarşı Street in the market district, where practically every interior surface is covered in tiles, here the tilework is used only in choice parts of the interior, to accentuate certain effects of the overall design against the mosque's rich, honey-coloured stone. First, or at least most noticeable, is the eastern wall of the mosque, where Sinan presents us with a big rectangle rounded off at the top by a semicircle, like a slice of an elongated dome seen face on.

This is the direction of Islamic prayer, and the *ensemble* frames and highlights the *mihrab*, that semicircular niche recessed into the front wall, surrounded by predominantly blue tiles, with cartouches of calligraphy, the lettering white as snow on the traditional Iznik blue that contains just a hint of violet. Medallions of brilliantly coloured *thuluth* calligraphy in blue and white are strategically placed throughout the interior. Since the floors are covered with predominantly dark red and blue prayer carpets, this deep richness sets off the more ethereal blues and whites of the tiles on the walls and pendentives – those curving triangular areas that provide the architectural transition from the massive supporting arches to the circular rim that holds up the dome.

Many of the windows are filled with stained glass. The Islamic approach differs greatly from what one sees in churches, because here what one sees is not figurative. No pictures tell us stories from the Bible or church tradition. Here all is pattern, with thirst-quenching greens, blues, ambers and reds intricately mullioned. The Sokollu Mehmed Paşa Mosque boasts a white marble *mimbar*, or pulpit, capped by a conical crown of Iznik tiles which, to my knowledge, is unique in Istanbul. One can imagine the challenge this posed for the craftsmen who made this amazing masterpiece of the tile-worker's art.

AFTER SPENDING SOME TIME around and inside the mosque, I like to leave by the steep stairs at the bottom of the courtyard and continue downhill to the little park at Kadırga. Now silted up, this harbour was originally dug in the fourth century on behalf of the Emperor Julian – known as Julian the Apostate because he attempted to restore paganism as the empire's state religion after Constantine had instituted Christianity. The park is a good place to take a breather. School children in their uniforms run through during recess, boys from the *lycée* (*lise* in Turkish) next door walk through in groups, and old men sit on park benches, talk man-talk and take their *keyif*.

The Little Holy Wisdom

From here it is not hard to find the sixth-century church of Saints Sergius and Bacchus, or the Mosque of Küçük Ayasofya as it has now become, even if one doesn't immediately locate Küçük Ayasofya Sokak, the long street that leads to the mosque and carries the enchanting name of The Street of the Little Holy Wisdom. How one would love to live out one's days on the Street of the Little Holy Wisdom! It is virtually impossible to get lost in this maze, because the interurban rail line running along the Marmara Sea to the south keeps you from straying too far in that direction, and as long as you keep walking east, you'll eventually find it. The neighbourhood is home to a working community of artists and artisans, and shopping for the things they make is much more leisurely here than in places like the Arasta Bazaar or the Covered Bazaar.

The pretty arcaded courtyard opposite Küçük Ayasofya formerly housed the *medrese* associated with the mosque. New construction for the mosque *külliye* covered up the Byzantine atrium serving both the Church of SS Sergius and Bacchus and an adjoining church, SS

Peter and Paul, no traces of which remain. This is a pleasant place to have a glass of tea and look at the ateliers and shops that sell framed calligraphy, marbled paper, jewellery, ceramics, and so on. Years ago I bought a nice pair of cufflinks with a *çintemani* design from a craftswoman from Erzerum whose studio is here. The courtyard was derelict not too many decades ago, as I found out from a group of regulars who take their *keyif* in the courtyard and who gave me lunch once. Homeless people, drunks and tramps used to sleep rough in this courtyard before it was restored, and leave their rubbish and empty bottles in ruined cells that had been built for dervishes and Muslim theological students.

THE FIRST THING TO DO is forget about looking for resemblances between this building and the great church of Haghia Sophia, except on a conceptual level. Not to say that the two churches are not similar, just that it is more enjoyable to see each individually. Built only a few years before Haghia Sophia, SS Sergius and Bacchus belongs to that fabled period from which few detailed records survive, when architects working under the patronage of Justinian and Theodora put their capacious imaginations to work on the questions of how to float a circular dome above a rectangular church building, and how the room below the dome could both support and harmonise with the upper storey. Artists and architects, like poets and musicians, often create their most exciting work when engaged with some technical problem to which the viewer, listener or reader is oblivious, enthralled by the beauty of what has been made.

The building evidently owes the irregularity of its floor plan to having been slotted in between the Byzantine Palace of Hormisdas to the north and, to the south, the Church of SS Peter and Paul, both now destroyed. Fragments of the church and palace, an archæologist's dream, perhaps lie underneath the mosque grounds and adjacent rail line. Istanbul is a palimpsest of rubbed-out markings left behind by the generations who, each in their turn, revised and erased what came before.

Both emperors and sultans liked to have easy access to their places of worship – witness the imperial loges in mosques such as the Nurosmaniye, Ayasofya Camii and the Yeni Cami – and Constantine Porphyrogenitus's *Book of Ceremonies* records that on Easter Tuesday the emperor would pass through the gallery of SS Peter and

Paul to enter his dining room in the Hormisdas Palace, moving seamlessly from the eucharistic to the culinary. It seems that the architect dealt with the problem of having to squeeze his church in between two existing buildings by constructing a square outer framework to line up with the walls of the existing palace and church, and then torquing the inner church so that the altar faced east: the direction of Christian prayer.

When the Ottomans converted the church to a mosque, they in turn shifted the direction of worship slightly by inserting a mihrab to point toward Mecca. In its Ottoman incarnation, the mosque's patron was Hüseyin Ağa, Chief Black Eunuch during the realm of Beyazit II, son of Mehmed the Conqueror. The Chief Black Eunuch was also known as *Kızlar Ağası* or Master of the Girls. This man, with his two impressive titles, served as manager of the Harem, and rose to become one of the most important figures in the Ottoman hierarchy, even commanding a corps of Janissaries. Hüseyin Ağa built the graceful little portico through which one enters the mosque, the *medrese* opposite it, and probably the minaret as well. His *türbe* stands amidst some interesting Ottoman tombstones in the little garden to the north of the mosque.

SS Sergius and Bacchus organises itself, somewhat similarly to Haghia Sophia, around massive piers supporting arches that in turn prop up the circular drum on which rests the dome, with the curious and appealing undulating appearance it presents to a viewer from the hill above. The architect of SS Sergius and Bacchus used eight piers in total, as opposed to the four at Haghia Sophia. The dome is comprised of sixteen sections, alternating flat and scalloped ribs. The names of its two saints in themselves tell a story of the transition between classical and late-Roman or Byzantine worlds and the struggles that the new faith underwent on the way to becoming the official religion of the empire. The details of the interior architecture are also transitional.

The capitals on the lower level are executed in the 'melon' or 'cushion' Byzantine fashion, undercut with lacy intricacy, like a Cavalier's frilly shirt-front, each capital displaying the monogram inscription 'Basileus', meaning Emperor, and most of them also bearing the intials of Justinian and Theodora. The capitals in the gallery above are also worth a closer look. Called 'pseudo-Ionic', they combine the classical and Byzantine, seating elaborately carved acanthus clusters atop little Ionic scrolls in an unlikely but fascinating way. Ionic scrolls are familiar to anyone who has seen neoclassical architecture, from the British Museum to a hundred provincial banks and government buildings throughout the world.

The columns, the sea-green hue of verd antique, support a horizontal entablature reminiscent of Greek and Roman temples. Readers will recall from art history classes that an entablature, that triple-level comformation that sits atop columns in classical architecture, divides itself into three parts: the architrave, that supporting beam that runs along the top of the columns or piers; the frieze, that strip that sits atop the architrave; and the cornice, which projects outward a bit to support the weight that rests above it. Still visible on the frieze that runs around the entire entablature of the lower level, stylish with its Greek lettering, is an elegantly carved inscription consisting of twelve Greek hexametres in praise of Justinian and of Theodora, 'whose mind is bright with piety, who works unsparingly to relieve the suffering of the poor'.

These verses, which the Muslims who have worshipped here since the early sixteenth century have, to their immense credit, made no effort to cover, also praise St Sergius, but curiously forget to mention his fellow saint, Bacchus. Who knows why? This is just one of many anomalies in this intriguing building, fifteen hundred years old. Regrettably the marble revetments that once covered the walls, sumptuous with veined patterns and seams, as well as the gold mosaics that covered its arches and dome, have disappeared. Regrettably because as Procopius wrote of this sumptuous little church: 'by the sheen of its marbles it was more resplendent than the sun, and everywhere it was filled profusely with gold.'

Between each pair of piers, two columns support the gallery above. Here, as in Haghia Sophia, the architect has alternated his arrangement of supporting columns. Pairs of them run parallel on the north, south and west sides, while in each of the four corners the pairs of columns curve outward, forming what are called, in the language of church architecture, *exedrae*, little bays that relieve the colonnades of what might have become a tiresome or predictable uniformity. If one compares this visual variety and love of what is graceful and various over what is geometrically regular, one can see how the Byzantine sense of beauty departs from that of the classical style that it inherited.

On the upper storey the dance of theme and variation continues. As the eye rises to the gallery, one sees the same pattern of straight rows of columns alternating with in-curving exedrae, but here, rather than supporting the horizontal, or what is called 'trabeated' entablature typical of classical buildings, the columns rise to support an arcade of small arches, creating a curvilinear arcade where, between each of the eight piers, rise smaller arches, in turn supporting larger arches which combine to hold up the drum on which the dome rests. The variation of this pattern is apparent at the eastern end of the church, where the upper gallery and the columns that support it on the other seven sides of the octagonal church interrupt themselves and open up into an apse filled with windows that light up with the rays of the rising sun, symbolic of the Resurrection.

The Church of SS Sergius and Bacchus played a role in the ongoing theological controversies that plagued the Byzantine Empire. In an attempt to put an end to the hair-splitting of his renegade theologians, Justinian and his church hierarchy condemned, as we have seen earlier, the pronouncements of three eastern ecclesiasts of the Nestorian persuasion who had published something called the *Three Chapters*, which argued in favour of the notion that Christ had two natures rather than one. When Pope Vigilius refused to fall in line with this condemnation, Justinian summoned him to Constantinople and subjected him to relentless pressure to conform. Justinian in effect forced the Pope to remain in the city until he came around. After a seven-year stalemate, the emperor ordered his men to arrest the stiff-necked Pope, whereupon Vigilius sought sanctuary in this church.

When Justinian's men tried to remove him from the church, the Pope clung to the altar. And even when the soldiers seized him by his feet and beard and tried to drag him out, he held on for dear life. The altar collapsed, and at this stage people who were in the church came to his aid, whereupon the soldiers had no choice other than to release him. Justinian was just as stubborn as Vigilius, however, and he refused to let the poor man return to Rome until he agreed to condemn the offending *Chapters*. This brought the Pope cold comfort, however, as he died on the return voyage.

BOTH AS CHURCH AND AS MOSQUE this building has tales to tell. The Little Holy Wisdom was a church dedicated to two little-known saints, one of whom bore the name Bacchus, the Roman god of wine and revelry, dramatising the Byzantine transition between the classical and Christian eras. Then it provided the setting for a confrontation in what may strike us as the Byzantines' peculiar and inexplicable fascination with theological pettifoggery. In its Islamic incarnation it became a mosque refurbished under the patronage of the Chief Black Eunuch, overseer of the sultan's harem, whose person and office both seem very alien to our twenty-first century understanding. The two saints, the unknown architect himself, the emperor and empress, the pope, the soldiers and the eunuch, have all left the stage, but this remarkable building remains as witness to it all.

Part IV

Modern Istanbul

21

Atatürk and the Difficult Birth of Modern Turkey

UNDERSTANDING THE STORY OF ATATÜRK is key to understanding how Turkey came to be what it is today, a modern nation with deep roots in tradition, a dynamic bridge between West and East. In a speech he gave in 1933 to mark the tenth anniversary of the proclamation of the Turkish republic, Atatürk concluded with the stirring words, 'happy is the one who says "I am a Turk"' [*Ne mutlu Türküm diyene*]. What this man did was not simply to save Turkey's fortunes after her catastrophic defeat in the First World War, but rather to create a new nation from the ruins of the Ottoman Empire. Before then there had been little sense of national or ethnic identity among the Turks. If we could go back several hundred years and ask a Turk who or what he was, he might have answered that he was a Muslim, or a subject of the *padişah*, or a native of one or another province of Anadolu or of Rumeli, the Asian and European sides of the Empire. The Ottoman Empire was, as we have seen, a multi-ethnic enterprise, from its soldiers and peasants to its rulers. There was no ethnically 'pure' line of succession in the royal family.

Genetically the Ottoman royal family stopped being of unmixed Turkish blood even before the Conquest. The sultans were the offspring of women in the harem who were almost exclusively non-Turkish – Greek or Armenian women, or the famously beautiful blonde Circassians and Bozniaks, or Europeans brought to Constantinople as slaves. Among the women in the royal family whose identities we know something about, such as Süleyman the Magnificent's wife Roxelana, palace rumour even had it that Roxelana's son Selim the Sot was fathered by an Armenian groom.

Roxelana was the first among many women of the harem who would exercise a strong, often controlling influence over their sons. Aimée Dubucq de Rivery, the mother of Mahmud II, the reforming sultan of the early nineteenth century, was a French-speaking Creole who, while on her way home from her convent school in France, was kidnapped by pirates who presented her as a gift to the ruler of Algiers, who in turn made a gift of her to the sultan. The sultan spoke French, and the reforms he would introduce during his reign were almost exclusively of French origin. Abdülhamid II, that shadowy, paranoid sultan who ruled for more than thirty years in the twilight of the Empire, was referred to behind his back as Bedros (Armenian for Peter); he had an Armenian mother and looked Armenian.

So when Atatürk said 'happy is the one who says "I am a Turk"', this could be interpreted as 'call yourself a Turk and you will know who you are. For the first time in centuries, you will be master in your own country'. The name that Atatürk gave himself when he decreed that every Turk must have a surname is usually translated as 'Father of the Turks', but literally what it means is 'Father Turk'. This great, flawed man was Father Turk – in important ways he embodied the nation's aspirations. Multiculturalism and multi-ethnicity were more characteristic of Istanbul than of the Anatolian heartland, and it is no wonder that Atatürk was initially unpopular in the city, and that he sought and found his base in Anatolia and made the little village of Ankara (Angora) – malarial, shoddy, muddy or dusty by season – the capital of modern Turkey. And yet this was a man of cosmopolitan tastes, a member of the Ottoman officer caste, an intellectual.

Early years

Atatürk was born in the city of Salonica, in Macedonia, which was then part of European Turkey. It is now a Greek city called Thessaloniki. Though Salonica was for many years a bone of contention between Turks and Greeks, a large segment of its population was Jewish until the Second World War, when the Nazis rounded up Salonican Jews and shipped them off to the death camps. There is a sad irony here. Had Salonica remained part of Turkey, a neutral country throughout most of the war until it aligned itself with the Allies shortly before the end of hostilities, its Jews would have been protected. During the war Turkey opened its doors to hundreds of German Jewish scholars and academics who were threatened by Hitler's policies of ethnic purity. Among these distinguished men was Erich Auerbach, author of *Mimesis*, one of the great works of literary criticism.

Of course Atatürk was not born Atatürk, the Father Turk. As a child he was simply Mustafa, a common name among Muslims, an attribute of the Prophet meaning 'The Chosen One'. Surnames were not usual in those days. He acquired his second name, Kemal, 'Perfection', from his schoolmaster, who added the second name to distinguish Mustafa the pupil from Mustafa the teacher. His appearance has given rise to speculation about his origins, because he was fair-haired with blue eyes. Lord Kinross, the Ottoman historian, wrote that he was 'as fair as any Slav from beyond the Bulgarian frontier' with 'fine white' skin and 'eyes of a deep but clear light blue'. He would appear to have had Turkish, Albanian and possibly Slavic blood, which would have been very common in this cosmopolitan empire. An ideal of Turkish ethnic purity was to loom large in the Republic which Atatürk invented, but it was always more invention than inheritance.

As a boy, Mustafa Kemal was enrolled in military school, became an officer, and served in the army of the Sultan. But he never fitted into the hierarchy. He could see that the Ottoman Empire was tottering, poorly led, and that its demise was only a matter of time. The Empire's Christian minorities longed for liberation. With the clandestine help of the British, Greece had liberated herself as early as the 1820s, with the Balkan states following Greece's lead. While many Greeks in Istanbul were content with their lives as Ottoman citizens, others were naturally sympathetic with the nationalist emotions of their brothers, and made no secret of their feelings. They had waited three hundred and fifty years to be free. Mahmud II, known as a reformer, was sultan. Alexis de Tocqueville once wrote that 'the most dangerous moment for a bad government is when it begins to reform itself', and this truth is sadly relevant to what happened under Mahmud. As John Freely narrates the tragic result in his *Istanbul, The Imperial City*:

> News of the revolt caused Mahmud to panic, for he feared that it would lead to a general uprising of the Greeks in the Ottoman Empire. He immediately sought a *fetva* from the *ulema* declaring

> a *cihad*, or holy war (jihad) against all of the Greek Christians in the empire, but the *Şeyhülislam* refused to grant it, having received assurance from the ecumenical patriarch Gregory V that his flock was loyal to the Sultan. Nevertheless, on 1 April 1821, Easter Sunday, armed soldiers seized Gregory after he had said mass at the patriarchal church of St George, whereupon they hung him from the Orta Kapı, the main gate of the Patriarchate. Orta Kapı was sealed shut and painted black after Gregory's body was cut down, and it has remained closed to the present day – a symbol of Greek-Turkish intransigence.

In the eyes of most Turks, the Greeks who rose in revolt were traitors. This was certainly the Sultan's view. When the Greeks on the island of Chios just off the coast of Turkey joined the rebellion, Mahmud sent troops, who massacred 30,000 of the islanders including most of the six hundred monks at the monastery of Nea Moni. Visitors may see a chapel where the bones of some of those massacred there are preserved. Axe wounds are visible on the skulls of some of the slain, including the skulls of children.

Every time a province of the disintegrating empire revolted and won its independence, tens of thousands of Muslim refugees fled from the reprisals of their former underlings, straggling into Turkey with their meagre possessions on their backs. What this felt like to ordinary Turks can be gathered from accounts like the following given by Mustafa Kemal's contemporary, Şevket Süreyya Aydemir:

> I was born during a war – the 1897 Turkish-Greek war….
> Ours was a refugee neighbourhood. The flotsam of torrents of refugees torn by wars and massacres from the Crimea, Dobruja, and the banks of the Danube, had been pushed back here step by step, as armies suffered defeat after defeat for one hundred and fifty, two hundred years, and as frontiers contracted … In our neighbourhood of refugees [on the outskirts of Edirne], every family had come from a different place, and every one had a different story to tell about the places where they had stopped and whence they had fled. Day by day the number of people grew, as new refugees made their way through the frontier. When they abandoned their homes, their land, their birthplaces, these newcomers threw supplies of food, cooking utensils, blankets and bedding into oxcarts and took to the road. Women

> and children were perched on top of the loads. These miserable convoys were the returning remnants of the conquering armies that had settled in the Balkans, the banks of the Danube, and further afield, and had built towns, castles and villages...

Even more than from Greece and the Balkans, Muslim refugees from the Russian-Turkish war of 1877–8 flooded in. Andrew Mango vividly sums up the multiplicity of nationalities and tribes in the introduction to his biography of Atatürk:

> First came hundreds of thousands of Turkic-speaking Tartars from the Crimea and the surrounding steppes, then the majority of Circassians and Abkazians from the western Caucasus, and large numbers of Chechens from the northern slopes of the Caucasus, of Lezgis and other Daghistanis from its eastern slopes, of Muslim Georgians from the Transcaucasia.

The Tsar had declared himself protector of all Orthodox Christians, and Armenians in the eastern provinces organised themselves into regiments and fought side by side with the invading Russian armies in the early years of the First World War.

The secretive and enigmatic Abdülhamid II isolated himself, for fear of assassins, behind the walls of Yıldız Palace above Beşiktaş. The Sultan was filled with an even stronger sense of insecurity and foreboding than were his subjects. Abandoning the Westernising policies of over a century of reformers, this much put-upon man chose retrenchment, looking for salvation as champion of the Empire's Middle Eastern Muslims. Terrified of being assassinated, he imagined plots everywhere, and surrounded himself with a network of spies. As Ali Fuat, one of Mustafa Kemal's companions in the struggle for independence, was to write:

> Sultan Abdülhamid II, in whose honour we had to shout 'long live our *Padişah*' several times a day, gradually lost lustre in our eyes .... As we heard that the government worked badly, that corruption was rife, that civil servants and officers did not receive their pay, while secret policemen and courtiers, covered in gold braid, received not only their pay but purses full of gold, our confidence in the Sultan, which was not strong at the best of times, was totally shaken.

It is at this juncture that Mustafa Kemal begins to appear on the pages of his country's history. The young officer fell in with the crowd of conspirators in the army who formed the Committee of Union and Progress (the CUP), whose purpose it was to address the abuses of the Sultan's government, bringing about a revolution in 1908. But even as a young man, Mustafa Kemal made it clear that only his own way would do, and that if he were given a free hand he could put things right. Over and over, because of his obstinacy and abrasiveness, his associates in the CUP assigned him to postings far from Constantinople. Unintentionally, this period of exile from the centre of things provided him with important lessons both military and cultural. In the Balkan Wars of 1912–13, and later, on the Syrian front against the advancing British army with their allies among Arab tribesmen led by Lawrence of Arabia, he fought rearguard actions, learning strategy from defeat and beginning to form his own ideas about the limitations of imperial power and territory, and how the Turks might defend themselves and retain what was left of their empire.

In the aftermath of the Balkan Wars, Mustafa Kemal was appointed to Sofia as military attaché. It was a position of little importance, but for the young officer it provided an education. In the eyes of sophisticated Constantinopolitans, Bulgarians were rustics. Cyrus Hamlin, an American missionary who founded Robert College, the elite school on the heights above Rumelihisarı which was to become the University of the Bosphorus – Turkey's Harvard – wrote: 'every spring, there was an advent of Bulgarian shepherds and ostlers in the streets of the capital – strong, rude men in sheepskin clothing, with their shrieking bagpipes and rude country dances, dashing their sheepskin caps upon the pavement to every passerby for *bakshish*. They seemed but little above savage life.'

Yet in the very brief period since Bulgaria had won its independence, the country's new capital, Sofia, had been transformed from a backwater into a place with broad streets and some of the amenities of a European city. Public buildings such as a theatre and an opera house had been built. Pleasant villas stood among gardens in leafy suburbs. 'This country where I went as ambassador', an Ottoman diplomat wrote, 'was but fifty years ago a province within our borders'.

While the sight of their former subjects succeeding in making a nation for themselves and going their own way in the world saddened and even outraged some Ottoman observers, Mustafa Kemal felt the transformation was something that could and should be emulated by the new nation he dreamed of. Europeanisation was clearly the way to a happier future. One evening at the opera in Sofia, he asked whether the singers and musicians on stage were Bulgarian. Hearing that they were, he replied, 'now I understand why the Bulgarians won the Balkan War'.

It was in Sofia that Mustafa Kemal learned ballroom dancing, which was to be a feature in the social life of the future Turkish Republic. He loved to waltz, and that meant everyone around him had to learn to waltz. For Turkish ladies to throw off their veils was traumatic enough; for them to get out on the dance floor and press their bodies against the bodies of men who were not their husbands was quite another matter. A ladies' man throughout his life, Mustafa Kemal was surrounded in Sofia for the first time by women who were the social equals of men. The handsome young officer appreciated their company and relished the rounds of dinner parties and theatre-going that made up diplomatic life in a European capital.

Invited to a fancy-dress party, he sent to the military museum in Istanbul for an authentic Janissary's uniform. A picture of him dressed as a Janissary survives, and he looks very dashing indeed in the uniform. He wrote back to his superiors that in replying to the questions of his fellow guests about his outfit, he was able to educate them to some degree about the Turks' former military prowess and prestige. This was Atatürk to a T: the elegantly dressed peacock who, underneath the costume, was busy educating people.

As the man who introduced Western dress to the Turks and forced them kicking and screaming into abandoning their traditional kaftans, veils and turbans, there was ever an element of fancy dress in Atatürk's persona. The pictures of the great man that one sees everywhere in Istanbul show him literally wearing different hats. In some senses, the early years of the Republic were a kind of fancy dress party in reverse, since traditional costumes were so much more colourful than drab European clothing. But Atatürk convinced his fellow countrymen that to be Europeanised was to be glamorous.

Atatürk's mission was not a simple one. The Turkish people needed to disentangle themselves from the wreckage of the dying empire and discover who they were as Turks. Most of those to whom his definition of the new nation would appeal were Ottoman Muslims. The Armenians and Greek citizens of the empire on the whole had their own national aspirations. Turkey's large Jewish minority entertained, in those days before the founding of the state of Israel, few thoughts of nationhood of their own. Both Muslims and Jews felt that their two religions had much in common. Both Islam and Judaism were monotheistic, untroubled by the mysteries of the Trinity, which had been the source of so much controversy among the Byzantines; both practised ritual circumcision; neither knew the pleasures of eating pork.

Paradoxically, this new Turkey, peopled almost exclusively by Muslims, would be a nation in which religion was de-emphasised. As the Ottoman Empire had simply not been able to respond to the challenges of modernisation, Atatürk felt that the road to Turkey's future lay through Europe, although ironically, he spent little time there. His brief posting as a cultural attaché in Sofia would form the basis of his notions about what a Europeanised Turkey would look like.

World War One and Gallipoli

The First World War was a disaster for the Turks. Enver Pasha, a member of the CUP triumvirate and commander-in-chief of the Turkish forces, led an army of 80,000 men against the Russians, who were attacking the Empire near Erzurum in eastern Anatolia. It was the middle of December, and Enver Pasha, a dreamer with delusions of grandeur and a less than firm grasp on reality, settled upon a plan of attack that required his army, in temperatures of minus 26° centigrade, to cross a mountain range called, ironically, *Allahuekber*, meaning 'God is great', which had been the centuries-old battle cry of many Ottoman military victories.

Poorly equipped and inadequately clothed, these poor devils froze to death by the tens of thousands. Those few who reached the field of battle were slaughtered by the advancing Russians and their Armenian allies, with the result that only 10,000 survived. The survivors were finished off by typhus. On the Egyptian front, Enver and his colleague Cemal Pasha attacked the Suez Canal, seized by the delusion that, as jihad had been declared, the Egyptian subjects of the Ottoman Empire would rise against their British occupiers. The Egyptian Muslims did no such thing, and the Turks were soundly defeated by the British.

NOW WAS MUSTAFA KEMAL'S moment to emerge as a national hero. Upon returning to the capital from his posting in Sofia, the young colonel was put in charge of a regiment on the Gallipoli peninsula overlooking the Dardanelles, the straits that lead from the Aegean into the Sea of Marmara. The Ottoman armies were under attack in the Caucasus by the Russians, and the British and French, allies of the Tsarist regime, thought this was an opportune moment to attack Turkey from the Aegean, force a landing of British, Anzac and Indian troops at Gallipoli with the purpose of overpowering the guns that prevented Allied warships from steaming through the narrow straits, and then to march on Constantinople. This would give the combined Russian, British and French forces control of the southeastern flank of Europe, and freedom to move at will from the Black Sea into the Mediterranean, connecting Russian forces with those of their European allies. Constantinople seemed ripe for the taking.

Perhaps the Turks had fought with less conviction in battles peripheral to their Anatolian heartland, but now their backs were to the wall. When the first British troops landed on the Southern tip of the peninsula, a Turkish sergeant named Mehmet found that his rifle had jammed. So he seized a rock from the ground and rushed the attackers. Mustafa Kemal, a public relations genius, wrote up the incident in his report on the campaign, and *Mehmetçik*, or 'Little Mehmet', became a national hero. While the British had their Tommy and the Americans their Doughboy, the Turks had their Mehmetçik. These days the Turkish army even has a new rifle called the Mehmetçik.

Had the British continued their offensive when they had the element of surprise, perhaps they could have reached Constantinople. But they stopped to retrench, and this delay gave the Turks, with their German officers and advisers, time to reinforce their positions. As always, Mustafa Kemal insisted on having things his own way, and he bitterly resented both the presence of German superior officers and the directives emanating from the CUP in Constantinople. The young lieutenant-colonel deployed his troops brilliantly, attacking furiously, even risking his own life by commanding from in front rather than behind his troops, at one point sitting out in the open and calmly smoking a cigarette while the enemy fired in his direction. He loved battle, and walked happily along the lines while bullets flew through the air, laughing and encouraging his men. 'Look to it that you have your bayonets sharp and fixed, and come out after me', he told them at the crucial moment.

His orders to his men have entered the legends of the Turkish Republic: 'I don't order you to attack, I order you to die. By the time we are dead, other units and commanders will have come up to take our place.' According to Andrew Mango, his actual words were slightly less dramatic and more nuanced. Mango quotes the order as found on the body of a dead Turkish soldier: 'I do not expect that any of us would not rather die than repeat the shameful story of the Balkan war. But if there are such men among us, we should at once lay hands upon them and set them up in line to be shot.' Even if the actual words of his orders were slightly less spectacular than those that have entered into the nationalist myth, heroes make their own legends, and Atatürk was a genuine hero.

THE VICTORY AT GALLIPOLI saved the Ottoman capital temporarily, and gave the Turks a reprieve from domination by the Europeans and their Russian allies, but it proved to be no more than a lull. World War I presented the empire with a humiliation that one must appreciate in order to understand the story of modern Turkey. At one time, controlling one of the greatest empires in history, they had ruled the world, riding herd over a mélange of religions and ethnic groups who remained free to worship as they pleased, practice their trades, and even amass fortunes in business.

Advancement in the Ottoman administration was not only open to non-Turks, high offices had in fact very commonly been occupied by these minorities, such as the Köprülüs, of Serbian origin, whose dynasty served wisely and well as grand viziers for half a century. Foreigners residing within the Empire negotiated tax breaks and other business advantages for themselves. In the early twentieth century a Greek businessman wrote, 'we lend them the vivacity of our intelligence and our business skills; they protect us with their strength, like kindly giants'. For several centuries it was a system that worked to everyone's advantage. But now this coalition had come unglued. The sick man of Europe was on his knees.

Ottoman weakness was greeted with shouts of joy by Greeks within the Empire, and the Turks were jeered at in Constantinople itself. The Patriarchate in Fener flew the Greek flag. Greeks took off their fezzes and stamped on them in the street. Only the Jews remained loyal. While Greeks on the Constantinople stock exchange worked to inflate the value of the drachma against the Ottoman lira so that Greeks could buy property more cheaply, Jewish financiers worked to prop up the lira.

The inevitable soon happened. The Turks admitted defeat and signed an armistice with the victorious Allies. They had no choice – Ottoman armies had lost on every front, and total defeat was inevitable if they kept on fighting. Their losses in the war had been catastrophic: an estimated 325,000 killed, 350,000 wounded and 250,000 taken prisoner. The government was bankrupt, and people were starving. When Mustafa Kemal returned to Constantinople in 1918 from Aleppo, where he had been in charge of the southern front, French and British battleships had already appeared in the Bosphorus; fifty-five of their warships cast anchor in front of the Dolmabahçe palace itself, the sultan's residence. It was clear that the Allies' intention was to dismember Turkey.

Three empires came to ruin in the world war – Ottoman, Austro-Hungarian and Tsarist Russian. The victors, as well as the newly liberated subject nations of these empires, were busy trying to create a new world from the ruins. In the spring of 1922 Lloyd George, Woodrow Wilson and Clemenceau made the decision in Paris to assist Greek troops in occupying Izmir on the Aegean coast, or Smyrna as it was then called. At a subsequent conference in San Remo on the Italian Riviera, the Allies formalised their plans to partition what was left of the Ottoman Empire. Lebanon and Syria were granted to the French. The Italians wanted their own zone of influence in the eastern Aegean. Meanwhile Mustafa Kemal was trying to get armaments from Bolshevik Russia.

Greek invasion of Anatolia and the War of Independence

The world picture the Allies were presented with after their victories over Germany and Austria in the west and over the Ottoman Empire in southeastern Europe and the Middle East was complex. War-weariness had set in, and the civilian rulers on the winning side were under pressure to demobilise their troops. In the eastern Mediterranean, meanwhile, there were the territorial ambitions of Greece to deal with. Late in the war the Allies had deposed the pro-German King Constantine and brought to power Eleftherios Venizelos, a man with the grand plan of recovering for Greece territories that had not been hers for well over half a millennium, since the fall of the Byzantine Empire. Venizelos envisioned a new Magna Græcia in control of the entire Aegean, as well as about half of Asia Minor, or Anatolia. It was a dream with great resonance even for Greek Constantinopolitans, accustomed as they were to thinking of themselves as Ottoman citizens. In the first flush of Greek triumphalism after the war, an enormous picture of Venizelos was erected in Taksim Square in the heart of Istanbul.

The idea of Magna Græcia also appealed to the Americans and the British, who had been brought up on the Bible and educated through the classics. Returning Asia Minor to the Greeks was of a piece with the Balfour Declaration, through which Britain expressed her support for a Jewish state in Palestine, which had not been Jewish for even longer than Asia Minor had not been Greek. The British Prime Minister, Lloyd George, presided over both these policies. Both were imperialistic gestures that had much in common with the British-French-Israeli seizure of the Suez Canal in 1956 and the Gulf wars late in the 20th century.

The English meaning of the word Turkey made puns inevitable, and a political cartoon of the day shows the Allies contemplating a roast fowl on a platter and discussing which cuts should go to whom. Meanwhile, remnants of the Ottoman army were plotting how to save their country. The armistice they had signed called for the demobilisation of Ottoman armies and the impoundment of their weapons, but Mustafa Kemal and his colleagues were determined not to let either of these things happen. They foresaw the struggle that was coming. With their massive losses, the sufferings and privations that had been inflicted on the civilian population, and the trauma of having lost their empire, the Turks were in no mood to mobilise for resistance.

This was where Mustafa Kemal's indomitable will and supernatural energy came in. Whatever *matériel* they could rescue from the defeat of their armies, he and his friends among the officer corps took care to ship to the Anatolian heartland and clandestinely store there. Meanwhile Mustafa Kemal's resistance activities were starting to arouse the suspicions of the occupying forces in the capital, and he escaped into the hinterland as soon as he could, having obtained a posting as inspector of one of the Ottoman armies. Mustafa Kemal was canny enough to know that few of his compatriots shared his predilections for secularism and parliamentary government. Most remained loyal to the religion of Islam, and to their *padişah*, 'the shadow of God on earth'.

Mustafa Kemal was aware that Turkish patriotism, religious fervour and fighting spirit coalesced around the dervish brotherhoods that had formed the heart of Turkish national identity since their ancestors had left the Asian steppes. A brotherly alliance between the dervishes and the Janissaries had been the heart and soul of the Turkish army throughout Ottoman history. Even the massacre of the Janissaries under Mahmud II in the early nineteenth century had not extinguished that spark of fervour that burned in the heart of the Turkish fighting man. So as part of the tour he undertook in Anatolia to secure weaponry and financial support and put backbone into those Turkish soldiers willing to pull on their boots again and continue to fight, Mustafa Kemal made a pilgrimage to the tomb of Haci Bektaş, the founder of the Bektaşi order of dervishes, in the winter of 1919.

Inland Turkey is famous for its hard winters, and even today the roads in Anatolia become impassable because of the snow. The 120 miles from Sivas to Kayseri in December 1919 took Mustafa Kemal and his party two days to cover, and upon arrival they were met by a procession of men carrying lanterns to light their way. In Kayseri he dined with Cemalettin Çelebi, head of the Bektaşi order. The rakı flowed freely, as the dervishes did not always follow the more troublesome prohibitions of the hard-shelled orthodox clerics, the hojas, (Turkish *hoca*), and soon the Bektaşis lined up to support the Kemalist cause.

This careful and painstaking marshalling of support for a coalition effort to defend what was left of Turkey fell into place none too soon. While the Allies remained in possession of Constantinople, with their warships anchored in the Bosphorus and their officers drinking in the bar of the Pera Palas, their soldiers flirting with the girls on the Grande Rue de Pera, Atatürk and like-minded patriots were forming what amounted to a government in exile in the heartland. Greek troops, disembarked in Smyrna harbour off British and French warships, opened fire on Turkish civilians, and the sectarian riots that followed set the tone for the bloody attacks and reprisals that would characterise the Greek-Turkish struggle for possession of Anatolia. The Greek army fought bravely and boldly, advancing deep into Anatolia almost as far as Ankara. But they suffered the fate of any army that penetrates into its opponent's homeland. The further they advanced, the longer their lines of supply and communications were stretched, and the harder it became to maintain coherent battle lines.

Under General Ismet the Turks won a strategic victory at Inönü. In a message to Ismet, Mustafa Kemal waxed eloquent: 'it was not only the enemy you have defeated, but fate itself – the ill-starred fate of our nation.' To another of his generals he wrote, 'our army has reappeared on the stage of history in thunderous majesty.' The Greeks regrouped and landed more troops in western Anatolia, mustering a force of 200,000. The epic battle fought on the River Sakarya on the outskirts of Ankara lasted twenty-one days, and in the end, the Greeks were turned back.

Later on, when Atatürk decreed that all Turks should have surnames, Ismet became Ismet Inönü and would later be Atatürk's successor as President of the Republic. In the aftermath the National Assembly voted Mustafa Kemal the title of *Gazi*, a term that reaches back to the beginnings of the Turkish experience as warriors for the honour of Islam, because it carries the implication of holy warrior. He was also elevated to the military rank of Marshall, and now stood head and shoulders above his erstwhile colleagues. He was able to sign himself as 'President of the Turkish Grand National Assembly, Commander-in-Chief, Gazi Mustafa Kemal Pasha'. Quite a mouthful. But he was now in complete control, and would remain so until his death.

The new Turkish nation

Of course it was not Mustafa Kemal alone who saved the nation. He did, however, lead the Turks, help shape their new identity, coalesce resistance against foreign occupation, and rally their forces at the darkest moments. Having done all those things, he set about shaping the nation into what he felt it should become if it were going to 'join the community of civilised nations', as he often expressed it. Shortly after turning back the Greek invasion, Atatürk abolished the Sultanate, and Mehmed VI, the last of the Ottoman rulers, was smuggled unceremoniously out of the Dolmabahçe Palace onto a waiting British vessel, eventually settling in San Remo, where he was joined by his three wives and his sister. Since the time of Selim I, the Ottoman sultan had simultaneously functioned as Caliph, or ruler of the world's Muslims. The Sultan's cousin, Abdülmecid, was given this office, in which he continued for two more years. In March 1924, Abdülmecid and his four wives, his son and daughter, his private physician and his secretary, left Istanbul in a private coach on the Orient Express. The last Ottoman Caliph died in Paris in 1944.

There was much to be done if Turkey was to become a modern nation. As Louis de Bernières put it in his novel, *Birds Without Wings*, 'the race that had preoccupied itself solely with ruling, tilling and soldiering now found itself baulked and perplexed, without any obvious means of support.' They considered menial trades undignified, disdained commerce, and had tended to leave such things to the minorities. Famous for their horsemanship, they relied on Armenian farriers to shoe their mounts. Atatürk's tailor in Istanbul was Greek, and his Jewish dentist, Dr. Sami Ginsberg, had brightened the smiles of the Ottoman ruling family. Pointing out that the nation depended on others for everything 'from needles to thread, from nails to pegs', Atatürk exhorted his audiences: 'the simplest trade is the most honourable. Shoemakers, tailors, carpenters, tanners, blacksmiths, farriers – these are trades most worthy of respect in our social and military life.'

Dress had always played an important role in the life of the Ottoman Empire, just as it had with the Byzantines. From as early as the reign of Mehmed the Conqueror, the different social ranks had been strictly assigned their own colours and styles of headgear, shoes and robes; different ethnic groups could also be identified by the colour of their boots. Women were both protected and subjugated by the veil. The size of a man's turban and the manner in which he wore it were subjects of manly pride. Even the poorest of the poor could scrape up a few *kuruş* to have their fezzes steamed and pressed at the corner shop.

Few people would have recalled that in the early nineteenth century spirit of modernisation under Mahmud II, the fez itself had been introduced as a replacement for the turban. In Istanbul's many cemeteries, those romantic and colourful cities of the dead, the various fezzes, turbans and dervish hats indicate the rank, status and profession of the deceased. Now this was all going to change. 'Shoes or boots on your feet, trousers on your legs, then shirt, collar and tie, waistcoat, jacket and, to complete it all', Atatürk announced in one of his many speeches to his fellow countrymen, 'headgear with a sun-shield, which I want to call by its proper name: it's called a hat'.

Next to go were the dervish orders. 'The Turkish republic cannot be a country of sheikhs, dervishes and disciples', he told a crowd in Kastamonu. 'The leaders of dervish orders will understand the truth of my words, and will themselves close down their lodges and admit that their disciples have grown up.' By eliminating the dervish orders Atatürk was making a radical change in the way the country operated. Almost every Turkish man had belonged, according to his station in life, to a dervish order. There were *tarikats*, or Sufi orders, for all sorts and conditions of men, from the cultivated and literary Mevlevis in Galata, to the salt-of-the-earth Helvetis in Fatih, to the scandalous Kalenders in the Kalenderhane Mosque, a converted Greek church with murals of the life of St Francis of Assisi, near the aqueduct of Valens.

A comparison can be made between the dervish orders of Islam and the monasteries of old Constantinople. On the eve of the Turkish assault in 1453, when the city's population had sunk below 100,000, there were still fifty monasteries; and the monks would not bear arms, even to save their city. Unlike the pacific traditions of the monks, however, there was a fighting edge to dervish culture, and as we have seen, the Bektaşis, with their long martial tradition, were among Atatürk's staunchest allies in the War of Independence. Unlike in Christian monasticism, there is no tradition of celibacy in Islam, and although cells were provided for dervishes who were bachelors, no spiritual cachet was attached to their status, and dervish sheikhs were almost always married men whose families lived with them in the *tekke*, or dervish lodge. Still, their attachment to things spiritual meant they had divided loyalties, and no doubt Atatürk was correct in thinking that the dervishes could not share fully in the cultural transformation of the Turkish nation if they remained the disciples of men whose world view was by definition theocratic and backward-looking.

The Muslim lunar calendar was abandoned in favour of the European solar, along with the twenty-four hour clock. In a new legal system modelled on that of Switzerland, women gained important civil rights, including the right to inherit equally with men. So that Turkey could more easily 'join the family of civilised nations', Atatürk decreed that every Turk should choose a surname. Some gave themselves patriotic names like *Öztürk* ['Pure Turk'], or inspirational names like *Korkmaz* ['Fearless'], *Cansever* ['Lover of Life'] or *Şafak* ['Dawn'], or called themselves after their occupations, like the family of the short-story writer Cemil Kavukçu ['turban maker']. The satirist Aziz Nesin, who lived through this period, has written:

> In 1933 when the surname law was passed which directed every Turk to select a last name, people's secret feelings of inferiority surfaced: Some of the world's stingiest became known as '*Eliaçık*' [Openhanded], the greatest cowards named themselves '*Yürekli*' [Stout-heart], and many of the laziest took the name '*Çalışkan*' [Industrious]. One of our teachers chose the surname of '*Çeviker*' [Dexterous] when he could barely sign his name to a letter. The rampant racism present caused people with mixed blood to grab for surnames which signified they were Turks.
>
> Invariably I came last in any kind of scramble; I was no different in this one for nice surnames. No surname remained that I could take pride in, so I assumed the name of '*Nesin*' [What-are-you?]. I wanted to think of what I was and pull myself together whenever anyone called 'What-are-you?'

The modified Latin alphabet that Atatürk mandated was one of his greatest contributions to the modernisation of Turkey. This replaced the old Arabic script, which was unsatisfactory both because it did not accurately reproduce the sounds of spoken Turkish and because it embodied what the reformers thought of as the dead weight of tradition. The language was revamped and simplified to eliminate vocabulary borrowed from Arabic and Persian.

As he got older, more infirm, and more assured of his secure position at the heart of his country, Atatürk began to spend more time in Istanbul, which he had earlier thought emblematic of all that was wrong with Turkey. He spent long periods of time at the Dolmabahçe Palace, like the sultans he had unceremoniously chucked out. It was to Dolmabahçe one day in the late twenties that he invited an audience of government officials, religious leaders, journalists and intellectuals, wealthy merchants and society ladies. Decked out in morning coat and striped trousers, he set up a chalkboard on a platform in the ballroom at the palace and gave a lesson in the new alphabet. Atatürk was a born teacher, and he was soon known all around the country as Turkey's 'Professor in Chief', bringing a slate and a box of chalks to towns and villages all over the country and teaching the new script. The Turks took to it with enthusiasm. For many in this land of mass illiteracy, the Latin alphabet was the first they ever learned.

Twilight years

The 1930s were an era of strong men and dictators in many nations of the world, but is it correct to call Atatürk a dictator? It was a label the man himself abhorred. He ruled, absolutely, in the name of the Turkish people, and entertained absolutely no doubts that his course was the right one for his country. Unlike Marshall Tito in former Yugoslavia and other dictators around the world, he did not live lavishly or line his pockets from the public exchequer. Unlike in Communist Russia and Nazi Germany, the ruling party in Turkey was never given pride of place above the institutions of government. As Andrew Mango has written, 'at a time when the Bolsheviks sought to create a culture "socialist in content and national in form", Atatürk's aim was that Turkish culture should become national in content, but Western in form, for only thus could it enter the field of universal culture.'

Though he and his henchmen dealt summarily with his political opponents, he preferred persuasion to violence. The people by and large adored him. The politicians were obsequious. An inspector of schools, when asked by Atatürk to define zero, replied, 'your humble servant in your presence', and soon became minister of education. Mango summarises, choosing his words carefully: 'Turkey in the 1930s, in the last phase of his rule, was a disciplined country under an unopposed pragmatic government which respected the forms of constitutional democracy.'

Atatürk ruled not like a dictator, Mr Mango suggests, but like a king. Certainly he kept a court; a group of cronies, 'the usual gentlemen', with whom he drank, played poker and engaged in long-winded discussions until the early hours of the morning. He rose in the afternoon. The presidential logbook is replete with entries such as the following: '*10 December*. H.E. the President got up at 17.30 hours. He did not go out and received guests in the evening, retiring at 5 a.m.' From the security of his informal, *rakı*-fuelled, late-night court he steered a prudent course for his nation, avoiding foreign entanglements and doing whatever was necessary to keep the country together. What he could not give Turkey was prosperity. This would come later, as would a weakening of military rule: an unfortunate legacy of Kemalism, as Mustafa Kemal Atatürk's approach to governance came to be called.

The great man appears to have enjoyed his twilight years, sailing the Bosphorus on the presidential yacht, bathing in the Sea of

Marmara from the modest house he built for himself in Florya, drinking and dancing in the night clubs and embassies of Istanbul. Once, when his yacht was surrounded at anchor by a crowd of little boats filled with admirers, he rose and addressed them: 'fellow-countrymen, this drink is called *rakı*. You must know that I have long been in the habit of drinking it. Now, I raise my glass and drink in your honour.' His vices were those enjoyed by many Turks, his virtues were the traditional martial qualities of courage and fortitude. At the same time he was an elegant man, a gentleman to his fingertips, and much loved by women. This combination of attributes, I think, is why he remains such a hero to his people. He liberated his country from foreign domination and set it on the path toward what it is today.

ONE EVENING IN THE AUTUMN OF 1938 Atatürk slipped out of Dolmabahçe unseen and was found late that night drinking and dancing with Greek fishermen up the Bosphorus in the little village of Arnavutköy. He was persuaded, with difficulty, to return to the palace. But this would be his last night on the town. His love for the rites of Bacchus had caught up with him. Like several of the Ottoman sultans, he was suffering from cirrhosis of the liver. The great man died on the tenth of November 1938 at the Dolmabahçe Palace. All the clocks in the palace were stopped at the moment of his death, five past nine. Contrary to Islamic tradition, where a corpse must be buried within twenty-four hours, Atatürk's body lay in state for seven days at the palace, where it was visited by huge crowds of mourners. Following the public viewing and days of mourning, his body was put on board a special train and carried back to Ankara, where he lies in the massive mausoleum that was erected for him there.

22

The Worldly City: Beyoğlu and Galata

THE GOLDEN HORN, or Haliç, has always divided the two sides of Istanbul. The old city, site of Byzantine Constantinople, with Haghia Sophia, the Hippodrome, and the palaces and administrative buildings of the old regime, is where the Ottoman Turks built in their turn. They situated their seat of power and patronage in the Topkapı Palace, with the imperial mosques of Ayasofya and Sultanahmet close at hand, and the market quarter just a few hundred metres up the Divanyolu. Beyond the bazaar quarter lie the Beyazit and Süleymaniye mosques, and along the Golden Horn the old Turkish neighbourhood of Fatih and the formerly Greek and Jewish quarters of Fener and Balat. Further up the Horn is the shrine of Eyüp el-Ensari, the holiest place in Istanbul, with its mosques and *türbes* and extensive and picturesque cemeteries.

Traditional accounts emphasise how dark and quiet the old city was at night. Everything seemed to shut down after dark. Across the Galata Bridge in Pera, now called Beyoğlu, things were different. In Byzantine times, this was the territory granted to the Italians – the Genoese and Venetians who carried on a rich trade with the empire and built the Galata Tower in 1348 as a fortress and lookout. Galata was virtually a separate city. There was no bridge: if you wanted to cross over, you had to row or be rowed. Until fairly recently the lingo of boatmen along the waterfront retained some nautical Italian vocabulary, or so I have heard. There was a rowdy collection of sailors' taverns and brothels along the waterfront at Karaköy, and further up the Galata Hill. Even as recently as the late twentieth century it was a place you wouldn't want to walk around alone late at night.

Karaköy literally means 'black village', but its true, or buried, meaning is 'the village of the Karaites', because Galata was from the eleventh century until modern times home to a community of Karaite and, later, Sephardic Jews. Ashkenazis came later. Many people from these communities were employed in the administration of the Ottoman Empire. Galata's Bankalar Caddesi, Bank Street, was the financial centre of the Ottoman Empire.

In 1860 the Ottoman-Venetian banker Abraham Salomon Camondo commissioned the elegant flight of Art Nouveau stairs down to Bankalar Caddesi known as the Camondo Stairs. These elegant stairs, which made it easier for the banker and his family to get from their home to their place of business, curve sinuously, and it is said that they were built this way so that the children of the family would be less likely to fall as they descended the steep street. Galata must have been a very curious place indeed – a financial centre as well as a family neighbourhood that also housed the red light district. A friend of mine who grew up there tells me that 'sometimes a synagogue and a brothel would literally be next door to each other'. You can still sometimes hear Ladino, the ancient version of Spanish spoken by Sephardic Jews, spoken in Galata.

High life in Pera

At the top of the hill in Pera, which was semi-rural in Byzantine days and remained so as recently as the eighteenth century, with villas and vineyards scattered as far back as present-day Taksim Square, the foreign powers built their embassies. One colourful observer of diplomatic life in Pera was Lady Mary Wortley Montague, whose letters we shall revisit later in this book. She lived in Pera in 1817 with her husband, the English Ambassador:

> In Pera they speak Turkish, Greek, Hebrew, Armenian, Arabic, Persian, Russian, Slavonian, Wallachian, German, Dutch, French, English, Italian, Hungarian; and, what is worse, there is ten of these languages spoke in my own family. My grooms are Arabs, my footmen, French, English and Germans, my Nurse an Armenian, my housemaids Russians, half a dozen other servants Greeks; my steward an Italian; my Janissaries Turks.

Up-market hotels arrived in the nineteenth century, along with shops run by Greek, Armenian, Jewish and Levantine merchants.

The Turks tended not to go into trade or banking. Wealthy Turks, like English gentlemen, thought trade was demeaning; usury was forbidden among Muslims, so banking was out as well. They lived as soldiers, men of letters, or gentlemen of leisure. Working-class Turks, who lived in traditional neighbourhoods which retained a kind of village atmosphere, scraped by or failed to scrape by, as the poor always do.

Pera was also home to a number of glamorous shops. The Grande Rue de Pera was lit up at night, and to Muslim Turks who had begun to chafe under the restrictions imposed by their traditional culture, Pera represented an earthly paradise. All the charms, liberties, luxury goods and vices of modern Europe were on display. In 1875 a French engineering firm built the Tünel, one of the first funicular railways in the world, so it was easy to get up the steep hill from the waterfront at Karaköy. Previously, the wealthy had employed sedan chairs to ascend and descend.

Meyhanes and *lokantas* sprang up in the neighbourhood of Tünel, and in Asmalımescit, the sinuous long street that runs between Istiklal Caddesi (the old Grande Rue de Pera) and Mesrutiyet Caddesi, where the British Consulate and the Pera Palas, Istanbul's most famous hotel, are located. In addition to vice, luxury, and its other charms, Pera developed in the Cold War period a reputation for espionage. Istanbul sat in a geographical crease between the 'free' world and the Soviet sphere, with lots of clandestine to-ing and fro-ing. Spies were posted here from both sides of the Iron Curtain, arriving from Europe on the Orient Express, coming down from Russia by Black Sea steamer. The Orient Bar at the Pera Palas is said to have been a favourite watering hole of Kim Philby's. Graham Greene's *Stamboul Train* captures this world of intrigue.

La vie bohème

In the mid-twentieth century, Tünel and Asmalımescit became a kind of *Rive Gauche*, Soho, Greenwich Village, or the Coast of Bohemia for Republican Turkey's artists and intellectuals. The Çiçek Pasajı, or 'flower arcade', so-called after the flower sellers who used to congregate here, some of whom were also prostitutes, was the prime hangout for Istanbul's bohemians. Turkey's two most visible twentieth-century poetic movements were enacted here: *Garip*, the 'Strangers' of the twenties and thirties, whose leading figure was

Orhan Veli, quoted in chapter one, and the *Ikinci Yeni*, or 'Second New' movement of the fifties and sixties. Edip Cansever, a selection of whose work Julia Clare Tillinghast and I have published under the title *Dirty August*, from Talisman House, described those days in an autobiographical sketch. Cansever inherited from his father an antiques shop in the Grand Bazaar which occupied him during business hours. But he spent his evenings in Asmalımescit.

> I have never in my life worn flowers in my lapel. But we were like flowers freshly cut and worn in the Flower Arcade. We were in the 1960s. It was as if there was no word for 'liver' in the dictionary. Drinks worked their way into us as a lover would do .... Everything was poetry, everything was a line, everything had not ripened yet to maturity, everything was something poetic that had not yet found its name. Even poetic disputes were inexhaustible. Degustasyon, the Nile, the Lefter were full of artists, row after row of them. Everyone was just a bit late ... to his home, to his lover, to his loneliness. Some were coming from Ankara, some were going to Izmir. Their railroad, their sea routes would pass through the Fish Market, through Asmalımescit, through the back streets of Beyoğlu. The barrel-organist at Lefter would open the lid of his barrel-organ and show photos of his Greek mistress. He brought out old pictures and each one was in worse taste than the last...

Many members of the avant-garde of the day, including the novelist Ahmet Hamdi Tanpınar, the painter and poet Bedri Rahmi Eyüboğlu, and the painter Aliye Berger, lived in the Narmanlı Han, that massive crumbling building on a corner of Istiklal Caddesi fronted with huge Doric columns. Built in the nineteenth century to house the Russian Embassy and later serving briefly as a Russian jail, it was bought in 1933 by the Narmanlıs, a family of merchants, and later became the unofficial headquarters of an avant-garde artistic movement known as the D group. Their first group show was held in the Mimoza Hat Shop, also located in the *han*.

Beyoğlu today

Such is Beyoğlu's history. Still today it is a prime destination for locals in search of a night on the town. When I first came to Istanbul, the neighbourhood was filled with transvestites. Every other man seemed to be wearing a dress. Brothels were to be found nearby. Now I am told that scene has moved to some other part of the city where there is less of a police presence. I'm sure one has only to ask around. There are still plenty of shady bars where you can put a serious dent in your credit card buying pricey drinks for young bar-girls, or *Nataşas* as they are called in Turkish slang, from the former Soviet Union, if that sort of thing appeals to you. I speak from experience. It's an easy scam to fall prey to, so watch yourself.

These days I am more interested in strolling around, doing some casual shopping, stopping at cafés, looking in the bookstores and shops, then spending an evening at a *meyhane* with friends, with terrific food and a glass or two of *rakı*. Istiklal Caddesi, Istanbul's wide, pedestrianised main street, with its antique tram that runs back and forth to Taksim Square, leads off to your right as you come out of Tünel station. Left takes you into the maze of streets where Tünel merges into the neighbourhood of Asmalımescit. Once you have wandered so far to the left as to reach the Büyük Londra Hotel and the Pera Museum on Mesrutiyet Caddesi, you are on the outer edge of the area. Think of it as a big V, with the narrow end at the Tünel station. Most of the interesting cafés, bars, bookshops, galleries, etc, are found between these two main streets. As you continue up Istiklal toward Taksim, halfway up you come to Galatasaray, where the street opens up and the action sprawls downhill a bit to your right.

There are lots of places to eat in this neighbourhood, and there is live jazz at the weekends. You can find plenty of good *meyhanes* in the streets of Asmalımescit where you can get a meal, a glass of *rakı*, and *meze*, though some of these places are less about the food than the atmosphere. Get the fried anchovies, *hamsi*, when they're in season. You crunch them up, bones and all. Order *pazi*, a kind of Swiss chard, when it's on the menu. Another dish to try is *tavuk beyti*, chicken grilled on a flat skewer. *Meyhane pilavı* goes well with the chicken.

Also keep an eye out for *beğendi tavuk*, chicken with puréed aubergine, and *vişne tiridi*, sour-cherry bread. As is the case on the restaurant scene in any city, service at the best-known places can become a bit perfunctory over time, and the cooks can get complacent; so try to get recommendations from the locals whenever you can. In most places that serve *meze*, the waiter will bring a whole tray filled with little plates and start putting them on your table. Point to the ones you fancy and say no to those you don't want. Sign language works fine. A good phrase to know is *Daha koymayın* (DAH KOY-ma-yin), 'don't bring any more'.

A prominent Beyoğlu landmark is the Mısır Apartmanı, Istiklal Caddesi 303–311, a six-storey apartment block that now houses a jumble of bijoux art galleries. Mısır means 'Egypt' in Turkish, as well as 'corn', because Egypt supplied the Ottoman Empire with grain, as it had supplied Byzantium. The Egyptian royal family, which owed its position to the Ottomans and saw itself as culturally Ottoman, maintained a presence in Istanbul with their Art Nouveau residence in Bebek, the Valide Paşa mansion, and the Hıdiv Kasrı, the summer palace they built above Kanlıca up the Bosphorus in the early years of last century. They also owned the Mısır Apartmanı. You can see photographic exhibitions at Fototrek Fotoğraf Merkezi on the first floor, or sculptures and installations at Galeri Nev, which represents a dozen contemporary Turkish artists. It is worth having a drink at one of the night clubs and restaurants serving *meze* and *tapas* atop some of the buildings in this part of Istanbul. They aren't cheap, but the views of the city from up there are worth it.

When it comes to shopping, the old *pasajlar* are great places to stroll and see what you can find in the way of souvenirs, jewellery, old coins, watches, medals and tat. For Turkish sweets including *halvah* and *lokum* (Turkish delight), I like Haci Bekir, which has shops in Eminönü, Kadıköy and elsewhere, but most convenient is their shop at Istiklal Caddesi 83. If you are looking for books, there are at this writing three good English-language bookshops in Beyoğlu: Pandora, Büyükparmakkapı Sokak No. 3, between numbers 103 and 105 on Istitklal; Homer, Yeniçarşı Caddesi No 28/A in Galatasaray; and Robinson Crusoe, Istiklal Caddesi No 389. Ottomania on Sofyalı Sokak close to Tünel is a good place to look for prints and old maps.

For music, perennially the two top places to go are Babylon and Nardis. You can find Babylon at Sehbender Sok 3. It's an eclectic, top-of-the-line venue that books well-known jazz groups as well as hosting popular hip-hop nights. Their website is www.babylon.com.tr/. Down by the Galata Tower is the venerable Nardis Jazz Club, Kuledibi ['foot of the tower'] Sok 14. Check out their calendar at www.nardisjazz.com.

A more recent arrival on the scene, and one of my own favourite haunts, is Molly's, at Camekan Sok No 1/a, very near the Galata Tower, which bills itself as 'the best little café in Istanbul', and I think that may be true. It's a funky, intimate place that hosts jazz and other music, as well as poetry readings: mollyscafeistanbul.wordpress.com. A great place to cool out, day or night. They also run a nice second-hand shop. Though Molly's has changed its location during the years I have been writing this book, with any kind of luck, along with Babylon and Nardis, it will be in business for many years to come.

23

Orhan Pamuk's Istanbul

ISTANBUL IN HER DAYS OF IMPERIAL GREATNESS never lacked for writers to celebrate her beauty. If we can believe the words of literary travellers and poets like Lady Mary Wortley Montague and Lord Byron, Pierre Loti and Gerard de Nerval, this was a city of gardens, of excursion boats and royal barges rowed by liveried oarsmen, of phaetons clattering imperiously down cobbled streets at midnight on secret missions, dark-eyed harem ladies peering out through latticed windows at the street life below, and moonlight shimmering on the Bosphorus, its waters unsullied by pollution and teeming with fish. Then as one catastrophe succeeded another throughout the two centuries leading up to the First World War – a trauma for the whole world but perhaps even more so for the Ottomans – the disappearance of empire gave birth to the diminished but still vibrant city of 'Istanbul as it used to be', which even as it sank into bankruptcy, managed to maintain a brave, even ostentatious façade well through the waning years of the nineteenth century.

Cities become legendary in the eyes of the world, countries become fabled lands, when a poet or bard comes along to celebrate them and give them a larger existence, a penumbra to surround the scenes of everyday life with suggestions of amplified significance. Sooty chimney pots over the roofs of eighteenth-century hipped roofs in dense fog become 'Dickensian', and the Thames seen from Blackfriars Bridge recalls Pip and Herbert Pocket rowing the convict Magwitch downstream in their futile attempt to escape his pursuers. The sea viewed from a hillside on the Peloponnesian peninsula becomes 'wine-dark' in the hot afternoon light. We know that

Odysseus sailed these waters. Istanbul, in its modern incarnation, was waiting for its defining voice.

Over the past couple of decades it has become clear that the city has found that voice. Istanbul's indispensable chronicler – both of its present tense and its used-to-be – is Orhan Pamuk, whose *Istanbul: Memories and the City*, gives the place a dimensionality that might not otherwise be apparent. Pamuk was born in 1952 into a diminished, post-imperial Istanbul at a time when it had become the drab, black-and-white city brilliantly captured in the photographs taken by Ara Güler – a drabness reflected even in the way people dressed.

Drab perhaps, but at the same time still oddly elegant. It was a city where, despite the proliferation of concrete apartment blocks, one came unexpectedly upon wooden mansions like those that once filled the city – elegantly carpentered, unpainted, the oriel windows of their *haremlik* upper stories projecting out over the street – abandoned, their windows the targets of stone-throwing boys, or occupied by squatters and gypsies, windows curtained off with bedspreads and old kilims. American cars, imported by the rich or brought here by GIs stationed on military bases that looked north toward the Soviet Union's encircling Cold War missile installations, were adapted as taxis and *dolmuşes*, and kept running with the Turkish auto mechanic's heroic ingenuity and improvisation. Above these rolling museum pieces from the New World rose the domes and minarets of Istanbul's imperial past – powerful, awe-inspiring and mysterious.

Witness to the city in decline

Part of what makes *Istanbul: Memories and the City* such an appealing book are its eye-witness accounts of how the city's past became its present. Pamuk is both a knowledgeable observer of the city's history and a participant in its on-going present tense. During the period when the *yalıs*, those exquisite wooden mansions that once lined the Bosphorus, were regularly being torched for the insurance money and the opportunity to build taller, more profitable apartment buildings, Pamuk was a teenager. 'My friends and I', he writes, 'would immediately phone each other, hop into cars and go out to Emirgan, say, and park our cars on the pavement, turn on our tape decks (the latest consumer rage) and listen to Creedence Clearwater Revival, ordering tea, beer and cheese toasts from the teahouse next door as we watched the mysterious flames rising from the Asian shore.'

Does every city have its own characteristic mood? According to Pamuk, Istanbul is permeated by an atmosphere of *hüzün*, a word mentioned previously in these pages. This Turkish word, literally translated as 'melancholy', has entered the vocabulary of book-reading foreigners who have succumbed to Istanbul's allure. English language authors ranging from Shakespeare to Sir Thomas Burton have analysed the various aspects of melancholy at length; but *hüzün* is different. While melancholy is the humour of an individual, *hüzün*, 'the smoky window' between the poet and the world, is a quality often found in Sufi poetry, where it is suggested that the sufferer from *hüzün* is ennobled by the burden that has been imposed on him. 'Imbued still with the honour accorded it in Sufi literature, *hüzün* gives [Istanbullus'] resignation an air of dignity, but it also explains why it is their choice to embrace failure, indecision, defeat and poverty so philosophically and with such pride ...'

THE PAMUK FAMILY FORTUNE was established by the author's grandfather, one of the *nouveau riches* of the Republican era who made their money from railroads and manufacturing. As was the custom among those who could afford it, they constructed their own apartment building to house the various family groupings in separate flats on different floors of the building. It made sense for the extended family all to live under one roof. In this bourgeois interior, Pamuk's grandmother's sitting room housed the family's books, treasures, curios and mementos that spoke of their status as an affluent, secular family in modern Turkey – even though Pamuk's father and uncle were running through the family money as fast as luxurious living and bad business decisions could deplete a large fortune. Sitting rooms like this, which can still be found in many an Istanbul apartment, showed off the family's crystal and good china, its bibelots and *objets d'art*.

Even the city itself could be seen as a museum: 'in Istanbul the remains of a glorious past and civilisation are everywhere visible. No matter how ill-kept they are, no matter how neglected or hemmed in they are by concrete monstrosities, the great mosques and other monuments of the city, as well as the lesser detritus of empire in every side street and corner – the little arches, fountains and neighbourhood mosques – inflict heartaches on all who live amongst them.' Pamuk goes on to distinguish the sense of Istanbul as a museum from the prideful way traces of an illustrious past are preserved and displayed in Europe. The past in Istanbul is accompanied by a sense of defeat and shame, in a way that reminds one of the former Soviet Union in decline. There are similarities. The sister religions of Islam and Marxism carry in their scriptures a promise of ultimate victory and triumphalism. Marx presents the ultimate victory of Communism over capitalism as historically inevitable, just as Islam's narrative claims that the true faith will win out over the infidels.

Istanbul: Memories and the City contains within its covers a priceless guide to many aspects of the city, but Pamuk's remarks about failure, indecision, defeat and even poverty had, for many Istanbullus, already become outdated by the time the book was published. That's how fast the city has been changing. One could mention 2001 as a turning point for the entire world, but especially for the Middle East. Al Qaeda's attack on the World Trade Centre was traumatic for the entire global community, and the Anglo-American response led to great losses of human life, money, prestige and influence in the Middle East. The West's loss has been Turkey's gain in that the 'moderate Islamicist' government of the ruling Ak Party has skillfully moved to fill the void left by America's diminishing presence in the region. Turkey has moved strategically to regain the pivotal role that it played in Ottoman days. Its economy boasts a growth rate that is the envy of Western nations.

PAMUK'S NOVELISTIC PORTRAIT OF ISTANBUL came into being in fits and starts throughout the 1990s – first in the form of *The Black Book*, set in the 1950s, and then as *My Name Is Red*, a historical novel that recreates the city in the late sixteenth century, probably during the sultanate of Murad III. Pamuk numbers among his precursors as chroniclers of his native city not only the novelist, poet, art critic and essayist Ahmet Hamdi Tanpınar, but also the the seventeenth- and eighteenth-century *şehrengiz* or 'city books' extolling the wonders of the capital, including its lovely boys, as well as the columnist and popular historian Reşat Ekrem Koçu, whose *Istanbul Ansiklopedisi* (*Istanbul Encyclopædia*) does, in a non-fictional form, something of what James Joyce's *Ulysses* did for Dublin. The encyclopædic if quirky knowledge of the city newspaper columnist who wrote for the Sunday supplements with an imagination and curiosity that could delve freely into whatever subject seized his fancy, no matter how far-fetched or tangential – acts as a kind of collective unconscious of Istanbul.

While Pamuk's grandmother's museum of a front parlour is a static, fly-in-amber kind of place, the remit of Jelal (*Celâl* in Turkish) Salik in *The Black Book* is to lay out his encyclopædic knowledge of the city in daily newspaper columns. His is a museum that mutates with time. A journalistic chronicler of Istanbul life, he amasses an archive of old clippings, curiosities, notes and jottings, and as a connoisseur of the city's low life, he is always on the prowl among Beyoğlu's gangsters, drug dealers, gamblers, prostitutes and hustlers. The stories he tells surely also derive to some extent from the Scheherazade tradition of storytelling in the Islamic Middle East.

As *Ulysses* gave readers an imperishable picture of Dublin in 1904, *The Black Book* accurately recreates the Istanbul of the 1950s, traces of which are still to be seen in out-of-the-way places. Galip, whose wife has gone missing, roams the city in the same way that Stephen Daedelus covered Dublin, stopping off 'at a pudding shop in Karaköy which had marble tabletops. He turned away from the mirrors that reflected each other and had some vermicelli chicken soup and potted eggs. On the only wall in the pudding shop that wasn't hung with mirrors, there was the view of a mountain inspired by postcards and Pan American Airways calendars.' Pamuk clearly relishes the period details. In the voice of a religious fundamentalist prone to the conspiracy theories so common in this part of the world, he also presents a convincing picture of Istanbul as a dystopia.

Ottomans and Franks

Supremely confident, arrogant even, in its glory days as the colossus that bestrode the world from the Arabian Sea to the gates of Vienna, from the Black Sea to the Atlantic Ocean, its resolve and self-confidence stiffened by the moral power of the young religion of Muhammad, the Ottoman Empire nevertheless from an early date suffered crises of self-doubt. These crises spanned several centuries, from the sixteenth right up to the twentieth. But the era of Muslim invincibility began to pass, and European Christendom increasingly dominated a world evolving from the Middle Ages into modernity.

The armies of the infidels, better trained and disciplined, with more modern weapons, began to win battles they had previously lost to the fearsome Turk. European warships, swifter and more manœuverable, took back control of the Mediterranean. As early as 1571, at the Battle of Lepanto, the stronger navy and greater firepower the Europeans were able to muster, as well as their better-trained troops, carried the day. The combined forces of Venice, the Spanish Empire, the Papacy, Genoa and other European powers brought to the battle more than twice the number of weapons the Ottomans brought, and they had an additional technological advantage with their arquebuses and muskets. Europe feared the Ottomans' bows, but they were no match against firearms. And the six galleans the Venetians built in their famed shipyards at the Arsenale, each a large galley capable of carrying heavy artillery, literally blew the Ottoman navy out of the water.

Certainly the power of European science, technology and military strategy was overwhelmingly clear by the beginning of the nineteenth century to the reforming sultan Mahmud II, who in an attempt to reverse the empire's decline, destroyed the power of the corrupt and nepotistic Janissaries and brought in French military experts to help him reform his army. By the time of the First World War, Ottoman troops were commanded by German officers. In the scientific realm, the earlier accomplishments of Arab thinkers, astronomers and mathematicians were outstripped by the scientific West.

Italian painting began in imitation of Byzantine art: the great Madonnas of Duccio and Cimabue look very much like Byzantine icons. But at the dawn of the Renaissance, in the Italian *quattrocento*, painters like Masaccio and Masolino discovered what they called a new, 'scientific' approach to painting that revolved around perspective. If you can get close enough to Masaccio's fresco, *The Tribute Money*, in the Brancacci Chapel in the church of Santa Carmine in Florence, you can see the nail that the painter drove into the wall to establish his perspective point.

THE PLOT OF PAMUK'S MASTERPIECE, *My Name Is Red*, revolves around attempts to modernise Ottoman painting through the adoption of 'Frankish' (European) methods in the early seventeenth century. The book is a murder mystery that takes place among court miniaturists. Speaking from beyond the grave, the victim appeals to readers of his story: 'open your eyes, discover why the enemies of the life in which you believe, of the life you're living, and of Islam, have destroyed me.'

A world of princely states stretching from Herat on the western borders of what is now Afghanistan, to Isfahan, Shiraz and Tabriz in what is now Iran, to Baghdad in what is now Iraq, where rival khans patronised workshops of calligraphers and miniaturists in their courts, provides the surround for the murder mystery plot in *My Name Is Red*. The novel animates the multifaceted life of the imperial capital in its glory days – the dervish sects, the many and differing neighbourhoods of the city, the various trades, and the coffee houses where men gathered.

If all one knows of the dervishes is derived from an evening of 'turning', chanting and music in the reverent atmosphere of the Mevlevihanesi in Tünel, or the appearance of young men in dervish costumes performing in some of the city's cafés, then Pamuk's account of some of the other dervish orders will come as something of a shock.

The Kalenderhane Camii, originally built as the Church of the Theotokos Kyriotissa, almost adjacent to the Aqueduct of Valens that runs to the west of the Süleymaniye Mosque in the old city, is one of the most interesting of the city's mosques. Mehmed II, on converting it from a church, gave it to the Kalenderis. Pamuk's account of these lads, 'opium-addicted madmen ... piercing themselves with skewers and engaging in all manner of depravity', springs to mind when one is visiting the mosque. These vignettes are part of Pamuk's project of reclaiming for readers much of traditional Turkish and specifically Islamic lore that Atatürk attempted, largely successfully, to exorcise from Turkish consciousness.

IN *THE BLACK BOOK*, the storyline revolves around the mysterious disappearance of Rüya, the main character's wife. In *My Name Is Red*, as in *The Black Book*, we meet a chronicler who provides sketches of life in the city, tangentially related to the plot. The journalist Jelal Salik is the city chronicler in *The Black Book*; his role is played in *My Name Is Red* by a coffee-house storyteller, a shape-shifter who brilliantly speaks in the voice of a horse, or a gold coin, or a dog, and whose stories inevitably poke fun at one Nusret Hoja from Erzerum, a Savanarola-like Islamic fundamentalist who wants to punish the free-thinking coffee drinkers, artists and illustrators for their deviations from what he considers the true path that the Prophet laid out in his holy book.

Pamuk's evocations of life in the seventeenth-century city give his modern day readers a feeling for what Istanbul must have been like in days gone by – back to a time when humans coexisted with beings from other dimensions: the spirits of the dead, even messengers from heaven. When we walk the streets around Topkapı Palace at midnight, we know, thanks to Pamuk, that we are venturing into the same neighbourhoods that the sultans used to prowl at night in disguise, to spy on their subjects. He deftly establishes the feeling of walking across the sleeping city five centuries ago, past 'mosque courtyards where angels reclined on domes to sleep, beside cypress trees murmuring to the souls of the dead, beyond the edges of snow-covered cemeteries crowded with ghosts'.

The Museum of Innocence

Pamuk sets his most recent book, *The Museum of Innocence*, which was published in Turkish in 2008 and translated into English in 2009, in the late seventies and early eighties among the wealthy, Europeanised residents of Istanbul who live in upscale neighbourhoods such as Nişantaşı which visitors to the city seldom frequent. Kemal, the narrator, is typical of the Turkish upper-middle classes. Speaking of the Kurban Bayramı, when sheep are slaughtered all over Turkey in commemoration of the time God ordered Abraham to sacrifice his son Isaac, and alms are given to the needy, the narrator comments: 'neither my mother nor my father was religious. I never saw either of them pray or keep a fast. Like so many married couples who had grown up during the early years of the Republic, they were not disrespectful of religion; they were just indifferent to it... . We left it to the cook and the janitor to distribute the alms. Like my relatives, I had always kept my distance from the annual ritual sacrifice in the empty lot next door.' But perhaps the sense of estrangement, the cultural isolation, that members of Pamuk's class feel, says more about the social disconnection between classes than about religious matters: 'the pain, it seemed to me from then on', Pamuk writes in his memoir, 'was not being far from God but from everyone around me, from the collective spirit of the city.'

This separation from the Turkish masses is common among well-educated, affluent Turks such as Kemal's father's wealthy friend who ventured out only once a day, to sip tea for two hours in the lobby or pastry shop of the Hilton Hotel, 'because it's the only place in the city that feels like Europe'. In the 1950s the newly built Istanbul Hilton came to symbolise modernity and westernisation. 'On Sunday evenings', Kemal recalls, 'we would go as a family to eat that amazing thing called a hamburger, a delicacy as yet offered by no other restaurant in Turkey... . In those days so many Western innovations made their first appearance in this hotel that the leading newspapers even posted reporters here'.

As Istanbul has become increasingly transformed by wave after wave of immigrants from Anatolia, with their village ways and their fundamentalist understanding of Islam, the native, worldly Istanbullu can find himself feeling increasingly isolated. Pamuk addresses this cultural disjunction head-on in *Snow*, his most political novel, where the poet Ka, an Istanbul intellectual, travels to the far eastern Anatolian city of Kars (*kar* means 'snow' in Turkish) to investigate a wave of suicides among young girls forbidden by the secular Turkish state from wearing headscarves to school. The native Istanbullu is more comfortable either in his own neighbourhood or suburb, or in older quarters whose mixture of ethnicities and origins harks back to the days of Constantinople as the great *mélange* it used to be. Çukurcuma, where the Keskin family lives in *Snow*, is now home to Pamuk's Museum of Innocence (an actual museum whose collections flesh out the lives of the middle-class characters from the novel).

Through Turkish eyes

Orhan Pamuk has done more to put his city on the world's literary map than any previous Turkish writer. He has brought a Turkish voice to a culture that has usually been seen through European eyes. In *My Name Is Red* he lets his characters, most of them artists, discuss in terms of their own world-view the relative claims of Middle Eastern miniature painting and Frankish painting, with its realism in portraiture and employment of perspective. This book gives us Istanbul on its own terms, rather than through the eyes of the foreign visitor, who is on the lookout for the exotic and, yes, Oriental. Not that Turkey has not previously produced other novelists – notably Ahmet Hamdi Tanpınar, whose 1949 novel *Peace* – translated in 2008 by Erdağ Göknar as *A Mind at Peace* – Pamuk himself has called 'the greatest novel ever written about Istanbul'. But no one else has opened as wide a window on the city and given such a detailed and informed view of it.

His now considerable and global audience probably gives him

little credit for doing this, but his Istanbul readership is undoubtedly very aware of Pamuk as a literary voice of the non-exotic middle class trying to live within the realities of life in post-imperial Republican Turkey, now that society has come to embrace the new, rising power of the more religiously observant Anatolian business class, with their wives who wear the headscarf – that potent symbol of everything Atatürk tried to lead his country away from.

The main characters in *The Black Book* exist within a diminished world where the city they have known has been transformed beyond recognition, where they live side by side with millions of immigrants from the countryside with whom they have little in common culturally. *The Museum of Innocence* tells its story of obsessive love within the *milieu* of Istanbul's upper-middle-class socialites who live in the posh neighbourhoods which visitors to the city rarely see unless they make a point of going there, which they seldom do, since the old historic neighbourhoods are of greater interest. I seldom venture into those parts of town myself, but whenever I do, having read Pamuk makes me feel I know the people I see in the chic shops and restaurants.

24

The Turkish Kitchen

MY OWN FREQUENT VISITS to Istanbul are as much about food as they are about architecture and art, Turkish history and culture, and all the other good reasons there are for coming here. A good Turkish breakfast is a glorious thing: crusty bread, yoghurt and *beyaz peynir* – the Turkish white cheese that the Greeks call feta – delicious honey and jams, boiled eggs, black and green olives, tomatoes and cucumbers, cups of strong tea. If your hotel has a touch of class about it, breakfast in the warm months will also include *karpuz*, or watermelon, and *kavun*, a luscious, sweet, yellow-fleshed melon. Lunch might be *zeytinyağlı* vegetables – peppers, tomatoes and aubergine stuffed with savoury rice, and fresh salads, all washed down with *ayran*, the salty yoghurt drink available everywhere, or *vişne suyu*, sour cherry juice.

The way to say 'Turkish cooking' or 'Turkish cuisine' in Turkish is *Türk mutfağı*, literally translated as 'the Turkish kitchen'. Turkish restaurants typically fall into four categories: (1) *kebapçıs* and *köftecis*, (2) *lokantas*, (3) *meyhanes*, and (4) fish restaurants. In a *kebapçı* or *köfteci*, the specialty is grilled meat. *Köfte* is a kind of meatball grilled on skewers. Practically every Turkish city is known for its own type of *köfte*. *Izmir köftesi* is cooked with tomatoes. In Adana they make it very spicy. From Urfa comes *çiğ köfte*, made with raw meat or bulgur, mild onions, scallions, parsley and green pepper. And everyone has his or her own favourite *köftecis*. I like Ali Baba in Arnavutköy [Albanian Village] and Arnavut in Balat, the old Jewish neighbourhood.

Second comes the *lokanta*, an ordinary kind of eatery that is found in every neighbourhood. A *lokanta* is a Turkish bistro, with the same connotations as the word *trattoria* in Italian. *Lokantas* serve stuffed vegetables, pilafs, and the delicious lentil soup called *mercimek*, one kind cooked with tomato paste, carrots, etc, the other plain. You squeeze lemon juice into the second, more common kind. Turks eat a lot of salad too; either *çoban salatası*, 'shepherd's salad', made with tomatoes, cucumbers, onion, green peppers, etc, or *mevsim salata*, made with mixed seasonal vegetables. *Mevsim* means 'season'.

Then there are *meyhanes*, where *mezes* are served, the *zeytinyağlı* vegetable dishes prepared with olive oil and usually stuffed with savoury rice – served on little plates along with cheese, olives, *kavun*, that delicious yellow melon, and *ezmes* – purées made with aubergine, hot peppers and so forth. Turks don't drink without eating, and when they are drinking *rakı* or beer, *meze* are on the table. Some of the best *meyhanes* are in the Tünel and Asmalımescit sections of Beyoğlu. When people want a night out on the town, they go to Tünel and Asmalımescit, or to the *Çiçek Pasajı* [flower arcade] or the *Balık Pasajı* [fish arcade].

Fourth in this grand scheme would be fish restaurants. The Turks can't have seen seafood until they reached the Black Sea and the Mediterranean, but over the years fish has become a favourite food of Istanbullus. Istanbul has some of the best seafood in the world, most of it coming fresh from the Bosphorus, the Black Sea and the Sea of Marmara. In the more elegant fish restaurants you can eat a splendid meal that may take several hours, complete with *meze* and *rakı*, and end up gasping in disbelief at the bill. I prefer the simpler, no-frills places like Adem Baba in Arnavutköy and Ismet Baba in Kuzguncuk, on the European and Asian sides of the Bosphorus, respectively. If you time it right you can go to either Arnavutköy or Kuzguncuk by ferry. Otherwise, take a bus or cab to Arnavutköy. For Kuzguncuk, take a ferry to Üsküdar, and then a *dolmuş*, or cab, the rest of the way.

A shared cuisine

The roots of Turkish cuisine, as I have said, are fourfold. First let us take the grilled meats that would have been part of the Turks' traditional nomadic life. Then there is the sophisticated cuisine of Ottoman court cooking, which involves sauces, purées, vegetables stuffed with rice, spices and meats. Ottoman cooking survives in the *mezes* served in *meyhanes*, the main dishes served in *lokantas*, the pastries like *börek* and *baklava*, and the fabulous dishes served in places like Kanaat in Üsküdar and a few old-fashioned Beyoğlu restaurants.

The demotic version of Ottoman cuisine is to be found in the many *lokantas* all over Turkey which serve a basic form of this cooking.

At one time, Greeks, Turks, Armenians and Jews in Istanbul all shared a common cuisine, though a few ethnic specialities do stand out, such as the cold Armenian *meze* called *topik*, which is made from chickpeas and potatoes, and is served in some *meyhanes* around town. Claudia Roden, author of many books about Middle Eastern cookery, acknowledges these shared cuisines in her book, *Arabesques*, which presents a common cuisine based on the typical, and typically delicious, elements such as stuffed vegetables, grilled meats, pilafs, sweet milk-based puddings and the like.

While I have been somewhat dogmatic about the types of restaurants to be found in Istanbul, there is some blurring of categories. Ismet Baba in Kuzguncuk is a *meyhane*, but after your *rakı* and *meze*, you can eat some terrific fresh fish. The great thing nowadays is that you can do some serious restaurant research online: www.istanbulfoodie.com is a terrific resource. And www.tripadvisor.com lets you read other people's comments on places where you are thinking about eating. The food writer David Rosengarten gives some sage advice about how to find the best food in a foreign country. 'Eat the breakfast they eat,' he writes. 'Eat the lunch they eat. Eat the dinner they eat. Eat these meals at the times they eat them. Eat between meals only as they do. Drink what they drink, when they drink it… After a week of following their schedule and habits, you will begin to have insights into that country's food that you would never have had otherwise.' Sound advice, that.

Hunter-gatherer fare

I have mentioned that there are four categories of restaurant in Istanbul. But there is in fact a fifth, and it is the principal subject of this section. This kind of place serves an inexhaustibly rich cuisine from Anatolia which I'll call hunter-gatherer food. Since the late eighties, *the* place to eat for serious foodies has been Çiya, in Kadıköy, the creation of master chef Musa Dağdeviren – Çiya is the name of a mountain in Anatolia. Take the ferry from Eminönü, and then good luck finding it! There's no point in my trying to give directions to Çiya; I always get lost in the labyrinth of neighbourhood streets, but eventually find the place after asking for directions a few times. Mr Dağdeviren actually has three restaurants here, two of them being *kebapçıs*. I would recommend Çiya Sofrası (*sofra* means a 'dining table') over the *kebapçıs*, even though the kebabs are really imaginative and different from what you would find anywhere else. If you do eat at one of the *kebapçıs*, try to get a table on the roof, for the wonderful views.

Recently a group of five of us ate a huge meal at Çiya Sofrası with beer and desserts, and ended up spending TL 50, less than £15, per person. You can get by for less. The management gave us complimentary *kekik çayı* between courses (*kekik* can mean either oregano or thyme, but I think this tea was brewed from thyme) as well as Turkish coffee after the meal. A friend of mine from Thailand, by way of New York, pronounced it the best meal he had ever eaten.

The restaurant itself is simple and functional; the emphasis is on the food. After you are seated and have ordered something to drink, you go up to the front, where the *meze* and salads are displayed on one side while the main dishes are set out in tubs in a kind of open kitchen, with perhaps a dozen choices on either side. On the *meze* side we found things like the familiar but delicious yoghurt-based aubergine *ezme*, cold chopped greens of several kinds with unfamiliar names and in unusual combinations, such as purslane with barley and lentils.

Even if you know Turkish food pretty well, there's little hope that you will recognise what everything here is, so just get whatever looks good. They put your plate on a scale and charge you by weight. I loved the *pazi*, which is a kind of chard prepared with grated carrots and radishes, and another salad of something like black-eyed peas stewed with greens and served cold. A soup that must be tried is *Ezo Gelin Çorbası*, a hearty peasant lentil soup with meat, lemon, oregano, red pepper and yoghurt.

As main dishes *mumbar* – sheep's intestines stuffed with bulgur – was terrific, as was lamb cooked with *ayva*, or quince. I love aubergine so I ordered the *patlıcan kebabı*, aubergine cooked with lamb. (Kebab can describe several kinds of meat dish, not just grilled meats.) Another night I had the *kuru sebze dolması*, aubergine stuffed with meat, rice and dried vegetables. The plums stuffed with ground lamb were delectable. See if they have the *köfte* made with cherries. As in a Dim Sum restaurant, when in doubt just point to things.

To be human is to forget. Perhaps every culture survives by forgetting. Modern Turkey sometimes strikes me as a culture based on trying, not always successfully, to forget as many things as possible about the country's past. One thing I admire about the contemporary Turkish novelist Elif Şafak is her relentless determination to remind her readers of things they would either prefer to forget, or never knew in the first place, such as the Armenian massacres of the later nineteenth and early twentieth centuries.

Musa Dağdeviren's stated mission is to restore to Turkish diners a cuisine that they have forgotten. Though I've never heard anyone say so, I think this mission of his has an implicit political side to it since the food he serves is derived from a reservoir of influences that is far more inclusive than the 'Turkey for the Turks' approach to national self-definition that has guided this country ever since Atatürk's revolution. Musa Dağdeviren is a bit of a scholar, a serious archæologist of forgotten dishes who comes from a family of chefs, and his mission has been to acquaint or re-acquaint Istanbullus with the cuisine of Anatolia. To become re-acquainted with this cuisine is, it seems to me, to become re-acquainted with Turkey's multi-ethnic heritage.

Mr Dağdeviren, who is half Kurdish, hails from Gaziantep in southeastern Anatolia, and he describes what he serves as 'Southeastern and East Mediterranean Cuisine', which his website calls 'a reflection of a vast geography from Anatolia to Mesopotamia and the variety of culturally prosperous people that have existed on that land. Here, all the Azerbaijani, Georgian, Turkish, Arabian, Armenian, Ottoman, Syrian, Seldjukian and Jewish dishes are prepared according to the original customs and beliefs'.

Kurdish cooking is not included in this list, but surely to discover the cuisine of southeastern Anatolia is to discover Kurdish cooking as well. My notion is that Kurdish contributions must be the secret ingredients in this ethnic stew. Çiya's website lists the day's dishes, citing their origin, geographical and ethnic. Mr Dağdeviren owns fields where he grows his own beans, and maintains an apartment complex for his chefs and their families. Like any successful master chef, he shops seriously for ingredients, and travels all over Turkey to get the ingredients he wants.

If one could sum up Mr Dağdeviren's philosophy of cooking aside from the rediscovery of forgotten dishes and ingredients, it would have something to do with unusual combinations. The night we were there he offered two different kinds of *sherbet* or 'fruit drink' – one made with blackberries, one with sumac. Another night he offered tamarind *sherbet*. The concept of using *recherché* ingredients comes especially to the fore with the desserts. We were presented with five choices. First came a walnut, shell and all, stuffed with aubergine that had somehow been preserved and candied. How he processed the walnut shell to make it edible I have no idea. Then, amazingly, a candied chunk of zucchini, candied green olives, aubergine and tomatoes. Amazing. But this is a man who makes jam out of *kebbet,* a huge, sour fruit that looks like a cross between a lemon and a winter squash.

Any cuisine with roots in antiquity must share some qualities with a hunter-gatherer culture, with emphasis on the gathering. A lot of what goes into the dishes at Çiya is not grown but gathered. It reminds me of how, as one reads in Danilo Dolci's wonderful book, *Poverty in Sicily*, people in a subsistence economy survive. One of the things they do is go out into the fields and gather herbs, greens and roots, some of which they eat, and some of which they sell in the city. This part of Dolci's book is a study in the relations between survival and cuisine. In cities in the American South, people from the country still come around in winter selling little bundles of sassafras roots, which can be used to make tea. Greens such as collards, 'poke salad', turnip and mustard greens, are part of the cuisine of the region. Mr Dağdeviren, by incorporating in many of his dishes these herbs and greens that one would hardly know the names of, perpetuates a 'gatherer' cuisine for the delectation of anyone in Istanbul who is serious about food.

25

Crossing over into Asia

ISTANBUL IS WELL KNOWN for being the only city in the world that spans two continents. Part of the metropolis lives across the Bosphorus in Asia. There are ferry terminals in Kadıköy, where Çiya is located, and in Üsküdar, to the north of Kadıköy. To get there you take the Üsküdar ferry from Eminönü, Beşiktaş or from an *iskele*, ferry stop, along the Golden Horn. Crossing the gangplank and hurrying on board to find a seat can be a bit of an adventure when the Bosphorus is rough. 'To be travelling through the middle of a city as great, historic and forlorn as Istanbul', writes Orhan Pamuk in *Istanbul: Memories and the City*, 'and yet to feel the freedom of the open sea – that is the thrill of a trip along the Bosphorus.'

You can sit in an enclosed cabin, on one of the open decks where smoking is allowed, or on benches set along the outside of the ship where you are closer to the water. I like to order a glass of tea from the waiter who moves among the passengers with his tray, and drink it as we sail. Jade-green waves lap against the prow of the boat as she pushes out into the channel. With its crowds, traffic, noise and smog, Istanbul can be oppressive, particularly in the heat of the summer; it is refreshing to get out on the open water, to see the hills of the city rise over the Bosphorus above the shoreline at Beşiktaş, with the Dolmabahçe Palace and the rococo excess of the Nusretiye Mosque downstream from it, and the dense piney green of Yıldız Park opening between the red-tiled rooftops. Halfway across you see the domes and minarets of Üsküdar approaching.

The ship's crew bustles about, performing their duties. Seagulls swarm round the boat, there is a smell of diesel and cigarette smoke, the salt air of the sea, and underneath it all, the heavy effort of the ship's engines. The Bosphorus, pushing down from the Black Sea toward the Sea of Marmara, runs very deep in places and has a powerful current. In heavy weather one hears the deep assertion of the foghorn's bass note, a sound that seems to come from inside the heart of things. The first Bosphorus suspension bridge spans the sky upstream from us, rising above the ornate baroque mosque at Ortaköy, the 'Middle Village' between Istanbul and the upper reaches of the Bosphorus.

The pace of life in Üsküdar is just that bit slower than on the European side, and you feel as though you have stepped back a tick or two in time. You have indeed, because this is a settlement with deep roots in antiquity. The Greeks built a city here called Chrysopolis, the 'City of Gold', in the seventh century BC. The mosque of Atik Valide Sultan, one of Sinan's most harmonious accomplishments, awaits at the top of the steep hill of Üsküdar. Along with women in headscarves and the modest working men of this conservative quarter, one can visit the shrine of Aziz Mahmud Hüdayi, for the *bereket*. *Bereket* (*baraka* in Arabic) is the blessing or, if you will, good feeling, that emanates from holy places, the tombs of holy men in particular. Finally, one can visit a restaurant called Kanaat, which means 'contentment' in Turkish, not far from the ferry landing. Three pleasures, then: one of the most sublime creations of Ottoman architecture, Turkish cuisine at its best, and a third, the blessing, for which no word properly exists.

Not that there are only three things worth seeing in Üsküdar. In the first place, right above the ferry landing is the Iskele Camii, an imperial mosque built in 1547–48 by Sinan for Mihrimah Sultan, daughter of Süleyman the Magnificent. Like the Sultanahmet Mosque, the Iskele Camii is more interesting from outside than inside, where it is rather dark and cramped. Sinan built a spacious double porch in front of the mosque which extends to cover an attractive *şadırvan*. Like the precincts of many mosques, it forms a natural gathering place, and whether or not they are going inside to pray, people congregate here to meet friends, chat on their mobile phones and converse. Walk round to the side and look at the old sundial on the mosque wall which indicates the hours for the five daily prayers – these vary according to the season. A more modest, but charming Sinan mosque, the Şemsi Paşa, stands along the promenade. There is a little café beside the mosque, and it's a nice place to sit and enjoy the view of Istanbul across the way. Üsküdar also has an attractive covered market which is entered across the street from Kanaat.

If you are young and hardy, then by all means walk up to Sinan's lovely Atik Valide Mosque. As I am neither, I take a cab. The fare is about five liras. Your walk would take you down the length of the boulevard that runs through the centre of town, then uphill to the neighbourhood of Toptaşı, 'the cannon ball', toward the crest of the hill, one and a half kilometres from the ferry station.

The Mosque of the Queen Mother

Sinan regarded the Selimiye in Edirne as his masterpiece, and no one who has seen it could easily dissent. His Süleymaniye Mosque in Istanbul, the peak of his achievement before he built in Edirne, is perhaps a more forceful statement of the classical Ottoman mosque than the Selimiye is, because it contains few of the more fanciful touches that characterise the Edirne mosque. But the great architect's more modest creations are in many ways more appealing because their very lack of monumentality allows Sinan more room for caprice and inventiveness. The Atik Valide mosque was built in 1583 for Nurbanu, the *Valide Sultan* or 'Queen Mother' – the widow of Selim II.

Istanbul is built on hills, as any walker in the city knows, and the site of this mosque presented Sinan with certain challenges, surrounded as it originally was with an extensive *külliye* incorporating a soup kitchen, hospital, insane asylum, religious school and quarters for dervishes. The hamam that would normally be part of a *külliye* is instead located down by the waterfront: one half of it has been demolished, while the other half has been made into a small department store. It is speculated that there was only one spring at the site of the mosque, and that all its water was used to provide water for the *şadırvan*. One ascends to the plateau of the mosque courtyard, which is pleasing in every way: a broad space defined with arcades and topped by little domes. Two huge plane trees in the courtyard are thought to date from the sixteenth century. At the centre of the courtyard stands a broad-roofed *şadırvan* under whose eaves mosque-goers performing their ablutions can be protected from sun and rain.

The Ottoman architectural genius is winningly characterised by a combination of strength and fancy. The fancifully painted red and cream strips of boarding on the ceiling of the *şadırvan*, one of the most beautiful in Istanbul, make it something one never tires of looking at. Atop the roof is the traditional round, segmented leaden dome, and underneath it the pointed dome of the little fountain where one washes before praying. I particularly enjoy this courtyard in summer, when it is filled with roses in bloom. Their scarlets and vermilions go beautifully with the red of the *şadırvan* ceiling. A good angle from which to look at the *şadırvan* is at the foot of the steep steps that go down to a usually locked gate on the street, where you can then look up into it from below.

The prayer space inside the mosque has, like the site itself, a sense of latitude. In the first place there are two porches, equivalent to the exo-narthex and narthex that usher one into Haghia Sophia. The inner porch serves as the *son cemaat yeri*, the space outside the mosque proper where latecomers can pray. Then there are galleries that overlook the mosque floor under the arches of supporting domes. All in all this is a very pleasing building. The origin of the two black flags with yellow borders that hang from the *mihrab* is unknown: either they have to do with one or another of the dervish orders, or they were put here by the Janissaries.

If you look closely along the west wall of the mosque, you will see a bow hanging from the south gallery. No one is quite sure what it is doing there, except that archery was once thought of as a sacred sport. As befits an imperial mosque, the details and materials inside are very fine. The Iznik tiles, particularly those on the mihrab, are of the best period, and the mother-of-pearl inlaid woodwork of the window shutters is very beautiful. In the middle of the eighteenth century a baroque *hünkar mahfil*, or royal loge, was added, with a really interesting *trompe l'oeil* fresco that tricks the eye into thinking that there is a further recess inside the wall.

Back down the hill into Üsküdar

Leaving the mosque by its main entrance, past its little library, a pleasant detour will take you to the Çinili Cami, or 'Tiled Mosque', attractively decorated with blue and white tiles. The mosque itself is very old, though the porch and minaret are baroque additions. From the Çinili Cami one can keep walking away from the centre of town to reach the Karacaahmet Cemetery, Istanbul's oldest and largest. It covers 750 acres and dates from the mid-fourteenth century. With its ancient cypresses and weathered tombstones, the cemetery epitomises the gloomy romance of death in this old city.

To return to the centre of Üsküdar, one only has to head downhill on Çavuş Dere Caddesi, eventually reaching the main street, Hakimiyeti Caddesi. Uphill off the main street three or four turnings toward the waterfront, you will find, on Aziz Mahmud Efendi Sokağı, the shrine of Aziz Mahmud Hüdayi, a Helveti dervish who was a spiritual adviser to Ahmed I and Murad III. *Aziz* may roughly be translated as 'saint'. Islam asserts that there is no God but God, and though no Muslim would dispute that, Islam, like Christianity, reserves a place for saintly intermediaries. The shrine of Aziz Mahmud Hüdayi is associated with sailors, some of whom visit the shrine before embarking on a long voyage.

Local shrines

The sites where local holy men are buried hold great appeal for ordinary people who visit them, who say a little prayer and ask for blessings, sometimes lighting a candle, leaving a few coins or flowers, or perhaps tying a bit of cloth or ribbon to the grille enclosing the holy man's *türbe*. The practice is ancient, and just as much disapproved of by orthodox Muslims four hundred years ago as by the religious authorities who post signs prohibiting the practice today. A fundamentalist preacher in Pamuk's *My Name Is Red* mentions it as a feature of life in the early sixteenth century: 'today, people plead before gravesites, begging for amends. They hope for the intervention of the dead on their behalf. They visit the tombs of saints and worship at graves like pagans before pieces of stone. They tie votive pieces of cloth everywhere, and make promises of sacrifice in return for atonement.'

Outside many *türbes* and other places of pilgrimage you will see a green sign erected by the office of the Muslim authorities. Translated as follows, it gives a clear indication of how widespread are the practices it warns against.

HONOURED PILGRIMS

- Pilgrimage to tombs is a prescribed practice in our religion. In the course of these pilgrimages greetings are given and the Qur'an is read to the spirit of the dead.
- In our religion it is forbidden, it is a sin, to light candles at the tomb, to tie bits of cloth, to attach 'wish beads', to leave money, to make a ritual sacrifice, and directly to make any specific request of the dead.

- Pilgrimages are made for the purpose of taking warning from death.

Mahmud Hüdayi's shrine is the centre of the little Gülfem Hatun neighbourhood, where shops sell religious materials and souvenirs for visitors to the shrine. One enters the solemn room with its two catafalques draped in green baize, and carpets on the floor, filled with people holding their hands open and upward in an attitude of prayer. I have never seen the chamber empty. The ornate Murano chandelier hanging from the ceiling, slightly the worse for wear, is a typical Ottoman touch and a reminder of the wealth and luxury that were once commonplace in the imperial city. All over Turkey and all over the Islamic world, you find little pockets of sanctity like this. The way people look after them, make sure the gardens that surround them grow and flourish, and stop off on their way to and from work or while out running the day's errands, enhances a sense of the sacredness of life. How different this is from most Europeans' and Americans' idea of Islam as a source of terror and threat.

The shamans of the Turks' older, pre-monotheistic religion had their ways of appeasing the spirits, warding off their anger and spitefulness, curing the sick and protecting the health of children. The *nazar boncuğu*, a blue bead with a white circle and a lighter blue circle inside, with a black pupil at the very centre, can be seen on almost every building and in every home in Turkey. I use one as a fridge magnet and have another one on my key chain to ward off the evil eye. To say *Maşallah*, 'as God has willed', and touch children's heads when you praise them, is perhaps no more than a harmless form of superstition, differing little from the way Catholics make the sign of the cross and qualify statements about the future by adding 'God willing'. We arrived at this point in our evolution well fortified with superstitions. Every culture has its own.

As a footnote, on a recent visit to the shrine I was given a little flyer describing the shrine in English. I'd like to know who wrote it, because whoever did was of a broad-minded Sufistic persuasion. This fits with my overall sense of the place, because unlike at some more orthodox sites, I have never been made to feel unwelcome here. The flyer describes the place as 'the centre of Gnostics (Wisdom Seekers)' and goes on to say that 'his literature, preaches (sic), sufistic poems, exhortations and advices guided both Sultans and common people'.

Contentment

Now it is time for lunch. Though the restaurant is well-known to Istanbullus, one of my sons and I first discovered Kanaat for ourselves by chance. I have two favourite waiters at Kanaat. One is a man perhaps in his early forties with a plump, porcine face and an agreeable manner, the other a slightly older man, bespectacled, with a distracted but not inattentive, almost scholarly manner, whose Turkish is sprinkled with pleasantly old-fashioned words. Both are thoroughgoing professionals who have been here as long as I have been coming to the restaurant. I enjoy their ritualistic welcomes, making a little bow when saying *hoş geldiniz* [It is pleasant that you have come], to which one replies *hoş bulduk* [We find it agreeable], their quick and efficient movements, and the way they repeat your order aloud as they write it in their little notebooks in such a way that implies you have ordered a well thought-out combination of dishes.

On each visit, Kanaat is exactly the same. It is always filled with diners, but is so spacious a place that one never has to wait for a table. The first thing you pass when you walk in is the big glass case displaying all the many desserts, so you can immediately start planning what you will have at the end of your meal. Just beyond the dessert case you pass the *zeytinyağlı* offerings – those meatless dishes, prepared with olive oil, which are eaten cold: stuffed cabbage and stuffed grape leaves and green peppers, the *ezmes*, the artichokes, the cold stuffed tomatoes, the white cheese and olives, the yoghurt dishes. I like to start my meal with two kinds of *ezme*, the subtly seasoned purées that are spread on bread and eaten as appetisers: *patlıcan ezmesi* and *acılı* – the cool and the hot, the white and the red. The smooth coolness of the aubergine nicely balances the spiciness of the hot pepper.

To survey the meat dishes you walk up a couple of steps to the left and back to the open front of the kitchen, with its heat and bustle, its ample display of stews, vegetables stuffed with meat, kebabs and mysterious dishes some of which one inevitably doesn't know the names of. I recently ordered something called *parmak kebabı* and was rewarded with a delicious concoction of sheep's knuckles prepared with aubergine and tomatoes. The *Özbek kebabı* is also good. Chunks of fatty meat from the sheep's tail are interspersed with chunks of lean meat, and seasoned with coriander, cumin and red pepper. It is very similar to what Russians and Ukrainians call *shashlik*.

Kanaat is famous for *patlıcan karnıyarık*, aubergine stuffed with minced lamb, tomatoes, parsley, onion and dill. The Turks have found a way of taking the bitterness and toughness out of aubergine, giving it a texture light and airy, which beautifully absorbs the flavours of the meat and other ingredients. A dish of greens for which there is no word I know of in English, sautéed simply and served with a yoghurt-garlic sauce, goes nicely with the *karnıyarık*, as does a plate of fava beans dressed in olive oil and lemon.

After the *ezmes* and aubergine, the meat dishes and greens and fava beans, with side dishes of yoghurt, you go up to the counter and order dessert. Stewed quinces with homemade ice cream is terrific, and there is a syrupy sweet biscuit with an almond stuck on top whose name I do not recall. *Fırın sütlaç*, or milk pudding, is heavenly. A good way to finish off your lunch is with a little cup of Turkish coffee.

26

Dervishes

IN THE 1920S WHEN ATATÜRK set out to westernise Turkey and establish a modern, secular republic, one of his first acts was to close the *tekkes*, the dervish meeting houses, and forbid people to frequent *türbes* like that of Aziz Mahmud Hüdayi in Üsküdar. *Tekkes* were everywhere in Istanbul. They were men's fraternal clubs as much as they were centres for the practice of Sufism, the mystical expression of Islam. To an extent they resembled Masonic lodges, giving men – and more rarely women – a chance to meet and to practise their spirituality in a less formalised way than in the mosque. *Namaz* is normally performed as part of the activities at a *tekke*, but there are other practises – breathing exercises, chants, the whirling or 'turning' which the Mevlevis do – that bring on a sense of exaltation and ecstasy. Many *tekkes* closed when the government crackdown was imposed, and others went underground. In the more tolerant climate of the past few decades, many dervishes now practise their ceremonies openly.

An evening at a tekke

Last year an American convert to Islam invited me to attend a Helveti *sema* at a *tekke* on a back street between Cihangir and Harbiye in Istanbul. A *sema* is an evening of sacred music, chanting, prayer and the recitation of poetry. We entered through an ancient gate into the precincts of a mosque that had been ruined by fire and was no longer in use. We stopped to pay our respects at the *türbe* of the saint, a typical little domed enclosure with a wrought-iron grille surrounding an area where the saint's imposing catafalque lay draped in the traditional green of Islam. Then we proceeded to the *sheikh*'s residence, an old wooden house from the eighteenth or early nineteenth century. The house had clearly seen better days.

The amazing thing was that it still stood. It was charming, with fretted wooden ceilings and walls painted with rococo designs darkened by time and smoke. Behind a curtain, food was being prepared in the kitchen while my friend and I were shown into a small sitting room where the *sheikh*, an old man with big eyeglasses, wearing a green robe tossed carelessly over his shoulders, was receiving visitors. We presented him with some fresh quinces and a box of *lokum*. Though he was severely crippled and only moved with difficulty, the *sheikh* welcomed us hospitably. Tea was served and cigarettes passed around. Other men came in one by one. It emerged that one of them was a policeman and another a schoolteacher, while another was a maritime engineer.

After several cigarettes and a few glasses of tea, it was announced that the time had come to move upstairs to the *sema* room. We made our way up a double staircase that had once been very grand to a broad landing off which the *sema* room opened. Along one side of it a spacious alcove rose to windows overlooking gardens which were a tangle of old roses, wisteria and oleander. The scent of night-blooming jasmine entered the room more and more powerfully as the evening progressed.

Once we were assembled – a dozen or so men in all – we were invited to sit on the floor at two round tables covered with table cloths which we spread over our laps in lieu of napkins. The women of the house, who were otherwise invisible that evening, brought food up from downstairs in big battered pots, and the *sheikh* himself dished it out. I wish I could praise the food, but it was very ordinary. A stew with lumps of mutton in it followed bread and a rather tasteless lentil soup. Then came pudding and tea.

After supper while *namaz* was performed, I sat on the sidelines. I don't call myself a Muslim. Years ago I would have joined in, but these days it would seem insincere to me. In a world where one could subscribe to all religions, I would gladly pray my heterodox prayers in any temple, mosque or church; but from what I can see, our world gets further and further from the ecumenical ideal rather than closer to it.

Afterwards I did join the *zikr* line, feeling that masculine solidarity which in my view is one of Islam's chief appeals. The long line of us stood and chanted *La ilaha, ill'Allah, Hu*. The old *sheikh* sat in his chair on the platform and led the chanting, setting the rhythm on a round hand-drum. Two of the young men chanted perhaps a bit too vigorously, and some of the veteran dervishes stepped in to steady them and lead them aside till their heads cleared. It was beautiful to hear the rhythm of the chant rise and fall, then rise again to an emotional crescendo toward the end, which was where the *sheikh* called a halt.

We sat down to relax, drink tea and chat amongst ourselves. Along with the others, I kissed the *sheikh*'s hand as we prepared to leave, but my friend did not do this, telling me afterwards that veneration shown in that manner to an individual was un-Islamic. There is no God but God. I could see his point, but to me the culture of the dervishes, the veneration of the tombs of saints and the rest of it, is of a piece with a system of belief – or superstition if you will – that I would call pre-Islamic, just as the veneration of holy wells in Ireland is pre-Christian. All this jumble of impulses, everything that flies below the radar of orthodoxy, says something about what it means to be human, vulnerable, in need of reassurance.

Outside the mosque complex we said goodnight, co-conspirators from a quiet room of sanctity who found ourselves thrust into the secular world again, heading our several ways out into the city. It was midnight, and I made my way downhill through the cobbled streets to Tophane, where I hailed a cab. Soon we were swept into the stream of cars heading north on the coast road up through Beşiktaş, through Ortaköy, and up to my room in Arnavutköy.

It's true I had found nothing remarkable about the dervishes in whose company I had spent the evening, and I know I sound like a food snob and an ingrate for criticising the supper we were served. Food nourishes the spirit, and mediocre food makes one feel glum, just as inspired food elates. Why, then, did I feel so light, so exhilarated, glowing I would almost say, as I rode home that night and then climbed the stairs to my little room?

'My opium hasn't kicked in yet'

Picture the Turks as they came riding out of Central Asia centuries ago on their manœuvrable little steppe ponies, their caravans accompanied not only by flocks of sheep and goats, but by wild-haired shamans with their herbal cures and fire ceremonies influenced by contact with the Zoroastrians of Persia as well as the varied sects of heterodox Christianity whom they would have encountered in the lands through which they travelled. These holy men were natural allies of the warriors, and in the early days when the Turks fought as mercenaries in Asia Minor, the *Kızılbaş* dervishes no doubt got them worked up for battle through chanting and coordinated breathing practices not too different from the ones I had just participated in.

It is clear that the dervishes put their stamp on what the Turks made of Muhammad's revealed religion. If you read the autobiographical book *Yol* by the popular satirical writer Aziz Nesin, who grew up in pre-independence Istanbul, you find that he was educated by a dervish, a man so ragged and poor that even the few pennies that Aziz's working-class family could afford to pay him were welcome. Dervish life once pervaded the entire fabric of life in Istanbul. There were dervish orders for every sort and condition of men.

Working men favoured the lodges of the Helveti, with their rough-and-ready camaraderie. The more refined and educated layers of society, people with a taste for music and poetry, gravitated toward the assemblies of the Mevlevi, the so-called Whirling Dervishes, where the poetry of Rumi was chanted, where exquisite music was played on the *ney* and *kemence* and *tambur*, and the dervishes did their ritualistic turning or whirling. At the Galata Mevlevihanesi on the last Sunday of every month you can observe, for a fee, a fly-in-amber version of their *sema* and see them turn: a dozen or so young men – and sometimes women now – moving in a stately circular motion over the parquet floors of the hall. The dervishes wear soft kidskin slippers, long white surplices and the Mevlevi order's tall felt hat, an untasselled camel-coloured fez. But dervish dancing is an inner practice, and a false note is struck, I feel, when an audience watches.

A different kind of ecstasy was the meat and drink of the Rafai, called the Howling Dervishes. These were the lads who would work themselves into 'a dance, an agony of trance', then run skewers through their cheeks or flagellate themselves with scourges. I have seen them in action in their *tekkes* in western Iran where, impervious to pain, like firewalkers in the Tibetan Buddhist tradition, they appeared, in the firelight, to be running the points of swords through the soft flesh of their arms, with no bleeding. If what people say can be believed, the most unorthodox dervishes of all were the Kalenders whom we have seen through the eyes of Orhan Pamuk in *My Name is*

Red, who lived a rootless, tramplike life and went in for hashish and buggery. Even today you will occasionally hear someone described as *kalender gibi*, 'like a Kalender dervish', i.e. unconventional, bohemian, not quite respectable.

Alcohol is forbidden to Muslims, and as a result of this prohibition, drugs such as opium and hashish have played the role that wine and spirits did and do in Christian countries. The street that runs in front of the Süleymaniye Mosque used to be called Tiryaki Çarşısı, the market of the addicts, because the cafés that used to do business here served opium as well as tea and coffee to their clientele. One of my favourite old-fashioned expressions in Turkish is *afyonum patlamadı*, 'my opium hasn't kicked in yet'. It is used to mean something like 'sorry, I'm not quite up to speed'.

The more innocent interpretation, since *afyon* means poppy as well as opium, is 'my flower hasn't opened yet'. Another interpretation, which as an old hippy I prefer, is that the expression comes from something opium addicts would do during the holy month of Ramadan. Because they were obliged to fast during the day, meaning they could neither eat, drink nor smoke once it became light enough to distinguish a black thread from a white, they would make up a pill of opium coated with something that would take several hours for the stomach's digestive juices to wear away. When morning came, they would be in the position of being both religiously observant and high at the same time.

27

The Lost World of the Pashas

TWO FAVOURITE OLD POSTCARDS, both reproduced from photos taken around 1910, present different aspects of the Ottoman city; one depicts street life and the other gives us a glimpse of the world of the elite. Both project something indefinable about Istanbul's vanished past that will always be inaccessible except through the imagination. In the first of the two a group of rough old Turks sit in a tea shop, a familiar postcard genre. Seated on those low, rush-bottomed stools still used in simple tea stalls, on a pavement of irregular flagstones, nine men enjoy the pleasures of the *nargile* while drinking tiny cups of tea. Their outfits mark them as tribesmen: fellows from the country. Albanians, perhaps, with their plus-fours, long stockings, hand-woven shirts and scarves tied round their fezzes – or else they are Anatolian Turks or Laz from the Black Sea coast.

A man in the foreground looks directly into the camera with the same deep, black-shadowed eyes, dramatic moustache and sunken cheeks you still sometimes see in the face of a day-labourer newly arrived from the countryside, standing expectantly on a street corner hoping someone will hire him. Behind him the teahouse is a rough-boarded wooden construction of a type that used to be common in Istanbul. In the midst of this group sits a bearded imam wearing a great turban, with a walking stick propped against his leg. All these men, if one looks closely, are dressed in fabrics that put to shame today's machine-woven materials. One has draped over his shoulders the long-sleeved open coat that can be seen in Afghanistan even today. The imam's blouse is a striped silk rep. All the men wear slippers that turn up at the toes.

The other card is a sepia photograph of carriages assembled on the top of a high hill in Istanbul above Üsküdar, perhaps Çamlıca, where people go for the view and the cool evening air. Of the dozen carriages visible here, some are open, and in them one sees only men. In the foreground stands a phaeton, its curtains drawn, its driver dressed in livery, sitting on the box wearing a fez, smartly holding in his gloved hands the reins of two bays. I surmise that there are women inside the closed cab, carrying their atmosphere of sequestration with them even when they go out for a drive. You can see a carriage like this, its windows latticed, in the little carriage museum at Topkapı. The image of the carriages adumbrates Istanbul's atmosphere of imperial grandeur as it began to fall into decline. It is a vanished grandeur one glimpses sometimes when one sees in an antique shop curtains of plum velvet, stiff with thread of silver, or looks at an old miniature of Constantinople when it was still a city of gardens, and its gardens were filled with roses.

I thought of those carriages when I read Irfan Orga's heart-breaking memoir, *Portrait of a Turkish Family*. Orga was born into a rich and cultivated family whose house stood near the Sea of Marmara somewhere in old Stamboul. When the Ottoman Empire entered its final decline in the years leading up to the First World War, the fortunes of families like Orga's began to disintegrate. Money was worth nothing, and his father and uncle both went to war, where they died. His mother might wait half a day at the bakery and then still return home without a loaf. Every day, trains from Aleppo and the Balkans, from the eastern front where the Turks were being slaughtered by the Russians, shuttled the broken armies home to the capital. Red Crescent carriages were filled with the wounded and dying.

The ground buckled under tombstones. In cemeteries all over Istanbul, old gravestones, topped with marble turbans, wreathed with suras from the Qur'an and verses of Ottoman poetry written in Persian, were displaced as the bones of the ancients were shovelled aside to make space for the freshly dead. Sultan Mehmed V Reşad, who reigned from 1909–18, was still in place, but he seemed like a figure from a wax museum. Irfan Orga and his mother saw him one day:

> In the main street of Beşiktaş soldiers were marching and a band played military music, whilst the police were roughly keeping back the curious crowds from the royal route. We waited to

> see the Sultan, and the Cavalry came first, mounted on their high-stepping Arab horses. As far as I can remember, they wore blue jackets with brightly shining brass buttons, scarlet trousers and great tall kalpaks on their heads, with flowing white plumes. They pranced towards us, their uniforms making a splash of welcome colour in all that drab humanity and their spurs clinked and jingled and gleamed in the watery sun. A carriage came after the Cavalry, drawn by elegant, aristocratic horses and, dimly, from the windows we caught a glimpse of an old small man with a little white beard. He was in uniform, many medals marching across his breast. A great, loyal cry went up from the people, half of them in rags, a deep-throated, rumbling roar of welcome: '*padişahım çok yaşa*! [Long live my Sultan!]' they roared and then he was past us and other voices took up the refrain.

Six centuries of marches and conquests were reduced to the dirt on a waiter's cuffs. Formerly proud old families scavenged coal from the cobbled streets to light their meagre fires. Suddenly it was all gone, that Ottoman past – the clatter of musketry, the war ponies that had galloped unstoppably across borders, the bronze siege-cannon pounding Viennese stone. It was an apocalyptic time for the Turks who, without knowing it, awaited the coming of Atatürk, the 'grey wolf' who would bring a kind of deliverance from the past.

28

The Call to Prayer

THE CALL TO PRAYER wakes me as I lie in bed in the dark. First a nearby *muezzin* declares *Allah hu Ekbar*. The Arabic phrase, which the *muezzin* pronounces as if it were Turkish, is often translated as 'God is great', but the morphology of Arabic is not simple, and in fact the word *Akbar* is the comparative adjective from *kabir*, 'big' or 'great'. As the Libyan poet Khaled Mattawa puts it in a letter, 'the idea is that Allah is great(er) than all other presumed deities or creatures or beings'.

Other *muezzins* from other mosques take up the call, sometimes seeming to compete with one another's renditions, sometimes seeming to set up a dialogue. *Ash-hadu an la ilaha illa Allah*, 'I declare that there is no God but God', *Ash-hadu anna Muhammadan rasulu Allah*, 'I declare that Muhammad is Allah's messenger'. How many of these voices are live and how many recorded, I have no idea. But listening every dawn, I fancy I hear variations in the *muezzins* whose voices I have come to recognise.

Haya ala Assala, 'gather in prayer'. *Haya ala Alfalah*, 'gather in goodness'. There are places in the city that lie within hearing distance of so many mosques that the effect can become like a surreal assault of voices and the echoes of voices, the hard surfaces of stone and concrete and asphalt providing an echo chamber for all the tones and half-tones and quarter-tones of these Arabic phrases sung with Turkish intonations. I am inevitably sorry when the mélange of voices ends and the last echo drops away.

Then I try to make myself comfortable again under my bedclothes, even with the words fresh in my mind, picturing what would be happening if I were among those going to the mosque to pray. I would rise in the dark, find my clothes and pull them on, walk down the marble stairs and out into the darkened street through the snow. In the mosque courtyard I would make my way to the *şadırvan*, pull off my shoes and socks, roll up my sleeves and perform the ablutions: washing my feet and hands, letting water run down my forearms to the elbows, then washing my face and ears, and running my wet hands over my hair.

Pulling on my socks and shoes, I would stop at the mosque door to leave my shoes there and enter with the others. Inside I would line up shoulder to shoulder with the other men and perform *namaz*. Praying in a mosque gives one a great feeling of solidarity with other men. I can see how much one would value it if one lived in a traditional Muslim society and it was an inherent part of one's daily life, just as it can be comforting to pray in a church.

But I am far too much of a rebel and freethinker, too much given to humour and irony – in short, too Western and individualistic to accept orthodoxy and authority of any sort. I am drawn to mosques as an outsider and a lover of architecture. When I first came to Istanbul I used to sit in the Blue Mosque, in those precincts that are now roped off to exclude outsiders, prop my interlinear copy of the *Aeneid* on a Qur'an stand, and read there the story of Aeneas's wanderings. The world has changed, and I don't think I would try that now.

29

The Bosphorus

WE GO TO SULTANAHMET to explore the roots of Istanbul's Byzantine and early Ottoman history, to Nişantaşı for upscale shopping, to Istiklal Caddesi for the evening *passeggiata*, to Çukurcuma to look for antiques, to Ortaköy to stroll through the Sunday crafts market and play backgammon in a café, or to Tünel and Asmalımescit to spend a night on the town drinking *rakı* and eating *meze* and fish in a *meyhane*. Istanbul remains a city of neighbourhoods.

But the soul of the city, its poetic centre and the focus of many Istanbullus' nostalgia when they are away from home, hovers around the Bosphorus, that fabled strait that runs through the centre of the city and separates Europe from Asia. Over the centuries, first Byzantion, then Constantinople, and now Istanbul have been defined by their strategic location on this body of water that joins the Black Sea with the Sea of Marmara, which is in turn connected to the Aegean, and thence to the Mediterranean.

A little research tells us that around 5,600 BC the Mediterranean rose – perhaps in the wake of a massive earthquake – and forced a passage for its waters to flow into the Black Sea. Apparently there was already a river flowing in the channel, and this accounts for the presence of a counter-current at the bottom of the Bosphorus running in a different direction from its primary flow. In any case the currents flowing through the Boğaziçi, as it is known in Turkish, meaning 'inside the throat', are notorious for their treacherousness, and tales of shipwreck on its waters abound, particularly during a storm.

The length of the channel is about twenty miles, and it gets quite narrow and twisty in places. Navigation is difficult, since a 45-degree course alteration is required at one point near Bebek, made even more difficult by currents that can reach seven or eight knots at the point where the helmsman must turn the ship. At Yeniköy, about halfway up the Bosphorus, the course alteration is 80 degrees! Add to this that ships approaching from the opposite direction cannot be seen round the bend here. In addition to a heavy traffic of tankers and freighters between the Black Sea and the Marmara, ferries ply the waters between the European and Asian shores.

There is a certain romance about any city situated on a body of water, but the Bosphorus eclipses the relative domesticity of rivers like the Seine in Paris or the Thames in London. It is more like the mighty Mississippi pushing against the levees in New Orleans before it empties into the Gulf of Mexico. Being out on the Bosphorus one smells salt air and feels the sea breeze on one's face. Istanbul can seem noisy, crowded, polluted – even overwhelming, particularly in summer – and this is why one wants to get away from it all and out on the water. I like to take a ferry even when I have no place in particular to go. Turkish Maritime Lines operate an inexpensive cruise up the Bosphorus every day, leaving daily – the last time I checked – from Boğaz Hattı (Bosphorus dock) No 3 at Eminönü at 10.35 am. There are also private tours which cost more, but the one the city runs suits me fine.

Summer houses

In the shadow of the first Bosphorus suspension bridge, which spans the continents just north of Ortaköy, stands the palace of Beylerbeyi ('Lord of lords'), built by Sultan Abdülaziz in the early 1860s. Abdülaziz was a man of parts, a composer and someone with friends among the royal families of Europe at a time when, with the opening of the Suez Canal – largely financed by Istanbul's Camondo family, incidentally – the Mediterranean was more than ever open to European influences. He built the palace as a summer residence, a place to retreat from the stultifying airs of Topkapı, and also as a showplace to entertain European visitors. Built by the Armenian architects Agop and Sarkis Balyan, who undertook several Baroque projects for the royal family, it is just the kind of showy, over-the-top, Orientalised European mansion that the Ottomans favoured in the declining years of the empire. One of the most appealing features of the palace is its bathing pavilions built right down on the shore – one pavilion for women, one for men.

In Byzantine days only the occasional monastery or remote church punctuated the greenery of the natural landscape along what was then a placid waterway. But as the city grew in population and became more prosperous during the seventeenth and eighteenth centuries, it became fashionable for the wealthy and powerful to build *yalıs* (from a Greek word *yialos*, meaning the sea-shore), large wooden summer houses, along the shores of the Bosphorus. Their spacious, airy rooms and their access to breezes off the water made them places to escape the heat, noise and bustle of the city. Private boats brought friends to the houses of friends, and boats did business from village to village, *yalı* to *yalı*, selling fruit, vegetables and fish to the residents. Many of these mansions have been pulled down now in favour of concrete apartment blocks, but many still remain as remnants of a vanished way of life.

Yalıs have an architectural style that is at the same time distinct and hard to pin down. Their *cumbas*, those cantilevered upper stories that typify the traditional Turkish house, project here not over a street, but over the water. As in Venice, a berth or two for boats is usually tucked underneath at water level. There was a typical floor plan, the main floor having a large central salon called a *sofa*, with private rooms issuing off its corners. At the centre of many of these rooms a marble fountain played, providing water music to please the ear and cool the air. Almost all *yalıs* are wooden, with little attempt at permanence. It was all about pleasure and ease. The great and the good of Ottoman society tended to rise through the bureaucratic meritocracy we have observed earlier. They were not a hereditary aristocracy, and they built for the moment, not for the ages.

Wood was favoured for construction in Constantinople for several reasons. One, it was cheap. Anatolia was heavily forested. Secondly, a wooden house could be finished in a few months' time. As well, Istanbul is, like San Francisco – a city it resembles in many ways – situated on a fault line and vulnerable to earthquakes. Wood is flexible, unlike stone. And wood also absorbs dampness, making it the ideal material for a waterside house.

Yalı architecture has traditionally been fanciful, and receptive to influences from Europe. Some are reminiscent of Swiss chalets, some sport onion domes that look distinctly Byzantine or Russian. Balconies open to views of the Bosphorus, and Art Nouveau windows let in the watery light. Their fretted wooden ceilings are especially fetching, adorned with crystal and pastel-coloured Venetian chandeliers from Murano. Passengers in *caïques*, the private skiffs that plied the Bosphorus, would have looked up from the water into these rooms, each one a private world of cultivated luxury.

Their rooms were divided in the Ottoman fashion between *selamlık* public rooms, and *haremlik* private rooms for the family only. Even Greek Constantinopolitans arranged their houses like this. Gardens played an important role in the life lived in *yalıs*, and little enclosed bridges allowed ladies to visit their relatives and friends who lived nearby without exposing themselves to the eyes of strangers. The oldest *yalıs* were painted red, in a shade called Turkish rose, but many are now bare of paint, and the weathered wood makes them look all the more romantic. Others, with prosperous owners, have been spiffed up, repaired and freshly painted in the pastel colours of the Mediterranean.

In contrast to the Turkification of Istanbul that has taken place over the last seventy-five years, these buildings remind us of an older, multicultural city where Turks, Greeks, Armenians, Jews, European visitors and expats mingled freely. Kuzguncuk, on the Asian shore, home to a community of artists and intellectuals, retains some of that Ottoman spirit of harmony and mutual tolerance. Before the founding of Israel and the anti-foreigner riots of 1955, Kuzguncuk had a large Jewish population. Most but by no means all of Istanbul's Jews have moved away now, many to Israel. Last year I was a guest at a bar mitzvah in Kuzguncuk. The sister synagogues of Bet Yaakov and Bet Nissim, with reduced congregations, have joined forces.

After the ceremony and the usual enormous meal, we walked down the street to the Greek church of Ayios Yorgios, Saint George, to look at the icons. As there was at one time no mosque in the centre of town, about fifty or sixty years ago the Armenian church of Surp Krikor Lusavoriç, St Gregory the Illuminator, donated part of their courtyard to make space for a mosque, and even contributed funds to help with construction.

Seafood from the Bosphorus

Down by the water next door to the ferry station an old and popular *meyhane*, Ismet Baba, is a good place to have a drink and eat *meze* and fish. I order the *dilbalığı*, or sole, when it is on the menu. Upstream from Kuzguncuk and Beylerbeyi is Çengelköy, another very pleasant waterside town. Its Çınaraltı Aile Çay Bahçesi, 'family tea garden under the plane trees', with its charming little village mosque and the ancient plane trees from which it takes its name, is one of the best places in Istanbul, or anywhere else in the world for that matter, to take one's *keyif.* On Sunday mornings it fills up with people reading the newspapers out under the *çınars*, drinking tea and breakfasting on pastries from the nearby *pastane*. During the winter months a warm stove keeps the place toasty inside.

THESE WATERS have always teemed with fish, and from the city's earliest days, Greek fishing villages have dotted its shores. Istanbullus love fish, and it is an essential and much-valued part of the city's cuisine. Fishing boats go as far north as the Black Sea and work their way down to the Sea of Marmara as well. There is good fishing the length of the Bosphorus itself. Fish have their seasons, and a great deal of local knowledge goes into deciding what to order at any particular time of year.

Palamut, or bonito, swim from the Black Sea down through the Bosphorus in the spring, but on their southern migration they run too deep to be caught. In the autumn, when the *palamut* return, they for some reason swim closer to the surface and are more fishable. Among fish lovers, the moment they return creates great excitement, almost like the moment in November when in Paris you see signs in wine-shop windows announcing, *Le nouveau Beaujolais est arrivé. Palamut* is a strong-tasting fish, oily like *uskumru* or mackerel, and for this reason both these fish are often filleted and baked with onion and tomato sauce. Mackerel are also made into *lakerda*, a pickled fish *meze*.

The scrumptious *barbunya*, or red mullet, come in season in spring and early summer. A small fish, highly prized, these are best pan-fried. You can see from the shape of the word that it is Greek in origin, as is also the case with *karides*, shrimp, which are readily available, and *ahtapot*, or octopus. *Hamsi*, a kind of anchovy, is delicious. The Bosphorus is full of them, and those fishermen you see on the bridges and along the quays, fishing with a many-hooked line carried down by a sinker attached to the end, are often after anchovies. Fishermen fill a bucket with their catch and sell them to a restaurant or take them home, bread them and fry them whole. You squeeze lemon juice on them and crunch them up, tiny bones and all.

Levrek, or sea bass, is farmed, so it is good to be on the lookout on menus for *deniz levreği* – *deniz* means sea – which tells you the fish are wild. (See chapter five for why the *k* changes to a *ğ* and adds a final *i* when linked to the previous word.) In fact, when you see *deniz* in front of any word for fish, that is a good sign. Order it. Bluefish are good in Turkey. When large, they are called *lüfer* and when very small they are *defne yaprağı*, 'bay leaf'. As the fish grows to a size where it will fit on a small plate, it becomes a *çinekop*. They are very popular at this size, but can be bony. Other good sea-going fish are the *kalkan*, turbot, and the *kılıç* or swordfish. *Kılıç* means sword.

As for where to eat fish, seafood restaurants can be shockingly expensive. Often the fish is brought to your table before being cooked, for you to examine for freshness; or your waiter leads you to the fish tank or ice chest. A full evening at one of the upmarket restaurants along the shores of the Bosphorus, with *meze*, *rakı*, *börek*, a fish course and all the trimmings, can go on for hours and involve a major assault on the pocketbook. But there are smaller places that serve very good, fresh fish at more reasonable prices. I like Adem Baba in Arnavutköy on the European side of the Bosphorus, a no-frills place that began by serving fish out of boat along the shore. The kitchen at Adem Baba has a way with *kalamar*, and the *balık köftesi*, fish balls, usually prepared with *palamut*, make a great starter. Their fish kebabs are tasty, and they are famous for the fish soup they serve on Sunday nights. No alcohol is served here. In addition to Adem Baba, Arnavutköy is famous for its *köfteci*, Ali Baba, also cheap, no-frills and always good.

Bosphorus villages

Arnavutköy, where I used to stay back in the nineties, traditionally had a large Jewish population, but most moved away after a large fire swept through the town in the late 1870s. Greeks, Armenians and other nationalities were also well represented here. The town's name means Albanian Village. It is pleasant to hear the Sunday bells and to stroll along the narrow streets lined with old wooden houses with grape arbours, and to watch the parade along the quay, where joggers trot by and people walk their trophy dogs. There is not just one Greek church here, but two, and still enough Greeks in the town to make Sunday mass possible in one of their churches. Just before the First World War the census revealed a population of 493 Turks and Muslims and 5,973 Greeks.

The next ferry stop up the coast from Arnavutköy is Bebek, a little sleeker than its neighbour to the south but equally attractive despite the presence of a McDonald's and other recent encrustations. Bebek's setting at the foot of green hills forested with cypresses and its beautiful little mosque down near the harbour make it one of the most picturesque waterside villages along the Bosphorus. Just south of the town along the shore stands a remarkable building I have mentioned earlier – the Egyptian Consulate, once the Khedive's *yalı*, built in an eclectic Art Nouveau style.

Uphill from Bebek stands Boğaziçi Üniversitesi, the University of the Bosphorus, 'the Harvard of Turkey'. It numbers among its graduates Tansu Penbe Çiller, Turkey's first woman Prime Minister, Orhan Pamuk, and his brother Şevket Pamuk, an economist and historian who is on the faculty. John Freely, author of the classic guidebook, *Strolling through Istanbul*, taught physics here for many years. Founded in 1863, the University, originally called Robert College, has deep roots in modern Turkish history. Its founder, Cyrus Hamlin, was an American missionary who was first attracted to Turkey during the Crimean War as a follower of Florence Nightingale and worked in her hospital for soldiers, where he baked bread and lent a hand in the laundry.

Since as a visitor one will have difficulty knowing exactly which boats are going where, it's good to be flexible. All these waterside villages are appealing in one way or another. I like to stop at Kanlıca on the Asian side. Kanlıca is renowned for its very thick yoghurt, made of sheep's milk mixed with cow's milk. You sprinkle powdered sugar on top of it. In the little square off the ferry landing is İskenderpaşa Mosque, one of Sinan's minor commissions. Before you reach Kanlıca on the way up from Anadoluhisarı, you will see the oldest *yalı* on the Bosporus – the Köprülü Amcazade Hüseyin Paşa Yalısı (the Köprülü Yalı).

Every time I come to Istanbul, I am amazed to find this *yalı* still standing, as it has been derelict for as long as I can remember, perennially looking as if tomorrow, or perhaps just later today, it would fall into the Bosphorus and its mossy planks wash down into the Sea of Marmara. A distinctive wooden block right on the shore, it has low windows just above water line. It was built by Hüseyin Paşa, Grand Vizier under Sultan Mustafa II. In this very *yalı* in 1699 the Treaty of Karlowitz was signed, formalising the Ottoman Empire's loss of territory in Austria, Poland and Russia, leading to Ottoman retrenchment and the period of prosperity and stability in the downsized empire that is described in my chapter on Ahmed III. Somehow it is fitting that this treaty was signed in the Köprülü Yalı, because no more romantic and forlorn place, emblematic of Ottoman decline, could be imagined.

A good way to see the Hıdiv Kasrı, an altogether amazing Art Nouveau palace built by the hereditary viceroy of Egypt, Abbas Hilmi II, in 1900, is to take a taxi up the hill from Kanlıca – or walk up, if you are fit enough. I certainly am not. The palace has been renovated and operates as a luxury hotel. Its dining room is a great spot for a romantic Sunday breakfast.

Venturing further up the Bosphorus on the Asian side, one reaches Beykoz, with an eighteenth-century fountain gracing the town square. The historical and the contemporary mix here, as sellers from the open-air market wash the dirt off vegetables underneath the fountain's sublime arches. Still further north, one eventually reaches Sariyer, home of the Sadberk Hanım Museum. Whether you like museums or not – and I do like them – this is a place that really should be seen. It consists essentially of two *yalıs*, one filled with objects from classical antiquity, one with objects and displays from the Ottoman Empire – choice embroidery, illuminated Qur'ans, costumes, pen sets, rare calligraphy. Not many of us have friends who live in *yalıs*, so a visit here may be our one chance of seeing one of these fabled mansions on the inside.

Moonlight on the Bosphorus

In the nineteenth century, when everyone must have realised that the Ottoman Empire was living on borrowed time – and borrowed money – poetic and musical culture enjoyed a last flowering. At least three Ottoman sultans were musicians and composers. Selim III (1761–1808), who would be deposed by the Janissaries because they opposed his attempts to westernise and modernise the empire, and was then assassinated in the Harem by the Chief Black Eunuch, is considered to be the most talented of these royal musicians. He is credited with creating a number of *makams* or scales; he was a Mevlevi and participated in *semas* at the *Mevlevihanesi* in Tünel with the dervish poet Şeyh Galip. Abdülaziz (1830–1876) not only wrote music, he also painted and wrote poetry. And the last of the line, Vahdettin (1861–1926) has left behind haunting compositions that hint at wind-swept parade grounds, cracked masonry and huge ballrooms whose gilded furniture stands sheathed in dust covers.

The Bosphorus is pure magic on moonlit nights, when urban sprawl and recent concrete mistakes are hidden by darkness. What I would give to go back to the end of the nineteenth century to experience a *mehtab*, or moonlight, evening, when water-borne processions formed, made up of hundreds of assembled boats – large and small, elegant and plain, from the humblest dory draped with drying nets reeking of fish, to the choicest mahogany *caïque* kitted out with *baldacchinos* woven of silk and cloth of gold under which veiled and chaperoned ladies ate sweetmeats and drank sherbet while their gentlemen friends recited elaborate, allusive *divan* poetry, its stanzas rich with obscure metaphor and latticed with levels of meaning.

The procession would be headed up by a boat fitted out with a small stage where musicians played. The cavalcade of boats paused at *yalıs* along the way to serenade those inside with *makams* wrung from the *ney*, that wooden flute favoured by the dervishes. The melodies are heart-piercing, with tunes plucked from the stringed *saz* and that long-necked fretted lute called a *tambur* and bowed on the little violin-like *kemence*, whose strains resonate with longing.

30

Foreigners, Expats and Blow-ins

BYZANTIUM, and later the Ottoman Empire, had complex – and sometimes surprising – relations with outsiders. The most vivid accounts we have of medieval Byzantium were written by Liudprand, Bishop of Cremona, who was dispatched on a diplomatic mission to Constantinople by Otto the Great, the Holy Roman Emperor, in the tenth century. Arriving by ship from Venice, he was granted an audience by Constantine Porphyrogenitus, where the Bishop beheld something wondrous and strange:

> Before the throne of the Emperor there rose a tree of gilded bronze, its branches full of birds fashioned of the same material, all singing different songs according to their kind. The throne itself was so contrived that at one moment it stood low on the ground and the next moment it would suddenly be raised high in the air. It was of immense size, made of either wood or bronze... and guarded by gilded lions who beat the ground with their tails and emitted dreadful roars...

The Byzantines liked nothing better than awing visitors from the provinces with the majesty of their royal court. But Liudprand's surprises did not end with the miraculous mechanical throne and the singing birds – which inspired Yeats's lines about being 'set upon a golden bough to sing / To lords and ladies of Byzantium / Of what is past, or passing, or to come'. As he raised his head after making his obeisances, 'lo! He whom I had seen only a moment before on a throne scarcely elevated from the ground was now clad in different robes and sitting on a level with the roof. How this was achieved I cannot tell...'

Had this been the Bishop of Cremona's only visit to the Queen of Cities, he would have cherished fond memories of the place. But as it happened, he was sent there some twenty-five years later on another mission. Byzantine emperors came in all shapes, sizes, and degrees of education and refinement. On his first mission to Constantinople Liudprand had been received, as we have seen, by the cultivated and urbane Constantine Porphyrogenitus, but by the time he returned, Constantine had died and the throne was occupied by a different sort of man altogether, the Emperor Nicephorus Phocas:

> He is a monstrosity of a man, a dwarf, with a broad, flat head and tiny eyes like a mole; disfigured by a short, thick, grizzled beard; disgraced by a neck scarcely an inch long; piglike by reason of the big close bristles on his head; in colour an Ethiopian. As the poet says, 'you would not like to meet him in the dark'. A big belly, a small posterior ... small legs ... dressed in a robe made of fine linen but old, foul-smelling and discoloured by age ...

Where Constantine had been happy to receive the Italian emissary, wine him and dine him, discuss diplomatic issues with him and let him go on his way, with Nicephorus things were quite different. This was the man, after all, under whose generalship the Byzantines had retaken Candia in Crete from the Saracens, and in the aftermath, as John Julius Norwich tells us: 'women, old and young, were raped, murdered and thrown aside; children, even babies at the breast, were strangled or impaled on lances.'

Upon arriving in Constantinople on his second mission, Liudprand and his party were made to stand for hours holding the reins of their horses in a heavy rain before being admitted to the city. Once inside, they were not even allowed to ride their mounts, but were forced to proceed on foot to their lodgings in what the Bishop described as a 'loathsome, waterless and draughty stone house'. The food, what little there was of it, was no better, 'washed down with oil after the manner of drunkards and moistened also with an exceedingly bad fish liquor.' It sounds perfectly disgusting. A few days into his stay, Liudprand had a conversation with the Patriarch, a eunuch, who while insulting the Pope of Rome, 'that fatuous blockhead', informed his visitor that the inhabitants of Rome were 'nothing but vile slaves, fishermen, confectioners, poulterers, bastards, plebeians and underlings'.

Liudprand's trip back to Italy turned out to be equally as unfortunate as his stay in Constantinople had been. Just to get to the place whence his ship was to sail took the Bishop 'forty-nine days of ass-riding, walking, horse-riding, fasting, thirsting, sighing, weeping and groaning'. Then his departure was delayed by a lack of favourable winds, and when he arrived in Patras his ship's crew deserted, he was received in a churlish manner by his host, a eunuch bishop, and he experienced no less than three earthquakes whilst on the island of Corfu, where thieves robbed him of his possessions. 'Poor Liudprand', Lord Norwich writes, 'he could not have known that his account of his journey would still be read a thousand years after his death, and found to be as fresh, funny and revealing as on the day it was written. A pity: it would have cheered him up.'

English ladies in Pera

England was already a trading partner with the Ottomans around the time Henry VIII dissolved the Roman Catholic monasteries. The Turks needed every scrap of metal they could get their hands on to manufacture armaments. Their navy had been decimated in the disastrous battle of Lepanto, and they were engaged in equally destructive wars against Venice and Persia. As we have seen, Queen Elizabeth I carried on a correspondence with Mehmed III and his Venetian mother Safiye. The English cheerfully melted down religious metalwork they had seized from wealthy monasteries and shipped it off to Constantinople, where the Turks put it to use in their cannon factories at Tophane making war *matériel*. Rood screens were reincarnated as cannon balls.

As the centuries passed and the British Empire gradually eclipsed the Ottoman imperium in the Mediterranean world, Britain's influence increased. Shaped by an educational system based on classical languages and culture, representatives of the Foreign Office, with their public school backgrounds, searched out the remains of that heritage, saw it deteriorating and began collecting – some would say stealing – antiquities. Today one can see fragments of the Golden Gate, the ceremonial entrance into the city through the ancient walls of Byzantium, in the Ashmolean Museum in Oxford. Lord Elgin, British Ambassador around the turn of the nineteenth century, famously brought sculpture from the frieze of the Parthenon back to London, where today it resides in the British Museum. And as early as the 1880s the Alexandrian Greek poet C.P. Cavafy wrote an essay called 'Return the Elgin Marbles'.

There have been some acute observers among Western visitors to the great city, and two of the most notable have been women. None was more acute or more amusing than Lady Mary Wortley Montague, who was active in London society during the time of George I. Her wit and liveliness led her to become friends with Alexander Pope and John Gay, author of *The Beggar's Opera*. When her husband was assigned to the post of Ambassador to Constantinople in 1716, she accompanied him, and during their two-year stay there she wrote her *Turkish Embassy Letters*, an invaluable glimpse into refined Constantinopolitan life in the eighteenth century. Upper class Ottoman women made a practice of visiting the hamam once every week or so, taking their servants and children, and packing elaborately prepared food and drink with them. These visits were still part of Ottoman life into the twentieth century, for they are fondly described by Irfan Orga in *Portrait of a Turkish Family*. Here is what Lady Mary has to say about them in her day:

> The first sofas were covered with cushions and rich carpets, on which sat the ladies and on the second their slaves behind them but without any distinction of rank by their dress, all being in the state of nature, that is in plain English stark naked without any beauty or defect concealed. Yet there was not the least wanton smile or immodest gesture among them... so many fine women naked, in different postures, some in conversation, some working [doing their needlework], others drinking coffee or sherbet, while their slaves (generally pretty girls of seventeen or eighteen) were employed in braiding their hair in several pretty fancies. In short it is the women's coffee-house...

Miss Julia Pardoe, who went to Constantinople with her father, a British army officer, was an observer of the city two decades or so after Lady Mary Wortley Montague's time there, during the sultanate of Mahmud II. She wrote a series of popular books catering to the British reading public's taste for glimpses of the exotic Levant. Her books carried titles like *The City of the Sultan*, *The Romance of the Harem*, and *The Beauties of the Bosphorus*, which must have been great lending-library favourites.

Miss Pardoe witnessed the resurgence of Greek or Phanariot

culture upon its return after the brutal repression Mahmud II carried out as a reaction to this minority's perceived support for the Greek War of Independence in 1821. Theirs was a *nouveau riche* culture *par excellence*. Viewing the costumes on display at a Phanariot ball in Pera, Miss Pardoe's English taste was severely censorious: 'such bright blues, deep pinks and glowing scarlets I never saw collected together; and this glaring taste extends even to their jewellery which they mix in the most extraordinary manner.' She was more approving of the taste expressed by Mahmud II's sister, Esma Sultan, in her palace at Ortaköy on the Bosphorus: 'the sleeping chamber, hung with crimson and blue satin and scattered over with perfumes and objects of taste had an air of comfort and inhabitation almost English.' What could be nicer!

LORD BYRON, who also visited Constantinople in the early nineteenth century, saw a different side of the city from the ones frequented by Lady Mary and Miss Pardoe. Byron wrote in a letter to a friend:

> I see not much difference between ourselves & the Turks, save that we have foreskins and they none, that they have long dresses and we short, and that we talk much and they little. – In England the vices are whoring and drinking, in Turkey, sodomy and smoking, we prefer a girl and bottle, they a pipe and pathic. They are sensible people... I can swear in Turkish, but except for one terrible oath, and 'pimp' and 'bread' and 'water' I have no great vocabulary in that language.

In case you haven't guessed, the OED defines 'pathic' as 'a man or boy on whom sodomy is practised; a catamite'.

Pierre Loti

The name inevitably conjured up by any mention of expats and travellers to Istanbul is Pierre Loti (1850–1923), a Frenchman who was born with the name Julien Marie Viaud, was a captain in the French navy, and went on to become a world traveller, best-selling author of fiction and memoirs, and one of the most celebrated literary figures of his day. His work represents the epitome of literary Orientalism.

His portrait was painted by Henri Rousseau, and his book, *Les Fleurs d'Ennui*, 'The Flowers of Boredom', playing on the title of Baudelaire's poetic masterpiece, *Les Fleurs du Mal*, reflects the European mood of decadence in the late nineteenth century. Loti's explanation of his adopted surname was that it was given him by the residents of Tahiti, after a kind of Polynesian flower. A master of self-invention, myth-making and colourful lies, he was fond of referring to himself in the third person, as when, upon the day he was accepted into the Academie Française, he proudly declared '*Loti ne sais pas lire*', 'Loti doesn't know how to read'.

Loti travelled all over the world during the French colonial era and wrote about most of the places he visited. He happily if superficially adopted Turkish culture in a way summed up by his statement in his best-known novel, *Aziyadé*, where at one point he describes himself in his house in Constantinople, 'seated by a cheerful blaze, with a fur coat around me and my feet on a thick Turkish rug. Just for fun I am pretending to be a dervish'. Like no other writer, he brings to life the cosmopolitan mélange of Constantinople in the mid-nineteenth century. Of a boat trip from Salonica to the capital he wrote that 'the voyage took three days... . The passengers consisted of one fair Greek, two comely Jewesses, a German, an American missionary and his wife, and a dervish.' And Pierre Loti's characterisation of one of his companions in *Aziyadé*, 'a Turk for convenience, a Jew by religion, and a Spaniard by virtue of his forefathers,' nicely sums up the situation of many of Constantinople's Sephardim. Perhaps no other writer has more winningly evoked the gloomy poetry of the ancient city. Even today, Istanbul's cemeteries, like Karacaahmet in Üsküdar and the ones near the fortress in Rumelihisarı and Loti's favourite, the cemetery that climbs the hill in Eyüp, retain the gloomy yet appealing beauty that Loti saw in them:

> The cemetery paths, which are paved with stone or marble, lie deep in shadow and are for the most part sunk. On either side stand marble buildings of great age, their yet unsullied whiteness in striking contrast to the black tones of the cypresses. Hundreds of gilded tombs with borders of flowers encroach upon these gloomy paths; they are the sepulchres of the great, of the pashas of olden days...

Loti's favourite word for Constantinople is 'gloomy', a word that seems appropriate for Sultan Abdülhamid II, who was powerless to check the inevitable Ottoman decline. The thinnest of lines runs between memoir and fiction in Loti's work – perhaps one reason why Marcel Proust admired his writing – and it is hard to know whether the following passage from *Aziyadé* was fictional or based on personal observation:

> I remember the day when the new Sultan went in great pomp to take possession of the imperial palace. I was one of the first to catch sight of him as he emerged from the old seraglio, the gloomy retreat where all the heirs to the Turkish throne are lodged. Immense *caïques* of state had come for him, and my own *caïque* actually grazed that of the prince.
>
> These few days of power have already aged the Sultan. He has lost his former look of youth and spirit... . He was pale and thin, with a melancholy, abstracted air, and there were dark rings round his great black eyes. His face bore the stamp of breeding and intelligence.

The Loti character in *Aziyadé* was privy to all aspects of Constantinopolitan life, from the palace to 'an underground den on the outskirts of the city, where young boys of Asiatic race, dressed as nautch girls, performed unseemly dances to an audience composed of all the sweepings of the Ottoman jails... . It was dawn when we returned home.'

Like Hemingway, Pierre Loti had a knack for being in the right place at the right time for the writing he wanted to do. He was also fortunate in being able to marry into money, which allowed him to furnish a house in his hometown of Rochefort where he created an 'Oriental room'. This is now the Pierre Loti Museum. A reproduction of an old postcard widely available in Istanbul shows Loti in full Ottoman drag in this room. He is dressed as something like a Bedouin tribesman, bandoliers strapped across his chest, seated on a *divan* covered with Turkish rugs, smoking a *nargile* and surrounded by all sorts of Middle Eastern bric-a-brac and old rifles with inlaid stocks, his old-fashioned moustache bristling, very pleased with himself.

Pierre Loti's name is still well-known in Istanbul, where the Pierre Hotel may be found on Piyer Loti Caddesi in Sultanahmet. There is even a Lycée Pierre Loti in Beyoğlu. But the quintessential spot commemorating this romantic, half-comical man is the Pierre Loti Café on the heights above Eyüp, the holy suburb where the 'little Circassian slave-girl called Aziyadé' in the novel by the same name slipped out of the harem where she lived and carried out her assignations with the fictional character called Loti. The café has a wonderful panoramic view of the city, and one can walk back down into Eyüp through the cemetery that Loti celebrated.

Russian refugees

Constantinople was an adventuresome destination for young Englishmen on the Grand Tour, but others came here not for pleasure but out of necessity. The city's location between the Black Sea and the Mediterranean positioned it along the escape route for White Russians fleeing the 1917 revolution. Two characters in Elif Şafak's novel *Bit Palas* [*The Flea Palace*], General Pavel Pavlovich Antipov and his wife Agripina, are among these aristocratic refugees.

Once they had sold their jewellery, decorations and other accoutrements for less than they had hoped they would fetch, Şafak writes in this novel, 'thousands of soldiers of all ranks from the Czar's army had long been scattered into the least expected and most excruciating jobs at hotels, concert halls, cabarets, gambling houses, restaurants, bars, café chantants, movie theatres, beaches, nightclubs and streets. They washed dishes and carried trays in restaurants, worked as croupiers in gambling houses jam-packed with lies, peddled dolls at street corners, and provided piano accompaniment to cabaret dancers in boisterous entertainment halls.'

A ragged remnant of General Baron Pyotr Wrangel's army escaped from the Crimea in November, 1920, just ahead of the victorious Bolsheviks. 150,000 of them, officers and their families, boarded fifty-six ships and, with British help, landed in Constantinople. Wrangel's words to his troops were stirring: 'we are going into exile – not as beggars, but with our heads held high.' Some of these once-proud refugees found shelter under upturned boats alongside the Bosphorus, others slept on straw in the stables of the Dolmabahçe Palace.

There is little trace of these refugees nowadays. Rajans Restaurant in Yeniçarşı Sokak serves Russian food, but its variety of vodkas is more notable than its cuisine. Most visitors never see them, but the green, onion domes of rooftop Russian churches such as St Andrei, St Ilya and St Panteleimon in Karaköy offer startling little glimpses of the old country among the soot-begrimed streets of the quarter, a rather dismal patch of the city that descends to the Golden Horn, where forlorn-looking Ukrainian ships rust into the waters of the harbour. These churches, topped with their distinctive Orthodox crosses, were built to house Russian clergymen and give hospitality to pilgrims on their way to Mount Athos. Their reproductions of gold-encrusted icons, set against the vividly coloured walls of these sanctuaries, survive as pockets of old Constantinople within the Turkish city.

Today these refuges have been reincarnated as cheap hostels for those who cannot afford other accommodation, and their halls are redolent of boiled cabbage and sad lives. Paint peels from the ceiling of a dome from which hangs a crystal chandelier. Elsewhere a heavy bronze bell hangs, seldom rung. A mere handful of elderly communicants intone the responses and cough as an ancient priest reads the service in Russian. A proud and handsome Czar Nicholas II looks down impassively from his portrait on a wall.

The Istanbul avant-garde

Istanbul has provided a haven not only for political refugees but for artistic and literary exiles. Édouard Roditi is a name that comes up again and again in accounts of artistic and bohemian Istanbul in the mid-twentieth century and is the subject of a fascinating monograph by Clifford Endres, a professor at Kadir Has University, called 'Édouard Roditi and the Istanbul Avant-Garde'. Roditi was a true literary cosmopolitan. He was born in Paris in 1910 into a circle of wealthy Jewish patrons of the arts with ties to Constantinople, and distant cousins to the Camondos.

According to Endres, 'Édouard's paternal grandmother had him read the Greek newspapers to her and taught him Ladino, the archaic Spanish of the Istanbul Sephardim...' He was something of a prodigy, recognised for his talent early on by T.S. Eliot, and enlisted, along with Samuel Beckett, to translate Joyce into French. He published in the magazine *Transition*, the *entre deux guerres* house organ of the avant-garde, then when the Second World War broke out, he moved to New York, where he worked for the Voice of America and translated French poetry into English.

After the war Roditi made his way to Istanbul, where he turned up among the avant-garde circle associated with the Narmanlı Han, and co-translated Yashar Kemal's novel, *Mehmed, My Hawk*, into English along with his cousin, Thilda Serrero, who was married to Yashar Kemal. Roditi's family had long-standing connections with Istanbul, as he wrote to the American Beat poet Gregory Corso years later, describing himself as being 'of Italian and Greek Jewish origin, with part of my family coming from... the former Venetian concession in Istanbul' – in other words Galata. The Roditis, at least according to Édouard, had literary connections early on, for as Clifford Endres writes, 'it was said that one of the first printing presses of the Ottoman Empire, in sixteenth-century Smyrna, bore the Roditi name'. Roditi's father worked for the Compagnie Internationale des Wagon-Lits, who ran the Orient Express, and according to his son, he had a part in building the Pera Palas hotel.

'Another Country'

In the late summer of 1961 the American novelist, playwright, and essayist James Baldwin turned up during a party at a friend's house in Istanbul – 'a small and bedraggled black man with a battered suitcase and enormous eyes' according to Claudia Roth Pierpont, writing in *The New Yorker* – after leaving New York for Paris and going to Israel on a writing assignment. At this particular party he fell asleep, exhausted, with his head in the lap of a Turkish actress. The city would provide a refuge for Jimmy Baldwin off and on for the next decade, and it was there that he finished his book, *Another Country*. Like others before and since, Baldwin was seduced by the vitality of the city's artistic community, and the dramatic version of his novel, *Giovanni's Room*, was produced in an Istanbul theatre.

Coming from a stiflingly repressive family in Harlem, where his stepfather was a very strict Baptist preacher, Baldwin was enchanted by the city's gay scene, and was amazed to see men holding hands in the street, even though his Turkish friends told him the practice had nothing to do with men being gay. Though Turkey had and has its own forms of racism, as does every country, the black-white dichotomy of the United States does not prevail there, and Baldwin relished the difference. Thilda Serrero wrote to Roditi that 'Jimmy Baldwin is like *un poisson dans l'eau* in Istanbul'. This is a city that loves jazz, and the American black man is a cultural hero as he is throughout Europe. Though Baldwin never wrote about his experience of Istanbul, its openness and its traditions of multiculturalism surely helped shape his world-view. In the end, perhaps the city on the Bosphorus turned out to be too much of a party town, and Baldwin eventually left it to find further refuge in the south of France.

31

Beyazit: Café and Mosque

ANY DAY WHEN THE SUN SHINES in Istanbul is a good day to spend a couple of hours looking at the Beyazidiye, the first imperial mosque complex built in the city. It dates from 1506 and is evidence of the powerful mosques the Ottomans were building even before Sinan came on the scene. The orientation toward Mecca of the Beyazit *qibla* was said to be so precise that mariners could set their compasses by it, and astronomers their clocks. I am drawn to the mosque courtyard, which offers a few square metres of sanctuary in the middle of the city.

Within these precincts, you see such contrasts as a little girl dressed all in pink prattling away to her mother, who is draped from head to foot in a black *çarşaf*, while a young man performs his ablutions at the fountain that dominates the centre of the courtyard and in another corner a grey-bearded man sits reading his newspaper. The arches of the arcade on four sides of this interior space are supported by stout columns of verd antique and dark-blood-red porphyry, all of which have recently received a good scrubbing to cleanse them of the effects of air pollution. Passing from one portal to another, north to east, west to north, people come and go on their daily journeys.

In the architecture here, there is a solemnity, a heaviness that typifies a certain aspect of Ottoman taste. One sees a nineteenth-century version of this quality in baroque palaces like the Dolmabahçe and Beylerbeyi that were built during the twilight of the empire. The ablutions fountain is as solemn, overbearing and likeable as a Gladstone bag or your old aunt. Part of the effect comes from the proportions of the courtyard it occupies: it is less spacious than the courtyards of the Sultanahmet Mosque and the Süleymaniye. Still, it has fanciful touches such as the wavy voussoirs of the arches in the arcade. Grey marble alternates with ornamentation of emerald-green and ruby-red stone, almost maroon. The main dome is supported by subsidiary domes, in a clustering effect that is part of the great beauty of Turkey's sacred architecture.

The Beyazit who established this mosque was not Yıldırım Beyazit, the Thunderbolt, who was captured and put into a cage by Tamurlane the Great. All that was before the Ottomans conquered the Queen of Cities. This was Beyazit II, son of Mehmed the Conqueror, perhaps the most spiritual and ascetic of the sultans. His father's collection of Christian icons, Italian paintings and sculptures, classical manuscripts, books and artefacts Beyazit, as we know, sold in the Grand Bazaar after his death. Beyazit also established the Galata Mevlevihanesi, where you can watch the dervishes do their turning, and he welcomed Sephardic Jewish refugees after their 1492 expulsion from Spain and Portugal, though he did settle most of them not in Istanbul but in subsidiary cities of the empire. He was later forced to abdicate and was probably poisoned by his son Selim the Grim.

It can be tricky translating key words from one language to another. Turks would normally use the word *ruh* to identify what we call the soul. A related word is *nefis* – defined by Redhouse as 'real self, essence, essential nature (of a person)' and also, 'bodily desires, cravings of the flesh'. In Islam *nefis*, as used by the seventeenth-century chronicler Evliya Çelebi, is usually translated as an appetite or desire which would lead men to evil, but not as a separate entity, as the soul is usually conceptualised. Here is the story of Beyazit's struggle with his *nefis* as told by Çelebi:

> The last seven years of his life he ate nothing which had blood and life in it. One day, longing much to eat calves' or sheep's feet, he struggled long in this glorious contest with his soul [*nefis*]; and as at last a well-seasoned dish of the feet was put before him, he said unto his soul, 'see, my soul, the feet are before thee; if thou wishest to enjoy them, leave the body and feed on them'. At the same moment a living creature was seen to come out of his mouth, which drank of the juice in the dish; and after having satisfied its appetite endeavoured to return from whence it came. But Beyazit having prevented it with his hand from re-entering his mouth, it fell on the ground, and the Sultan ordered it to be

beaten. The pages kicked it to death on the ground. The *mufti* of that time decided that, as the soul was an essential part of a man, this dead soul should be buried; prayers were performed over it, and the dead soul was interred in a small tomb near Beyazit's *türbe*. This is the truth of the famous story of Beyazit II having died twice and twice been buried.

Across the space between the mosque and its *medrese* – now home to the calligraphy museum to the west of the mosque, with Ordu Caddesi, the Avenue of the Army, on the south – stretches a wide courtyard shaded by huge *çınars*. The courtyard provides a good vantage-point from which to look at the mosque from a distance. The afternoon sunlight brings out the slate-blue panels with which the exterior of the mosque is faced, and the brick and stone fancy-work that decorates the larger of the two minarets. The stone of the mosque is a warm, brownish-grey, almost buff, topped by grey leaded domes that look almost blue in today's mild sunshine. Throughout, the exterior of the mosque is complemented by little decorative touches of burnt red.

After having a good look at the Beyazit from the west, it is pleasant to sit for a while in the tea garden situated under plane trees that are as large as any in Istanbul, alongside one entrance to the mosque, just outside the gates of the Sahaflar Çarşısı, the Bookseller's Bazaar. Most of the tea drinkers here are men. No one seems to be in a hurry. Conversation proceeds at a leisurely pace. On a typical day a young man at one table might have a suitcase full of clothes he is offering for sale. Another man might have a screwdriver out, trying to repair a mobile phone.

At a little folding table an older gentleman has prayer beads for sale, some of them wooden, some amber, some made from plastic that looks like amber. One could tell whether the amber is real by lighting a match underneath the beads and seeing whether they burn. Amber doesn't burn. A cleric in a white turban and a long camel-hair coat joins the clump of men who are examining the prayer beads. Each *tespih* should have ninety-nine beads, one for each of the ninety-nine beautiful names of Allah. Meanwhile many cigarettes are smoked, and conversations proceed at a leisurely pace in this crowd of ruminative, grandfatherly men taking their *keyif*. One feels that these conversations have been taking place here for centuries, and that they could go on into eternity.

32

Constantinople, Cavafy and the Mediterranean World

IN PORTS ALL OVER THE MEDITERRANEAN, whether in Palermo or Malta, Tangiers, Venice, the Dalmatian Coast, or in the Greek islands, the atmosphere lingers of a timeless maritime world that existed for millennia before the age of air travel. Along the waterfront in Piraeus, the port of Athens, ferries and tugs manœuvre in and out among white cruise ships which loom sleek and enormous above the fleet of lesser craft. Along the quay, *souvlaki* stands and lemonade vendors do a brisk business. Women in black dresses, shawls and broken shoes are roasting ears of corn over smoky braziers. Ancient Mercedes trucks overloaded with five-gallon olive oil containers and burlap bags stuffed with who knows what rumble over the cobblestones, mixing their diesel exhaust with the fragrance of roasting lamb and corn on the cob amidst the noise of clanking metal, loud conversational Greek, internal-combustion engines, boat whistles and horns.

You locate a bookshop on a quiet street off the quay, no larger or better lit than a cobbler's or locksmith's shop. It's in business to supply the reading needs of travellers like yourself, in search of something in English to read on the beach, on trains, on a hotel terrace, in a café with little zinc tables and rough chairs set out under a big plane tree, where an old man pulls a white handkerchief out of his back pocket and ceremoniously dusts off the seat of his chair before sitting down, then claps his hands imperiously until the waiter appears with iced water and *ouzo*. In Istanbul it would be iced water and *rakı*.

Poorly stacked, in no kind of order, stand orange and blue covered

Penguins and Pelicans – Graham Greenes, Iris Murdochs, Evelyn Waughs and Lawrence Durrells, somebody's dog-eared college text of Plato's *Republic* with a dorm address at Wellesley College in Massachusetts written on the inside fly-leaf, a copy of Mary Renault's *Bull from the Sea* with a lurid cover. Here's *Prospero's Cell*, Lawrence Durrell's book about Corfu; *The Station*, Robert Byron's book about Mount Athos; and a volume of poems by C.P. Cavafy with Greek on one side and English on the other.

Cavafy the Alexandrian, the Constantinopolitan, the patron saint of poets who love the demotic civilisation of the eastern Mediterranean. Forced out of the family home in Alexandria by political unrest in 1882 and subsequent bombardment by the British, who occupied Egypt in that year, Cavafy's mother brought her sons back to Constantinople and settled them in her father's house in Yeniköy, not far from what is now the Sadberk Hanım Museum, until the trouble blew over. The nineteen-year-old Cavafy walked beside the Bosphorus, became acquainted with the city and had his first sexual adventures here; and it was in Constantinople, the city of forgetting and remembering, that he wrote the first of his poems that survive.

With his book in your pocket, you find a taverna. Your freighter sails at midnight, and you know you'll get hungry during the night. Walk through to the kitchen as is the custom both in Greece and in Turkey, and point to one or two dishes simmering in big copper pots on the stove. Achilles, Menelaos, Mark Antony, early Christians and late Pagans, the fourteenth-century Byzantine emperor John Kantakuzinos – the *dramatis personæ* of Mediterranean history from the Trojan War to the Cavafy's own afternoons in the tavernas and *meyhanes* of *fin de siècle* Alexandria – populate the little taverna as you read.

The food is delicious – lamb and aubergine, the juices sopped up with thick chunks of bread, washed down with *retsina*. Out of nowhere you recall that Liudprand, Bishop of Cremona, complained bitterly about the wine in his reminiscences of Constantinople. 'To add to our calamity', he wrote, 'the Greek wine, on account of being mixed with pitch, resin and plaster was to us undrinkable.' All the human drama of the Mediterranean world feels, at this moment, contemporary. Or more precisely, contemporaneous – the fall of Troy and the fall of Constantinople encompassed in one long continuous moment.

Midnight comes. You board the rusty old ship bound for Istanbul, provisioned for the night with a half-litre of *ouzo* and some bottles of cold water. Find a deck chair amidships on the starboard side, wrap your legs in a rough blanket, and open the book of Cavafy's poems. A tomato-hued, butterfly-shaped stain colours one of the pages from the stew you have eaten in the taverna. Light escaping the saloon makes it just possible to read. Here are a couple of lines from a poem called 'Ithaka':

As you set out for Ithaka
Hope the voyage is a long one...

The Mediterranean is a cat's cradle of connecting threads, where space and time have become fused through trade, conquest, and the seepage of ideas. The robust bronze horses at St Mark's Cathedral in Venice were plundered from the Hippodrome in Constantinople during the Fourth Crusade. The most perfect Greek temples are to be seen at Pæstum in southern Italy, and at Agrigentum in Sicily.

Remember the cathedral at Siracusa, built in the shell of the ancient temple of Diana, and the gasps and smiles and cries of *Che bella!* on Santa Lucia's Day from church-goers who crowded the darkened sanctuary holding up candles? They were seeing what seemed to be an apparition: a swarthy man with Arabic features carrying on his shoulders a blonde angelic child, radiant bearer of Norman genes from the medieval rulers of Sicily – the Norman kings who built the Palazzo Normano in Palermo and brought Byzantine craftsmen in to adorn its rooms with mosaics.

As for the prison camp on the far side of the island of Leros where enemies of the Colonels' regime were hidden away in a secret prison, the brutality of it would not have shocked the Byzantines, one of whose favourite punishments for deposed royalty was to cut off the offender's nose and split his tongue. Black Ali, Murad IV's Head Executioner, with his seventy-seven instruments of torture, would have been in his element there. Cavafy's Hellenism reflects not the morning of civilisation we associate with classical Greek culture but rather its late afternoon, when human nature wore thin and became debased. These are latitudes that Cavafy's book navigates. As you doze in your deck chair, feeling the ship roll, its engines strain and the old craft pushes north and east toward Byzantium.

AT DAWN THE SHIP docks at a harbour whose name is unfamiliar to you. It's hard to make out the Greek letters stenciled on the wall at the quay. Cavafy seems to have got here first. In 'Ithaka' he writes:

> May there be many a summer morning when,
> With what pleasure, what joy,
> You come into harbours seen for the first time.

On the quay you see a half-effaced marble bas-relief of the winged Venetian lion of St Mark, his stone paw propping up the gospel. There's one just like it in Üsküdar, and a couple of others that I have seen placed randomly in the park in Sultanahmet. Probably they are left over from the days when the houses of Venetian merchants were marked by the lion of St Mark.

Overhead the blue and white Greek flag snaps in the sea breeze like the square sail of a Phœnician sloop. From the market on the quay a potpourri of scents blows offshore: pepper and cloves, sun-beaten Greek oregano, thyme and lavender. Perhaps this is the very harbour into which a ship packed with refugees from the Queen of Cities sailed on the ninth of June, 1453, ten days after the decisive battle along the walls of Constantinople. A sailor on board cries out the news to those waiting on the quay.

Short Chronology

324	Emperor Constantine I initiates construction of the new city on the site of Byzantium
330	Constantinople consecrated as the capital of the Byzantine Empire
360	Dedication of first church of Haghia Sophia
378	Battle of Adrianople, defeat by the Visigoths
381	Christianity becomes the official imperial religion
413–414	Theodosius II builds triple-wall fortifications
527–65	Reign of Justinian, Byzantine Empire at its peak territorially
532–37	Justinian I rebuilds Haghia Sophia
541–42	Plague of Justinian kills 40 per cent of the city's population
565–717	City under attack from Arabs and Persians
628	Heraclius defeats the Persians, who surrender their conquests
726	Leo III issues decree against graven images, start of Iconoclast movement
780	Empress Eirene restores the veneration of images
1096	First Crusade arrives at Constantinople
1204	City sacked by Fourth Crusade
1204–61	City becomes seat of Latin Empire – Byzantine nobility scattered
1347	Black Death spreads to Constantinople, exacerbating decline
1453	City besieged and captured by Ottoman Sultan Mehmed II, later 'the Conqueror'
1459	Construction begins on Topkapi Palace

1512–1520	Rule of Selim I, expansion of the eastern and southern borders into Egypt and Safavid Persia
1517	Selim conquers the holy cities of Mecca and Medina, and the Ottoman Dynasty claims status of Caliphate
1520–66	Reign of Süleyman the Magnificent, time of artistic achievement
1699	Treaty of Karlowitz, concluding Austro-Ottoman War of 1683–97 and recognising loss of territory in Central Europe
1526	Süleyman establishes Ottoman rule in modern-day Hungary, going on to lay siege to Vienna
1574–1617	So-called 'Rule of the Women', series of chief concubines and Valide Sultans dominated court
1812–13	Mahmud II reconquers Mecca and Medina
1827	British, French and Russian armies defeat Ottoman forces at Battle of Navarino
1832	Treaty of Constantinople, recognition of Greece and beginning of break-up of the Ottoman Empire
1839	Tanzimat reforms, Europeanising clothing, architecture, legislation and political institutions
1918–23	City occupied by Allied forces
1920–22	Turkish War of Independence
1922	Last Ottoman sultan deposed
1923	Creation of Republic of Turkey; Ankara replaces Istanbul as capital city
1930	City's official name changes to Istanbul
1938	Death of Mustafa Kemal Atatürk
1950	First democratic elections
2005	Start of Turkish membership negotiations with the European Union

Rulers of Istanbul

Among the Byzantine Emperors were:

Constantinian Dynasty

324–337	Constantine I – 'The Great'
337–361	Constantius II
361–363	Julian – 'The Apostate'

Valentian Dynasty

364–378	Valens
378–379	Gratian

Theodosian Dynasty

379–395	Theodosius I – 'The Great'
395–408	Arcadius
408–450	Theodosius II
450–457	Marcian

Leonid Dynasty

457–474	Leo I – 'The Thracian'
474–491	Zeno
475–476	Basiliscus
491–518	Anastasius I

Justinian Dynasty

518–527	Justin I
527–565	Justinian I – 'The Great'
565–578	Justin II
578–582	Tiberius II Constantine
582–602	Maurice

Heraclian Dynasty

610–641	Heraclius
641–668	Constans II
668–685	Constantine IV – 'The Bearded'
685–695	Justinian II – 'The Slit-Nosed'

Twenty Years' Anarchy

695–698	Leontios
698–705	Tiberius III
705–711	Justinian II – 'The Slit-Nosed'
711–713	Philippikos Bardanes
713–715	Anastasios II
715–717	Theodosios III

Isaurian Dynasty

717–741	Leo III – 'The Isaurian'
741–775	Constantine V – 'The Dung-Named'
775–780	Leo IV – 'The Khazar'
780–797	Constantine VI
797–802	Eirene of Athens

Nikephorian Dynasty

802–811	Nikephoros I – 'The Logothete'
811–812	Staurakios
812–813	Michael I

Amorian Dynasty

820–829	Michael II – 'The Stammerer'

829–842	Theophilos
842–867	Michael III – 'The Drunkard'

Maedonian Dynasty

867–886	Basil I – 'The Macedonian'
886–912	Leo VI – 'The Wise'
912–913	Alexander III
908–959	Constantine VII Porphyrogenitus
959–963	Romanus II
963–969	Nikephoros II
969–976	John I
976–1025	Basil II – 'The Bulgar-Slayer'
1025–1028	Constantine VIII
1028–1050	Zoë
1028–1034	Romanos III
1034–1041	Michael IV – 'The Paphlagonian'
1042	Theodora
1042–1055	Constantine IX
1055–1056	Theodora

Doukid Dynasty

1059–1067	Constantine X
1067–1078	Michael VII
1068–1071	Romanos IV
1078–1081	Nikephoros III

Komnenid Dynasty

1081–1118	Alexios I
1118–1143	John II
1143–1180	Manuel I
1180–1183	Alexios II
1183–1185	Andronikos I

Angelid Dynasty

1185–1195	Isaac II
1195–1203	Alexios III

1203–1204	Isaac II
1203–1204	Alexios IV
1204	Alexios V

Latin Empire (founded by leaders of the Fourth Crusade)

1204–1205	Baldwin I
1206–1216	Henry
1217–1219	Yolanda
1219–1228	Robert I
1228–1237	John of Brienne
1237–1261	Baldwin II

Palaiologan Dynasty

1261–1282	Michael VIII
1261–1328	Andronikos II
1294–1320	Michael IX
1328–1341	Andronikos III
1341–1391	John V
1391–1425	Manuel II
1425–1448	John VIII
1448–1453	Constantine XI

Sultans of the Ottoman Empire

1453–1481	Mehmed II – 'The Conqueror'
1481–1512	Beyazit II – 'The Saint'
1512–1520	Selim I – 'The Grim'
1520–1566	Süleyman I – 'The Magnificent'
1566–1574	Selim II – 'The Sot'
1574–1595	Murad III
1595–1603	Mehmed III – 'The Just'
1603–1617	Ahmed I – 'The Fortunate'
1617–1618	Mustafa I – 'The Intestable'
1618–1622	Osman II – 'The Young'
1622–1623	Mustafa I – 'The Intestable'
1623–1640	Murad IV – 'The Warrior'
1640–1648	Ibrahim I – 'The Mad'
1648–1687	Mehmed IV

1689–1691	Süleyman II – 'The Warrior'
1691–1695	Ahmed II – 'The Warrior Prince'
1695–1703	Mustafa II
1703–1730	Ahmed III
1730–1754	Mahmud I – 'The Hunchback'
1754–1757	Osman III – 'The Devout'
1757–1774	Mustafa III
1774–1789	Abdülhamid I – 'The Servant of God'
1789–1807	Selim III – 'The Composer'
1807–1808	Mustafa IV
1808–1839	Mahmud II – 'The Reformer'
1839–1861	Abdülmecid I
1861–1876	Abdülaziz I – 'The Unfortunate'
1876	Mehmed Murad V
1876–1909	Abdülhamid II – 'The Sublime Khan'
1909–1918	Mehmed V – 'Follower of the True Path'
1918–1922	Mehmed VI – 'The Unifier of Religion'

Presidents of the Republic

1922–1938	Mustafa Kemal Atatürk
1938–1950	İsmet İnönü
1950–1960	Celâl Bayar
1960–1966	Cemal Gürsel
1966–1973	Cevdet Sunay
1973–1980	Fahri Korutürk
1978–1983	Kenan Evren
1989–1993	Turgat Özal
1993–2000	Süleyman Demirel
2000–2007	Ahmet Necdet Sezer
2007–present	Abdullah Gül

Further Reading

Fiction

Altun, Selçuk, *Songs My Mother Never Taught Me*, translated by Ruth Christie and Selçuk Berilgen (Telegram, London: 2008)
——*The Sultan of Byzantium*, translated by Clifford Endres and Selhan Savcigil-Endres (Telegram, London: 2012)
De Bernieres, Louis, *Birds Without Wings* (Vintage, London: 2005)
Faik, Sait, *Sleeping in the Forest*, translated by Talat S. Halman and Jayne L. Warner (Syracuse UP, New York: 2004)
Freely, Maureen, *The Life of the Party* (Warner, London: 1986)
Goodwin, Jason, *The Janissary Tree* (Picador, London: 2007)
Karasu, Bilge, *The Garden of the Departed Cats*, translated by Aron Aji (New Directions, New York: 1991)
Kemal, Yashar, *The Sea-Crossed Fisherman*, translated by Thilda Kemal (Minerva, Frankfurt: 1985)
——*The Birds Have Also Gone*, translated by Thilda Kemal (Minerva, Frankfurt: 1985)
Loti, Pierre, *Aziyadé* (Dodo, Gloucester: 2008)
Nesin, Aziz, *Turkish Stories from Four Decades*, translated by Louis Mitler (Passegiata, Colorado: 1991)
——*Memoirs of An Exile*, translated by Joseph S. Jacobson (Southmoor Studios, Houston: 2001)
Nicolson, Harold, *Sweet Waters* (Eland, London: 2008)
Pamuk, Orhan, *The Black Book*, translated by Maureen Freely (Vintage, London: 2006)
——*My Name Is Red*, translated by Erdağ Göknar (Everyman's Library, London: 2010)
——*The Museum of Innocence*, translated by Maureen Freely (Vintage, London: 2010)

——*The White Castle*, translated by Victoria Holbrook (Vintage, London: 1998)
Roditi, Edouard, *The Delights of Turkey* (W.W. Norton and Co., London: 1977)
Şafak, Elif, *The Bastard of Istanbul* (Penguin, London: 2008)
——*The Flea Palace*, translated by Müge Göçek (Viking, New York: 2010)
——*The Forty Rules of Love* (Viking, New York: 2010)
——*The Gaze*, translated by Brendan Freely (Viking, New York: 2006)
——*Honour* (Viking, New York: 2012)
Tanpınar, Ahmet Hamdi, *A Mind at Peace*, translated by Erdağ Göknar (Archipelago, New York: 2009)
Tekin, Latife, *Dear Shameless Death*, translated by Saliha Paker and Mel Kenne (Marion Boyars, London: 1983)
——*Swords of Ice*, translated by Saliha Paker and Mel Kenne (Marion Boyars, London: 2007)
——*Berji Kristin: Tales from the Garbage Hills*, translated by Ruth Christie and Saliha Paker (Marion Boyars, London: 2000)
Ziyalan, Mustafa, and Spangler, Amy (eds), *Istanbul Noir* (Akashic, New York: 2008)

Guidebooks

Able, Vanessa, *Istanbul Insight Step by Step Guide* (Berlitz, London: 2009)
Bainbridge, James, *Lonely Planet: Turkey* (Lonely Planet, London: 2011)
Baring, Rose, *DK Eyewitness Travel Guide: Istanbul* (Dorling Kindersley, London: 2011)
Freely, John, *Companion Guide to Istanbul and Around the Marmara* (Boydell and Brewer, New York: 2000)
Freely, John, *Istanbul* (Blue Guide Ltd, London: 2011)
Karmi, Ilhan, *Jewish Sites of Istanbul: A Guide Book* (Isis, Istanbul: 1992)
Kerper, Barrie, *Istanbul: The Collected Traveler: An Inspired Companion Guide* (Vintage, London: 2009)
Richardson, Terry, *The Rough Guide to Istanbul* (Rough Guides, London: 2009)

Sumner-Boyd, Hilary, and Freely, John, *Strolling Through Istanbul* (Kegan Paul, London: 2005)
Time Out Istanbul, fifth edition (Time Out, London: 2012)

Non-fiction: Histories, Travellers' Accounts, Memoirs, Art and Architecture

Abbott, G.F., *Turkey in Transition* (Nabu, South Carolina: 2010)
——*Under the Turk in Constantinople: A Record of Sir John Finch's Embassy, 1674–1681* (Bibliobazaar, South Carolina: 2009)
Andersen, Hans Christian, *A Poet's Bazaar* (Nabu, South Carolina: 2011)
Andic, Fuat, *Farewell, Homeland* (Booksurge: 2008)
Anon., *Letters Historical and Critical from a Gentleman in Constantinople to his Friend in London* (Gale, Oxford: 2010)
Atamian, Sarkis, *The Armenian Community* (Philosophical Library, London: 1955)
Byron, Robert, *The Byzantine Achievement*, 12th edition (Axios, Virginia: 2010)
Bury, J. B., *A History of the Later Roman Empire*, 1889–1923 (Nabu, South Carolina: 2010)
Croutier, Alev Lytle, *Harem: The World Behind the Veil* (Abbeville, New York: 1989)
Clark, Peter, *Istanbul, a Cultural History* (Signal, Oxford: 2010)
De Amicis, Edmondo, *Constantinople*, Revised edition, translated by Stephen Parkin (Alma Classics, London: 2011)
Doukas, *The Decline and Fall of Byzantium to the Ottoman Turks*, translated by Harry J. Magoulis (Wayne State UP, Michigan: 1975)
Dufferin and Ava, Dowager Marchioness of, *My Russian and Turkish Journals* (Nabu, South Carolina: 2011)
Dwight, H.G., *Constantinople: Settings and Traits* (Harpers, London: 1927)
Dwight, Henry O., *Turkish Life in War Time* (British Library, London: 2010)
——*Constantinople and Its Problems* (Nabu, South Carolina: 2010)
Edip, Halide, *Memoirs* (Gorgias, New Jersey: 2005)
——*The Turkish Ordeal*, (Hyperion, New York: 1981)
——*Turkey Faces West: A Turkish View of Recent Changes and Their Origins* (Nabu, South Carolina: 2010)

Epstein, Mark Alan, *The Ottoman Jewish Communities and Their Role in the Fifteenth and Sixteenth Centuries* (Klaus Schwarz, Berlin: 1980)

Evliya Çelebi, *Narrative of Travels in Europe, Asia and Africa in the Seventeenth Century*, 1834–50, Reissue edition, translated by Joseph von Hammer (Cambridge UP, Cambridge: 2012)

Finkel, Caroline, *Osman's Dream: The History of the Ottoman Empire, 1300–1923* (Basic Books, New York: 2007)

Freely, John and Ahmet S. Çakmak, *Byzantine Monuments of Istanbul* (Cambridge UP, Cambridge: 2004)

Freely, John, *Stamboul Sketches* (Redhouse, Istanbul: 1974)

Freely, John and Brendan, *A Guide to Beyoğlu* (Archaeology and Art Publications, Richmond: 2005)

Garnett, Lucy M.J., *The Dervishes of Turkey* (Octagon, London: 1990)

——*The Women of Turkey and their Folklore* (Bibliobazaar, South Carolina: 2010)

Gautier, Theophile, *Constantinople* (Nabu, South Carolina: 1990)

Gibbon, Edward, *The History of the Decline and Fall of the Roman Empire*, edited by J.B. Bury (Nabu, South Carolina: 2010)

Gilles, Pierre, *The Antiquities of Constantinople*, translated by John Ball (Italica, New York: 1988)

Goodwin, Godfrey, *The Janissaries* (Saqi, London: 1988)

——*A History of Ottoman Architecture* (Thames and Hudson, London: 2003)

——*Sinan: Ottoman Architecture and Its Values Today* (Saqi, London: 2001)

Goodwin, Jason, *On Foot to the Golden Horn* (Penguin, London: 1993)

——*Lords of the Horizons: A History of the Ottoman Empire* (Picador, London: 2003)

Göçek, Fatma Müge, *East Encounters West: France and the Ottoman Empire in the Eighteenth Century* (OUP, Oxford: 1987)

——*The Transformation of Turkey* (Tauris Academic Studies, New York: 2011)

Göktürk, Deniz, Soysal, Levent and Türeli, Ipek (eds), *Orienting Istanbul: Cultural Capital of Europe?* (Routledge, Abingdon: 2010)

Gül, Murat, The Emergence of Modern Istanbul: *Transformation and Modernisation of a City* (Tauris Academic Studies, New York: 2009)

Güler, Ara and Orhan Pamuk, *Ara Güler's Istanbul: 40 Years of Photographs* (Thames and Hudson, London: 2009)

Gülersoy, Çelik, *The Dolmabahçe Palace and Its Environs* (Turkiye Turing ve Otomobil Kurumu, Istanbul: 1990)

——*The Story of the Grand Bazaar* (Turkiye Turing ve Otomobil Kurumu, Istanbul: 1990)

——*Taksim: the Story of a Square* (Turkiye Turing ve Otomobil Kurumu, Istanbul: 1991)

——*Yıldız Parc and Malta Pavilion* (Turkiye Turing ve Otomobil Kurumu, Istanbul: 1983)

Gürsu, Nevber, *The Art of Turkish Weaving: Designs Through the Ages* (Turkish Yellow Pages, Istanbul: 1988)

Hamlin, Cyrus, *Among the Turks* (Forgotten Books, London: 2012)

Hellier, Chris, and Veturi, Franco, *Splendours of the Bosphorus: Houses and Palaces of Istanbul* (Thames and Hudson, London: 1993)

Hester, Lucy Stanhope, and Meryon, Charles Lewis, *Travels of Lady Lester Stanhope* (Nabu, South Carolina: 2010)

Hope, Thomas, *Anastasius or Memoirs of a Greek* (Nabu, South Carolina: 2010)

Inalcık, Halil, *History of the Ottoman Empire: The Classical Age 1300–1600* (Phoenix, Washington: 2001)

——*The Ottoman Empire: Conquest, Organisation and Economy* (Phoenix, Washington: 2001)

——*The Middle East and the Balkans under the Ottoman Empire* (Indiana UP, Indiana: 1993)

Jones, J.R. Melville, *The Siege of Constantinople 1453: Seven Contemporary Accounts* (Hakkert, Las Palmas: 1972)

Kent, Marian (ed), *The Great Powers and the End of the Ottoman Empire*, second edition (Routledge, Abingdon: 1996)

Kinross, Lord, *Atatürk: The Rebirth of a Nation* (Weidenfeld & Nicolson, London: 1993)

——*Atatürk: A Biography of Mustafa Kemal, Father of Modern Turkey* (Quill, Whitby: 1992)

——*The Ottoman Centuries: The Rise and Fall of the Turkish Empire* (Harper Perennial, London: 1979)

Kortepeter, Carl Max, *The Ottoman Turks: from Nomad Kingdom to World Empire* (Isis, Istanbul: 1991)
Kritovoulos, *History of Mehmed the Conqueror*, translated by Charles T. Riggs (Greenwood Press Reprints, Westport: 1954)
Köprülü, M. Fuad, *The Origins of the Ottoman Empire*, edited by Gary Leiser (State University of New York Press, New York: 1991)
Kuran, Aptullah, *Sinan, the Grand Old Man of Ottoman Architecture* (Ada, Chicago: 1987)
Lane Fox, Robin, *Pagans and Christians: In the Mediterranean World from the Second Century AD to the Conversion of Constantine* (Viking, London: 1986)
Lane-Poole, Mrs Stanley (ed) *The People of Turkey: Twenty Years Residence among Bulgarians, Greeks, Albanians, Turks and Armenians by a Consul's Daughter and his Wife* (Nabu, South Carolina: 2010)
Lang, David Marshall, *The Armenians: A People in Exile* (Unwin Hyman, New South Wales: 1989)
Lewis, Bernard, *The Emergence of Modern Turkey*, Third edition (OUP, USA: 1960)
——*Istanbul and the Civilization of the Ottoman Empire* (Oklahoma UP, Oklahoma: 1972)
——*The Jews of Islam* (Routledge, Abingdon: 2007)
——*Race and Slavery in the Middle East: a Historical Enquiry* (OUP, USA: 1992)
Liddell, Robert, *Byzantium and Istanbul*, Second edition (Jonathan Cape, London: 1956)
Lifchez, Raymond (ed), *The Dervish Lodge: Architecture, Art, and Sufism in Ottoman Turkey* (University of California Press, Berkeley: 1992)
Liudprand of Cremona, *The Complete Works of Liudprand of Cremona*, translated by Paolo Squatriti (Catholic University of America UP, Washington DC: 2007)
Llewellyn Smith, Michael, *Ionian Vision: Greece in Asia Minor, 1919–22* (Hurst, London: 1973)
MacFarlane, Charles, *Constantinople in 1828*, second edition (Kessinger, Whitefish: 2009)
Majeska, G.P., *Russian Travellers to Constantinople in the Fourteenth and Fifteenth Centuries* (Dumbarton Oaks Research Library and Collection, Washington DC: 1984)

Mango, Andrew, *Atatürk: The Biography of the Founder of Modern Turkey* (Overlook, New York: 2002)
——*Turkey: The Challenge of a New Role* (Praeger, Connecticut: 1994)
Mango, Cyril, *Byzantine Architecture*, second edition (Electa, New York: 1985)
——*Byzantium: the Empire of New Rome* (Weidenfeld, London: 1980)
——*The Oxford History of Byzantium* (OUP, USA: 2002)
Matthews, Henry, *The Mosques of Istanbul* (Scala, New York: 2010)
Mears, Eliot Grinnell, *Modern Turkey: A Politico-Economic Interpretation, 1908–1923* (Macmillan, London: 1924)
Mihailovic, Konstantin, *Memoirs of a Janissary* (Markus Wiener, New Jersey: 2011)
Miller, Barnette, *The Palace School of Muhammed the Conqueror* (Ayer Company, Stratford: 1941)
Moore, Thomas, *Life of Lord Byron Vols 1 and 2* (Cambridge UP, New York: 2012)
Moorehead, Alan, *Gallipoli* (Harper Perennial, London: 2002)
Necipoğlu, Gülru, *The Age of Sinan: Architectural Culture in the Ottoman Empire* (Reaktion Books, London, 2010)
——*Architecture, Ceremonial, and Power: The Topkapi Palace in the Fifteenth and Sixteenth Centuries* (MIT Press, Massachusetts: 1992)
Nesin, Aziz, *Istanbul Boy, The Autobiography of Aziz Nesin*, Vols 1–4, translated by Joseph S. Jacobson (Texas UP, Texas: 1977–2000)
Nicolson, Nigel, *Alex: Life of Field Marshall Earl Alexander of Tunis* (Macmillan, London: 1976)
Norwich, John Julius, *Byzantium Vol 1: The Early Centuries* (Penguin, London: 1990)
——*Byzantium Vol 2: The Apogee* (Penguin, London: 1992)
——*Byzantium Vol 3: The Decline and Fall* (Knopf, London: 1995)
——*The Middle Sea: A History of the Mediterranean* (Vintage, London: 2007)
Obolensky, Dimitri, *The Byzantine Commonwealth* (ACLS Humanities, New York: 2009)
Orga, Irfan, *Portrait of a Turkish Family* (Eland, London: 2003)
Ousterhout, R., *Master Builders of Byzantium* (Pennsylvania Museum of Archaeology, Pennsylvania: 2008)

Palmer, Alan, *The Decline and Fall of the Ottoman Empire* (M. Evans, New York: 1992)
Pamuk, Orhan, *Memories and the City* (Vintage, London: 2006)
——*Other Colours: Essays and a Story* (Faber and Faber, London: 2007)
Pardoe, Julia, *The City of the Sultan, and Domestic Manners of the Turks*, (Nabu Press, South Carolina: 2010)
Porphyrogenitus, Constantine VII, *De Ceremoniis Aulae Byzantinae Libri Duo*, Vols 1 and 2, edited by J. Reisky (Nabu, South Carolina: 2012)
Procopius, *Secret History*, translated by H.B. Dewing (Kessinger, Whitefish: 2010)
Schimmel, Annemarie, *Calligraphy and Islamic Culture* (New York UP, New York: 1990)
Seal, Jeremy, *A Fez of the Heart: Travels around Turkey in Search of a Hat* (Mariner Books, New York: 1996)
Setton, Kenneth M., *Venice, Austria and the Turks in the Seventeenth Century* (American Philosophical Society, Philadelphia: 1991)
Seyhan, Azade, *Writing Outside the Nation* (Princeton UP, New Jersey, 2000)
Settle, Mary Lee, *Turkish Reflections: A Biography of a Place* (Touchstone, Florida: 1992)
Skilliter, Susan, *Life in Istanbul 1588: Scenes from a Traveller's Picture Book* (Bodleian, Oxford: 1977)
Talbot Rice, David, *Byzantine Art*, Revised edition (Penguin, London: 1968)
——*Byzantine Icons* (Faber and Faber, London: 1959)
——*Byzantine Painting: the Last Phase* (Dial, New York: 1968)
Talbot Rice, Tamara, *Everyday Life in Byzantium* (Hippocrene, New York: 1967)
Toledanco, Ehud R., *The Ottoman Slave Trade and its Suppression 1840–1890* (Princeton UP, New Jersey, 1982)
Tuglaci, Pars, *Armenian Churches of Istanbul* (Pars Yayin ve Tic, Istanbul: 1991)
——*The Role of the Balian Family in Ottoman Architecture* (Pars Yayin ve Tic, Istanbul: 1990)
——*The Role of the Dadian Family in Ottoman Social, Economic and Political Life* (Pars Yayin ve Tic, Istanbul: 1993)

——*Turkish Bands of Past and Present* (Pars Yayin ve Tic, Istanbul: 1986)
——*Women of Istanbul in Ottoman Times* (Pars Yayin ve Tic, Istanbul: 1984)
——*The Ottoman Palace Women* (Pars Yayin ve Tic, Istanbul: 1985)
Vacalopoulos, Apostolos E., *The Greek Nation 1453–1669* (Rutgers UP, New Jersey: 1976)
——*Origins of the Greek Nation: the Byzantine Period 1204–1461* (Rutgers UP, New Jersey: 1970)
Van Millingen, Alexander, *Byzantine Churches of Constantinople* (Macmillan, London: 1912)
Vassilaki, M., *Images of the Mother of God: Representations of the Theotokos in Byzantium* (Ashgate, Surrey: 2005)
Vryonis, Speros, *The Mechanism of Catastrophe: The Turkish Pogrom of September 6–7, 1955, and the Destruction of the Greek Community of Istanbul* (Greekworks, New York: 2005)
Wortley Montagu, Lady Mary, *The Turkish Embassy Letters*, edited by Malcolm Jack (Little, Brown, London: 1994)

Poetry

Andrews, Walter G., Najaat Black and Mehmet Kalpakli, *Ottoman Lyric Poetry: An Anthology* (Washington UP, Washington: 2006)
Andrews, Walter G., *Poetry's Voice, Society's Song: Ottoman Lyric Poetry* (Washington UP, Washington: 1985)
Ash, John, *The Anatolikon* (Talisman House, Greenfield, Massachusetts: 1999)
——*Parthian Stations* (Carcanet, Manchester: 2007)
——*To the City* (Talisman House, Greenfield, Massachusetts: 2004)
Ayhan, Ece, *Blind Cat Black and Orthodoxies*, translated by Murat Nemet-Nejat (Sun and Moon, Los Angeles: 1997)
Batur, Enis, *Ash Dîvan: Selected poems of Enis Batur*, edited by Saliha Paker, translated by Clifford Endres, Mel Kenne, Saliha Paker and Selhan Savcigil-Endres (Talisman House, Greenfield, Massachusetts: 2006)
Berk, Ilhan, *A Leaf About To Fall: Selected Poems*, translated by George Messo (Salt, London: 2006)

——*Madrigals*, translated by George Messo (Shearsman, Bristol: 2008)
——*The Book of Things*, translated by George Messo (Salt, London: 2009)
Cansever, Edip, *Dirty August: Selected Poems*, translated by Julia Clare Tillinghast and Richard Tillinghast (Talisman House, Greenfield, Massachusetts: 2009)
Cavafy, Constantine P., *Collected Poems*, translated by Edmund Keeley and Philip Sherrard (Princeton UP, Princeton: 1992)
Erözçelik, Seyhan, *Rose Strikes and Coffee Grinds* (*Gül ve Telve*), translated by Murat Nemet-Nejat (Talisman House, Greenfield, Massachusetts: 2009)
Halman, Talat S. and Jayne L. Warner, *A Brave New Quest: 100 Modern Turkish Poems* (Syracuse UP, New York: 2006)
Hikmet, Nâzım, *Beyond the Walls: Selected Poems by Nâzim Hikmet*, translated by Ruth Christie, Richard McKane and Talât Sait Halman (Syracuse UP, New York: 2004)
Hikmet, Nâzım, *Human Landscapes from My Country: An Epic Novel in Verse*, translated by Randy Blasing and Mutlu Konuk (Persea, New York: 1983)
Hikmet, Nâzım, *Poems of Nâzım Hikmet*, Revised and expanded edition by Randy Blasing, Mutlu Konuk (Persea, New York: 2002)
Kenne, Mel, *The View from Galata / Galata'dan Şiir* (Yapı Kredi Yayınları, Istanbul: 2010)
Menemencioglu, Nermin, *The Penguin Book of Turkish Verse* (Penguin, London: 1978)
Messo, George, *Ikinci Yeni – The Turkish Avant-Garde*, (Shearsman, Bristol: 2009)
Messo, George (ed), *From This Bridge: Contemporary Turkish Women Poets An Anthology of Turkish Women Poets* (Conversation, Kent: 2010)
Müldür, Lale, *Water Music*, translated by Leland Bardwell and others (Poetry Ireland, Dublin: 1998)
Nemet-Nejat, Murat, *Eda: An Anthology of Contemporary Turkish Poetry* (Talisman House, Greenfield, Massachusetts: 2004)
Orga, Ates, *Istanbul: Poetry of Place* (Eland, London: 2008)
Trypanis, C.A., *Fourteen Early Byzantine Cantica* (Byzantine Institute, Vienna: 1968)

Veli, Orhan, *I, Orhan Veli*, translated by Murat Nemet-Nejat (Hanging Loose, New York: 1989)
Yeats, William Butler, *Collected Poems* (Vintage, London: 1990)
Yücel, Can, *The Poetry of Can Yücel*, translated by Feyyaz Kayacan Fergar (Papirus Yayinlari, Istanbul: 1993)

Historical Gazetteer

The **Aqueduct of Valens,** or *Bozdoğan Kemeri,* 'Aqueduct of the Grey Falcon', was built in the fourth century during the reign of the Roman Emperor Valens to pipe water into the city. Crossing Atatürk Boulevard in Fatih, it is one of the city's most visible monuments from the classical age. **204, 221, 307**

Arnavutköy is a waterside neighbourhood on the European side of the Bosphorus between Ortaköy and Bebek. The name means 'Albanian Village': the Ottomans settled refugees from Albania here. In the nineteenth century the population of Arnavutköy was predominantly Jewish, but most of its Jewish residents left after the catastrophic fire of 1877. Up the hill is the University of the Bosphorus, formerly Robert College. **20, 207, 225–6, 241, 254–5, 296, 308**

Asmalımescit, meaning 'vine-clad small mosque', is a Beyoğlu nightlife neighbourhood that takes its name from the long street that runs between Istiklal Caddesi and the Pera Palas Hotel, filled with meyhanes and lokantas. It has traditionally been the haunt of artists and intellectuals. **21, 24, 210–12, 226, 249**

The **Atik Valide Camii,** 'The Mosque of the Old Queen Mother', was built in 1547. One of Sinan's best mosques and his last major work, it stands atop the hills that rise behind the centre of Üsküdar on the Asian side of Istanbul. The mosque was commissioned by the Sultana Nurbanu, the Venetian-born wife of Selim II and the mother of Murat III. **114, 232–3**

The **At meydanı**, literally translated as 'horse field', is the Turkish name for the Byzantine Hippodrome, a stadium holding 100,000 spectators where chariot races, circuses and other popular entertainments were held in Byzantine times. Political demonstrations also sometimes took place here, including some events associated with the Nika riots of 532 when, after mobs destroyed much of the town, including the original church of Haghia Sophia, Justinian put the uprising down by slaughtering 30,000 people in the At meydanı.

Ayios Yorgios, the Greek Orthodox Church of Saint George in Kuzguncuk, once ministered to the needs of the large Greek population in this multi-ethnic community. Its side chapel contains some notable icons. **252**

Balat is located on the shores of the Golden Horn. Traditionally the main Jewish neighbourhood in Istanbul, it is home to the Jewish hospital and the Ahrida (Ochrid) and Yanbol synagogues. Few Jewish inhabitants remain, but Balat remains an old-fashioned place of narrow, cobbled streets and family businesses. **11, 208, 225, 301**

Bebek – means 'baby' or 'doll' – the full name is 'Boğaz'ın Gözbebeği' which roughly means 'Apple of the Bosphorus's Eye'. Located on the European side of the Bosphorus above Arnavutköy, Bebek began life as a waterside village, and grew to be a popular residential area in Ottoman Istanbul. **19–20, 159, 213, 250, 255, 295**

Beyoğlu encompasses what the Greeks called Pera, meaning 'beyond', since this Venetian and Genoese enclave was situated beyond the Golden Horn. The Turkish name for the area north of the Golden Horn means 'son of the lord, or ruler', probably referring to the Venetian emissary Lodovico Gritti, whose father, Andrea, was the chief Venetian diplomat in Constantinople and later became Doge of Venice. Lodovico's palace was located here. Beyoğlu extends from the shores of the Horn to Taksim Square and beyond and is Istanbul's main nightlife and shopping district. **16, 19, 28, 71, 124, 208–14, 219, 226, 265, 287, 295, 299, 301, 304, 308, 311, 312**

Beşiktaş – the name for this neighbourhood on the European side of the Bosphorus is thought to have come from the Turkish *beşik taş*, meaning 'cradle stone', deriving from a Byzantine church that housed a relic of Christ's stone cradle from Bethlehem – possibly the same relic that passed into the collection of Mehmed II. Beşiktaş is a transportation centre, with buses pulling in and out from various points, a taxi stand, and terminals for ferries crossing the Bosphorus to Üsküdar on the Asian side. But this district is perhaps best known as the home of Beşiktaş Jimnastik Kulübü (Beşiktaş Gymnastics Club), founded in 1903. The club is famous for its fanatical supporters, who include both the novelist Orhan Pamuk and Turkish Prime Minister Recep Tayyip Erdoğan. Beşiktaş has won 13 Turkish Super League titles and participated five times in the UEFA Champions League. **18, 21, 118, 193, 231, 241, 245, 311**

Beyazıt is a district in the old city of Istanbul named after the Sultan Beyazıt II. The centre of the district is Beyazit Square, site of the Forum Tauri in the Roman city, some remains of which may be found on Ordu Caddesi, the extension of Divanyolu, the big avenue that runs along the southern side of the square from Sultanahmet. The square opens on the north to Istanbul University, with the landmark fire tower near the entrance gate. A large flea market is held here at the weekend. To the east, past the mosque, is the entrance to the Sahaflar Çarşısı, the booksellers' bazaar, a shady refuge of calm at the edge of the Grand Bazaar. **107, 137, 146**

Beyazıt Mosque was built in the opening years of the sixteenth century for Beyazit II, son of Mehmed the Conqueror. The second of the imperial mosques to be built, after the Fatih Mosque, it sets a precedent in its scale and overall design for the great mosques to come, including those of Mimar Sinan. **107, 119, 208**

Beylerbeyı Palace – the name means 'Lord of Lords' – was built in the Second Empire style for Sultan Abdülaziz by Sarkis Balyan, of the Armenian family of architects who also designed the Dolmabahçe Palace. **97, 252, 269**

The Blue Mosque is the name Westerners have given to the Sultanahmet Mosque, the interior of which is extensively revetted in tiles, predominantly blue in colour. Located in the heart of the district that takes its name from the mosque, the Blue Mosque was built between 1609 and 1616 during the rule of Ahmed I by Sedefkar Mehmed Ağa, who succeeded Sinan as chief architect of the empire. **24, 71, 73, 113, 166–8, 176–7, 248, 311**

Bodrum Camii translates as 'Basement Mosque', so called because of its large lower storey. The building began life as the Church of Myrelaion, 'the place of myrrh' and was built in the early tenth century near a Byzantine palace of the same name. **57**

The **Bosphorus** translates in Greek as Βόσπορος, or Vosporos, meaning 'Ox-ford', as according to Greek mythology it was here that the goddess Io, who had been transformed into a cow by Zeus, crossed the strait in her wanderings. This stream that connects the Black Sea and the Sea of Marmara is the demarcation between the continents of Europe and Asia. According to the so-called 'Black Sea deluge theory', the Bosphorus was formed in about 5,600 BC when the rising waters of the Mediterranean surged through to the Black Sea, which at the time was a low-lying body of fresh water. **5, 7, 12, 16, 19, 20–1, 29, 78, 91, 99, 132, 135, 153, 194, 201, 206–7, 213, 215–6, 226, 231, 232, 249–57, 261, 262, 268, 273, 288, 295–7, 300–1, 304, 307, 308–9, 311, 327**

Büyük Valide Han, or 'The Large Han of the Queen Mother', was built in the seventeenth century by Valide Kösem Sultan, mother of Sultan Murat IV, and is the largest of the large commercial buildings in the bazaar area, occupied by wholesale textile firms and often filled with the sound of looms. **21**

Büyükada is the largest of the Princes' Islands. The name literally translates as 'The Big Island': in Greek it is Πρίγκηπος (Prinkipos) or Πρίγκιπος (Prinkipo), meaning 'Prince' or 'Foremost'. The Byzantine Emperor Justin II built a palace and monastery on Büyükada in the early sixth century, and a convent on Büyükada was the place of exile for Byzantine empresses. The hill above where the ferry docks is home to the monastery of Agios Nikolaos. Leon Trotsky, exiled from Russia, lived here between 1929 and 1933. **12, 79**

Büyükçekmece Bridge was built by Sinan on a commission from Selim II to span a tidal estuary in what is now a suburb of Istanbul. Over 2,000 feet in length, the bridge is considered Sinan's major engineering feat as a builder of secular structures. **128**

The **Church of the Holy Apostles**, built in the fourth century under Constantine the Great to house his mausoleum and those of his successors alongside relics of the apostles, was at one time second in importance only to Haghia Sophia, and much frequented by Constantinopolitans, as it stood in one of the busiest parts of the capital. It was rebuilt under Justinian and Theodora in the sixth century and enlarged in the ninth century under Basil I. The Crusaders and Venetians plundered the riches of the church in 1204. Immediately after the Conquest, Mehmed II gave the church to his first Patriarch, Gennadius, but after a short time the Sultan had the dilapidated church pulled down so that his Fatih Mosque could be built, between 1463–1470, on this prominent hilltop site. According to contemporary accounts and surviving depictions, the church was built in the cruciform style later imitated by the architects of the Cathedral of Saint Mark's in Venice. **44, 92–3, 302**

The **Church of San Antonio di Padua** is located just off Istiklal Caddesi in Beyoğlu. It is the largest Roman Catholic church in Istanbul, built in the Venetian Gothic style for the Italian community in the eighteenth century. As the Vatican's ambassador to Turkey before his election to the papacy, Pope John XXIII preached in this church for ten years. He was popularly known as 'The Turkish Pope' due to his fluency in Turkish and fondness for Istanbul and the Turkish people. **114**

The **Church of Santa Maria Draperis** is a Roman Catholic Church on Istiklal Caddesi, known in Turkish as Meryem Ana Draperis – 'Meryem Ana' translates as 'Mother Miriam', since the Arabic word for Mary is Miriam. The church was originally constructed in the sixteenth century, on a site donated by one Clara Maria Draperis; hence the name. The location was moved after the original church burnt down in 1660, and after two subsequent fires and demolitions by both earthquakes and a hostile state, the current building was constructed in the eighteenth century. Run by Franciscan friars, who say Mass every Sunday in Italian and Spanish, Santa Maria catered to a large congregation of Levantines and Arab Christians in Ottoman days. On the main altar is an old wooden icon of the Virgin Mary which was rescued after each catastrophe.

The **Church of Saints Peter and Paul** was an earlier church existing on the site of the Church of Saints Sergius and Bacchus that was demolished to make way for the construction of the new church in the early sixth century. **180–1, 306**

The **Church of Saints Sergius and Bacchus**, after its conversion to a mosque, came to be called the Küçük Ayasofya or 'The Little Haghia Sophia'. It was built in the years immediately preceding the construction of Haghia Sophia, probably between 527 and 536. The church was the scene of a dramatic chapter in the history of Byzantine theological controversy in 551 when Pope Vigilius, who had been summoned to Constantinople from Rome by the Emperor Justinian, sought sanctuary in the church from the Emperor's soldiers who were sent to capture him here. Later, during the Iconoclastic period, the monastery became one of the centres of the movement. **28, 125, 176, 180–5, 306**

Cibali is a neighbourhood in the district of Fatih named after Cebe Ali Bey, the Ottoman soldier and dervish who led his men in an attack on the Byzantine walls in 1453 at the point where the Cibali Gate stands today. He was called Cebe Ali, 'Armoured Ali', on account of his buffalo-skin armour, which, as legend would have it, terrified the defenders, allowing him to break through at this point in the fortifications. **23**

The **Column of Constantine**, standing beside the Divanyolu, which is now known as Yeniçeriler Caddesi, is a monumental column erected by order of Constantine the Great in AD 330. The Turkish name Çemberlitaş Sütunu, combines *çemberli*, 'hooped' and *taş*, 'stone'. Constantine erected it to commemorate the declaration of his new city as the New Rome, the new capital city of the Roman Empire. **18, 44**

Çengelköy is a neighbourhood (formerly a separate village) in the Üsküdar district on the Asian shore of the Bosphorus near Beylerbeyi. The name has been translated as 'hook village' – Turkish *çengel*, because the village sits on a bay where the Bosphorus shore takes a sharp curve, and has also been said to derive from the word *çenkar*, 'crab', as the village was famous for its crabs. **252**

The **Çinili Cami** is a small, pretty mosque in Üsküdar, on the hill of Toptaşı, a short walk from the Atik Valide Mosque. The mosque was built in the seventeenth century and has some of the prettiest Iznik tiles in Istanbul. While the body of the mosque dates from 1640, the porch and the minaret are later, baroque additions. **144, 234**

Çukurcuma is a gentrified, formerly Greek neighbourhood in Beyoğlu that is home to some of the best antiques shops in Istanbul. Designer boutiques share its winding streets with shops offering antique furniture and Ottoman knick-knacks. The origin of the name is obscure, but may refer to a mosque built here on low-lying ground at some point in the past. **249**

Dolmabahçe Palace is an ornate rococo palace, built during the reign of Abdülmecid I. It was home to the sultans and the centre of the Ottoman government between 1856 and the dissolution of the sultanate in 1922, except between 1887 and 1909, when Abdülhamid II ruled from Yıldız Palace. The name means 'filled garden', as the palace was built on land reclaimed from the Bosphorus. The architects were members of the Armenian Balyan family, and catered to the late Ottoman taste for sumptuous display and ostentation: one of the great staircases has banisters of Baccarat crystal. The world's largest Bohemian crystal chandelier hangs in the main hall – a gift from Queen Victoria, weighing 4.5 tonnes. **9, 132, 202, 205, 207, 231, 265, 269, 288, 297, 311–2**

Edirne is a city in eastern Thrace, known as Hadrianopolis, the city of Hadrian, in classical times, and as Adrianople in English until the 1930 postal service laws enforced the use of the modern name. It served as the capital city of the Ottoman Empire from 1365 to 1453, before the conquest of Constantinople, and continued to be important as the gateway to the capital after this date. In 1575 Sinan built his masterpiece, the Selimiye Mosque, in Edirne. **112, 117, 123, 128, 148, 170, 192, 233, 298, 310**

Eminönü is the busy area at the tip of the Stamboul peninsula, located roughly on the site of the old city of Byzantium. Before the eighteenth century this was a neighbourhood of Karaite Jews, but they were moved to Balat so that the new mosque could be built. The first Galata Bridge across the Golden Horn in 1912 made it possible for the first time for the two sides of European Turkey to have easy access to each other. The ferry docks along the shore take passengers back and forth to and from all parts of the city. Sirkeci Station nearby is the terminus of trains from Europe. **11, 23, 73, 130, 152, 174, 213, 227, 231, 250, 302, 305**

Eyüp is an ancient neighbourhood up the Golden Horn, reachable by ferry from Eminönü. It takes its name from Abu Ayyub al-Ansari, the companion and standard bearer of the Prophet Muhammad who participated in the first Muslim attempt to seize Constantinople in 674. Eyüp-el-Ensari (in the Turkish spelling) is considered a hero of the faith, and his tomb is much visited. Cemeteries and shrines to illustrious figures from Turkish history surround the türbe. Pierre Loti loved Eyüp and made it the setting for his novel *Aziyadé*. **20, 111, 171, 208, 263, 265, 302**

Fatih – encompassing the district of Eminönü, the administrative district of Fatih is a large urban area stretching from the Golden Horn to the north to the Sea of Marmara in the south, and comprising most of the historic city of Constantinople before its nineteenth-century expansion. As a neighbourhood, however, Fatih is usually defined more narrowly as the part of town centring around the Fatih Mosque. As host to millions of villagers from Anatolia, it has a reputation for conservatism and religious fervour. **20–1, 204, 208, 295, 297, 300**

Fatih Mosque – Mehmed II had the Church of the Holy Apostles pulled down and in its place built the first imperial mosque in Istanbul between 1463–1470. Unfortunately the mosque was damaged by earthquakes in the sixteenth and eighteenth centuries and the current baroque building, constructed during the reign of Mustafa III on a different plan from the original mosque, dates from only 1771. The graveyard, planted with roses, is well worth visiting. The türbe of Sultan Mehmed II is an elaborate baroque fantasy, while that of his wife Gülbahar Hatun is more in line with the classical Ottoman style. Inside the mosque courtyard, the şadırvan, in the shape of a witch's hat, is charming. **20, 44, 124, 297, 299**

Fener is an old neighbourhood centred around the Greek Orthodox Patriarchate roughly halfway up the Golden Horn between Eminönü and Eyüp that used to be predominantly Greek. The name comes from the Greek word φανάριον, meaning lightpost, streetlight or torch. During Byzantine days a column topped with a lantern that sailors used for navigation stood here on the shores of the Horn. During the eighteenth and nineteenth centuries wealthy and powerful Greeks called Phanariotes, who occupied positions of power in the Ottoman state and served as governors of provinces in European Turkey built their mansions in Fener, some of which survive in varying degrees of dilapidation. **11, 23, 64, 93, 198, 208**

Fethiye Camii, the Church of Theotokos Pammakaristos or 'All-Blessed Mother of God', was built in the eleventh and twelfth centuries. Late in the Byzantine era a parekklesion or side chapel was built on the south side of the church and decorated with exquisite mosaics. The church was converted into a mosque in 1591 by Murad III, in honour of his conquest (fetih) of Azerbaijan and Georgia. While the main body of the building is still used as a mosque, the parekklesion of the church has now been made into a museum, its mosaics sparklingly cleaned and restored. It is located in a rather remote part of Fatih. **63, 93**

Florya is an upmarket neighbourhood along the shore of the Sea of Marmara to the northeast of Yeşilköy, where the Atatürk International Airport is located. Originally a Greek fishing village, Florya became well known when a summer house and bathing pavilion for Atatürk designed by the architect Seyfi Arkan was built here in 1935 and used by the Turkish leader until shortly before his death. It was here that he entertained prominent guests such as the King of England, Edward VIII, and Mrs Simpson. After his death the pavilion was used by the Republic's Presidents Ismet Inönü, Celal Bayar, Cemal Gürsel, Cevdet Sunay, Fahri Korutürk and Kenan Evren. **207**

Galata is a neighbourhood on the northern shore of the Golden Horn known for its cosmopolitan population. Nowadays Galata is often called by its modern name, Karaköy, particularly in reference to the waterfront area. As the downhill part of Pera, this area was a colony of the Republic of Genoa between 1273 and 1453: a walled and self-governing entity. The Genoese built the Galata Tower, one of Istanbul's most recognisable landmarks, in 1348 at the northernmost and highest point of the citadel. Galata had a large Jewish population from the eleventh century onward and has traditionally been a centre of banking and prostitution. **11, 17, 78, 159, 204, 208–14, 267, 270, 293**

Galata Bridge is an important and beloved landmark, the bridge connecting the old city, Stamboul, with the Europeanised neighbourhood of Pera. It features prominently in Turkish literature and has great cultural importance for Istanbullus. A wooden toll bridge in the nineteenth century was superseded in 1912 by a floating bridge which was destroyed by fire in 1992 and replaced by the current structure. **15, 23, 96, 124, 139, 152, 208, 301**

The **Galata Mevlevihanesi**, a tekke or dervish meeting house of the Mevlevi order, was founded in 1491 during the reign of Sultan Beyazit II. The tekke's first *şeyh* (sheikh, or leader) was Muhammad Semaî Sultan Divanî, a descendant of Mevlâna Jelaleddin Rumî, founder of the Mevlevis. The building has been remodelled several times over the centuries. It is essentially an eighteenth century structure built after a disastrous fire in 1765; but it was renovated during the nineteenth century, and again, most recently, in 2008. **242, 279**

The **Golden Horn** is a curving tidal estuary about four and a half miles long running inland from the confluence of the Bosphorus and dividing the old city from Beyoğlu. The English term is a rough translation from the Greek *Κεράτιος Κόλπος*, *Keratios Kolpos*; in Turkish it is called Haliç, meaning a gulf. The natural harbour the Horn provides is a great advantage of Istanbul's setting. **4, 11, 16, 19–21, 23, 43, 49, 64, 71, 91, 96, 124–5, 159, 171, 208, 231, 266, 287, 296, 301–3, 310**

The **Golden Gate** was a triumphal arch built during the reign of the Emperor Theodosius the Great (378–395), perhaps to celebrate his victory over the Visigoths in 386. It was called the Golden Gate because the city walls here were covered with gilded plates of bronze. Throughout the Byzantine period the Golden Gate was used for triumphal entries by emperors and generals returning from important campaigns. One such illustrious occasion was the triumphal entry of the Emperor Heraclius in 628 from his successful campaign against the Sassanian Persians, when he defeated them in battle and returned the relic of the True Cross, which they had stolen from Jerusalem, to Constantinople. His chariot was drawn by four elephants. Under Mehmed II the Turks built the Yedikule ('Seven Towers') fortress here to defend the city in case of attack from the European side. **51, 59, 260**

The **Grand Bazaar** – in 1455 Mehmed II ordered the construction of a large covered bazaar for the sale of cloth and jewels near his first palace in Constantinople. In Turkish it is called the *Kapalıçarşı*, meaning the 'Covered Bazaar'. Containing 3,000 shops and stretching over 61 streets, the bazaar is one of the largest covered markets in the world. In its centre lies the Cevâhir Bedestan, or jewel market, a secure enclave within the bazaar that can be locked at night to protect the treasures that are kept here. **5, 17, 21, 24, 101, 110, 150, 172, 180, 211, 270, 288, 297, 309**

The **Great Palace of Byzantium** was the large palace complex located in what is now known as Sultanahmet. Construction began under Constantine the Great, and the Byzantine royal family and court lived here from 330 to 1081. Little remains of the Great Palace other than some floor mosaics to be found in the nearby Mosaic Museum and a few fragments in the Archæological Museum. The army of Boniface of Montferrat, one of the Crusaders, plundered the palace; and Baldwin II, the Latin emperor, even stripped the palace roofs of their lead. An extensive archæological dig on the site of the palace behind the Four Seasons Hotel is ongoing. **49, 52, 55–6, 66, 159, 312**

Gül Camii, 'The Mosque of the Roses', began life as a Byzantine church built with a Greek cross floor plan, as is clear from the lines of the building. The original church was identified as either belonging to the nunnery of Saint Theodosia, or to the monastery of Christ the Benefactor, and played a role in the events of May 28, 1453. On that day, the eve of the Saint's feast, the Emperor Constantine XI went with the Patriarch to pray in the church, which was adorned with garlands of roses. It was one of the last times Constantine was seen in public, as he left shortly afterwards to return to the defence of the city walls. Many people remained all night in the church, praying for the salvation of the city. In the morning Ottoman troops, breaching the city walls nearby, entered the church, which was still adorned with flowers, and captured all the people gathered inside. **23, 57**

Gülfem Hatun is the neighbourhood in Üsküdar where the türbe of Aziz Mahmut Hüdayi is located. It takes its name from one of Süleyman the Magnificent's wives. **236**

Gülhane Park, located in Eminönü, is a large urban park occupying most of what in Ottoman days were the pleasure grounds of Topkapı

Palace. The sultans and their retinue used these acres for hunting, archery practice and so forth. Gülhane was opened to the public in 1912. **73**

Haghia Eirene, or 'The Holy Peace', which is now enclosed within the walls of Topkapı Palace, is the second largest Orthodox church in Istanbul. A church was built on the site of the present Haghia Eirene in the fourth century. Destroyed during the Nika riots under Justinian the Great, it was restored by Justinian in the sixth century when he was rebuilding the city. Only the shell of the church remains. **51, 83, 134**

Haghia Sophia, The 'Church of the Holy Wisdom', was dedicated in 360, but later destroyed, like Haghia Eirene, during the Nika riots, and rebuilt during the reign of Justinian the Great. Its Greek architects during the rebuilding were a physicist, Isidore of Miletus, and a mathematician, Anthemius of Tralles. After the Conquest, the church was converted to service as a mosque, and Islamic prayers were conducted here until it was made into a museum under Mustafa Kemal Atatürk in 1935. **8, 24, 28, 45, 46–7, 51–2, 55–6, 59, 61, 68, 71–85, 90, 104, 118–20, 125, 127, 130, 132, 134, 150, 153, 167, 169, 171, 173–8, 181–3, 208, 234, 277, 296, 298, 300, 308, 311**

Harbiye is part of the neighbourhood of Şişli, and home to the Military Museum. **133, 140, 239**

Hıdiv Kasrı or 'Pavilion of the Khedive', is an Art Nouveau palace built in 1907 by the Italian architect Delfo Seminati, on a ridge in Çubuklu, above Kanlıca. The Khedives were hereditary rulers of Ottoman Egypt. When Egypt gained its independence from the Ottoman Empire, Abbas Hilmi Paşa, the last Khedive of Egypt, was dismissed from his position by Sultan Mehmet Reşat V, the 35th Ottoman Sultan. At this point Abbas Hilmi Paşa settled with his family in the Hıdiv Kasrı. After they left Istanbul in the 1930s, Hıdiv Kasrı was purchased by the Istanbul Metropolitan Municipality, and subsequently fell into disrepair. In 1982 the Touring and Automobile Association of Turkey (TURING) restored the Pavilion, and it was reopened in 1984 as a hotel, restaurant and cafeteria. **213, 256**

Hippodrome – see **At meydanı**

The **Hormisdas Palace** stood on a site now covered by the train tracks that run along the Sea of Marmara from Sirkeci Station to the city's southern suburbs. The Emperor Justinian lived here before his accession to the throne, and in the sixth century he built the Church of Saints Sergius and Bacchus between this palace and the Church of Saints Peter and Paul in what is now called Kadırga, down the hill from Sultanahmet. **181–2**

Iskele Mosque is the informal name for the Mihrimah Sultan Mosque located on the waterfront in Üsküdar. *Iskele* means quay or ferry station in Turkish (from the Italian *scala*, stair or landing), and the mosque perches above the landing here. It was built by Sinan in 1546–48 for Mihrimah Sultan, daughter of Süleyman the Magnificent and wife of the Grand Vizier Rüstem Paşa. It is distinguished by its broad, overhanging awning-like porch that faces the landing. **123**

Kadırga is a neighbourhood at the foot of the hill below the Hippodrome and the Sultanahmet Mosque. The Turkish name means 'galley', because before it silted up, there was a harbour here – dug out during the reign of Julian the Apostate in the mid-fourth century – where galleys in the Byzantine fleet docked. **178, 189, 310**

Kalenderhane Mosque is in the neighbourhood of Vefa. This is a former Orthodox church, most probably the Church of Theotokos Kyriotissa, 'The Most Holy Mother of God Enthroned', built in the ninth century. It stands almost adjacent to the Aqueduct of Valens that runs to the west of the Süleymaniye Mosque in the old city. Mehmed II, on converting it from a church, gave it to the Kalenderi order of dervishes. The lines of the beautiful old church, with its marble revetments, are very plain to see, as it has been altered very little. **204**

Kanlıca is a waterside village on the Asian side of the Bosphorus famous for its yoghurt. In Ottoman times Kanlıca was a popular destination for moonlit boating parties. The İskenderpaşa Mosque in the square by the landing was commissioned by Gazi İskender Paşa and built by Mimar Sinan in 1560. Time has not treated the mosque well, and the dependent buildings of its külliye have not survived. **21, 213, 255–6**

Karaköy See **Galata.**

Kariye Camii, or 'The Church of Saint Saviour in Chora', is a Byzantine church dating from the eleventh century. In the fourteenth century Theodore Metochites, a high official in the Byzantine administration and adviser to the emperor, commissioned mosaics to decorate the entrance hall and side chapel. These mosaics are among the glories of late Byzantine art. **55, 68, 80**

Kuzguncuk is a quiet neighbourhood on the Asian side of the Bosphorus which embodies the cosmopolitan and ethnically diverse atmosphere that was typical of the Ottoman Empire at a time when Greeks, Jews and Armenians were still much in evidence in the city, before the anti-foreigner riots of 1955. Kuzguncuk is home to two synagogues, an Armenian church and two Greek churches. **226–7, 252, 296, 308, 311**

Küçük Ayasofya or 'The Little Haghia Sophia'. See the Church of SS Sergius and Bacchus. **28, 176, 180, 300**

Mecidiyeköy is a commercial and residential neighbourhood on the European side of Istanbul beyond Beyoğlu. Mecidiyeköy takes its name from Sultan Abdülmecid I (1839–1861), during whose reign the district was settled. **23–5**

Nişantaşı is an upmarket neighbourhood on the European side of Istanbul known for its shopping and restaurants. Nişantaşı encompasses the district of Teşvikiye, or 'encouragement' in Ottoman Turkish, because Sultan Abdülmecid I encouraged citizens to move here in the middle of the nineteenth century, building a new mosque and police station as cornerstones of the new district. The name Nişantaşı itself means 'Aiming Stone' or 'Target Stone', as this was where Ottoman soldiers would take target practice. **1, 20, 222, 249**

Ortaköy, literally translated as the 'middle village', has a pleasant, mildly bohemian atmosphere and is a good place for tea, a stroll or a leisurely meal. Its picture-postcard baroque mosque, commissioned by Abdülmecid from the Armenian architect Nigoğos Balyan in 1853, makes a nice visual contrast with the Bosphorus suspension bridge rising just above. Like Arnavutköy and Kuzguncuk, Ortaköy was known in Ottoman days for its cosmopolitan and multi-religious makeup, and is home to two mosques as well as two synagogues and two Armenian churches – the synagogues and churches now little used since these populations have largely moved away. **13, 232, 241, 249–50, 262, 295**

The **Palace of Ibrahim Paşa** is an early Ottoman mansion at the western edge of the Hippodrome in Sultanahmet, built in the sixteenth century by the Grand Vizier Ibrahim Paşa, a Greek promoted in the ranks of government by Süleyman the Magnificent. **47–8, 176**

Pera See **Beyoğlu.**

Pera Palas Hotel – This historic hotel was built in 1892 for the purpose of hosting passengers arriving on the recently completed Orient Express line from Europe. In its blend of Art Nouveau, Beaux Arts and Orientalist decorative styles, the hotel exemplifies the Levantine culture for which Constantinople was famous. The architect, Alexander Vallaury, was also responsible for the Ottoman Bank building in Karaköy and the Archaeological Museum in Sultanahmet. The hotel has hosted many famous people over the years. Room 411 was Agatha Christie's room while she wrote *Murder on the Orient Express*, and Room 101 is an Atatürk museum in miniature, displaying many personal items belonging to Mustafa Kemal Atatürk, including some of the books and magazines he was reading when he stayed here. King Edward VIII, Queen Elizabeth II, Emperor Franz Joseph, Sarah Bernhardt, Alfred Hitchcock, Pierre Loti, Jacqueline Kennedy Onassis, Ernest Hemingway and Greta Garbo have all been resident here at one time. **163, 267, 295**

The **Princes Islands** are a group of nine islands in the Sea of Marmara. In Byzantine times exiled royalty and others in official disfavour were sent here. Later, the islands became a popular site for the summer homes of a wealthy cosmopolitan elite of Greeks, Jews, Armenians and other Levantines, notably Ismet Inönü, second President of the Republic, who had a summer home on Heybeliada. The poet Nâzım Himet and the humorist and memoirist Aziz Nesin both attended the Naval Cadet Academy on Heybeliada. The Islands, or Adalar, as they are familiarly called, are still redolent of a vanished way of life. **11, 79, 298**

The **Sahaflar Çarşısı** is the booksellers' bazaar at the edge of the

Grand Bazaar. It is entered from the courtyard outside the Beyazit Mosque. **107, 271, 297**

The **Sea of Marmara** was known during classical antiquity as the Propontis. It is connected by the Bosphorus to the Black Sea, and the Dardanelles join it to the Mediterranean. The Sea takes its name from the island of Marmara, which the Greeks called Proconnesus, whose quarries have provided a seemingly inexhaustible source of marble since classical times. **11, 16–7, 49, 56, 71, 135, 159, 169, 173, 176, 180, 197, 206–7, 226, 232, 245, 249–50, 253, 255, 298, 302, 306**

Şehzade Mosque – this enormous building was Sinan's first large mosque, completed in 1548. It commemorates Süleyman the Magnificent's son, Prince Mehmet, who died in 1543. Mehmet's türbe is, in contrast to the monumentality of the mosque itself, one of Sinan's most beautiful works executed on a small scale. **112, 119–20**

Selimiye Mosque – situated in Edirne, this mosque was constructed in 1568–74 and was considered by Sinan to be the greatest of his works. It is today listed as a UNESCO heritage site. **128, 301**

The **Serpentine Column** is a bronze column that Constantine the Great had brought from Delphi on the Peloponnesian peninsula in 324. The column, made up of three intertwined serpents originally supporting a golden tripod which held up a golden bowl, is said to be at least 2,500 years old. Celebrating the Greek victory in the Battle of Plataea, the column was fashioned, according to Herodotus, from the melted-down weapons belonging to the defeated Persians. Various stories, probably apocryphal, account for the missing serpents' heads. According to Gibbon, Mehmed II struck and damaged one of the serpents' heads with his mace upon entering the city in 1453, while another story has a drunken Polish nobleman knocking them off toward the end of the seventeenth century. **48**

Sokollu Mehmet Paşa Mosque is one of Sinan's finest small mosques, built in the Kadırga neighbourhood in 1572 for Grand Vizier Sokollu Mehmet Paşa, who married one of the granddaughters of Sultan Süleyman the Magnificent, Princess Esmahan. Sinan skilfully positioned the mosque and its appurtenant structures on this steep hillside that descends to the Kadirga harbour from the plateau where the

Hippodrome is located, using the finest Iznik tiles of the period for the restrained but sumptuous decoration of the interior. **114**

Stamboul – when foreigners tried to imitate the way Turks pronounce the name of the city, is-STAN-boul, this is the pronunciation they came up with. The name thus entered the English lexicon and is a by-word for intrigue and exoticism in novels such as Graham Greene's *Stamboul Train*. Stamboul describes the old city, roughly encompassing the walled city of Byzantine Constantinople on the southern side of the Golden Horn. **16, 130, 152, 210, 245, 287, 301, 303**

Süleymaniye Mosque was the fourth imperial mosque to be built in Istanbul. Commissioned by Süleyman I and designed by Sinan, it crowns one of the city's seven hills and dominates the Golden Horn. This is perhaps the grandest of Sinan's works, and though he did not describe it as his best (this accolade was granted to the Selimiye Camii) he chose to be buried within the Süleymaniye complex, and his *türbe* can be found outside the walled garden. Approximately 3523 people worked on the construction of the mosque, which was built between 1550 and 1557. It has survived an earthquake in 1766 and a fire during the First World War, when it was used as a weapons depot, and was set alight when some of the ammunition ignited. It has since been restored. **104, 116, 124–8, 208, 221, 233, 243, 269, 307**

Surp Krikor Lusavoriç (St Gregory the Illuminator), is an Armenian church in Kuzguncuk. **252**

Sultanahmet – The neighbourhood surrounding the Mosque of Sultanahmet (see Blue Mosque) from which the area takes its name. This is where most of the historical sites in Istanbul are to be found, including Haghia Sophia and the Topkapı Palace. The Sultanahmet Mosque was completed in 1616. **20–1, 24, 44, 48, 52, 66, 71, 83, 166–7, 173–5, 232, 249, 264, 269, 275, 297, 304, 306–8**

Taksim – the name of the central area of modern Istanbul, as well as of the large square there. The word, from the Arabic *taqsīm*, 'distribution', refers to the distribution of Istanbul's water supply from a stone reservoir situated here. Taksim Square has been the centre of many protests and demonstrations in recent years. **18–9, 23, 133, 159, 200, 209, 212, 288, 296**

Tophane – a neighbourhood of Beyoğlu, the name can be literally translated as 'cannon house', or 'armoury'. Mehmed II had his arsenal built here on the waterfront between Karaköy and Beşiktaş, and it was here that munitions for the Ottoman armed forces were manufactured. The Istanbul Modern Art Museum was established in one of the warehouses of the area in 2004. **91, 241, 260**

Topkapı Palace was the home of the sultans for 400 years until 1856, when Sultan Abdülmecid I moved his court to the recently completed Dolmabahçe Palace on the banks of the Bosphorus in Beşiktaş. Work began on the palace as early as 1459 under Mehmed II, and renovations and improvements were carried out almost continuously under Mehmed's successors. **9, 51, 72, 83, 93–5, 100–1, 111–2, 117, 118, 123, 129–59, 170–1, 173, 208, 222, 305, 312, 325, 328**

Tünel, or 'The Tunnel', is the second oldest subterranean rail system in the world after London's Underground. This short funicular railway, built by a French company, was inaugurated in 1875. From a terminus in Karaköy, it carries passengers up the steep hill to Beyoğlu. **21, 24, 27, 210, 212–3, 221, 226, 249, 256**

Üsküdar – in classical times this was the Greek city of Chrysopolis, the 'City of Gold'; so called either because of the wealth of its citizens or because of its appearance in the rays of the setting sun when seen from the opposite shore. It came to be called 'Scutari', after *skutari*, the leather shields borne by the soldiers who guarded the town under the Romans. The current name comes from the Turkish corruption of *skutari*. **21, 24, 114, 119, 123, 171, 178, 226, 231–2, 234–5, 239, 245, 263, 275, 295, 297, 300, 305–6**

Yeni Cami is the abbreviated Turkish name of the Yeni Valide Camii, 'the New Queen Mother's Mosque'. Construction on the New Mosque was begun in 1597 under Safiye Sultan, mother of Mehmed III, but discontinued after the Sultan's death when the Valide Sultan lost influence at court. After a lapse of half a century, Valide Turhan Hadice, mother of Sultan Mehmet IV, took an interest in the project, and, under the imperial architect Mustafa Ağa, construction was at last completed in 1663, and the mosque was inaugurated in 1665. **11, 152, 174, 181**

Yerebatan Saray Sarnıcı, 'the underground palace cistern', is also known as the Basilica Cistern since a church once stood on this site in the early Byzantine period. The enormous cistern, with 336 columns supporting its roof, stored water piped by aqueduct from the Belgrade Forest twelve miles north of the city. It supplied the Great Palace of Byzantium, and during the Ottoman years, Topkapı Palace. **51**

Yıldız Palace, or the 'Star Palace', became the centre of the Ottoman government in 1880 under Sultan Abdülhamid II, though it had already been developed as an imperial estate in the early seventeenth century under Ahmed I. Abdülhamid, an exceptionally paranoid man, feared that the Dolmabahçe Palace would be attacked from the water, so he moved his headquarters up the hill to Yıldız, which he felt could be more easily defended. Like Topkapı, Yıldız is a complex of buildings, rather than a single palace. **13, 97, 193, 301**

A Brief Guide to Turkish Pronunciation

BEFORE ATATÜRK'S 1928 "language reform", Turkish used the Arabic alphabet. Nowadays, the Latin script is used, with a few small modifications, for a total of 29 characters. Turkish pronunciation is for the most part completely regular and phonetic, allowing the newcomer to the language to pronounce almost any new word on sight. Every letter is pronounced (with the exception of the silent ğ), so that *fare*, mouse, is 'fah-ray', not like the English 'fare'. There is one sound per letter with almost no variation, and there is no combining of sounds as with the English 'sh' (which is produced in Turkish with the letter ş).

Aa as 'a' in father
Bb as 'b' in button
Cc as 'j' in joke
Çç as 'ch' in chap
Dd as 'd' in dear
Ee as 'e' in get
Ff as 'f' in food
Gg as 'g' in gap
Ğğ 'yumuşak g' or 'soft g', a silent consonant which provides a transition between two vowels and/or lengthens the proceeding vowel, so *tura*, drumstick, is prounounced 'toora', while *tuğra*, the Sultan's monogramic signature, is pronounced more like 'toooora'
Hh as 'h' in hat
Iı a short 'i' sound somewhere between the 'i' in 'pin' and the 'u' in plus. Note that this 'ı' is always undotted.
İi as 'ee' in see. Note that this 'İ' is dotted even in the upper-case, as in İstanbul.

Jj as French 'j' in 'jour', or English 'z' as in 'azure'
Kk as 'k' in key
Ll as 'l' in lip
Mm as 'm' in moon
Nn as 'n' in need
Oo as 'o' in phone
Öö as in German ö, similar to English 'u' in fur
Pp as 'p' in paper
Rr as 'r' in red, or, at the end of words, slightly aspirated, making it sound closer to an 'l'
Ss as 's' in silk; always the unvoiced 's' sound like lease and never the voiced 'z' sound like tease
Şş as 'sh' in shave
Tt as 't' in ten
Uu as 'oo' in look
Üü as 'ü' in German *für Elise* or French *tu*
Vv a soft 'v' sound, half-way between the 'v' in volvo and the 'w' in water [note that Turkish has no 'w']
Yy as 'y' in yellow
Zz as 'z' in zebra

Glossary of Turkish Words

ahi: historically, a member of an Anatolian sufi brotherhood; also a generic word for 'brother', with positive connotations of generosity, honesty, etc.
acılı: a spicy spread made from peppers; lit. hot, spicy
afiyet olsun: bon appetit, enjoy your meal, lit. 'may it be healthy'
afyon: opium
ağa: landowner; Ottoman title for a military commander or other important officer
ahtapot: octopus
aile: family
akbil: a 'smart card' used as a pass for public transportation
akşam: evening
alem: the bronze or copper crescent placed on the domes of mosques and the peaks of minarets
aleyküm selam: the response to selamün aleyküm; 'and God's peace be upon you!' from the Arabic 'waleikum-salam'
am: a vulgar word for vagina
anlattı: she or he explained or related
ansiklopedi: encyclopedia
araba: car
arabesk: arabesque, commonly referring to a highly emotional style of pop music with an Eastern or Arabic flavour
arz: presentation; petition; offering
at: horse
av: hunting
avlu: courtyard
aya: holy person
aynalı: mirrored
ayran: a traditional Turkish salted yogurt drink

aziz: saint; reverend
baba: father
bahçe: garden
bahşiş: tips
bakkal: corner-store or bodega
balık: fish
banka: bank
barbunya: red mullet
başıbozuk: an irregular soldier of the Ottoman army, particularly known for disorderly conduct, lit. 'damaged-head'
bayram: religious holiday
bekir: bachelor; virgin
bektaş: of the Bektashi Sufi order
bereket: blessings
bey: a traditional Turkish honorarium meaning sir or gentleman
bir: one
bit: flea
boğaz: throat
börek: a flaky savoury Turkish pastry filled with meat, cheese or spinach
bugün: today
büyük: large
cadde: boulevard
cami: mosque
Cansever: a common surname meaning 'lover of life'
cemaat: congregation
cıkmaz: cul de sac or dead end
ciğ: raw
cihad: jihad, religious war, struggle or cause
cin: djinns, spirits, who, according to the Koran, are one of the three categories of rational creatures in the universe, including angels and humans; the origin of the English 'genie'
cumba: bay window, oriel window
çamışır: laundry
çamışırhane: commercial laundry
çarşı: market
çay: tea
çeri: troops
çeşme: fountain
çınar: plane tree

çiçek: flower
çinili: tiled
çintemani: an Ottoman design motif thought to have been influenced by Chinese art
çoban: shepherd
çok yaşa: the equivalent of 'bless you,' offered when someone sneezes; lit. 'live long'
çok: many, much, a lot, very
daha: more
defne yaprağı: bay leaf; another name for the smaller lüfer, bluefish
deli: insane
delibaş: see başıbozuk
deniz: sea, ocean
derviş: dervish, Islamic mystic, any member of a number of diverse sufi sects
devri: period or era
devşirme: 'gathering'; the Ottoman practice of forcibly plucking talented young boys from Christian families within the empire to be enrolled in imperial institutions
dilbaliğı: sole (fish)
dip: foot (of a mountain), base
divan: a metonymic name for the imperial council of the Ottoman Empire; also as in English 'divan', a couch-like piece of long furniture for sitting, usually along a wall and covered in cushions
diyene: 'when I say'
dolmuş: a shared taxi
döner: doner kebab, or gyro, in Greek
effendi or **efendi:** a term of respect for Turkish men correlating to 'sir', or 'mister' but used especially to honour scholars and the learned; now seldom used
elma: apple
enderun: inner rooms or other private quarters
erkek: boy
Ermeni: Armenian
ev: house
eyvan: vaulted room, usually open to a court
ezme: puree, especially pureed spices and vegetables made into a spread
fetva: fatwa, religious ruling
fırın: oven

fıstık: generic word for any variety of nut
garip: strange, weird
gazi: tribal hero or veteran, especially in the defeat of infidels
geçmiş olsun: 'get well soon', lit. 'may it be passed'
gel!: come!
gelin: bride
gül: rose
günaydın: Good Morning
haci: hajji, pilgrim
halife: caliph, the political leader of the Muslim world, traditionally regarded as the successor of the Prophet Muhammad's worldly authority; the caliphate was abolished by Ataturk in 1924 and the title has remained inactive worldwide
halı: rug
hamam: bathhouse; Turkish bath
hamsi: European anchovy
han: roadhouse, inn, or caravansary, commonly used to refer to a particular kind of large public structure of various uses
hane: house
harem: harem, the most private part of a traditional Muslim household, the domain of women, forbidden to men outside the family
haremlik: the generalized noun for 'harem,' denoting women's space in the household with less historical and architectural specificity than 'harem'
haseki: a woman in the harem favored by the Sultan
hazret/hazrat: a religious honorific
Helveti: an important dervish sect known in English as Khalwati, known for asceticism
hepimiz: all of us
hisar: fortress
hoca: teacher, an honorarium applied to secular and spiritual instructors alike
hoşbulduk: the response to hosgeldiniz
hoşgeldiniz: 'welcome!', lit. 'it is nice that you have come'
hünkar: sultan
hüzün: sadness, melancholy, ennui
iç: inside
iftar: the evening meal breaking the fast during the month of Ramadan

İsa: the Arabic and Qur'anic word for Jesus
iskele: pier; dock
Istanbul'lu: Istanbulite
iyi akşamlar: Good Evening
iyi: good
İznik: a town in central Turkey known in Greek as Nicaea, site of the ecumenical councils that developed the Nicene Creed. Known in Turkish art for its pottery, especially İznik tiles, which were inspired by Chinese porcelain and decorate many of the most famous mosques in Istanbul
kabir: great
kafes: cage; in Ottoman history, the part of the Imperial harem where potential successors to the Ottoman throne were confined
kalamar: calamari
kalem: pen
Kalender: Kalenderi, a dervish sect associated with Shi'ism
kameriye: arbour
kanaat: contentment
kapalı: closed, covered
kapı: door
kapıcı: doorman, gatekeeper
kara: black or dark; land
Karadeniz: The Black Sea
kardeş: sibling
karides: shrimp
karnıyarık: a dish of baked aubergine stuffed with minced lamb
kasap: butcher
kaşıkçı: spoon-maker
kavukçu: turban-maker
kavun: musk-melon
kebabçi: kebab-seller
kebbet: a large, melon-sized citrus fruit
kekik: thyme, oregano
kemence: a classical Turkish stringed instrument resembling a violin
keyif: pleasure
kız: girl or daughter
kızılbaş: any number of shia or alevi heterodox religious groups originating in Anatolia; lit. redheads

kible: the part of a mosque faced by worshippers; the generic word for the direction of Mecca
kilim: woven tapestry or rug, commonly originating from Anatolian Turkey
köfte: a Middle-Eastern, Turkish and Southeast Asian meatball dish
köfteci: kofta-seller
kolay gelsin: formulaic expression to wish well to someone who is working, lit. 'may it come easy'
konak: mansion
koymak: to place
köprü: bridge
Köprülü: Ottoman appellation for Serbian minorities, lit. 'bridge people'
Korkmaz: a common surname meaning 'fearless'
kösk: pavillion or other decorative outbuilding
köy: village
kul: slave
kule: tower
kurban: sacrifice; victim
kuru: dried
kuruş: a sub-unit of Turkish currency equivalent to British pence or American cents. 100 kuruş make up one Turkish lira
küçük: small
külliye: complex of buildings adjacent to a mosque devoted to charitable and educational purposes, including hospitals, schools and soup-kitchens
kütüphane: library
Ladino: a Romance language derived from Old Castillian and Hebrew
lakerda: pickled mackerel
lale: tulip
Lale Devri: The Tulip Period, a brief time in early eighteenth-century Ottoman Istanbul (1718–1730) known for the cultural prominence of tulips and tulip designs, as well as for leisure, consumerism and tranquility
levrek: bass
lise: high school
lokanta: restaurant, usually of the more humble sort
lokum: Turkish delight

lüfer: large bluefish
mahfil: elevated lodge, usually on a mosque grounds
makam: musical scale
manav: greengrocer or produce shop
manzara: view
masal: legend, tale or story
medrese: school; historically a religious or theological school built as a part of the complex of a mosque
mehtab: moonlight
mercimek: lentil
Mevlevi: of the Mevlevi dervish order, originating from the teachings of Jalal-ud-din Rumi, who is known as Mevlana in Turkish
meydan: city or town square
meyhane: tavern or saloon, in Istanbul particularly one serving rakı and meze
meze: starters or side-dishes, often served as a light meal, especially with rakı
mısır: corn
Mısır: Egypt
millet: nation, nationality, ethnicity or citizenry; in the Ottoman empire the Millet System allowed limited political autonomy for conquered nations, and afforded religious freedom to minority groups
mimar: architect
muezzin: the singer who performs the five-times-daily call to prayer from the minaret of a mosque
muhallebici: a shop where traditional Turkish milk-based puddings are sold
mumbar: a dish made from sheep intestines
mutfak: kitchen; metonymically, cuisine, as in Turk Mufağı, Turkish cuisine
mutlu: happy
namaz: Muslim ritual prayers, performed five times a day by the devout
nargile: hookah
nataşa: an ethnically-based slur for Russian prostitutes
nazar boncuğu: an eye-shaped amulet, usually blue in colour, believed to ward off the evil eye
ne: what or how

nefis: personal essence or essential nature; also id, or inner appetite
ney: a classical Turkish reeded instrument
o: she, he, that
oda: room
oğlu: boy, son
onun: his or hers
orta: medium; middle
Osmanlı: Ottoman
Özbek: Uzbek
Özturk: a common surname meaning 'pure Turk'
padişah: sultan; sovereign leader invested with divine mandate
palamut: bonito, a kind of fish related to tuna but smaller
palas: 'palace', used in the names of luxury hotels
parçe: variant of Turkish parça; part, bit
paşa: pasha, an honorary title granted to high-level officials in the Ottoman Empire, similar to the British 'lord'
pasaj: arcade
pastane: patisserie
patlamak: to explode or go off
patlıcan: aubergine
pazarlık yapma: bargaining
pazi: chard
pilav: cooked rice
piyaz: a cold white bean dish
rakı: an anise-flavoured alcoholic drink similar to Greek ouzo, the national alcoholic beverage of Turkey
sade: plain
sağ ol: a more informal way to say 'thank you' in Turkish
sağ olun: the second-person plural/polite form of 'sağ ol'
sahaflar: booksellers
salata: salad
saray: palace
sarhoş: drunk
sarnıçı or **sarniç:** cistern
saz: classical Turkish stringed instrument
sebze: vegetable
selamlık: parlour or receiving room, public part of a household (as opposed to the private harem)
selamünaleyküm: 'God's peace be upon you', the traditional Muslim greeting, from Arabic As-Salamu-Alaykum

sema: a Muslim devotional musical and dancing ceremony, often performed by dervishes of varying sects, originating with the thirteenth-century poet Rumi and his whirling dervishes
soba: stove
sofa: large hall or anteroom
sofra: dining table
soğuk: cold
son: last
sülüs: Arabic thuluth, an elegant variety of Arabic caligraphy originating in the eleventh century
sünnet: circumcision; also the general word for worldly acts of the Prophet to be imitated by believers, sometimes translated into English as 'mitzvah'
susam: sesame
sütlaç: a traditional Turkish rice pudding
şadırvan: fountain used for ritual ablutions found in the courtyard or grounds of a mosque
Şafak: a common surname meaning 'dawn'
Şam: old Turkish word for Syria
şehirde: in the city
şehzade: sultan's son, or prince
şekerli: with sugar
şerefe: the balcony on a minaret; also the Turkish ritual 'cheers' commonly exchanged while drinking
şerengiz: a kind of light, literary guidebook to a city
şeyh: sheik
tabhane: guesthouse or hostel, especially in Ottoman times, those built for itinerant dervishes
tambur: a classical Turkish drum
tarikat: dervish sect
tavuk: chicken
tekke: dervish lodge
teşekkur ederim: thank you
tespih: Islamic prayer beads, usually containing either 33 or 99 beads, to remember the 99 names of Allah
tiryaki: addict
topik: a type of meze of Armenian origin made from chickpeas, potatoes and tahini
toptaşı: cannonball
torun: grandchild

tuğra: the official calligraphic signature of the Ottoman sultan
tünel: tunnel; subway
türbe: a tomb or mausoleum, especially those of individuals of religious significance, often a domed shrine or outbuilding on mosque grounds
Türkçe: Turkish
Türkiye: Turkey
Türküm: 'I am a Turk'
uskumru: mackerel
uzun: long, or tall, depending on the context
üniversite: university, college
valide: the queen mother
vezir: a high-ranking political advisor or minister in the Ottoman state
vişne: sour cherry
yalı: a particular type of large wooden house or mansion, usually by water; shore
yedi: seven
yeni: new
yer: space, place; floor, ground
yeşil: green
yıldırım: thunderbolt
yıldız: star
yokuş: a slope, particularly a street on a very steep incline, common in Istanbul
yol: street, road or way
yolculuk: journey
yumuşak: soft
zeytinlağlı: a savoury vegetable dish in Turkish cuisine usually made with olive oil and served cold; lit. 'with olive oil'
zikr: dhikr, an Islamic devotional practice involving the repetition of a phrase, often the Shahada ('there is no God but God, and Muhammad is his prophet'), the 99 names of Allah, or some other sacred utterance; lit. 'remembrance,' or 'pronouncement'

Acknowledgements

The author would like to thank the authors and publishers of the following works for their kind permission for the reproduction of copyright material:

Aydemir, Şevket Süreyya, quoted in Andrew Mango, *Ataturk: The Biography of the Founder of Modern Turkey* (John Murray, London: 2006)
Cansever, Edip, *Dirty August, Selected Poems* (Talisman House, Greenfield, Massachusetts: 2009)
Endres, Clifford, *Edouard Roditi and the Istanbul Avant-Garde* (*Texas Studies in Language and Literature*, Austin: 2012)
Freely, John and Sumner-Boyd, Hilary, *Strolling through Istanbul* (Kegan Paul, London: 2005)
Freely, John, *Istanbul: the Imperial City* (Penguin Books, London: 1998)
Fuat, Ali, quoted in Mango, *Atatürk*.
Goodwin, Godfrey, *A History of Ottoman Architecture* (Thames and Hudson, London: 1971)
Hamlin, Cyrus, quoted in Mango, *Atatürk*.
Mango, Cyril, *The Oxford History of Byzantium* (Oxford University Press: Oxford, 2002)
Mansel, Philip, *Constantinople: City of the World's Desire 1453–1924* (John Murray, London: 1997)
Necipoğlu, Gülru, *The Age of Sinan: Architectural Culture in the Ottoman Empire* (Princeton University Press: 2005)
Necipoğlu, Gülru, *Architecture, Ceremonial, and Power: The Topkapı Palace in the Fifteenth and Sixteenth Centuries* (Architectural History Foundation, MIT Press, Cambridge, Massachusetts: 1991)

Nemet-Nejat, Murat, 'Istanbul Noir', *Istanbul: Metamorphoses in an Imperial City*, edited by M. Akif Kirecci & Edward Foster (Talisman House, Greenfield, Massachusetts: 2011)

Norwich, John Julius, *Byzantium: the Apogee* (John Murray, London: 1993)

Norwich, John Julius, *Byzantium: the Early Centuries* (John Murray, London: 1989)

Orga, Irfan, *Portrait of a Turkish Family* (Macmillan, London: 1950)

Şafak, Elif, *The Bastard of Istanbul* (Viking, New York: 2007)

Author's Note

MANY IMPRESSIONS AND INFLUENCES go into one's experience of a city, and in the case of this book there are many people to thank. Two who come to mind immediately are no longer with us. The poet Hulusi Özoklav, a graduate student of mine at the University of Michigan in the 1980s, corresponded with me about his native city and was my companion on rambles around Istanbul in the early nineties. He also introduced me to the novels of Orhan Pamuk. Another native Istanbullu, James Stewart-Robinson, welcomed me as an auditor in his Turkish classes at Michigan and was an exacting guide to this rich and challenging language. Belgin Eraydin, Feyza Sayman and Beste Kamali were generous conversation partners, and Gerjan van Schaik helped me read Turkish fiction. Travelling companions in the city have been important to me and, among many, I want to mention Suzy Papanikolas, Mary Tillinghast, David Nicolson Freidberg, Grace Wells, Mesut Ilgim and David Clough. Three of my children, Andrew Tillinghast, Josh Tillinghast and Julia Clare Tillinghast, have strolled through the city by my side. Thanks to Julia for compiling the glossary and to Leslie Richardson for reading the book in manuscript form. Ellie Shillito at Haus has been a sympathetic and exacting editor, and I thank her as well.

It is an honour to be associated with the Istanbul community of writers and translators, especially Saliha Paker of the University of the Bosphorus, and Mel Kenne, Clifford Endres and Selhan Savcigil-Endres of Kadir Has University, all of whom have helped me in many ways, both as guides to the city and in suggesting things to read. Professor Paker's generous work on my Further Reading section is greatly appreciated. To these friends I owe many unforgettable meals, expeditions and *rakı*-fuelled nights on the town. Murat Nemet-Nejat's take on Turkish poetry has been stimulating. Ed Foster of Talisman

House has been a pioneer in bringing Turkish poetry to English-language readers. My conversations with Elif Şafak while she was living in the US provided many insights into Turkish culture.

The authors of books one loves come to feel like friends as well: among the great dead, Evliya Çelebi, Gibbon, Ruskin and Yeats stand out. I wish to thank the staffs of several libraries where I did research: the public libraries in Clonmel and Kilkenny in Ireland; the libraries at the University of the South in Sewanee, Tennessee, the University of California in Berkeley, and the Istanbul branch of the American Research Institute in Turkey. Thanks to Anthony Greenwood, the director at ARIT, where I stayed on several occasions. John Freely's *Strolling through Istanbul* was my first guide to the city, and I am heavily indebted to it and to Mr Freely's other books, as well as to Cyril Mango's work and John Julius Norwich's masterly three-volume history of the Byzantine Empire, which I have had constant recourse to in my chapters on Byzantium. I have found Gülru Necipoğlu's books on Sinan and the Topkapı Palace brilliant, informative and exciting to read; anyone who is familiar with her work will see at once how much my chapters owe to her erudition and insight. The same is true of my chapter on Atatürk, where Andrew Mango's 2002 biography of the great man, particularly in terms of Mr Mango's access to Turkish-language sources not available to other biographers such as Lord Kinross, has informed my understanding in important ways.

Index

B

C

H

I

P

Q

R

T

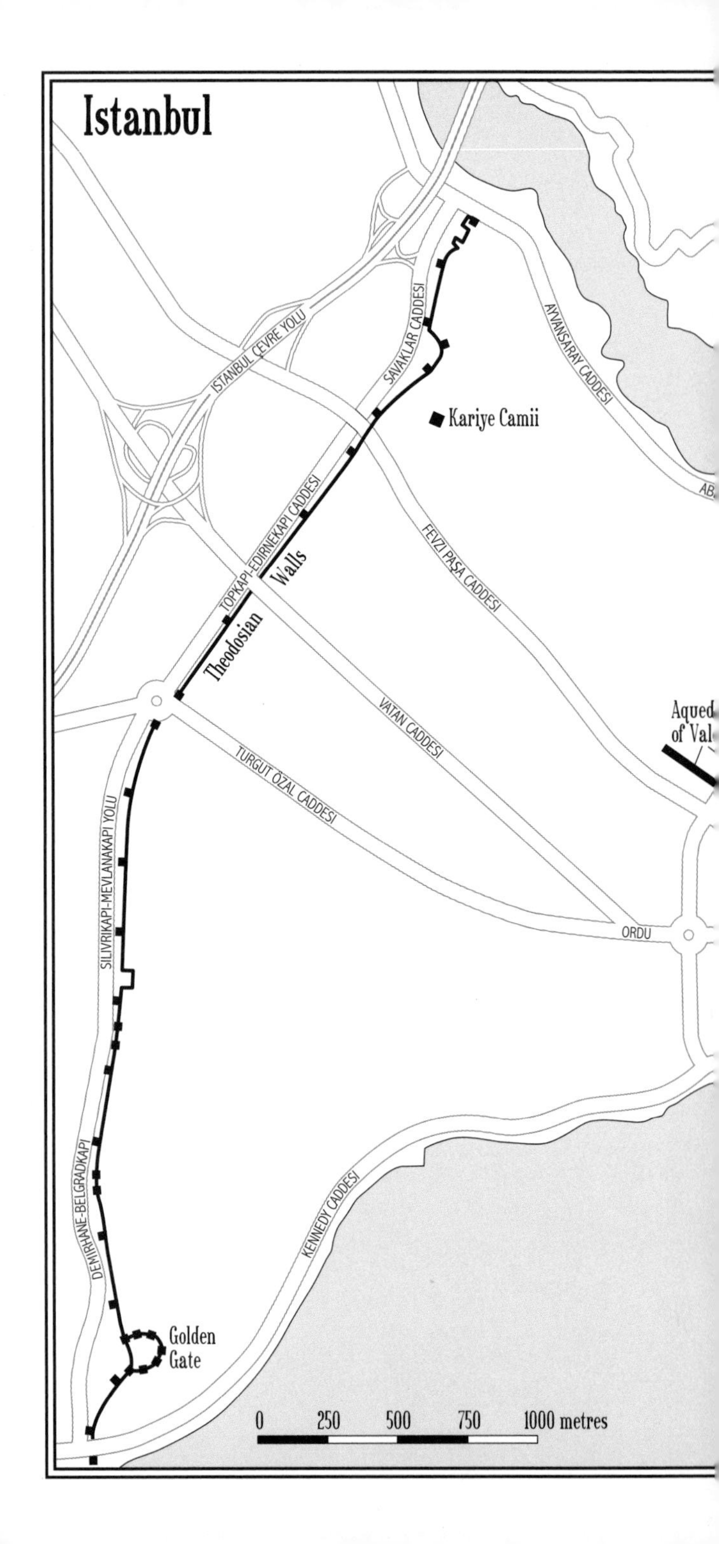

Istanbul
ISTANBUL ÇEVRE YOLU
SAVAKLAR CADDESI
AYVANSARAY CADDESI
Kariye Camii
TOPKAPI-EDIRNEKAPI CADDESI
FEVZI PAŞA CADDESI
Theodosian Walls
VATAN CADDESI
TURGUT ÖZAL CADDESI
SILIVRIKAPI-MEVLANAKAPI YOLU
ORDU
DEMIRHANE-BELGRADKAPI
KENNEDY CADDESI
Golden Gate
0 250 500 750 1000 metres